THE
HOOD HEALTH
HANDBOOK

A PRACTICAL GUIDE to HEALTH and WELLNESS in the URBAN COMMUNITY
VOLUME TWO

Edited by
SUPREME UNDERSTANDING and C'BS ALIFE ALLAH

supreme Design Publishing
www.SupremeDesignOnline.com

Supreme Design Publishing books are printed on long-lasting acid-free paper. When it is available, we choose paper that has been manufactured by environmentally responsible practices. These may include using trees grown in sustainable forests, incorporating recycled paper, minimizing chlorine in bleaching, or recycling the energy produced at the paper mill.

Supreme Design Publishing is also a member of the Tree Neutral™ initiative, which works to offset paper consumption through tree planting.

TreeNeutral

ISBN-13: 978-1-935721-33-8

LCCN: 2010934314

Wholesale Discounts. Special discounts (up to 55% off of retail) are available on quantity purchases. For details, visit our website, contact us by mail at the address above, Attention: Wholesale Orders, or email us at orders@supremedesignonline.com

Individual Sales. Supreme Design publications are available for retail purchase, or by request, at most bookstores. They can also be ordered directly from the Supreme Design Publishing website, at www.SupremeDesignOnline.com

Visit us on the web at

www.HoodHealthHandbook.com

TABLE OF CONTENTS

8. EMOTIONAL HEALTH **251**

9. DYING TO BE BEAUTIFUL..**281**

10. SURVIVAL TACTICS..**328**

DISCLAIMER

Let's get one thing clear before we go anywhere. We're not doctors. Well, technically Supreme Understanding has a doctorate, but we're not medical doctors, bound to the rules and regulations of the Western medical establishment. Then again, some of the authors are medical doctors, but just pretend they aren't either. Just treat us all like people with opinions (opinions that some people disagree with very strongly), and we're simply providing our person opinions for informational purposes only. We don't hold ourselves to the code that binds many doctors to ineffective practices and corporate-sponsored madness. Yet we can't help but be bound to U.S. law, which some nut-job may try to use one day to ruin our lives. We don't want anybody suing us because they think we're prescribing medicine (we're not) or telling people to ignore their doctors and listen to us (we're not), so we've got to provide this sucky legal disclaimer.

Here goes: The information provided in this book should not be construed as personal medical advice or instruction. No action should be taken based solely on the contents of this book. Readers should consult appropriate health professionals on any matter relating to their health and wellbeing. The information and opinions provided here are believed to be accurate and sound, based on the best judgment available to the authors, but readers who fail to consult appropriate health authorities assume the risk of any injuries. This book is not responsible for errors or omissions.

INTRODUCTION

IT'S DEEPER THAN FAST FOOD
BY SUPREME UNDERSTANDING

We're sick. And it isn't just food poisoning. It isn't just heart disease and cancer. The scope of this sickness is so wide and so deep that we're affected on every level. Meaning our minds, our bodies, our emotions, our relationships, our children, our entire communities. And some of us know this all too well, but because the situation seems so overwhelming, we've given up on the idea of change. But change is possible. Change is very possible. But change, like any process, begins with knowledge. And while some people "think" they know the kinds of problems we face, their knowledge is in fact quite limited, because they don't seem to know how much we can do about it. Otherwise they wouldn't be so hopeless!

The Hood Health Handbook was written to spread this knowledge, to educate people about everything from the toxic chemicals that cause our babies brain damage before they're even born, to the mental illnesses we're never adequately treated for. There's so much more to know beyond our sorry diets and the diseases they cause. That's certainly the first piece of the puzzle, but in order for us to truly develop comprehensive solutions for our struggle, we've got to learn about mental and emotional issues, survival and first aid, how to raise healthy children, how to avoid the chemical stew that surrounds us, and why everything is the way it is now.

This is a continuation of the journey that started with *The Hood Health Handbook, Volume One*, but there's no reason why you can't read this book first if these are the topics that interest you most. In the end, we need people who are willing and able to create change in the community – wherever change in needed – beginning with the change they make in their own lives. If that sounds like too much to expect, don't stress yourself. Just read the book, and use it as a reference. Make small changes, a day at a time. And soon enough, you'll be surprised to see that this "expectation" wasn't so unrealistic after all. In fact, it's almost the only direction you can take, with knowledge like this.

Is this Book for You?

If you can answer "Yes" to any of these questions, this book is for you:

- ❏ I want to exercise, but don't have the time, money, or equipment.
- ❏ I want practical advice on how I can lose weight without a crazy diet.
- ❏ I want to keep my home clean, but don't have much time or money.
- ❏ I want to know about the best way to have a safe, healthy pregnancy.
- ❏ I've heard more and more children are developing diabetes and cancer, and I need to make sure my children don't end up that way.
- ❏ I can't find any information on mental health that speaks to me and my background.
- ❏ I know someone in a toxic relationship and I want to help them.
- ❏ I want to improve myself, but I hate boring books that don't speak to me.
- ❏ I want to know how all the chemicals in my environment will affect me.
- ❏ I want to know what to do if the people close to me are mentally unstable.
- ❏ I want to understand why today's youth act the way they do.
- ❏ I'm interested in becoming stress-free and happy with my life.
- ❏ I'm considering getting a piercing, tattoo, or surgery and want to know the risks.
- ❏ I'm into "natural beauty" but that natural stuff seems too expensive for me.
- ❏ I want to know how to have an emotionally healthy relationship.
- ❏ I want to be prepared in an emergency, especially if someone's hurt.
- ❏ I want to teach others about how to get themselves and their communities healthy.

What this Book is NOT

This book is a lot of things, and it will definitely reach different people in different ways...but there are some things this book is certainly NOT. This book is not...

Only for people who are already healthy: There's a lot of "health" books (especially natural/holistic titles) that don't address the way most of us are living right now. Instead, they preach to the choir, talking only to readers who are already on the right path. Not this book.

A guide on how to take your medicine: It's fairly easy to see that "more medicine" hasn't made our people "more healthy." Instead of promoting the Western medicine model (diagnosis of symptoms → prescription of chemicals), we're going to show you how to prevent sickness and how to heal without the chemicals (which actually make us sicker).

A diet/weight loss book: Our health problems are deeper than obesity. And while it's good to be in shape, we're not going to teach you how to starve yourself to do so. We're also not going to promote the idea that a skinny person is healthy just because they are skinny. "Holistic" health means "everything."

Super-holistic, super-natural, and super-difficult: Our books are written to address the needs of people who normally don't enjoy books about health, so we're not going to promote a lifestyle that is unrealistic for many of our readers. Our goal is to provide practical, sensible advice that almost anyone can use. Along the way, we'll throw in more challenging concepts here and there to keep things interesting.

Medical advice, replacing that of a professional, or meant to diagnose you: We're not trying to pass ourselves off as doctors giving you medical advice. We are simply providing information that you can take into consideration when you make your lifestyle decisions. If you have a condition requiring serious or immediate attention, then by all means, seek out a professional you trust.

Race-specific: The topics addressed in this book focus on Black and Latino people, but many of the health issues we talk about are relevant to just about anyone interested in improving their health. That means you don't need to be Black or Latino to benefit from this book.

Class-specific: Similarly, you don't need to live in the hood to benefit from this book.

A bunch of opinions: We are not "quacks" with crazy ideas. We have spent countless hours making sure that our information and recommendations are research-based. As often as possible, we've drawn on clinical studies and medical journals to develop our positions. When we came across an idea that "sounded good" but had no evidence to support it, we refused to publish it.

A scientific journal: At the same time, we have avoided including hundreds of footnotes and citations throughout the text. We have simplified the language to the point where everyone can read it without a dictionary on hand (though it wouldn't hurt). Our goal is to make this information accessible, not to sound smarter than everyone else.

A 'what you're doing wrong' lecture: We're not here to make you feel bad. While the hood is certainly very sick, nothing is hopeless. We're more interested in providing easy recommendation for change than to harass readers about the mistakes they've made.

A 'change everything now or die' sermon: Revolutionary change is a process, not a one-time event. It made more sense to promote one step at a time than to tell you to change everything immediately.

A walk in the park: In spite of all of the above, this book will challenge you mentally and physically. It will challenge your pre-conceived notions as well as your current lifestyle. And the truth might hurt occasionally. But without pain, there's no real growth. We promise it will be worth it.

WHAT'S UP WITH THE "WELLNESS" THING?

Oh yeah, that. We almost didn't put the word "Wellness" in the subtitle of this book. Sounds kind of "New Age," we thought. "People will think we're pushing something weird and expensive instead of something practical and affordable." But we kept the word because "wellness" has a meaning that's worth keeping. Wellness means more than just being in a state of good health. Wellness is being on the road to getting there. And wellness is things that the doctor often can't measure.

"As I see it, every day you do one of two things: build health or produce disease in yourself." – Adelle Davis

According to John Travis, author of *The Wellness Index*, "Wellness is not a static state. High-level wellness involves giving good care to your physical self, using your mind constructively, expressing your emotions effectively, being creatively involved with those around you, and being concerned about your physical, psychological, and spiritual environments." He goes on to explain that it doesn't matter what side of the 'healthy-unhealthy' spectrum a person is on but which direction they are facing.[1]

"To wish to be well is a part of becoming well." – Seneca, ancient Roman philosopher

So how do we know where we're at – and where we're going – on the road to wellness (or the road away from it)? Simple. Take every test, quiz, and questionnaire in this book. Read every article and see where you fall in terms of your daily practices. This book is the first COMPREHENSIVE guide to health in the urban community because it covers nearly EVERY aspect of health AND wellness. When you're done with these two volumes, you'll know exactly where you stand…and where to go from there. From there, you can set your goals and move fast or slow. But the critical first step is KNOWLEDGE. And once you KNOW, wisdom – and wellness – follow.

"He who has health has hope; and he who has hope has everything." – Arabian Proverb

HOW TO READ THIS BOOK

- ❏ You can start from the beginning and work your way to the end, or you can find interesting headings in the Table of Contents and hop around from essay to essay. This book can be read in any order.
- ❏ When you come across a word you don't know, first see if you can figure out the meaning based on the rest of the sentence. If not, the word may be defined in the glossary in the Appendix of this book. If it's not there either, grab a dictionary or go to www.dictionary.com. You can also find basic definitions at http://medical-dictionary.thefreedictionary.com.

---

[1] As holistic health writer Gretchen Goel writes: "If a person is currently suffering with cancer he or she can be moving forward or backward depending on their daily practices. They can decide to do chemotherapy and continue the same poor diet and health practices they had prior to diagnosis. The person may have decided in their mind that death is imminent. This would cause the person to continue to move backwards toward increased ill health and ultimately death. Whereas a person who decides they want to be well can move forward on the continuum. Their daily choices might look like this: eating a diet of mostly raw fruits and vegetables, exercising daily, practicing meditation and positive thinking, getting 8 or more hours of sound sleep daily."

☐ The same thing goes for any person, place, event, or idea that's new to you. We don't want you to simply "believe" us. Look it up. If you don't feel like grabbing a book, you can start at www.wikipedia.org, www.webmd.com, health.about.com, or one of the many other websites we suggest in the book.

☐ Bring it with you wherever you go. Instead of smoking a cigarette or text messaging when you're bored or waiting for something, *read*.

☐ Find a partner or two who can get a copy of the book to read as well. When you meet, talk about what you're reading and what you think about it.

"The best preservative to keep the mind on health is the faithful admonition of a friend." – Sir Francis Bacon

☐ Don't get overwhelmed. All this information can be difficult for someone who thinks they have to start changing everything all at once. As we said earlier, optimum health is a path, not a destination.

☐ Take notes. Highlight. Circle important sections. But only if this is *your* book. Otherwise the owner's going to be pissed.

☐ Work to understand every idea that is discussed in this book. If you can do that, we guarantee that you'll know more than the average pre-med student.

☐ We didn't make everything easy. Some of this book is written in very simple language that anyone can understand, dealing with basic issues like weight loss. Other parts are more challenging, dealing with issues like herbal treatments for OCD. If this book didn't challenge every reader somehow, we wouldn't be proud to present it to the general public.

☐ Above all, the single most important thing you can do with this book is APPLY WHAT YOU LEARN. We cover everything from the low end to the high end, so EVERYONE can start using SOMETHING in this book to improve their lives. The key isn't to do it all at once, or even to do it all period, but to begin the process by doing something you haven't done before. That's all it takes. The journey of a thousand miles begins with one step.

Let me reiterate that last point. There are some parts of this book that will *totally* blow your day. You'll be feeling dusted and disgusted. You'll feel like you can't do *anything*, because *everything* out there is so unhealthy. Don't fall victim to that kind of thinking. The goal, again, is to simply **start doing better**, and to constantly be doing the best you currently can. Meaning, for example, you'll know that canned food isn't that good for you, but eating canned vegetables is better than NO vegetables.

THE 23 KEYS TO HEALTH AND WELLNESS

Your health is the most important thing you possess. When it all falls down, it's one of the only things that matters. These are 23 keys to health and wellness that one should keep in mind regardless to race, creed, class or environment. The chapters and articles of this book are written around these core principles, so you'll find yourself revisiting these ideas as you read.

1. The traditional lifestyles of Original People (otherwise known as "Indigenous People" or "People of Color") all over the planet were always in tune with their environment (even if they lived in cities).

2. Optimum physical health requires a nutritious diet, avoidance of toxins and other stressors that cause disease, and life's essentials: clean water, clean air, sunlight, exercise, and rest. Deficiency in any area causes most of the health problems we experience.

3. The eating practices of Original/Indigenous/People of Color all over the planet leaned toward diets that were focused on vegetables, fruits, grains, legumes, and other plant based foods. The consumption of meat has traditionally been a minor, if at all, part of the diets of Original people.

4. You can eat some meat and still be pretty healthy, but not if you're eating S.A.D. (Standard American Diet) amounts of it, or eating the chemical and parasite-filled kind we find at most grocers.

5. Clean on the inside, clean on the outside. We should be free of nastiness and parasites inside our body, and this cleanliness should be reflected on our exterior as well. With healthy practices, we won't need to depend on artificial cosmetic processes and products to feel attractive. And because we live in a toxic environment, it's important to fast and cleanse our internal systems regularly, no matter what kind of diet we're on.

6. Western culture through White Supremacy (slavery, genocide, colonialism, terrorism) initiated the current downward spiral of sickness and disease amongst Original/Indigenous People all over the planet.

7. White Supremacy is anti-life. Through its doctrine of Manifest Destiny they seek to be the ultimate consumers, devourers, users, conquerors with no thought as to how resources are to be renewed in the environment.

8. Original People don't need the help of white people to assist in the recovery of their health and wellness. The way that most "health-conscious," liberal white people approach our communities is patronizing at best. It's just another manifestation of colonization. Also, in actuality, their information and resources about a holistic way of life were taught to them by Original/Indigenous People.

9. We are not anti-Western medicine yet we do reserve the right to critique it and take the best part that is beneficial to our communities

10. Too much of anything is no good. Some things are more dangerous in their excess than their lack, other vice versa. (For example, too much salt is more dangerous than too little, but too little Vitamin A is more dangerous than too much, etc.)

11. At least 75% of disease is nutritional, either in terms of how disease is developed or how it could have been prevented. Junk food, fried

food, red meat, and other popular foods are killing you slowly.

12. Eating dead, burnt, toxic, chemically altered, genetically tampered, and/or inorganic matter leads to obvious consequences.

13. Everything that tastes good is not good for you. Yet we eat these things because certain ingredients in our foods can be as addictive as hard drugs.

14. You can also overuse (abuse) parts of your body, particularly the organs that are in place to clean and filter your system. When you overload those organs with toxins, they eventually shut down and disease emerges.

15. Whenever a part of your body (such as a muscle) is not in use, it atrophies, meaning it dies. People who are not physically fit die sooner than those who are.

16. Losing weight is not about dieting, but about changing your habits. By eating right and exercising, it's easy to lose any amount of weight you desire.

17. Hospitals, doctors, drug companies, and the whole "industry" of Western medicine, is a big business. We understand that its goal is to maximize profits and that they may go against the goal of healing the people.

18. Healing and Wellness must be holistic. It is mental and physical. The individual and the environment.

19. Healing starts where you are at. It took you years, months, and days to get to your current state of dysfunction and will take an equal amount of time to rise out of it. Utilize the resources right around you realizing that health and wellness is a journey not a destination.

20. One of the most powerful elements of health and wellness is preventative medicine.

21. Children are born with all the stress and toxins we put in our systems, even those from before they were conceived. Whatever they see us eating and doing, they will also want to eat and do. But children are more susceptible to toxins in the environment, as well as those in the foods we eat. In order to keep them healthy, we have to be healthy as well.

22. Get your mind right. Mental/emotional health is as important, if not more so, as physical health. Without a sound mind, it does us no good to have a sound body. But mind and body are interdependent, so living healthier can have us thinking and feeling healthier.

23. When you heal yourself, you'll, in effect, be healing the hood.

1. GETTING FIT...THE CHOICE IS YOURS

GETTING RID OF DEAD WEIGHT

BY SUPREME UNDERSTANDING

In my spare time, I'm a historian and social scientist. So I spend a lot of time studying the culture and traditions of Original/Indigenous people throughout the world, especially those that are ancient (sometimes called "primitive"), because those are the ones with the least "outside" influences. And I look for similarities across those cultures that reminds me of stuff we do today.

At one point, I wondered why indigenous people would let their women work as hard as the men, gathering in the fields while the men went out on long hunts. I thought we prized our women so much that we wouldn't make them work like that. But now I understand how the old way worked for us. Exercise was how everyone, male and female, even the old, stayed healthy. Historically, Original people have almost always been slim and trim or muscular and well-built. Our women might have had some weight in their hips ("mother's hips"), but not ankles that looked like fireplace logs. We walked hundreds of miles carrying everything on our backs, sometimes – such as among the Aboriginal people of Australia – just to relay a message carved into a stick.

> **Did You Know?**
> America's not a particularly healthy country by other measures either. As Steve Plog, Founder of the Results Project, has written: "According to the World Health Organization (WHO), America is the 37th healthiest nation in the world. Basically the American Medical Association's team is in 37th place. When was the last time you took the word of a 37th place team as Gospel?"

Only the wealthy upper classes were fat and sick. Why? They ate diets high in fatty meat and low in the vegetables and grains eaten by the common people.[2] Meanwhile, the poor though overworked, were

---

[2] This typically only happened in societies where there was a strong divide between the rich and poor. These are the ancient societies we tend to celebrate as "civilizations" while ignoring the amazing societies that lived off the land and didn't build gigantic tombs and stuff.

healthy as could be!

America is the fattest country in the world, a strange place where the poor are actually fatter than the rich. Our unbeaten rates of obesity are known to nearly everyone in the world, except perhaps us. And despite the two or three "be healthy" campaigns you see on TV, the numbers are on the rise in 28 of our 50 states.[3] **Our fattest state? Mississippi, where 34% of adults are obese. That's one out of every three people!**

And while the overall numbers might be disturbing, what's worse is the rates of Black and brown obesity in this country. For example, **44% of Black people in Wisconsin are obese. In fact, everywhere you look, Black and Brown people are disproportionately fatter than white people. And it's the same for Latinos. For example, 40% of Latinos in Tennessee are obese. And the health problems are the same.**

Recent surveys put Black females at a mind-blowing 78% overweight and 50% obese. Now, SOME of that might be overestimated (See "Am I Fat?" in Volume 1.), but let's be real, go outside and you'll see those numbers aren't THAT exaggerated. It's more bootydews than badonks out there.

And the numbers aren't going down; they're rising, even in cities where overall rates are improving. For example, in 2009, obesity increased among Black and Native American girls in California, even while declining for white girls. This can be because Blacks and Latinos are less likely than white people to receive advice and information about the benefits of exercise or healthy eating habits.[4] Black adults are 50% less likely to engage in physical activity than whites and it's even worse for children.

But it's deeper than being addicted to the television (though we watch more TV than any other group). 31% of Black women identify "hair care" as their primary reason for not working out. Diet is another issue. Some of it is by choice ("I don't like vegetables,"), and some of it is not ("There's no Whole Foods in the hood," "I don't know how to cook any other way," etc.). But one thing is clear: SOMETHING's got to change. At this rate, we're all going to be fat and dead. Plain and simple, we ALL

---

[3] One place that doesn't follow the national trend? The nation's capital, Washington D.C., is actually losing weight. D.C. also has the highest rate of fruit and vegetable consumption. The full report, "F as in Fat: How Obesity Threatens America's Future 2010" can be found at www.healthyamericans.org

[4] You can check the websites of the Office of Minority health (http://minorityhealth.hhs.gov) or the newly formed National Institute on Minority Health and Health Disparities (www.ncmhd.nih.gov) for details.

know that being fat isn't good for us.[5]

But it's all about when are we going to decide to *really* make a change, and how much are we prepared to give of ourselves to do so. The thing is – you're giving yourself extra years of life, your children a chance to introduce you to your great-grandchildren, a better love life, you're giving yourself more mobility, flexibility, and just plain ease in doing everything you couldn't do before and freedom from illness that will make you miserable.

And it's not about being anorexic or looking like a European model. It's about being healthy. In the words of Dr. Mary Charleson, director of ORBIT (Obesity Related Behavioral Intervention Trials), an education program working to reduce obesity and obesity-related deaths in New York City's Black and Latino communities:

> If you're overweight and you're able to run a marathon, then that's a big difference from being overweight and you can't go up the subway stairs. And we're not necessarily targeting them to be a certain size. It's really just being fit in the size that you're in.

Identify one unhealthy habit that you want to get rid of a month.

HIP HOP AND WEIGHT LOSS
BY SUPREME UNDERSTANDING

I can name more than a dozen artists who gained crazy weight and health issues once their albums started selling. On the other hand, folks like Coolio are in the best shape of their career now that their careers are over. All jokes aside, Coolio really is in good shape, here he explains why:

> The key is taking care of yourself. I don't drink or smoke excessively, and I don't eat pork. I only go to McDonald's or Jack in the Box when I can't get anything else. If I see myself getting a gut, I'll start eating less and doing extra sit-ups. You have to kick your own ass.

The following are a few examples of weight loss and dieting in the hiphop world, as well as what we can learn and apply to our own lives.

Paul Wall (100 lbs.)

If you followed Paul Wall's career as he emerged from the Houston

---

[5] If not, you're either in denial, or you're one of the small percentage of obese people who are considered "Metabolically Healthy Obese," who usually eat healthier and are physically active (and thus less likely to have major health issues, but still likely to have minor issues like joint problems and increased risk of infection). FYI, there are also many people who the Mayo Clinic calls "skinny fat", meaning they have elevated body fat percentages, low HDL, and elevated LDL levels, but low BMI. Still out of shape, still unhealthy.

underground, he's an obvious case. As his star rose, so did his weight, until he hit 320 pounds. His doctor told him he was morbidly obese and needed to change something or die. Paul recounted: "I tried doing it the legit way. I stopped sippin' syrup, stopped takin' pills...all that, but it ain't work...So I went out, went on and got surgery man." He was advised to get gastric sleeve surgery, which basically reduces your stomach to a tube.

> I lost 100 pounds, so I'm back at my fight weight. I'm ready. The champ is back...[The surgery] saved my life for real...I really didn't have too much of a choice, because the doctor told me I was morbidly obese. So, I really didn't have a choice. I was like 'Man, I'm morbidly obese, I need to do something. Man, I got to save my life.'

Mike Jones (100 lbs.)

But surgery doesn't need to be your only choice. Case in point, fellow Houston rapper, Mike Jones. He got fat too then lost 100 pounds. Maybe it helped that he fell out of the limelight. When the people at www.BallerStatus.com caught up with him, they asked how he'd lost so much weight. According to Mike:

> I was almost 300 pounds man. I lost almost 100. I'm 190 right now...That goes from eating Subway, running on the treadmill, and watching what I eat. I'm trying to make sure I'm the urban Jared right here, baby.

Mike says that with his "long absence from the music scene," he felt compelled to "come back" with a "new look, image and sound." Perhaps the desire to come back on the scene was the motivation Mike needed to get in shape.

Yung Joc (35 lbs.)

There's nothing wrong with having some motivation. For many of us, it's the opposite sex. But as Drake tells women on "Fancy":

> Hit the gym, step on the scales, stare at the number/ You say you dropping 10 pounds, preparing for summer/ And you don't do it for the man, men never notice/ You just do it for yourself, you're the f*ckin coldest

So what's your motivation? Maybe you need a competition in your family, clique, or company for whoever loses the most weight – like a toned down version of *Celebrity Fit Club*.[6] That's what they did at Yung Joc's record label:

> Block Entertainment, we all just made a bet...We started dieting, eating [small meals] like five times a day, exercising three to four times a week...Weights and curling. I [started out] with 20 pounds; now I'm gonna curl up a 90-pound weight. And crunches – you have to do crunches...Do cardio every

---

[6] Speaking of which, you may have noticed that several rappers have done incredibly well on this show, proving that we can lose weight if we really want to. These include Biz Markie (lost 40 lbs., winning the first season and setting the record for total weight loss); Young MC (lost 38 lbs. and won Season 3); BoneCrusher (lost 51 lbs. and broke the record for total weight loss in Season 4); Bizarre of D12 (lost 31 lbs); Warren G (lost 31 lbs.); and Da Brat (lost 26 lbs.)

time you work out. Just stay on the treadmill and work your way up. I would run for 20 minutes.

Joc won the bet, losing 35 pounds, and collecting the winnings of $1,000 each from his CEO, manager, and manager's assistant. "A lot of women notice it," the rapper says, "and a lot of 'em want to get closer." He was talking about his new physique, not the money...though I'm sure both help.

Jazze Pha (73 lbs.)

Multi-platinum producer Jazze Pha lost over 73 pounds in just three months after announcing a similar $1,000 weight loss contest (this one for fans) with celebrity trainer Kenya Crooks, aka "The World's Greatest Weight Loss Expert" in April of 2010 **The super-producer said a rigid, variety of daily exercises, like boxing, running and swimming, helped him shed the pounds in such a short period of time.**

"I never know what to expect," Jazze Pha told AllHipHop.com. "He'll have me doing a boxing workout one day and then doing one of his famous pool workouts the next day. That's why I haven't hit a plateau, it's always something different every day."

8Ball (?)

Memphis Rap legend 8Ball is another "XXL rapper" who's gone "low carb," has quit red meat as well. According to the Fat Mack, or "Fat Boy From Da Mound," he's stopped eating beef, pork, bread and has cut out on sippin' soft drinks – even trying yoga – all in the name of health:

> I been doing a change in the way I eat. I got youngin's. I'm getting older every day, so I just changed the way I eat man. Lost a little bit already...I made little minor changes. I ain't trying to get 'heroin chick,' but I want to be healthy...I'm walking, walking dogs, tread mills etc.

Bow Wow

Lotta rappers going low carb...and then there's Bow Wow, who's gone "high fiber." He sticks to this strict fiber-heavy diet to prevent a relapse of the stomach illness which hospitalized him back in 2007. Although Bow Wow is now fully recovered, he says he's battled gastrointestinal problems his whole life – prompting him to turn to healthier food. He told *Hip Hop Weekly*:

> I've always had bad stomach problems. That's why I went to the hospital a year and a half ago when me and Chris Brown were on tour. Now me and all my team, we're starting to work out more and stuff like that. I had to go on a special diet. Bananas, rice, apples and toast. It's crazy, but so far so good.

Eminem (28 lbs.)

Eminem's another one who got big fast, in more ways than one. But he also recently dropped about 28 lbs. by eliminating fatty, greasy fried foods and alcohol from his diet. That sounds like great news, but doctors were concerned the addiction-prone Eminem could become anemic if he continued to crash diet while embarking on a strenuous 70-date European tour. According to an insider close to Eminem:

> He used to live off fried chicken, fries, burgers and his real favorite, drumsticks. Now he's eating only grilled meats and fish, fruit and vegetables, but no refined carbs. His riders (performance request lists) are unrecognizable from those of four years ago.

So what seems to be the problem? Em is eating healthier, claims he's gotten sober, works out on a treadmill and took up running in 2009. Britain's Dr. Morris Missler was one of many who expressed concern:

> Even without a wildly energetic and adrenalin-charged job, crash dieters risk heart attacks and strokes, liver and kidney failure and most certainly death in extreme cases…This would be bad enough if he wasn't living the non-stop life of a music superstar. Crash diets are extremely dangerous for your heart, liver, kidneys and brain because you lose tissue around them. If you don't eat enough, your body will actually burn the muscle tissue of the organs themselves to provide you with sufficient energy to function.

Crash dieting helps you lose weight, but you might also lose your life. That was the main criticism of the TV show, *The Biggest Loser*. Critics said that losing THAT much weight that FAST could not possibly be safe. And it isn't. **Losing a bunch of weight quickly requires that you send your body into shock.** Not only are you cutting your calorie intake significantly and denying your body all the things it has grown addicted to all at once, you're also changing the nutritional intake of your diet (and usually not in the right way). Beyond all the health concerns, crash dieting doesn't LAST. You'll get so sick and miserable you'll have a hard time keeping the weight off.

Big Pun (80 lbs.)

In 1999, rapper Big Pun – at the urging of friends and family concerned about his health – enrolled in a weight-loss program in North Carolina. He quickly lost 80 pounds, but he quit the program before completing it. He just couldn't take it. He returned to New York and promptly gained back the weight he had lost. On February 7, 2000, Big Pun suffered a fatal heart attack and respiratory failure. Pun was pronounced dead at the hospital after paramedics could not revive him. He was over 400 pounds when he passed.

NORE (65 lbs.)

N.O.R.E. is probably the last rapper you'd expect to make a conscientious change in lifestyle. I mean, hell, his name stands for "Niggas On the Run Eatin." But now, he's eatin VEGAN! And claims that switching to a vegan diet plus exercise helped him lose over 65 pounds. He also started a serious workout regimen with the Bartendaz (See "Exercise without

Equipment") thanks to a weight loss competition with Busta Rhymes. To top it all off, he quit drinking as well, replacing liquor with herbal tonics (See "Magic Potions")!

Mike Tyson (130 lbs.)

Although not a rapper, his story is just as good as NORE's. Turns out that even former human-biter Mike Tyson has left flesh alone:

> I became a vegan. Vegan is where [there's] no animal products. No livestock products. Nothing. I just did a lot of training and try to become more faithful in life. I wanted a different life. I felt like I was dying. I had an incident in life where I lost my 4 year old daughter in a tragic accident at home. I don't know. I didn't want to live anymore. So I said that in order to go there, I had to change my life. I am going to change everything I dislike about myself...I don't smoke anymore. I wanted to give up everything. I had to change my life. I didn't have a problem with drugs or nothing. I had a problem with thinking. My thinking was broken. That was the solution of my broken thinking, using drugs, and living crazy. It was just the way I was thinking.

In addition to helping him eliminate drama from his life and increased energy, Tyson also credits his vegan lifestyle with his 130 lb. weight loss.

What Diet Will Work For Me?

Haven't you been reading this book? Did you even read the last essay? "Diets" are NOT the answer. LIFESTYLE changes are. Just look at the words themselves: <u>DIE</u>t. <u>LIFE</u>style change.

Which one do YOU think is gonna be better for you? If you're stuck on the idea of dieting, here's a quick review of some of the popular diets out there and their pros and cons.

The South Beach Diet	One of the most dangerous diets ever designed. The fact that it was written and promoted by a cardiologist makes it more threatening because heart patients, thinking it's safe, are encouraged to eat this way. You are told to move from a carbohydrate-restricted, high-protein phase back to a less restricted phase, but when you start to regain your weight (as you will inevitably do), you are instructed to return to the more restricted phase. **This pattern of changing dietary phases accelerates the progression of atherosclerosis and promotes electrolyte swings that not only increase the likelihood of you getting a heart attack, but can predispose you to a life-threatening cardiac arrhythmia.** Many are aware that ketogenic diets are dangerous if maintained long-term, but if done for a short-time on and off, as recommended in the South Beach plan, it's even more dangerous to your heart and health. Full of incorrect, unscientific and fraudulent dietary advice on almost every page.

The Atkins' Diet	Also known as the "no carbs" diet because it claims you can lose weight by avoiding breads, pastas, sweets, and other carb-heavy foods, while still enjoying as much meat as you want. You can lose some weight but it's difficult to lose a significant amount, long–term. More importantly, this diet is bound to hurt your health no matter what it does for your waistline. Studies have shown that it causes constipation, kidney insufficiency, bad breath, fatigue, high cholesterol, atherosclerosis, life-threatening cardiac arrhythmias and even sudden death due to electrolyte imbalances. This diet is the richest in saturated fat, the food element best associated with cancer. Also associated with cancer is aspartame, which is the sugar substitute preferred by most people avoiding carbs.
Weight Watchers	This involves calorie counting and portion control. Like Atkins and other diets, most people do not keep the weight off permanently. More importantly, reducing calories and nutrient levels simultaneously, raises your risk of chronic diseases such as diabetes, arthritis and cancer. You can include other "programs" in this category, including Jenny Craig and whatever else is next on the "meals mailed to your door" bandwagon.
The Eat to Live Diet	This isn't based on The Honorable Elijah Muhammad's books *How to Eat to Live, Vol. 1 and 2*. This "Eat to Live" diet, created by Dr. Joe Fuhrman, focuses on two primary objectives: weight loss and optimal health. Fuhrman pushes a "nutritarian" diet based on foods with a high nutrient to calorie ratio such as fruits, vegetables and legumes, as well as limiting (but not eliminating) the amount of meat, dairy and processed foods that one consumes. According to Fuhrman, you can eat as much as you want on this diet (within reason). How? He says: "Foods high in fiber tend to be plant-based foods. Foods high in fat tend to be animal-based foods. As you change your diet to include daily fruit, vegetable, green salad and bean consumption, you will have more energy, feel fuller and lose weight."
The RAVE Diet	The Rave Diet was created by Mike Anderson after watching family and friends suffer from disease. Deciding that there had to be a better way to live, he embarked on two years of research and formed the principles of the Rave Diet and Lifestyle. The "rave" part of the name is an acronym for the four most important aspects of the diet. They are: no Refined foods, no Animal foods, no Vegetable oils, no Exceptions. The lifestyle also emphasizes exercise, if you can get past the strict requirements of the diet! But if you've got a disease rooted in nutrition (heart disease, cancer, etc.), the RAVE diet is the next best thing to a RAW diet.

Make a health weight loss bet/wager with your friends or co-workers to motivate you.

RBG FIT CLUB

BY STIC.MAN OF DEAD PREZ

"To keep the body in good health is a duty…otherwise we shall not be able to keep our mind strong and clear." – Buddha

Here's just a few of the ways you can start getting stronger, faster and more toned:

1. Calisthenics. There are many bodyweight exercises out there. For the lower body: lunges and squats are a good start. For upper body: pull-ups, push-ups, and shoulder press ups. For your core: crunches and twisting sit ups will get you going. Bodyweight exercises build functional strength and stability. They're natural movements you would use in real life situations like sports, self-defense, gardening, or doing chores.

2. Isometric exercises. These are basic bodyweight exercises where you hold your body in a static position. Examples of these are the frog sit, v-sit, horse stance, hanging from a pull-up bar, and the plank. Isometric exercises are great for joint and stabilizing strength.

3. Yoga. The best exercise I've found for range of motion and flexibility. It does not require equipment and has tons of free online sources with routines.

4. Dynamic exercise. Dynamic exercise is anything constantly changing. You're moving in more natural movements, rather than continuous repetition of fixed patterns. This includes Jeet Kune Do and other self-defense martial arts, tennis, handball, basketball, and even dance.

There are other opportunities to exercise. Hiking, jogging, skiing, swimming, running, yard work...The list goes on. Just use your imagination to make it fun and change it up.

Find one new "dynamic exercise" (martial art, dance, or sport) that you would to try out.

EXERCISE WITHOUT EQUIPMENT
BY NASIM ALLAH

It really doesn't take much, and what it does take, can be found at no expense. Knowledge and resistance are two of our most abundant resources. Understanding these two concepts is key to living a fulfilling and healthy life.

Your body was not exclusively designed to sit, walk, and lie down. Your body can essentially become the wildest roller coaster ride you step into. As a baby, you struggled to crawl, struggled to walk, then took off. What's the next step in this natural progression? Well, that all depends on how far you want to go, and how fun of an experience you want. Just remember three things:

- When you're old, you won't be able to do what you could while young.
- The human body is as deep as the universe itself.
- The body is designed to constantly build itself, not to self-destruct.

Calisthenics and Free Weight Exercises

The most basic of exercises in calisthenics are the pushup, pull up, squat, dip and abdominal crunch. These exercises work most if not all the major muscles in the body and from these four exercises countless variations can be created.

The following are some basic callisthenic exercises:

- Dips - can be done on parallel bars or pull up bars. More advanced dips can be done with knees or legs extended in front of you.
- Pushups - diamond pushups (hands 1-6 inches apart), wide pushups (arms wider than shoulder length), incline pushups and clap pushups.
- Pull ups - close grip pull ups, wide grip pull ups, hammer pull ups (pull ups on monkey bars with palms facing each other), muscle ups.
- Squats - lunges, wide stance squats, one leg squats,
- Crunches - reverse crunch (bring knees toward chest, lift hips off floor), lying scissor kicks, planks, abdominal twist.

Regarding free-weights, it's easier to label the exercises by body region. **I recommend you visit bodybuilding.com for video demonstrations and variations of many exercises.** No recommendations on purchases from their supplement store.

- Shoulders - shoulder press, front raises, lateral raises.
- Traps - upright rows, shrugs.
- Chest - bench press, flies.
- Biceps – curls.
- Triceps - triceps extensions.
- Abdominals - the best abdominal exercises involve calisthenics.
- Legs - leg curls, deadlifts, squats.

With resistance always present, because of gravity, there are many ways to exercise. In calisthenics you use your body weight to workout. You can adjust the amount of resistance by adjusting the amount of weight you use. A classic example is found in pushups; if you can't do a full pushup, do a pushup on your knees. It's not cheating if you're breaking a sweat. Remember you learned to walk before you ran. **If you're ready to go beyond running, search for "Parkour" and "Free running" on YouTube.**

You can also perform raising motions such as lateral raises, bent-over lateral raises, and front raises. These motions target your shoulders. They're great to do with dumbbells and you won't need heavy amounts of weight. If you can't afford dumbbells don't worry, take a milk jug and fill it with water, sand, and/or small rocks. Cheapest adjustable dumbbell you'll get.

(For more great and inexpensive equipment you can make at home, search for "Homemade Fitness equipment" on YouTube). You'll see everything from medicine balls, mace bells, tornado balls, Bulgarian training bags, kettle bells, and more things you may not have heard of but will have you feeling and looking right.

Your muscles can also be stimulated WITHOUT movement (See "RBG Fit Club"). By positioning your body in a way that muscles need to contract in order to maintain posture or stability you can get a hell of a workout. Don't be fooled and think that you can only get in shape with heavy amounts of weight. Typically, the longer the range-of-motion the less amount of weight is needed. This is because the muscles will be contracted for longer periods of time and will fatigue quicker. The "No pain, no gain" saying is in full affect here. When exercising your muscle fibers actually get "ripped" and are rebuilt stronger. In a way you're destroying yourself to build yourself back up stronger. But don't overdo it, "rest" is just as important as "work" in ensuring optimum health. **How much rest you need is determined by your ability to recover from your workout.** I suggest you exercise 3-5 times a week and rest at least two days. The following is an example:

Sample Workout Schedule

Tuesday: back, bicep, shoulders.

Wednesday: rest

Thursday: chest and triceps.

Friday: back, biceps and abdominals

Saturday: rest

Sunday: abdominals and legs.

Monday: rest

Note: "Rest days" aren't lazy or "bum days." Play basketball or football on your rest day. Go for a jog, walk, or a swim. If your friends are moving into a new place that day, help them out. Don't shut down on your rest day! Your body won't suffer if you're active, in fact it will benefit from it because you are warming up those sore muscles and speeding up their recovery. You probably took note that some muscles appear to be worked out only once a week. If you play sports, you probably have certain muscles that you may want to focus on more than others (i.e. in boxing you may need stronger abdominals, legs, and shoulders instead of a big chest). But make sure you target all major muscles at least once a week, what you don't use, you'll lose.

I have a simple rule when I need a quick but great workout. The trick is to spend less time resting than you do actually exercising. For example, if you do 20 pushups, rest 10-15 seconds, then do 20 more pushups and repeat. This short rest period is very demanding and after the third set, will be difficult to keep up. But if you want a longer rest period and still make your workout time efficient perform "super sets," i.e. do a shoulder exercise then a chest exercise right after or a back exercise followed by triceps. (To learn more and see examples, search for "Interval Training" on YouTube)

Everything from health, strength, relationships, talents, households, integrity, and so on, needs maintenance. There may always be some sort of resistance present in your life or around your community. Overcome it and you'll get health and wealth from it.

Create a workout routine that exclusively uses callisthenic exercises.

WHAT'S CARDIO?

BY NASIM ALLAH

Aerobic exercises are exercises that strengthen your cardiovascular system (heart, lungs, and blood vessels). While resistance based exercises like weight-training can increase strength, develop muscles, and strengthen bones; aerobic exercises increase stamina, burn more calories, lower blood pressure and bad cholesterol.

Aerobic workouts include jogging, walking, jumping rope, bicycling, swimming, and even dance. **For an exercise to be considered aerobic it must increase your heart rate by 60-90% of your maximum heart rate potential and maintain that target zone for 10-20 minutes.** Any rhythmic, repetitive activity you can maintain for 10-20 minutes can keep you in that range. Aerobic exercises should be low-medium in intensity and long in duration. You want to feel slightly winded, sweaty, and warmed up; not gasping for air, dehydrated, and overly tired. Control the intensity of your workout by controlling your pace. Make sure you are jogging, not sprinting, at a rate you can keep up for at least 10 minutes. If jogging is too difficult, work your way to it by walking and/or jumping rope for 10-20 minutes.

In aerobic, meaning "with air," activities your body relies on oxygen more than anything else. It strengthens your heart and lungs as your body needs an external energy source (oxygen) to keep going. Keep in mind when you perform an exercise that's too intense it's no longer aerobic. Remember, jump rope, swimming, and bicycling can become anaerobic based on their intensity.

Anaerobic, meaning "without air," exercises are short in duration and high in intensity. This includes Weightlifting, sprinting, because these activities are short, your body has enough stored energy to use as fuel and does not rely on oxygen (external energy) as much.

Aerobic exercises complement anaerobic workouts, especially weight training, by building muscle and losing fat quicker. A brief 3-5 minute jog can be the perfect warm up while a 10-15 minute run at the end can further increase weight loss and prevent heart disease, high blood pressure, and even diabetes.

You can measure your heart rate by purchasing a "heart rate monitor." This is a small device you strap around your chest or wrist and will accurately measure your heart rate as you exercise. These monitors can range from $50-$300. Less expensive models simply measure your heart rate, while more expensive models can keep track of and compare results from multiple workouts, nothing you can't do on your own though.

To measure your heart rate yourself, you'll need to find your pulse by placing two fingers on your wrist (specifically 1-3 inches below your hand). You can also locate your pulse by softly placing 2 fingers into either groove lining your Adam's apple. I find this to be the easiest way to feel your pulse. Once you have that, count how many heart beats you feel in 15 seconds then multiply the number by four. This is how many times your heart beats in a minute.

To establish your target zone follow this formula: 220 − age= maximum heart rate. Maximum heart rate x 0.9 = top of the target zone. Maximum heart rate x 0.5 = bottom of target zone. For a more specific evaluation of your target zone, you can see a doctor, personal trainer, or other health professional.

Aerobic equipment such as treadmills, elliptical machines, and rowers can be useful but they aren't necessary. They're a luxury you may want to look into if you can afford it. With a decent pair of running shoes alone you're set.

Take your pulse before, during, and after your workout. Try staying within the target zone.

WHAT TO EAT AND DRINK ON A WORKOUT REGIMEN

Who said you got to eat meat to be tough? Mike Tyson's a vegan now, homey. So are dozens of bodybuilders, MMA fighters, football players, track and field athletes, rappers, and in-the-streets gangsters. So don't let anyone tell you that you got to eat meat to build muscle. In fact, if you trying to get lean and mean, all that fatty meat is working against you.

N.O.R.E.'s Story

When N.O.R.E. (of Capone N Noreaga) decided he wanted to get healthy and basically save his own life (and image), he embarked on a serious journey that he called the hardest thing he's ever done in his life, even "harder than jail." In case you didn't know, N.O.R.E. went from being totally flabby and out of shape to doing upside down push-ups with the Bartendaz and 4 mile runs through the streets of Miami. On his video blog at www.57thAve.com, he explains what he went through to get to that point:

You know it's crazy, man…I had a history in my career of having a hit record and not having a great look, or having a great look and not having a hit record. You know I'm a person that's pretty confident in myself and right now I feel like New York you know I shouldn't have any excuses for New York when I come back out, you know it's really about me just being healthy… Being able to live, you know what I'm saying? And I got tired after a while living the same life you know drinking every day and you know going to parties. So I haven't had a drink since September 8th and, for me, ya'll should be clapping right now, ya'll should be clapping, give me some claps or something going on!

So, I lost like 25 pounds B but, but I ain't nowhere near done. I still have a stomach…So, that's the basic thing this time, it's to lose the stomach and to just get healthy. Big ups to the God giant from Bar-tendaz, I don't know if ya'll know about Bar-tendaz, but he's incredible. He came out here – he really showed me the basics – he showed me how to get my life together and ever since then I've been doing it. I became a vegan, I don't even eat meat, you know what I'm saying?

I woke up and the God Giant was like, "Yo, you know they talking about you and sh*t. They talking about that workout sh*t." And I said it on there…yo this is the hardest thing I've ever done. It's crazy, you know, to stop eating meat, cold turkey…that's dedication, to stop drinking, that's one part of the dedication. I gave up bread, you know what I'm saying? …Then I turned around and started eating bread and stopped eating meat in its totality…That goes to show you…once I get it, I'm really gon try to lose it, cause this is the hardest thing I have done in my life, it's harder than jail.

Around the same time N.O.R.E. made his video blog about shopping for organic food at Whole Foods (followed by a stop at Winn Dixie for the things he didn't need organic versions of!), Lil Cease also did a video blog on how he chooses what to eat, as part of his Hardbody Fitness series. In case you didn't know, Lil Cease was another dude who'd gotten fat until he decided to make a serious change in his lifestyle. You've got to see his workout videos to believe where he's at now. Here are some excerpts from the video of his trip to the supermarket:

Lil Cease on How to Eat

It's always good to get some salad. You ain't gotta work out to know that, naw mean? …I was trying to starve myself to lose weight. I would eat like one big meal, but then people told me, "Yo you gotta eat, that's how you burn off the food." So…I eat like 5, 6 times a day. Sometimes when I want to eat something and I'm hungry, I don't want nothing big, I'll get some salad, some tuna fish on some wheat bread. Stuff like that is healthy. Now the mayonnaise might not be too healthy, but you can find healthy mayonnaise. Everything that you would probably find to eat – "regular food" – they got it in a healthy form, naw mean?

Lil Cease on Breakfast

Now before, I couldn't stand oatmeal. You could never get me to eat oatmeal. But when I used to work out, I would ask the trainers what's good to eat in the morning?… I couldn't stand oatmeal but when you come here it's a whole bunch of different kinds you can get, you know what I mean? You see the oatmeal: it's got fiber too, fiber is good when you working out too. But you see: no sugar, 80 grams of sodium, that's not bad, and only 2 grams of fat. You see the iron? Yo this is good, you know a lot of vitamins and stuff.

Lil Cease on Soy Milk

This is the healthiest milk you wanna mess with. People know regular milk ain't good. A lot of people that's trying to diet or want to get healthy, they drink skim milk and all that, but this is the healthiest milk right here.

Lil Cease on Protein Shakes

I stress the peanut butter a lot, cause I drink protein shakes a lot, like when I work out. The best time to get a protein shake is right before you work out, another one after you work out. They say that if you really on the workout tip that you should have one before you go to bed, so I was having like 3 protein shakes a day. Those protein shakes are like meal replacements, so when you want to eat, that's how I used to replace it, naw mean? Like if it's 2 o'clock in the morning and I'm in the studio and if I'm like hungry, I just keep a blender in there and make me a shake real quick and I like my sh*t with peanut butter. You can make like different kinds of protein shakes. You can make one with just all fruits, but usually I do the peanut butter with half of a banana, 2-3 strawberries in my sh*t, with like some soy milk, make me a shake like that.

Styles P

Styles P is another celeb who fell out of shape (and into bad health) once he fell out of the spotlight. This is what he told Martin Berrios of www.AllHipHop.com:

I got back into working out hard while I was in the county penitentiary when I did that stabbing. I was mad stocky, I was big when I came home. A year later I was fat - I wasn't on the TV or none of that and I got mad big…[And] I kept f*cking up parts of my body. After I broke my leg I said "F*ck it. After this heals, I'm going in." I won't gain weight while my leg broke. I was on my hands a lot, hopping up and down on the steps, doing some push ups; crazy sh*t. What you don't know is that they thought I wasn't going to walk. I got hit by a Mack truck. My joint was broken in five places but everything was lined up right. They don't know what happened. When I first I got there they didn't think I would be able to walk. I feel if I wasn't on my work out sh*t I would have been finished.

AllHipHop.com: How many pushups can you do without stopping?

Styles P: In one clip, probably a buck and change [over 100] - it depends on how I'm feeling and my day. I work out frequently. I try to go extremely hard. I go to the juice bars, and get my wheat grass, my garlic, my ginger, my pineapple, my roots; a dab of honey. I don't eat chicken, I don't eat beef. I only eat fish.

AllHipHop.com: Do you miss any of those fatty foods?

Styles P: Sometimes, like on Thanksgiving - I haven't done this in three years. I'll have some organic turkey if my whole family is there. The next day I'll just eat mad watermelon, grapes, apples, ginger. It's not for no religious [reason], mine is just for health. If I wanted to do chicken? I can't do it though. Like three years ago I had a relapse and I had some chicken but I was dumb tired. It tasted good, I didn't get sick. Even when I came home from jail when I ate chicken, I ate organic and farm-raised. Ultimately I want to get to all juices one day. That's in my older life for a clear mind state. What you eat helps your mind. I might get some organic turkey bacon to eat for Thanksgiving, and then never eat it again.

Make a list of healthy alternatives to your favorite unhealthy dishes.

WORKOUT IDEAS YOU WON'T HATE
BY SUPREME UNDERSTANDING

We all know we live in the fattest, most out-of-shape country in the world. Nonetheless, people make all kinds of excuses for why they don't get in shape. Out of the following excuses, I've used at least three at any given time. But working on this book has inspired me to do better, actually putting a few of the ideas below to work. After all, it's not enough to be an intelligent revolutionary if you can't run a mile without passing out.

Common Excuses

No Discipline. If you're not disciplined, join a neighborhood league or association that follows a schedule (no matter whether it's for football or daily walks), or invite your friends to remind you of your own schedule. Better yet, find a partner and push each other to stay on track. Or you can sign up to an online site of personal trainers, www.freetrainers.com.

No money for equipment. Using the methods in this book, you can exercise at home or outdoors without spending any money at all. (See, "Exercise Without Equipment.")

No time. Before school or work, exercise for 15-30 minutes. This is enough to meet the 150 minutes of moderate exercise needed weekly to stay fit.

No space. You can transform your living room into a space for exercise in 30 minutes. Play a workout DVD, catch a scheduled TV program. You can do different types of cardio routines such as boxing, martial arts, or dance.

No interest. Or "I hate exercise." Then don't think of it as exercise. There's plenty of activities suggested in the next articles that are so much fun, you won't even think of them as exercise.

Don't want to get sweaty. Or "I don't want to mess up my hair." Believe it or not, these are actually common excuses. We've got to let go of our distorted perceptions of health and beauty. A 300lb woman with diabetes and a beautiful weave is NOT what you want to be. Nor do you want to be a man who has cancer, arthritis, and gout, but is still too pretty to sweat. As far as hair, either go natural or schedule your workouts around your hair appointments.

Don't want to become muscle-bound freak. When you start working out, first you'll burn fat and cellulite. Next, you'll be nice and toned. And if you go past THAT point, then you might start seeing ripples and ridges. But trust me, that's not happening overnight.

No partner(s) to work out with. Then exercise in a public place like a city park. Better yet, invite family or friends out to jog, cycle, do yoga or swim.

Exercise Ideas that Anyone Can Do

Dancing to Hip Hop. You can clown the "silly" new dances you see on BET nowadays, but they're a real workout for any man or woman. You can hit the club and dance all night, or you can save money by dancing at home. There are plenty of Hip Hop dance programs available via DVD, on daytime TV, and On Demand.

Belly-dancing. If you're trying to get your waistline in shape, and add to your sex appeal, this is a sure bet. I assume you know that I'm talking to women here, not men.

Pole-dancing. There's a reason why corporate women and homemakers are registering for these "dance like a stripper" classes. First, practicing those moves will get you in terrific shape. Yeah, all that booty-shaking will actually trim your waistline pretty fast. Second, women find that it increases their confidence, body image, and sex life (with their husbands, not strangers in clubs, of course).

African Dance. This is actually where most Hip Hop dances come from (if not all dance, including the moves performed by the strippers we just talked about), and it's an even more intense workout. And it's not just for women. Visit a class or performance and you'll be impressed.

Video Games. I'm talking about the Nintendo Wii here. And you can step up that work out even further with the Wii Fit Plus. If you don't have a Wii, you can go online and find cheap copies of Dance, Dance Revolution (plus the dance pad) for most other video game systems. Still fun, especially if you actually let your kids play too.

Jogging. This can be something as simple as running around your block 5 times before you take your morning shower, or you hit the local high school (or college) track and do 20 laps every other day. In addition to bringing some water and an iPod, you can add arm weights to build your muscle tone evenly throughout your body. It also helps you get your daily requirement of sunlight and outdoor oxygen!

Baby Lifting. You can lose that stubborn baby weight by using your baby as a weight, like Ione Jamison, wife of NBA star Antawn Jamison:

> "It's always that last 10, 15 pounds to lose. My stomach area, it kind of needs some work now. I have three babies under four years old so it's kind of gotten a little stretched out. With the Mommy and Me Pilates, it's really helpful to get the core back, and just bonding with your baby too while doing it."

"It's functional training because you're going to be carrying around the baby anyway. So we're going to use it in a way that challenges your core," Instructor Jennifer Hunter says. How does it work? You might lift the baby overhead, hold them up while doing crunches, and even incorporate them into traditional Pilate's movements. There's other benefits beyond the exercise: bonding/quality time spent with your baby, and getting used to handling/carrying your baby. And men can do it too, though it's not as much of a workout for us to bench press a 16-pounder.

Baby Making. Good sex means you're both dripping sweat by the time it's over. Which means both of you will have to move through a number of positions on the way there (See "Sex is Good for You").

Gymnastics/Cheerleading/Tumbling. A lot more fun than plain step aerobics, and a much better workout for your whole body. But there are also risks, particularly to your neck and back. The hood version of "tumbling" is a common sight in many communities, where Black boys can do backflips down the street as young as eight years old. But people have seriously injured themselves this way, including one teen that broke his neck practicing a backflip in March 2010. **Similarly, the hood version of gymnastics, known today as "parkour" and "free running" (after white people caught on and made an "extreme sport" of it), is also ridiculously dangerous.** I recommend you stick to workouts that don't involve being airborne and upside down.

Yoga. (See "Yoga's Not Just for Hot Chicks")

Reducing Luxury. This just means that you stop taking the easy way on

> **Did You Know?**
> Exercise does more than slim your waist. It also changes the way you feel...about anything. Thanks to several studies, exercise is well-known known for its ability to lessen the symptoms of depression, but now there's also research on its effects on anxiety. In a study published in the *Archives of Internal Medicine*, researchers studied 3,000 study sedentary individuals who had chronic illnesses but were still able to exercise in sessions of at least 30 minutes. Compared with similar individuals who did not exercise, the people who exercised had a 20% reduction in anxiety symptoms. Exercise helped people no matter what kind of health problem they had: cancer, depression, heart disease, fibromyalgia, etc. "We found that exercise seems to work with just about everybody under most situations," said Pat O'Connor, a co-author of the paper. "Exercise even helps people who are not very anxious to begin with become more calm."

everything, such as taking the stairs (instead of the elevator or escalator) and walking or riding a bike (instead of driving).

Martial Arts/Boxing. With things the way they're going these days, you NEED to be able to defend yourself. So this is HIGHLY recommended. Not only do you learn something useful, you'll be in better shape in no time.

Sports. Of course, all sports don't require the same amount of strength, agility, and endurance, so different sports give you different benefits. The best all-around workouts are probably basketball (which leans more towards building agility and reflexes) and football (which leans more towards building strength and muscle mass).

Paintball. This is what finally got me back in the game. I made tons of excuses until my brother DJ Rebellion invited me out to play paintball at a spot that had an "urban warfare" field. Not only did I learn that shooting at a piece of paper is TOTALLY different from shooting at a target that runs at you and shoots back, but I nearly passed out trying to run that field in the 100 degree sun.

Participate In fun, non-traditional exercise activities. Toss in some calisthenics into a game of basketball for an aerobic/anaerobic workout.

YOGA'S NOT JUST FOR HOT CHICKS
BY SUPREME UNDERSTANDING

Long-time advocate Russell Simmons says a yoga class is the best place to meet fine women. While most guys don't like the idea of having their ass in the air, Russell is right. Yoga is a great way to develop flexibility, peace of mind, and get in good shape. It's so good for that last part that it's even spawned the "yoga booty," which is just another way for white women to say they have Black girl butts. And Russell's not the only man hitting up classes these days. Even Jay-Z took yoga, inspired by friend Chris Martin of Coldplay. So do Evander Holyfield, Serena and Venus Williams, Diddy, Shaq, Grant Hill, Kevin Garnett, and Lisa Leslie.

Hatha Yoga is the aspect of yoga that focuses on physical development and control of the body. **Research has shown that Hatha Yoga can:**

❏ Improve aerobic conditioning	❏ Improve sports performance
❏ Improve flexibility	❏ Assist with weight loss
❏ Improve strength	❏ Reduce stress
❏ Improve health	❏ Prevent cancer
❏ Help prevent injuries	

Yes, studies have even shown that Hatha Yoga has preventative effects against CANCER.[7] While it might still be a tough sell convincing a guy to do yoga, I encourage any single, hot-blooded male to simply VISIT a class. I'm pretty sure you'll want to stay. Thank me later.

How to Find a Decent Yoga Class

According to the authors at www.holisticmed.com:

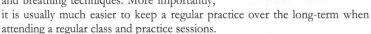

> It is difficult to overemphasize the important of learning yoga in a class. Experienced yoga teachers can help with the correct postures and breathing techniques. More importantly, it is usually much easier to keep a regular practice over the long-term when attending a regular class and practice sessions.

They say you should look for a yoga class that meets the following criteria:

- ❏ Located close to your home or work if possible.
- ❏ Taught by a certified yoga instructor, not by a health club instructor teaching glorified stretching exercises that they decide to call "yoga" or teaching "relaxation exercises."
- ❏ The yoga instructor is willing to adjust the routine to your abilities and develop a routine that'll improve your overall wellbeing without injuring or frustrating you. Speak with the yoga instructor on this subject before starting classes.
- ❏ I feel that it's best to start with a form of yoga that emphasizes the asanas (postures), includes a "final relaxation" pose and over time begins to add a couple of breathing exercises (pranayama). For many people, it's best to leave meditation and the spiritual aspects of yoga until later. (On the other hand, I know several people who have gotten enormous benefits from meditation without first practicing yoga postures or breathing. So, you will have to find what works for you with a little experimentation.)
- ❏ If possible, locate a yoga instructor who has several low-cost practice sessions per week. This way, it'll be easier to perform short yoga routines regularly.

---

[7] Yoga is only just beginning to be studied by the Western scientific community. Following are the findings of just a few of the completed scientific studies. Several studies have shown that yoga significantly improves the condition of bronchial asthmatics, even patients who were childhood asthmatics. Yoga has been shown to significantly decrease hyperglycemia in non-insulin dependent diabetics and improve mental and physical energy levels and alertness as compared to relaxation exercises and visualization. One study showed that yoga produced a gradual, significant decrease in body weight. In addition there was an increase in alpha wave activity in parts of the brain which corresponds to an increase in patient calmness. Yoga has been shown to produce a significant increase in serum LDH levels (the enzyme which provides energy to contracting muscles during exercise). Other studies have shown that yoga can help conditions of arthritis, arteriosclerosis, chronic fatigue, varicose veins, and heart ailments. Specific yoga breathing postures and breathing exercises have been led to significant improvements in patients with Obsessive-Compulsive Disorder (OCD). Yoga stretches and tones the muscles and joints, has a positive effect on the entire skeletal system including the spine, and has a postive effect on all of the organs, glands, and nerves. Many of the yogic postures and breathing exercises bring much needed blood and oxygen to bodily tissues and organs which speeds the healing of the practitioner.

- As you become more experienced, the yoga instructor should be able to teach you yogic cleansing exercises.
- Some very experienced yoga teachers may be able to customize treatment routines for persons with a chronic illness. Some of the research mentioned earlier included customized yoga exercises.

How to Do Yoga When No One is Looking

In spite of all the above, some of us (like me) would prefer to try those moves in the privacy of our own homes. It only takes about a half hour a few days a week to feel results, so why not? You don't even need to buy a yoga mat. A folded blanket will do.

Recommended Reading

There's a ton of decent books (and videos) on yoga out there, even some catering specifically to Black people. The following are two book reviews on popular yoga books worth checking out.

The No Om Zone

The No Om Zone bills itself as a "no-chanting, no-granola, no-Sanskrit practical guide to yoga." This book by Kimberly Fowler, founder of the L.A.-based YAS Fitness Centers, is geared to athletes and others, who want to improve muscle tone and flexibility, take away aches, alleviate pain and calm the mind. Fowler promises you won't have to go sit on a mountaintop and chant to achieve these results. The former triathlete started doing yoga in 1983 to rehabilitate after an injury and became a fan after seeing the benefits to her body and athletic performance. She was turned off, however, by "elitist" classes targeted to the few who could do pretzel poses and handstands. Today, the motto in her yoga classes is "safe, fun and effective." Her book offers short workouts for 13 parts of the body, including the neck, arms, core/abs, lower back, hips and knees. Each body part gets its own chapter describing and showing the anatomy of the area, common injuries, recommended yoga poses for it and a workout routine typically lasting about 10 minutes. Poses are accompanied by photos, step-by-step guides, difficulty ratings, descriptions of benefits, tips and modifications to make them easier. Fowler does manage to slip some mind-body material into the book. The first body part addressed is the head, for example, and here she talks about the benefits and practice of meditation and describes how to do yoga breathing. This is a good book for those who want yoga workouts targeted to individual body areas as opposed to a one-size-fits-all workout. Fowler also offers a "No Om Zone" DVD containing three 15-minute workouts.

The Yoga Body Diet

The Yoga Body Diet, by Kristen Schultz Dollard and John Douillard, is everything "The No Om Zone" is not. Not only is it not a no-granola book, it even includes recipes for granola. Dollard, digital director at Self magazine, is a yoga teacher and former editor of www.iyogalife.com. Douillard directs LifeSpa, an ayurvedic retreat center in Boulder, Colo., and has written and produced numerous health and fitness books, CDs and DVDs. Their pretty book – generously illustrated with colorful pen-and-ink drawings – says it can help you get a "yoga body" in four weeks through eating, exercising and de-stressing according to the principles of yoga and Ayurveda. The book describes Ayurveda as yoga's sister science, one of the world's oldest medical systems practiced by 80% of India's population today. Dollard and Douillard say their mission is to present "Ayurveda's greatest hits" and teach you how to use it for weight loss. "Yoga Body" kicks off with a quiz to determine what ayurvedic "type" you are: vata (airy), pitta (fiery) or kapha (earthy). Each type is told what kinds of foods to eat and avoid, yoga moves to do and lifestyle changes to make. Recipes for chai tea, pad Thai, roti pizza and other dishes include variations for each ayurvedic type. The book's illustrated yoga pose guide is easy to follow, with about 75 positions that range from the simple corpse pose to the more challenging revolved half-moon.

For anyone who thinks Yoga is only for feminine people who wear spandex pants (which includes a lot of men nowadays, especially since skinny jeans are made with spandex), I'll end with some words from my brother Anton Bridges:

If anybody got anything against yoga or is just ignorant of it, I suggest linking up with some of the Brothers and Sisters in the community who actually who practice it. All you big strong cats, I GUARANTEE you will be sweating an ocean waaayyyy before the halfway session. Or go to YouTube, find a workout, follow along, and FEEL the burn. Then imagine how someone who isn't as physically fit would benefit from it. Personally I use the P90X yoga workout, but I DON'T suggest that for folks new to the art.

What people say about the esoteric/metaphysical nature of it *is* often on point, but I don't even get that deep into it. It's HARD and it physically builds you in a way that is unique in all the physical and spiritual arts. It's very good for building your CORE. Anybody doing anything highly physical/defensive/combat-related understands the importance of core strength. You *can* also use it meditatively/internally, similar to Tai Chi, and it certainly has that value, but again I, personally, don't take it to that level right now.

To be frank, we need more people practicing martial arts, yoga, and all the other things that are purposeful, as opposed to running around putting a brown ball through a white hoop for exercise. Let's not forget there is still a conflict going on…

Find a form of yoga that fits your personality and lifestyle needs.

LIST OF STRETCHES

There are many more stretches than there are muscles in the body. Here are just selections of common stretches for all parts of the body.

Basic Stretching Protocol

Here are some points to follow for any passive stretching session:

❒ Always complete a warm-up session prior to stretching
❒ Stretch until a mild tension is felt, then hold
❒ All stretches should be held for up 30-60 seconds unless otherwise stated

- Avoid stretches to the point where numbness or a tingling sensation is felt
- Focus on the stretch and avoid any distractions
- Try to relax the muscles throughout the passive movement of the stretch, as this will help to alleviate any unnecessary tension within the muscle.
- Don't hold your breath, breathing freely helps you relax and get the best stretch

Trunk

cat stretch   knees to chest   spinal twist

side trunk   back extension

Hips

forward lunge   side lunge   sitting hip stretch

Legs

hamstring (standing)   quadriceps (side lying)   hamstring (supine)

calf (gastroc) calf (soleus) hamstring (sitting) quadriceps (standing)

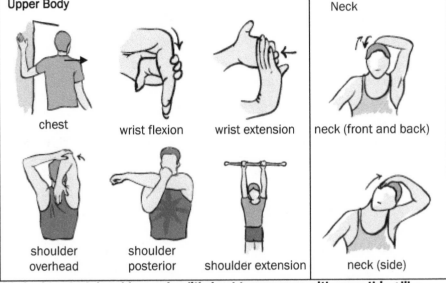

Upper Body Neck

chest wrist flexion wrist extension neck (front and back)

shoulder overhead shoulder posterior shoulder extension neck (side)

It's bad to stretch cold muscles (it's best to warm up with something like a short jog), so create an "after workout" stretch routine.

THREE WAYS TO TEST YOUR FLEXIBILITY
BY SUPREME UNDERSTANDING

Test One: Hamstring Flexibility test

Materials: tape measure and either a small sticky note or piece of tape.

Starting Position: Sitting tall against a wall with your legs straight out in front of you, trying to keep your legs as straight as possible. Legs are a couple of inches apart with your knees and toes facing the ceiling.

Directions: Place your hands on top of each other holding your sticky and reach arms out in front of body, extending the spine from the lower back, leading with your breastbone first. Place your sticky on the floor between your legs as far as you can reach forward, keeping good form.

Tip: Be careful not to round over as you reach forward this will give you a false result.

What to Measure: Measure from the wall to the sticky and record your result. Each week do the same test again and see how much your flexibility has increased.

What it Tells You: The object of this test is to measure the flexibility in the hamstrings. Tightness of these muscles can cause lower back pain and quality of movement/function of your daily activities.

Test Two: Upper Body Flexibility Test
Materials: Rolled up medium-sized towel and two pieces of tape.

Starting Position: Standing with feet hips-width apart holding a rolled up towel above your head, with your hands at each end to the extent that's comfortable.

Directions: With your hands reaching straight up holding the tightly rolled towel; gently move your hands slightly behind the body. Stop when you feel a comfortable stretch in the chest, biceps and shoulders.

Tip: Keep your arms as straight as possible.

What to Measure: Wrap the tape around the towel in the two spots exactly where your hands were. Measure the distance from each mark and record your number. In a week's time, perform the same test placing your hands a little bit closer together. If you can keep good form and comfortably hold the test position, place tape where your hands were and measure the distance between the new tape and see how much your flexibility has increased.

What it Tells You: The object of this test is to see what range of motion you have and how it has improved the flexibility in your chest, shoulders and biceps. The flexibility of these muscles has a huge impact on your posture. If any of these muscles are tight, they can cause you to be round shouldered and slightly hunchbacked.

Test Three: Lateral Side Stretch and Lower Back Flexibility Test
Materials: Sticky tape

Starting Position: Standing tall against the wall with your butt and back resting against the wall.

Directions: Holding a piece of tape in your right hand, bend sideways over to the right without collapsing or buckling your knee. Place the piece of tape or sticky note as far down the leg as you can while still maintaining good form.

Tip: Think of reaching up and over as you side bend.

What to Measure: Measure from the floor to the tape on your leg and record your number. Repeat this in a week's time with the same test and compare results to see if your flexibility has increased.

What it Tells You: The object of this flexibility test is to test the flexibility and range of motion in your lower back and oblique's (side abdominal muscles).

Do you Have Flat Feet?

Stand with your feet shoulder-width apart, toes straight. While keeping your feet on the ground, bend each knee, one at a time. If your kneecap falls toward the inside of your big toe, you have pronating feet (or "flat feet"), making you more susceptible to exercise injuries. There's a number of ways to treat flat feet, ranging from the cheap (buying arched insoles for all your shoes) to the expensive (seeing a podiatrist). But you'll never guess the cheapest way to prevent flat feet: Walking around barefoot. **Studies in India have found that children who walked everywhere with no footwear were less likely to develop flat feet than children who wore sandals and shoes.** I'm not saying to hit the hood barefoot, because there is that rule about "No Shirt, No Shoes, No Service," (plus there's broken glass everywhere), but it does prove that, once again, natural (or "Original") is better.

Test your flexibility after your next workout. Try to become more flexible and test your progress once a week.

THE GODBODY WORKOUT ROUTINE

BY ALLAH SUN TRUTH

P.roper E.ating A.nd C.alesthenics E.veryday!

I am a former United States Marine, former Certified Personal Trainer, and a twenty year veteran of the Martial Arts. I have studied American Boxing, Kempo Goju Karate, Shaolin Kung Fu, Aikido, VSK Aikijitsu and Escrima.

The Godbody routine below was designed for Original people of any age or fitness level. As always, obtain approval from your doctor before beginning any exercise program.

While I was in the USMC, I was an avid body builder. I used to spend hours in the gym, 5-6 days a week. During this time I also came into the acquaintance of many skilled individuals with very high levels of fitness.

After suffering my third back injury from lifting weights, I met an individual named Gunnery Sergeant Nurse. Gunny never lifted weights but was in incredible shape. He trained me in many different martial arts forms and calisthenics routines. Gunny's line of reasoning was, as long as he was strong enough to break bones, he was happy. I agree with Gunny 100%. **If you're looking for a workout program that makes you look like a steroid-fed Mr. Olympia, keep looking. If you're looking for a program that will give you speed, flexibility and strength, keep reading.**

If you're a beginner, start out slow and pace yourself so you don't burn yourself out too quickly and quit. No matter your level of fitness, make sure you stretch for at least 15 minutes before beginning any workout. One should take in an adequate supply of the necessary nutrients and water since rest days are few and far between.

The Routine

First 9 Weeks:

Week 1

Running: 2 miles, 8:30 pace, Mon/Wed/Fri

Pushups: 4 sets of 15 pushups, Mon/Wed/Fri

Sit-ups: 4 sets of 20 sit-ups, Mon/Wed/Fri

Pull-ups: 3 sets of 3 pull-ups, Mon/Wed/Fri

Swimming: Swim continuously for 15 min. 4-5 days/week

Week 2

Running: 2 miles, 8:30 pace, Mon/Wed/Fri

Pushups: 5 sets of 20 pushups, Mon/Wed/Fri

Sit-ups: 5 sets of 20 sit-ups, Mon/Wed/Fri

Pull-ups: 3 sets of 3 pull-ups, Mon/Wed/Fri

Swimming: Swim continuously for 15 min. 4-5 days/week

Week 3

Running: No running

Pushups: 5 sets of 25 pushups, Mon/Wed/Fri

Sit-ups: 5 sets of 25 sit-ups, Mon/Wed/Fri

Pull-ups: 3 sets of 4 pull-ups, Mon/Wed/Fri

Swimming: Swim continuously for 20 min. 4-5 days/week

Week 4

Running: 3 miles, 8:30 pace, Mon/Wed/Fri

Pushups: 5 sets of 25 pushups, Mon/Wed/Fri

Sit-ups: 5 sets of 25 sit-ups, Mon/Wed/Fri

Pull-ups: 3 sets of 4 pull-ups, Mon/Wed/Fri

Swimming: Swim continuously for 20 min. 4-5 days/week

Weeks 5-6

Running: 2/ 3/ 4/ 2 miles, Mo/Tu/We/Fr

Pushups: 6 sets of 25 pushups, Mon/Wed/Fri

Sit-ups: 6 sets of 25 sit-ups, Mon/Wed/Fri

Pull-ups: 2 sets of 8 pull-ups, Mon/Wed/Fri

Swimming: Swim continuously for 25 min. 4-5 days/week

Weeks 7-8

Running: 4/ 4/ 5/ 3 miles, Mo/Tu/We/Fr

Pushups: 6 sets of 30 pushups, Mon/Wed/Fri

Sit-ups: 6 sets of 30 sit-ups, Mon/Wed/Fri

Pull-ups: 2 sets of 10 pull-ups, Mon/Wed/Fri

Swimming: Swim continuously for 30 min. 4-5 days/week

Week 9

Running: 4/ 4/ 5/ 3 miles, Mo/Tu/We/Fr

Pushups: 6 sets of 30 pushups, Mon/Wed/Fri

Sit-ups: 6 sets of 30 sit-ups, Mon/Wed/Fri

Pull-ups: 3 sets of 10 pull-ups, Mon/Wed/Fri

Swimming: Swim continuously for 35 min. 4-5 days/week

Second 9 weeks:

Week 1 and 2

Running: 3/ 5/ 4/ 5/ 2 miles, Mo/Tu/We/Fr/Sa

Pushups: 6 sets of 30 pushups, Mon/Wed/Fri

Sit-ups: 6 sets of 35 sit-ups, Mon/Wed/Fri

Pull-ups: 3 sets of 10 pull-ups, Mon/Wed/Fri

Dips: 3 sets of 20 dips, Mon/Wed/Fri

Swimming: Swim continuously for 35 min. 4-5 days/week

Weeks 3-4

Running: 4/ 5/ 6/ 4/ 3 miles, Mo/Tu/We/Fr/Sa

Pushups: 10 sets of 20 pushups, Mon/Wed/Fri

Sit-ups: 10 sets of 25 sit-ups, Mon/Wed/Fri

Pull-ups: 4 sets of 10 pull-ups, Mon/Wed/Fri

Dips: 10 sets of 15 dips, Mon/Wed/Fri

Swimming: Swim continuously for 45 min. 4-5 days/week

Week 5

Running: 5/ 5/ 6/ 4/ 4 miles, Mo/Tu/We/Fr/Sa

Pushups: 15 sets of 20 pushups, Mon/Wed/Fri

Sit-ups: 15 sets of 25 sit-ups, Mon/Wed/Fri

Pull-ups: 4 sets of 12 pull-ups, Mon/Wed/Fri

Dips: 15 sets of 15 dips, Mon/Wed/Fri

Swimming: Swim continuously for 60 min. 4-5 days/week

Week 6 and Beyond

Running: 5/ 6/ 6/ 6/ 4 miles, Mo/Tu/We/Fr/Sa

Pushups: 20 sets of 20 pushups, Mon/Wed/Fri

Sit-ups: 20 sets of 25 sit-ups, Mon/Wed/Fri

Pull-ups: 5 sets of 12 pull-ups, Mon/Wed/Fri

Dips: 20 sets of 15 dips, Mon/Wed/Fri

Swimming: Swim continuously for 75 min. 4-5 days/week

Cut the exercise requirements in half for a "beginner's level" of this regiment. Then make the necessary adjustments to get GodBody.

HOW TO PREVENT MUSCLE CRAMPS

Muscle cramps can be one of the downsides to serious exercise. But they don't happen to everyone. There are a number of factors and something you can do about all of em. The following are common causes:

Mineral Deficiencies: A mineral deficiency of potassium, calcium, magnesium and/or sodium can lead to your muscles not working right and cramping painfully.[8]

Dehydration: This can occur when you exercise hard, especially in hot conditions, and don't drink enough liquid.

Over hydration (is that a word?): Drinking too MUCH fluid (2-3 liters or more of water in addition to your normal daily fluid intake) can 'wash' the above-mentioned minerals out of your body and lead to cramps.

Being Out of Shape: Well-trained muscles are less likely to cramp. People who are not fit often develop cramps when they start exercising because their muscles are so poorly used. Work your way into your routine gradually, giving your body a chance to get ready.

Tight Clothes: Wearing tight clothes, even to bed, can constrict the blood supply to your muscles, causing them to contract painfully. I'm not sure if this includes Spandex since it stretches, but unless you're a fine female, you probably should not wear Spandex either way.

Balance fluid intakes, mineral consumption and exercise intensity.

LOSING 240 POUNDS

WINNING MY BATTLE WITH OBESITY

BY VICTORIOUS LANASIA EARTH

ORIGINALLY PUBLISHED IN THE 14TH DEGREE AND BEYOND

As Original people continue to put on pounds at a rapid rate, many of us are going from being overweight to dangerously obese.[9] **High blood pressure, diabetes, cancer, and a shorter life expectancy are all health risks associated with obesity.** While we are generally aware of these terms and illnesses, many of us don't consider them as seriously as we should. While many of us think losing weight is about vanity, for the severely overweight, it can become a matter of life and death. Life expectancy is a figure that strives to predict how long we will live. It's a number that scientists figure based on all kinds of complicated methods that would bore you to tears if we explained it. But take a look at what the chart looks like:

LIFE EXPECTANCY (in years)			
White Female	White Male	Black Female	Black Male
78.0	75.3	76.1	69.0
Data taken from US Life Tables, 2003, Natl. Vital Statistics Reports, 54(14)			

The numbers speak for themselves. There is a tremendous gap between Black men and everyone else. Too many of us are needlessly dying too young. There are many reasons, but the major one is our higher rate of heart disease, diabetes, and stroke. We can begin to close the gap and improve not just the length of our lives but the quality as well. It's up to us to start making better food choices, time to exercise, and get the necessary screening tests such as breast mammograms for women and prostate exams for men.

> **Did You Know?**
> By definition, obesity means to be overweight by over 30% of the ideal weight. Morbid obesity means to be more than 100 lbs. overweight.

---

[9] By definition, obesity means to be overweight by over 30% of the ideal weight. Morbid obesity means to be more than 100 lbs. overweight.

My Story

All my life I have been overweight, fat, obese, and finally morbidly obese before I decided to make change.

When I was first introduced to the idea of "Knowledge of Self" through the Nation of Gods and Earths in 1998, my "self" was tipping the scale at almost 450 lbs. I could barely walk a couple of blocks without back and knee pain; just the thought of conceiving and bearing children was a joke. I suffered immense depression and was at risk for an early physical death from complications such as heart failure and/or diabetes. I tried every diet known to man and exercise was not an option since every part of my body was in constant pain. Everyone thought I was flaky because instead of saying "oh sorry I didn't come. I'm too fat and could barely get out of bed." I would make up any and every excuse for why I couldn't be there, or participate.

Three major events happened in my personal cipher that finally led me on a path to winning this battle and begin to educate myself on how to shed this weight. The KNOWLEDGE came in the summer of 1998, when I got knowledge of myself while pursuing graduate school in Bridgeport, CT. The brother who gave me knowledge was a strict vegetarian and anytime he came to my rest to give me lessons or to go over some tracks, he went through my cabinets and refrigerator and chastised me about just about everything that was in there. This is when I first heard of the book, *How to Eat to Live* by the Honorable Elijah Muhammad and was given certain highlighted sections to read. I recall the sections having to do with swine, another about eating too much and too often, and overindulgence. I also read about how the wrong foods can promote dis-ease and illness, and even general ugliness. It wasn't until recently, around 2005, that I realized that all of this was true. The funny thing is, although my first enlightener spent many hours building with me on dietary law and exercise, I really didn't pay him any attention. I still ate what and when I wanted, and still did not do any exercise, other than when I had step practice with my sorority.

The WISDOM came in December of 1999 when my Mother had a major heart attack and almost passed. My Mother is about 5'2" and maybe 140-150 lbs. By no means was she overweight, but she had horrible eating habits. The same eating habits that I grew up with. In our West Indian household, we ate a LOT of stewed meals (Stew Peas, Stew Beef, Stew Chicken), THICK soups, and foods very high in sodium and fat such as curry chicken, jerk chicken, and of course, all types of pork and fried foods, particularly dumpling bammy, etc. We also ate a lot of heavy starches like hard dough bread, potatoes, rice and peas. Sweet drinks included sorrel, ginger beer, eggnog (the one with Guinness Stout in it), and carrot juice. Like with many Original households, food was a source of comfort (aka soul food), celebration, mourning, etc. So in addition to growing up with generally bad eating habits, I also grew up learning to use food as my comfort when I was down, sad, lonely, bored or even when I was happy and joyous.

I thought, if my Mother was not even fat and could have a heart attack, what will these eating and living habits do to me?

The UNDERSTANDING came September 11, 2001 with the attacks on the World Trade Center. This was an extremely scary day for me. In addition to not being able to contact my Mother at her office just a few blocks from the World Trade Center, I also realized that all 452 lbs. of me was going to have a hard time trying to get home. My office was on 61st Street and Broadway in Manhattan, and I lived, at the time, in East NY Brooklyn—about a 15 mile distance. I could not take a cab, or subway, so my only recourse was to either squeeze on the bus or walk home in 90 degree weather. To make a long story short, I was terrified that either I would drop dead walking home, or would be in such grave pain I would want to kill myself. It was during my walk across the Brooklyn Bridge that I decided that I would make a change so that if I was ever in this position again, I would be more comfortable in my alternatives.

Here are some things that worked and I am still working at, to battle obesity:

1. The very first thing I did was see a doctor. I found a doctor through my employer's health plan that specialized in weight loss. He did a total physical exam, and then recommended me to a nutritionist and an exercise regimen that I could utilize once I dropped some of the weight.

2. I had to educate myself. I really had to learn moderation, nutrition, and healthy eating. I went to a holistic nutritionist that did a body makeup. I would highly suggest this first step for anyone looking to lose weight, or even how to maintain their current weight. During my 3-session nutritional counseling, we discussed good foods/bad foods, meal plans, and caloric intake, but also this was the first person who identified much of my eating issue, had nothing to do with eating. I had to find other ways to deal with my boredom, loneliness, sadness, fear, anger, frustration, happiness, and celebratory aspects without it always being about food. This was extremely difficult.

3. I had to get active. It wasn't until I lost my first 100 lbs. that I could start working out the way I wanted to. Prior to that, I would force myself to do a walk around the block, or a couple of sit-ups here and there. Once I got to my first milestone, I joined a gym and got a friend to be my "personal trainer" just to help get me started on all of the machines and weights. In addition, it was a great motivation to have someone in my life that wanted to see me succeed as much as I did.

4. I got my cheerleading section together. When I was going through my issues of obesity, I went through it alone. I rarely spoke to anyone about what I was going through and often times isolated myself from others to avoid having to face reality. However, when I made the decision to change my life, I told any and every one that I could. Those who were naysayers of my journey, I exiled them and kept it moving. Those who were supportive of me, I kept closer and let them know how I was doing every step of the way.

5. Get your children involved...for their own sake. When I was bearing my young queen Nyaa, I took time off from the gym. That "break"

eventually became a 4-year hiatus from any and all physical activity! I only recently started going back to the gym, but now I have Nyaa at the same gym in swimming and gymnastics classes. It's now become as important for me to continue my weight loss battle for my child's sake as it was to do it for myself.

Today, although I am not at my goal weight, I have dropped almost 240 lbs. and still working to lose about another 40 lbs. to reach my goal weight of 180 lbs. However, I am healthy and happy, and finally winning my lifelong fight with obesity. Trust me...you can do the same.

Make losing weight and getting healthy a team effort. You don't have to fight obesity alone.

---

2. SEXUAL HEALTH

SEX IS GOOD FOR YOU

BY SUPREME UNDERSTANDING

Sex is not evil, dirty, or impure. Sex is good. After all, without it, you wouldn't be here. But we all know that sex ain't all good…at least not in today's society, which has turned just about everything healthy toxic. Without even mentioning the problems caused by "unwanted" pregnancies, **there are 19 million new cases of sexually transmitted diseases (STD) every year in the U.S., and more than half occur in young people between the ages of 15 and 24.** At least one in four U.S. teenage girls has a sexually transmitted disease. **In the US, about 30% of 15-17 year old adolescents have had sexual intercourse, but only about 80% of 15-19 year old adolescents report using condoms for their first sexual intercourse.** More than 75% of young women age 18–25 years felt they were at low risk of acquiring an STD. And when you're ready to get one, you've got a whole buffet table full of choices. There's Gonorrhea, Chlamydia, Hepatitis B, Syphilis, Herpes, HIV, HPV, and combination platters where you can get two or three at a time. So, next time you get naked with somebody, ask yourself if it's worth a slow death, a miserable pregnancy, or the sensation of pissing razor blades.

> **Did You Know?**
> In humans, sex has been claimed to produce health benefits as varied as improved sense of smell, stress and blood pressure reduction, increased immunity, and decreased risk of prostate cancer.

Sex Relieves Stress. According to studies published in the journal *Biological Psychology*, people who had sex handled stress better than those who didn't.

Sex Lowers Blood Pressure. Another study published in the same journal found that frequent sex was associated with lower blood pressure (in couples living together, not people having sex with strangers). Studies have also found that getting hugs from their mates helps lower blood pressure in women.

Sex Boosts Immunity. Having sex once or twice a week (but not more) has been linked with higher levels of an antibody which can protect you from getting colds and other infections. Again, this does not apply to sex with strangers, which increases your risk of "other infections."

Sex Improves Body Maintenance. One of the health benefits of sex is that it helps to keep you fit and it can keep you in constant awareness of your body image. Everyone likes to know that they have a nice physique and continually being naked in front of another person can be somewhat of a good incentive to stay in shape. Also, 30 minutes of sex burns 150 calories or more (especially if you're "putting in work").

Sex Improves Cardiovascular Health. Studies found that having sex twice or more a week reduced the risk of fatal heart attack by half for men, compared with those who had sex less than once a month.

Sex Boosts Self-Esteem. Boosting self-esteem was one of 237 reasons people have sex published in the *Archives of Sexual Behavior*. According to sex therapist, Gina Ogden, PhD, "Great sex begins with self-esteem, and…if the sex is loving, connected, and what you want, it raises it."

> **Did You Know?**
> Vivica Fox might need to rethink dating those young dudes. It turns out that being a cougar can be bad for your health. Researchers from the Max Planck Institute found that being with a younger man increases a woman's chances of an early death by up to 20%. The study found that women in relationships with men seven to nine years younger had "a less joyful and more stressful life, reduced health, and finally, increased mortality." On the other hand, men who were with women seven to nine years younger lowered their chance of death by 11%. In general, marriage is good for men's health. Studies show that being unmarried can actually shorten a man's life by ten years.

Sex Improves Intimacy. Having sex and orgasms increases levels of the hormone oxytocin, the so-called love hormone, which helps us bond and build trust. Researchers found that women who had warm contact with their husbands or partners, including frequent hugs, also had higher oxytocin levels.

Sex Reduces Pain. As oxytocin surges through your body, endorphins increase, and pain declines. Oxytocin can also raise our pain thresholds significantly. So sex can actually help that headache.

Sex Helps You Sleep Better. A healthy sleep is part of a healthy life. But you should know that men release the sleep-inducing oxytocin, while women release *another* hormone after orgasm that gives them energy, which explains why dude is snoozing while his girl is still trying to cuddle and kick it.

Sex Heals Wounds. Several experiments have shown that oxytocin can help even stubborn sores, like those suffered by diabetics, to heal by regenerating certain cells.

Sex Prevents Old Age Problems. Maybe it's the rejuvenation, the happiness, or all of the above. One thing's for sure: "Use it or lose it" is literally true. For example, **postmenopausal women often suffer from "vaginal atrophy," which is what it sounds like and can lead to all sorts of complications like urinary tract infections.** What's one way to prevent it? More sex.

Sex Reduces Prostate Cancer Risk. Frequent ejaculations (5 or more weekly), especially in 20-something men, may reduce the risk of prostate cancer later in life by about 30%.

Sex Strengthens Pelvic Floor Muscles. For women, doing a few pelvic floor muscle exercises known as Kegels during sex offers a couple of benefits. You will enjoy more pleasure, and you'll also strengthen the area and help to minimize the risk of incontinence later in life. To do a basic kegel exercise, tighten the muscles of your pelvic floor, as if you're trying to stop the flow of urine. Count to three, then release.

Sex Increases Blood Flow. When we get aroused our blood starts to pump at a quicker rate and, thus, blood flow to our brain increases. This results in better performance (in and out of the bedroom), providing the organs with a healthy dose of oxygen and rids the body of old and wasteful products.

Sex is a "Fountain of Youth." Researchers in a large British study found a 50% reduction in overall mortality in men who had the most orgasms. The more orgasms, the better. Every time you reach orgasm, the hormone DHEA (Dehydroepiandro-sterone) increases in response to sexual excitement and ejaculation. **DHEA can boost your immune system, repair tissue, improve cognition, keep skin healthy, and even work as an antidepressant.** Therefore, a health benefit of sex is potentially a longer life.

Sex Increases Testosterone or Estrogen. Both testosterone and estrogen levels experience a boost through regular sexual activity. Testosterone does more than just boost your sex drive, it helps fortify bones and muscles, and it keeps your heart in good working condition as well. In women, estrogen protects against heart disease and provides a number of other important health benefits.

> **Did You Know?**
> There may be a medical reason why it just "feels better" without a condom. A recent study of college students suggests that semen acts as an anti-depressant. Females in the study who were having sex without condoms had fewer signs of depression than women who used condoms or abstained from sex. "These data are consistent with the possibility that semen may antagonize depressive symptoms," the authors wrote, "and evidence which shows that the vagina absorbs a number of components of semen that can be detected in the bloodstream within a few hours of administration."

An active and responsible sex life can improve your overall health.

HOW DOES MY DIET AFFECT MY SEX LIFE?

As Dr. Joe Esposito has written on the connection between sex and diet:

> The body responds to sensual stimulant, such as erotic touch, sight, scents, sounds and thoughts of becoming aroused. One of the physiological responses is increased blood flow to the erogenous zones of the body. The blood vessels to these areas must be able to carry blood freely in order for you to perceive the maximum pleasure. There are mounds of research showing that certain foods will directly or indirectly clog your blood vessels and prevent normal blood flow. The consequences can range from mildly

decreased sensation to a complete shutdown of an erogenous area or organ of the body. A classic example of this is impotence. Many men are in search of some miracle pill, potion or lotion to solve their problem when in fact all they need to do is change their diets. **The arteries, if given the proper nutrition, can clean themselves out and the men can act as the young strapping bucks they used to be.**

Not only is blood flow involved in arousal but also a complex combination of brain function, hormonal releases and nerve impulses that must work together in order to achieve optimum performance. Certain medications, alcohol, poor diet, cigarettes, and pinched or damaged nerves can all play a part. When we start putting the good nutrients in our bodies and ensuring our nerves are functioning at 100%, in most cases; the body will give us the pleasure we are seeking.

3 Foods That Get You Down

Fried Foods: All that saturated fat is sure to give you the "itis" and make you feel too tired to move a muscle.

Sugary Sweets: The high amount of carbs and sugars in cookies and other sweets leads to a serious "crash and burn" effect.

Soda: Caffeine and sugar will have you crashing and "out of it" even worse than cookies.

Medication: Not really a "food," but prescription medications, particularly anti-depressants, can lower sex drive and prevent orgasm.

6 Foods That Get You Up

Almonds: Almonds are a great natural source of energy, which are also said to arouse passion in women. Almonds are packed with Vitamin E, a natural sex hormone stimulant.

Avocado: With its 25 essential nutrients, including Vitamin E, folic acid and iron, avocadoes are said to be one of the healthiest fruits in the world.

Bananas: The large amount of potassium, which is an energy booster, helps muscles contract leading to stronger orgasms.

Chocolate: Cocoa contains a chemical stimulant called phenyl ethylamine, which affects your mood by changing the chemical makeup of the brain and inducing a sexual high.

Garlic: Eating garlic helps your body release a chemical called allicin, which increases blood flow in the body to all the right places. It also contains inulin, a fiber that gives you energy. Just make sure you brush your teeth, buddy.

Ginseng: There's a reason they sell those little bottles of ginseng root at gas stations and corner stores. Ginseng has been used for thousands of years in Traditional Chinese Medicine to increase male virility and stamina. It's nature's Viagra.

Now that you know what foods your body needs to perform at its sexual peak, head down to the grocery store and fill your shopping cart with all the ingredients you need to make a better sex life.

Consume natural food sources and avoid fried, sugary and modified foods for an optimum sex life.

PUT IT IN YOUR MOUTH
BY SUPREME UNDERSTANDING

National statistics show that most Americans have some experience with oral sex, beginning in the early teen years. More than half of teens and about 90% of adults aged 25-44 have had oral sex with someone of the opposite sex, according to a 2002 survey.

While that popular email about the "health benefits of swallowing" turned out to be an internet hoax started by a college student, there actually are some health benefits to oral sex and swallowing (though preventing breast cancer, as the email hoax claimed, isn't one of them). For example, **a recent study found that women who gave their men oral sex, and swallowed, had a lower risk of a high blood pressure disorder that sometimes accompanies pregnancy.** Another obvious benefit is avoiding some of the risks associated with regular intercourse. HIV and all other viruses are inhibited by saliva and destroyed by stomach acid. However, those risks jump back up if somebody's got cuts or open sores on their mouth or genitals. And **for those of you that put your mouth on everyone and anyone, your risk of catching the human papillomavirus (HPV) is high, and HPV increases your risk of oral or throat cancer.** That's right, you might get throat cancer from giving away too many blowjobs. Don't laugh men, because you can get it too.

10 Tips on Tasting Better

Your "taste" is affected by what you eat, like any other secretions from your body, like sweat. Here's some advice on how you can get more head by NOT tasting like bleach and boogers.

☐ Cut out alcohol, caffeine, drugs and nicotine because they're all pollutants.

☐ Drink lots of water and exercise regularly to flush out body toxins.

☐ Eat plenty of fruit. Pineapple, kiwi, papaya, mangos, apple, melons, and grapes are all good choices because they offset the bitter taste.

☐ Eat vegetables but avoid asparagus, cabbage, cauliflower, or broccoli.

☐ Cut red meat and dairy because this makes you salty.

☐ Avoid heavy spices, especially garlic and onions. They're big offenders because they have a high sulfur content.

☐ Parsley, wheatgrass, and celery have been recommended because of their high chlorophyll content.

☐ Cinnamon, cardamom, peppermint and lemon are also recommended.

☐ Avoid junk food, they're loaded with chemicals and preservatives that also pollute your body's chemistry.

- Try and eat food "from the earth" i.e. as naturally as possible, especially foods high in zinc and selenium.
- If nothing works, you might have a damn infection. Sorry you had to find out this way.
- What you put into your body takes between 12 and 24 hours to come out. You should keep your sex schedule in mind before eating!

Making these small changes to your diet will improve the oral sex experience for both you and your partner.

NOW YOU'RE JUST BEING NASTY

SEX AND SEXUALLY TRANSMITTED DISEASES

BY TAMIKA HOGAN

> **Did You Know?**
> In some countries and states even here in the US, anal sex is still a criminal offence punishable by "long custodial sentences, corporal or even capital punishment." Of course, most of this is due to the gay stigma (rather than health concerns), but if we're gonna be real, you have to consider that bisexual men in heterosexual relationships ("On the Downlow") are statistically one of the notable sources of HIV transmission among Black heterosexual women. And studies report that many HIV-positive Black men who are having sex with men don't reveal their HIV-positive status (or sexuality) to their HIV-negative female lovers. In fact, 12% of ALL men say they wouldn't tell a partner if they were HIV positive.

What was once done in the dark is now in the light. In fact, it's right out in public at 3 pm, while your kids are getting out of school. Sex is now a common trend that is popularized through every form of media and entertainment that we view. Cartoons, reality shows, sitcoms, videos, movies, music, sports, even M&M commercials, etc. Sex is in there.

We all know how much rap culture influences the way people view sex. We also know, from rap, how easily being promiscuous can lead you to an early grave. On March 16, 1995, the infamous rapper Eazy E announced publicly that he was infected with the HIV virus, caused by the promiscuous ways that he engaged in while entertaining the world as a member of the rap group NWA. Eazy E talked about having unprotected sex with hundreds of women during wild parties (orgies) and with women who he did not even know (or cared to know, for that matter).

Eazy E even rapped in his song, "Gimme that Nutt":

> I took her to tha pad and we started tah kiss/ Now my d*%k's on hard ya know what I'm thinkin'/ Took tha panties off and the p%@*y wasn't stinkin'/ Pulled off my draws and we started to begin/ Now tha p@*%y's wet so my dick slides in.

How many males share the same concept? The same men who either already have contracted HIV/AIDS or will contract it and pass it along to others at some point. Eazy E died within days of making his public announcement. He couldn't help himself but he hoped to help others by telling the truth.

But did his announcement help, or did it fall on deaf ears? **According to recent statistics, Blacks have the highest number of diagnoses of HIV and AIDS in the United States.** So regardless of your believes on the origins of AIDS or the nature of the HIV/AIDS connection, if you're in the hood, you need to practice safe sex.

Anal Sex

Not only is sex trendy, but so is pornography, which has given us all kinds of "imaginative" ideas about how to get pleasure. Before porn blew up in the Black community, you'd rarely, if ever, hear Black people admit that they were into "doing it in the butt." Now everyone from Slick Rick to Nicki Minaj got songs talking about it! But if you didn't know, one of the most common and easiest methods of contracting HIV/AIDS is anal sex. Anal sex was once looked upon as a sexual act practiced only by gay men. However, anal sex is now practiced by plenty of heterosexual couples. What many people don't know is that **anal sex carries a greater risk of HIV/AIDS and STD's than almost any other sexual activity.**

Anal sex is so unsafe because it causes bleeding from torn tissues in the anal area. Other health risks associated with anal sex are: Human Papilloma Virus (HPV warts can turn into cancer within the anal canal); Hepatitis A (a viral infection usually transmitted by oral-anal contact); Hepatitis B (spread through infected blood and body fluids and use of contaminated needles; Hepatitis C (though it is rarely spread through anal sex, but usually by the sharing of needles for drug use); and E. coli (usually spread through a urinary tract infection in females and can be transferred if the anal sex immediately follows vaginal sex). **Many of us don't know this, but Hepatitis B and C together infect 3-5 times more Americans than AIDS does.** So if you're not with it, stick to your script and don't agree to let someone put you at risk.

Herpes

According to statistics from the Center for Disease Control, Genital Herpes is the most common STD with nearly one in every two African American women ages 14-49 being infected with it. **The Herpes virus known as Herpes type 2 or HSV-2 affects every 2 out of 5 Blacks in every age group, 80 % who don't even know that they are infected with it and 21% of women being infected in comparison to 11.5% of men.** Why is it more susceptible to women than men? Women's genital tissues are more vulnerable than men's genital areas making transmission greater.

The two types of Herpes are oral and genital. Oral herpes appears as fever blisters and can be spread by kissing or touching the infected area and then touching someone else. Oral herpes can be spread to the genital area by oral sex (mouth to genital area). The Herpes virus stays in the body normally in a nerve located in the cheekbone. It may stay there and be inactive or it may travel down to the nerve in the skin's surface causing a reoccurrence of fever blisters. Reoccurrences (outbreaks of Herpes) are often triggered by emotional stress, fever, illness, injury and exposure to sunlight. Let's also note that there is NO cure for Herpes, there are only treatments for the blisters which include medications that relieve the pain, ointments that numb the blisters, ointments that soften the crusts of the sores, and antibiotics that control secondary bacterial infections.

Additionally, with pregnant females, herpes can be spread through the birth canal to the baby which can cause significant health risks to the infant. To stop the spread of this infection we must: get tested; talk to our doctors about treatment options if you are infected; use condoms (they also have condoms for the vagina); and most importantly, talk to you partner (ask them about their status and avoid sex if you or they have visible lesions or sores).

There is a high percentage of teen pregnancy as well as the transmission of STD's and/or STI's. Statistically, in the U.S., nearly 1 million young women under the age of 20 become pregnant each year (that comes out to about 2800 teens getting pregnant each day) and 1 in 4 sexually active teens become infected with an STD or STI every year. Common STD's among teens are: Chlamydia, gonorrhea, genital warts (HPV) and herpes. It is a fact that our government and media have admitted that teens are not only having sex but are having unprotected sex. Due to the racial disparities in the rate of contracting STD's and STI's, this calls for Black parents to WAKE UP, educate yourselves and your children.

Chlamydia and Gonorrhea

Chlamydia and gonorrhea are the most common infectious diseases in the U.S. among Blacks (accounting for 71% of reported gonorrhea cases and half of Chlamydia and syphilis cases – with Black women having the highest rates of Chlamydia and gonorrhea). These infections can cause PID (Pelvic Inflammatory Disease) which is an infection of the uterus, fallopian tubes and other reproductive organs. PID can cause long term complications such as chronic pelvic pain, ectopic pregnancy, and infertility. **What is even worse is that Chlamydia and gonorrhea are two highly treatable bacterial infections that can be cured with antibiotics,** but how can sexually active teens seek out services, screening and treatment when these STI's are not even talked about by parents?

Always keep condoms in your home and car. Safe Sex is about no excuses.

Do Cold Sores Mean You Have Herpes?

BY PATRA AFRIKA

What are cold sores (fever blisters)?

Cold sores (also called "fever blisters") are an inflammation of the skin accompanied by the formation of clusters of small bumps and blisters that is usually on the lips or close to the mouth. Pus sometimes oozes from the blisters, which can make eating difficult. Most people know these sores are associated with Herpes. But there are actually two types of herpes simplex virus, "Type 1" and "Type 2."

Type 1 Herpes Simplex Virus

Herpes simplex virus type 1 ("HSV1") generally only infects the body tissues that lie "above the waistline" and it's HSV1 that causes cold sores in most cases. If uninfected, they dry up in about 7-10 days. In those with HSV1, any little "upset to the health may bring on an attack. The infection tends to break out repeatedly in people who carry the virus in their skin. If cases occur persistently on the same area, there may be an infection from the teeth, nose, etc. to blame.

Treatment. There's no "cure" for either form, but neither is going to kill you. Those who recognize the early signs of HSV1 can limit an attack considerably by bathing the part with very hot water, or applying collodion. The blisters should be protected by a mild antiseptic powder.

Type 2 Herpes Simplex Virus

Herpes simplex virus type 2 ("HSV2") usually only infects the body tissues that lie "below the waistline" and it's this virus that is also known as "genital herpes." Herpes simplex virus Type 2 is not usually the virus that causes cold sores, although it can. It attacks the skin of the penis, resembles facial herpes, but also can "ulcerate." It's a pain (and definitely a condition you want to avoid if you don't have it), but it's not going to kill you. However, make sure you don't have some OTHER venereal disease that is masked by your Herpes symptoms.

Treatment. Again, no cure. But in an uncomplicated case the only treatment required is an antiseptic dusting powder, such as one or two percent salicylic acid in boric acid. All sex or stimulation must be avoided for at least six weeks.

What can trigger an outbreak of cold sores?

Under normal circumstances a person's immune system would be able to fight off a cold sore but if the immune system is overwhelmed a cold sore can easily develop. By observing which factors typically trigger a cold sore, a person can learn when to expect an outbreak. Common signs are emotional upset and stress, physical stress and fatigue, illnesses (including a cold or the flu), injury to the lips or skin, such as physical trauma or severe chapping, menstruation or pregnancy and an immune system deficiency.

What you can do to reduce cold sores or prevent them?

❑ Tea contains tannic acid and tannic acid possesses antiviral properties (some over-the-counter medications for cold sores contain tannic acid). Placing a tea bag on a cold sore when it first begins to form (especially during the tingling stage) can possibly help to stop or minimize the cold sore.

❑ Applying ice (for five to ten minutes each hour) during the first stage of a cold sore (tingling stage) will help lower the temperature of the tissue where the cold sore is forming and lessen the uncomfortable pain and itching.

❑ Eat plenty of raw vegetables daily

❑ Eat a handful of pumpkin seeds (no salt or oil added) or take a Zinc with C lozenge (NOW brand) every 3 waking hours for 2 days, then 2 lozenges daily until healed, making sure not to exceed more than l00 mg daily from all supplements

❑ Take 3,000-6,000 mg daily of buffered vitamin C in divided doses to raise your immune system. Take both a good multivitamin and good multi-mineral supplement daily. To heal your tissues, take 50,000 IU vitamin A daily in an emulsion form for safety at high doses, but don't exceed 10,000 IU daily if pregnant. Use a high-stress vitamin B-complex supplement (150 mg twice daily) to help your immune system to heal

❑ Take maitake, sh*take or reishi mushroom as directed on the label to fight viruses and increase your resistance to disease

❑ Use powdered organic garlic on all your food or take 2 capsules of Kyolic garlic 3 times a day as a natural antibiotic and immune enhancer

Treating Herpes Outbreaks

Some find that keeping the sores moist prolongs the healing process, others find the comfort of salves and ointments very healing. Try both methods and see which works best for you. If you find that your particular case responds better to an astringent, drying type medication than to a salve, make a St. Johns' wort/lemon balm tincture. **Aloe Vera gel soothes, dries, and effectively helps to heal herpes sores.** Apply the aloe vera gel directly to the sores. You can use the gel pressed fresh from the leaf of a plant, or you can buy aloe gel. Apply both topically.

Anti-Herpes Paste: One part goldenseal powder, one part black walnut hull powder, one part Echinacea root powder. Mix the powdered herbs together, then moisten the mixture with a bit of St. Johns' wort/lemon balm tincture.

Warm herbal baths are soothing and healing. You might wish to alternate both types or find the one that works best for you. The first is a soothing, relaxing bath that relieves the itching. The second bath is an astringent cleanser. After bathing, gently but completely dry the groin area.

Relaxing & Soothing Herbal Bath Blend: Three parts chamomile, one part instant oatmeal (dry), one part hops, one part comfrey leaf, two parts calendula, one part comfrey root. Mix these ingredients together and place a big handful or two in a large handkerchief or cotton bath bag. Tie it onto the nozzle of the tub and let hot water stream through it for several minutes. Adjust the temperature of the water, untie the bag, and let it float with you in the tub.

Astringent Bath: One ounce dry chaparral leaves, 1-2 drops tea tree oil, 4 tablespoons baking soda. Mix dry ingredients thoroughly, then mix in oil. Place mixture in a large cotton handkerchief or bath bag. Tie it the same way you would above.

NOTE: Cold sores are very contagious, so you should avoid using anyone's cup, glass, washcloth, toothbrush or kiss anybody with a cold sore.

Although there's no "cure" for HSV type 1 or 2, use the above treatments can help soothe or reduce symptoms.

SEX ED: BIRTH CONTROL AND TEEN PREGNANCY
BY TAMIKA HOGAN

Whether you are a teen or an adult, if you are at the point in your life where you are sexually active, or considering becoming active, it's very important you educate yourself. Sex is not just "what you do" as a part of romance and relationships. **The act of sex involves biological, psychological, physical and emotional factors, which is the reason why young people under a certain age** (mostly 16 yrs. of age) **are considered legally unable to consent to any sexual act. There is a mental stage that teens have not reached that consists of the ability to not respond based on one's biological drive, but to be able to make a sensible, responsible and rational decision to engage (or not) in sex and to have knowledge of what the outcomes may be.** Now that I look at it, it seems that many adults haven't reached that stage either.

Teens have an alarming and increasing rate of unwanted pregnancies as well as sexually transmitted diseases. This is mainly due to a lack of proper sex education and the failure to at least practice safe sex. While some (not all) STDs can come and go, another obvious consequence of sex – children – do not. Adults may be in the position to care for a child, financially, emotionally, physically (or not). But most teens don't have the means or the mental or emotional capabilities to do so. This often results in teens killing their infants, relying on or giving custody to adults, parents/caregivers, giving the baby up for adoption, or simply doing a piss-poor job of raising their children. This is why it's important that teens (whether sexually active or not) be educated on sex and to instill in them the importance of practicing safe sex.

One method of preventing unwanted pregnancy is by using oral or other means of contraceptive (contraceptive injections such as Depo Provera). However, these methods don't reduce the risks of getting STDs, HIV or AIDS, not to mention that there are risks and side effects associated with these contraceptives. In fact, **some of these contraceptives that were being pushed in the Black and Latino communities (like Norplant) are also being used in forced sterilization campaigns in Africa and India, often with disastrous health consequences for the women affected.**

We call it "birth control." They call it "population control." Anything that causes a woman to STOP ovulating is unnatural and bad for your health.

This is why it's important to always use condoms, to know which condoms to use and how to use them. Here are a few tips on the correct usage of condoms:

❏ Use a condom every time you have sex. (See, "Which Condom Are Best.")

❏ Always make sure that the expiration date on the condom has not passed and that the manufacturing date does not indicate that the condom is too old (note that if the package is not opened, condoms are good up to 5 years after the manufacture date).

❏ Keeping a condom in your wallet for more than a week is not a good idea. The constant friction and temperature changes can create microscopic tears in the condom that allow sperm (and other things) to get through.

❏ Be careful how you open that little packet. Don't think you're being smooth by tearing it with your teeth, or ripping it like some animal. Tear it at along an edge so you don't damage the actual condom.

❏ Put the condom on as soon as it's hard and before coming into contact with any vaginal, anal or oral fluids.

❏ Roll it down the right way. It's real cute if the girl can put it on with her mouth (you probably don't want to ask where she learned), but make sure the reservoir tip is pointed upwards.

❏ If you can barely roll it down to the base, you probably need a bigger size. But if it can move once it's on, it's too loose. Downgrade from that Magnum XL big boy. "Regular" will do.

❏ Keep the condom on from the beginning until the end (no starting off raw).

❏ Use a new condom for each site of penetration (vaginal, anal, oral), or else you'll spread bacteria from one site to the other.

❏ Always pull out immediately after ejaculation. Don't try to get a few more strokes in, because you might end up leaving something else behind. Make sure that when you pull out, you're holding the base of the condom in place to keep it from sliding off.

Finally, dispose of the condom properly. You can wrap it up in some toilet tissue and put it in the bathroom wastebasket. That way, you won't be polluting the water supply any more than you have to. However, if you're NOT with someone you trust, you should probably flush it. As nasty as it sounds, there are confirmed stories of women extracting semen from disposed condoms and impregnating themselves. Now ask yourself, if that's something I'm worried about, why am I sleeping with this girl in the first place?

Note: Many women who smoke are also on birth control. Many of us don't know, but this is a harmful, potentially deadly mix. As in heart attacks, blood clots and strokes. Reconsider smoking, birth control, or both. Is it worth having a stroke and losing the ability to speak or to use certain parts of your body?

Educating children reduces teen pregnancy and other sexual health risks – Silence increases it.

WHICH CONDOMS ARE BEST?

BY QUEEN CIVILIZED ZAG

At this point, your question should not be whether to use a condom, but which condoms are best...

No Frills Condoms

These are the ones you sometimes get from shady free clinics that won't spring for a decent brand or the kind you find at the very BOTTOM of the condom rack in the store. You should already know that you get what you pay for. If you think Durex has a bad reputation for breaking, just imagine the results you'll get messing with a Flurex. NOT recommended.

Male Novelty Condoms

These are the edible or specialty condoms that you often see in sex shops, adult bookstores and in condom machines in bathrooms. They are **NOT good for protection against HIV/AIDS, sexually transmitted diseases (STDs) or pregnancy.** As their name implies, they're just for fun and for something different. Which makes you wonder, why use a condom just for fun? It's either for protection or it's not.

Male Natural/Sheepskin Condoms

These are around $30 or more for a dozen. These are only good for protection against pregnancy, not against STDs (including HIV/AIDS). People prefer them because they "feel more natural." In fact, these are the modern versions of the world's earliest condoms. Yes, that means they're made from lamb intestine. You can use any type of lubricant (oil or water-based) with these condoms. If you know your partner's status and are just trying to avoid pregnancy, these are an option.

Male Latex Condoms

Male latex condoms are the most common types of condoms on the market. They cost about $6 to $20 a dozen, but cost can vary widely from brand to brand (check www.condomdepot.com for user reviews and ratings). Used consistently and correctly, these will protect you against HIV/AIDS, other STDs and pregnancy. Their drawbacks are their bad taste for oral sex (but see below for an alternative), and that you can only use water-based lubricants with them. **Oil-based lubricants like hand lotion, Vaseline etc. can make a latex condom break.** A condom can also break due to lack of lubrication! There are some people out there who are allergic to latex, who therefore cannot use latex condoms (but see below for an alternative).

Male Polyurethane (Plastic) Condoms

This condom is sold under the brand name, "Avanti." It costs about $8 for six condoms. If your life ain't worth that, you shouldn't be having sex. The benefits of these condoms is that they **can be used by people who are allergic to latex, and that they don't taste bad if you're using them for oral sex.** These condoms **can be used with any type of lubricant, oil or water-based.** It is still not known for sure how much protection they will offer against HIV/AIDS and STDs as long as they don't break or come off, since HIV and other STDs will not pass through polyurethane.

> **Did You Know?**
> In 2009, *Consumer Reports* tested condoms for reliability. Seven condoms achieved a perfect score of 100. Those condoms include the following models: Durex Performax; Lifestyles Ultra Sensitive Lubricated; Lifestyles Warming Pleasure; Trojan Her Pleasure Ecstasy; Trojan Magnum Lubricated; Trojan Ultra Ribbed Ecstasy; and Trojan Ultra Thin. The lowest score was for Night Light Glow in the Dark condom, which often had holes in it, but did a damn good job of glowing. A similar study in 2005 found that Planned Parenthood's Honeydew and Assorted Colors condoms scored the worst of the 23 condoms tested.

Female Polyurethane (Plastic) Condoms

The female condom is sold under the brand name, "Reality." These are only good for vaginal intercourse. Since they're made of polyurethane, you can use any type of lubricant with them, although they do come with their own lubricant. They cost $4 each, and are usually sold in packs of 3 (for $8). **They have a higher failure rate than latex condoms, primarily since they're much more difficult to insert and to use.** If you don't use enough lubricant, they can also make a squeaking noise when you use them.

Get what works best for you. If you don't want to pay for condoms, know which centers give them away for free.

HOW TO BOOST YOUR TESTOSTERONE
BY SUPREME UNDERSTANDING

Did you know that eating a poor diet and drinking all day is actually weakening your masculinity? I'll explain.

Besides cultural factors, most of the differences between males and females can be attributed to one biological factor: Hormones. And while all humans have varying levels of each, it's testosterone that makes you a man.

Testosterone is the primary male sex hormone. The majority of which is produced by your testes, as the name would suggest. Women have some too (just as men have some estrogen – some more than others), but men have 40-60 times more in their bodies. Testosterone is what gave us all the physical features that distinguish us from women, and even plays a role in the difference in our brains. Testosterone maintains your manly characteristics throughout your whole life and regulates several systems in your body.

The Benefits of Testosterone

Testosterone has been proven to:

❏ Improve your mental and physical energy
❏ Increase your competitive drive
❏ Increase your muscle size and strength
❏ Increase your metabolism
❏ Help prevent Alzheimer's and dementia
❏ Increase libido (sex drive) and erectile function

So testosterone is pretty damn important to a man (and probably to that man's woman, too!). It's a major part of what makes you feel like a man. So if you haven't been feeling too manly lately or maybe ever, perhaps it's time for you to grow some

> **Did You Know?**
> If your index finger is shorter than your ring finger, you may have an aggressive trait. The shorter a man's index finger is, when compared to his ring finger, the more aggressive and rowdy he is likely to be, according to a new study by Canadian researchers. The authors say the connection may have something to do with testosterone, as there is definitely a correlation between finger lengths and the amount of testosterone men are exposed to in the womb. This may be true of women too, as testosterone is not exclusive to men.

testes, or at least put them to use. Ask yourself these questions to see if you're "losing" testosterone.

❏ Do you feel like your sex drive has been decreasing?
❏ Have you been having a hard time "getting it up"?
❏ Have you been carrying some extra pounds that won't go away?
❏ Do you often feel physically and mentally tired?
❏ Do you feel depressed and unhappy?
❏ Do you feel shiftless and lack drive?
❏ Do you wish you felt more like a "real man" some days?
❏ Do you eat a lot of soy products?

I know the last question may have seemed a bit odd, like I was saying all vegetarians are soft, but I know enough gangster vegetarians to know better than that. I'm talking about the endocrine-disrupting influence of the chemicals found in soy (See "Is Soy Bad For You?"), as well as many other products. They can offset your natural balance of testosterone and estrogen (See "Gay Bomb"). Combined with several other factors, such influences have testosterone levels dropping throughout the Western world. According to a recent study of 8,000 men:

> [Testosterone levels in the U.S. are] substantially lower – by about 15 to 20% – than they were fifteen years ago. Scandinavian studies show similar declines, and in younger men too; a man born in 1970, for example, had about 20% less testosterone at 35 than a man of his father's generation at the same age.

Meanwhile, the average U.S. male's sperm count has dropped over 30% in the last three decades. While I'm not sure if people of color outside of North America and Europe are doing any better, I'm pretty sure it's not just white people being affected.

Here are some of the other factors behind the decline in testosterone:

Stress: Stress increases our level of cortisol and decreases our testosterone.

Lack of sleep: Testosterone rises while you sleep, particularly during the REM phases. Today, men are often skimping on their shut eye, which in turn is sapping their testosterone.

Drinking alcohol: Alcohol decreases the body's ability to produce testosterone. We may act on impulse when drinking, but our ability to sense stimulation is diminished when we drink.

Eating a "low-fat" diet: Low-fat diets that don't distinguish between "good" fats (like EFAs in plants and seeds) and "bad" fats (like those in meat products) also have been widely proven NOT to be healthy or helpful, but another reason to reconsider a low-fat diet is because they have been proven to decrease your testosterone.

Smoking: The nicotine and cotinine in cigarettes inhibits and reduces testosterone production.

Age: Every man is born with different levels of testosterone to begin with, but the average man's testosterone level peaks at age 20 and then slowly declines for the rest of his life. **You lose about 1% a year** – not bad – **but loss can cause obesity, brittle bones, muscle loss and impotence by the time you reach your 60s** – if you live that long. There's even a condition known as "male menopause." Testosterone levels in the low range may increase chances of heart attacks, prostate problems, or other serious conditions.

So how do you boost your testosterone? There's medical treatments involving injections, gels, and patches…but the side effects include acne, high cholesterol, shrunken testicles and liver damage. Supplements like

DHEA or androstenedione increase your risks of prostate cancer and heart disease. And steroids – in addition to other negative health effects – will results in the exact opposite of what you were going for (breast development and shrinking testes). So, uh, no. Here's 12 natural ways to increase your testosterone:

1. Get Rid of the Flopping Belly. Carrying excess body fat elevates your estrogen levels, and that may cause your testosterone levels to sink. All it takes is being 30% over your ideal body weight, which is pretty common nowadays.

2. But Don't Overdo the Weight Loss. Losing too much weight too fast can hurt you in more ways than one. In addition to the dangers listed elsewhere in this book, cutting your calorie intake significantly can make your brain think you're starving. As defensive response, your brain shuts down testosterone production until normal eating resumes. It's nature's way of keeping us from making babies during a time of famine. Ironically, this drop in circulating testosterone stops you from burning body fat efficiently, so you're actually hurting your weight loss goals.

3. And Don't Bother with the Atkins Diet. Research suggests that eating a high-protein, low-carbohydrate diet is bad for you for several reasons. For one, it can hurt your testosterone level. **Your protein intake should only be about 16% of your daily calories. Otherwise, high amounts of dietary protein in your blood can eventually lower how much testosterone you produce.** On the other hand, not getting enough protein can reduce testosterone as well. The key is a balanced diet. A diet with a carb to protein ratio of 2:1 is ideal for testosterone production.

4. Have Morning Sex. German scientists found that simply having an erection causes your circulating testosterone to rise significantly, and your body will produce even more if you prolong it with morning sex.

5. Work Out. To beef up your testosterone levels, the bulk of your workout should involve "compound" weight-lifting exercises that train several large muscle groups, and not just one or two smaller muscles. For example, studies have shown that doing squats, bench presses or back rows increases testosterone more than doing biceps curls or triceps pushdowns, even though the effort may seem the same. Start off by using a heavy weight that you can lift only five times. That weight is about 85% of your one-repetition maximum. Finally, do three sets of each weight-lifting movement. This fosters greater increases in testosterone than just one or two sets. Rest a full minute between sets, so you can regain enough strength to continue lifting at least 70% of your one-rep maximum during the second and third sets.

6. But Don't Overdo the Workouts. If you over train – meaning you don't allow your body to recuperate adequately between training sessions

– your circulating **testosterone levels can plunge by as much as 40%.** The symptoms of overtraining are hard to miss: irritability, insomnia, muscle shrinkage, joining the Reform Party. To avoid overtraining, make sure you sleep a full eight hours at night, and never stress the same muscles with weight-lifting movements two days in a row.

7. Eat Nuts. Research has found that men who ate diets rich in monounsaturated fat – the kind found in nuts, seeds, fish, olives, and avocados – had the highest testosterone levels. Aim to get at least 30% of your calories from this "good" fat daily and spread your consumption of it throughout the day.

8. Stop Skipping Meals. Your body needs a ready supply of calories to make testosterone, so regularly skipping meals or going for long stretches without eating can cause your levels of the hormone to plummet.

11. Eat More Vegetables. Veggies like broccoli, cauliflower, radishes, turnips, cabbage and Brussels sprouts contain Diindolylmethane which helps balance your estrogen and testosterone levels and increases the amount of free circulating testosterone in your body.

What about Too Much Testosterone?

According to a study of 4,393 military men, published in the April 1999 Journal of Behavioral Medicine, men whose testosterone levels were slightly above average were healthier than others. They were 45% less likely to have high blood pressure, 72% less likely to have experienced a heart attack and 75% less likely to be obese than men whose levels were slightly below average. These men were also 45% less likely to rate their own health as fair or poor.

However…these men were also 24% more likely to report one or more injuries, 32% more likely to consume five or more drinks in a day, 35% more likely to have had a sexually transmitted infection and 151% more likely to smoke. At very high testosterone levels (1000 Nano grams), men were even more likely to engage in risky behavior – and less likely to reap the positive health benefits of testosterone.

Taking all the factors together, researchers found that the healthiest men overall had testosterone levels that were in the average range, which is basically the point of this entire book: Balance.

Proper sleep, a good diet and exercise will keep you going stronger for longer. Don't neglect any of these things.

KEEP IT TIGHT...AIGHT?

BY SCIHONOR DEVOTION

Can you consciously relax and contract your vaginal muscles? Can you even find em? **Strengthening these muscles will help you with** avoiding **urinary incontinence, uterine prolapse** (yes, your uterus can fall right out of place if the muscles around it aren't strong)**, improving sex, avoiding hemorrhoids and even having an easier childbirth.**

Let's start with the basics. Get a mirror if you must and follow along. You may eventually want to purchase a vaginal speculum to help with this but you can do this without one. Come on, if you can let some strange man dig in there because he has the letters "MD" behind his name, you sure can.

Pelvis –Your pelvis is that big bone that you feel when you put your hands on your hips. It wraps all the way around your body and it open at the top and bottom. It has a bunch of other openings too that allow muscles and blood vessels to flow through it. Your pubic bone just above your pubic hairline along with other bones are all part of your pelvis. We call this whole area of muscles that run throughout this area, the Pelvic Floor.

Vulva – This includes all your external sexual organs that you can see.

Mons – The soft area that covers the part of your pubic bone where pubic hair grows.

Outer Lips – These are connected to the Mons, are covered with pubic hair and are different sizes and colors depending on the woman.

Inner Lips – They are underneath the outer lips and are hairless. At least most of them are. These lips get darker in color when sexually aroused.

Hood of Clitoris – This covers the clitoris and under this is the clitoral shaft connected to the bone by a soft, rubbery cord.

Clitoris – The most sensitive spot in the genital area, known to swells during sexual arousal.

Urinary Opening – I can't believe that some women don't even know where their urine comes from! Well, let me tell you. It comes from a little hole behind the clitoris.

Vaginal Opening – This is the opening that is used for menstruation, sex and childbirth. This opening leads to a canal with leads to the cervix which is the mouth of the uterus.

Hymen – If you have never had sex before, or inserted anything into your vagina, you may still have a hymen. Females are born with a thin layer of skin partially covering the vaginal opening. It used to be thought that girls lost it only if they've had sex, but we know that is can be broken during other activities like bike riding, dancing, or other sports.

Bartholin's Glands –These are two holes, one on either side of the vaginal opening. I had a friend whose glands got backed up, clogged and swollen. They became full of fluid and grew as big as oranges. She was in so much pain, she had to go to a doctor to get them drained. She was advised to be careful when wiping after using the bathroom. Just in case your Mamas didn't teach you, we are supposed to wipe from front to back as to keep any bacteria out of our vaginas after using the bathroom.

Perineum – This is the area of skin between the lips and the anus.

Anus – The opening of the rectum.

Those are the basics of the outer sexual organs. The breasts are also considered to be external sexual organs. Let's talk about them just a bit before we move on to our internal sexual bodies.

Breasts – Interestingly enough, each woman has about the same amount of glandular tissue, which makes milk when she is nursing. The glandular tissue is supported by fat. **Breast size is determined by genetics and hormones.** Meaning, it's possible for a skinny woman to have huge breasts, just as it's possible for a larger woman to be "small chested." **Although, If your weight changes, you may also see a change in breast size.**

The areola is the darker round area which houses the nipple which milk comes out of for our babies. During pregnancy and nursing, this area may get dark and look like a "bull's eye" for baby's to easily see. Some areolas have bumps around them, which are oil glands and are normal. Just as there are many sizes and shapes of breasts as a whole, there are many sizes and shapes of nipples too. Sometimes, a milky fluid may come from them even if you are not pregnant or nursing. This fluid should not be yellow or green though. Especially if you have a fever or your glands are swollen. If so, get it looked at. Breast health is so important.

What's Inside of There?

Now, let's get back to getting ourselves, tight and right. There is so much going on inside our bodies. Let's take a look.

Vagina – The vagina itself is about 3-5 inches in length and connects the uterus to the outside genitals. It produces a discharge which is made of old cells and secretions. This discharge should be clear and thin but can thicken and even turn white during ovulation. But, if you have discharge that is funky, foul yellow, green, thick, lumpy, or frothy, you may have an infection and should get it looked at and treated. If you have a fishy odor, you may not be cleaning yourself properly, using the wrong cleaners and may need an internal detox.

Cervix – This is the mouth of the uterus and at the top of the birth canal. Sometimes, it is bumped into during sex. Have you felt it before? If you are brave enough, touch it. It feels like a nose with a hole in the middle. If you have had a baby pass through it, yours may have a little smiley face shape in the middle. A plug seals this opening to keep it from being infected. It opens to about 10 centimeters to allow the baby to come out of the uterus and into the birth canal and eventually out of the vaginal opening into the world.

Uterus – This organ is sometimes called a Womb. It is usually the size of a fist but can grow to be as large as a melon in order to carry a placenta, baby and a bunch of other stuff during pregnancy. The lining of the uterus is called the endometrial and is lost during menstruation along with blood and fluid. This is what makes up menstrual blood. The uterus is a strong muscle.

Ovaries – These are two organs on each side of the uterus and just under the fallopian tubes. These organs are small and about the size of an almond. Eggs and female sex hormones like estrogen and progesterone along with many other hormones that we don't even understand are produced in the ovaries. When the ovaries release an egg, the little fingers of the fallopian tubes rub against the ovary and kind of sweep the egg into the tube.

Fallopian Tubes – Once an egg is swept up into the fallopian tubes, tiny hairs push the egg in the direction if the uterus. The hairs also push sperm towards the egg. If the egg and sperm meet up then the fertilized egg will stick itself to the wall of the uterus. Sometimes, although rare, the sperm may fertilize the egg outside of the fallopian tube sometimes in the ovaries, cervix or abdominal cavity causing what is called an ectopic pregnancy. This can end in miscarriage and can lead to infertility.

Exercises that Help

You may have heard of kegal exercises are used to keep your pelvic floor muscles toned, strong and controlled. When you try the following exercises, do them with either the vaginal muscles or anal muscles or both. Strengthening these muscles is beneficial and you won't be disappointed.

The Build and Destroy – A whole pyramid with your vaginal muscles. Here we go… Pull the muscles that you use to stop the flow of urine upwards. Imagine levels to your pyramid matching the walls of your vagina. Try to feel them as you squeeze the muscles upwards to the 1st level, 2nd level, 3rd level and so on. Then release the muscles slowly going in reverse down each level back to the foundation. Take a power break for about 5 seconds and repeat. When you start the exercise, you may not be able to distinguish the different levels, and may be squeezing many levels all at one time. That's ok, as you practice, you will be able to isolate and move your levels individually.

The Anxious Anus – Find the muscles that you use when you got to move your bowels but are nowhere near a toilet. Found em? OK, squeeze them and hold them for 5 seconds, then release. Pause for about 2 seconds and repeat another 9 times.

Healthy, Strong, Good – You can do this exercise with vaginal or anal muscles. Spell each word out loud or in your head. However you choose, squeeze with each letter spoken. Start with the "H" in Healthy and end with the "D" in Good. Take a break and say, "I Am" and then start again. There are 17 letters total in this statement making 17 squeezes. Then start again.

Cop a Squat – Squatting is one of the best things a woman can do with her body. Squatting is a great way to tone your pelvic muscles. Traditionally, women have always moved our bodies and squatted when handling our

business. Squatting for 5 to 10 minutes with flat feet can also prove to be a benefit during childbirth.

Dancing – Swing your hips! Tighten your butt! Try some Polynesian dance (Hula), Raqs Sharqi (Belly Dance), and of course some Booty-Shaking (African dance, West Indian wining and dancehall, and even Hip Hop)

There's much more about pelvic floor health and exercise that you can look into on your own, like the g-spot, ovarian breathing, maintaining wetness, and posture. You may want to check out Dr. Sunyatta Amen's Sexual Kung Fu, Sexual Tai Chi, Womb Yoga and Belly Dance classes. You may even want to look into egg exercises. These eggs are made of stone, usually jade or obsidian just like they used in ancient times and are still weighty and used the same way. So ultimately, you will be doing vaginal weight lifting with a stone egg to tighten your internal muscles. When you get real nice with it, you can even add weights to your egg. But that's a whole notha level of Coochie Kung Fu that we won't be going into now.

Knowing yourself "inside" and out is important for organ health. Dancing, squatting and contraction exercises are all things you can do to keep it tight and right.

SEXUALLY "OUT THERE": ADDICTS AND DERELICTS
BY SUPREME UNDERSTANDING

Some of Us are Addicts

Do you remember when Kanye West said he was addicted to porn? No? Maybe I pay too much attention to Hip Hop media. Speaking on his abstinence from the drugs that most rappers indulge in, Kanye confessed, "My only drug is porn. I have porn with me all the time. Whenever I go to the porn store, I call it the crack house." Maybe his huge porn collection is the reason why he's inseparable from the laptop he carries everywhere. Before sex hit the internet, a young Kanye was bringing smut magazines to school as a child. I'm not saying that looking at porn will make you a pervert, but we all know that being exposed to sex at a very young age can have some screwy effects on your psychology as you mature.

Kanye later confessed that he did have a problem with sex: "When Marvin Gaye made Sexual Healing, it was a fun song but he really had a problem with sex. And I think I have a sexual problem, a sexual addiction. I want to do it all the time." I'm sure Ye's got some issues, but I don't think people like Kanye have the clinical level of sex addiction experienced by people who are really sick. Halle Berry's ex-husband Eric Benet realized the same thing once he checked into rehab for sex addicts. He explained, "Sex addiction is a real thing, you know. In retrospect, it's not what I would label my situation." Hold on! If he wasn't addicted to sex, how does he explain his cheating? "Making some stupid-ass, stupid-ass mistakes." Benet continued:

> We all know I cheated. It was out there. It's a betrayal. But I never did have sexual intercourse with anyone while I was with Halle. Going into rehab was presented to me by her mother that in order for the marriage to have a shot, this is what you need to do...But I'm not a sex addict. I wanted to save my marriage and do anything necessary to do that. I went and heard other people's stories and realized this is really not my struggle.

Are you a sex addict? Probably not. If you're an adult who constantly craves sexual satisfaction, you might have developed a "compulsive behavior" which can resemble an addiction, but you're not really an addict (you just play one in real life).[10] Since it's not a "real" addiction, there won't be a "real" withdrawal if you get yourself back in check. And for some people, getting over a psychological fixation/obsession can be just as hard as beating an addiction. For the strong-minded among us, it's much easier.

Some of Us are Derelicts

Now, what about if your sexual cravings are a little, ahem, odd? Commonly dubbed 'perversions' or 'sexual deviations', a "paraphilia" is a condition in which a person's sexual arousal and gratification depend on fantasies, urges or behaviors that are out of the ordinary and often extreme. Of course, paraphilia's are reportedly more common in men than in women.

According to the DSM-IV, the paraphilia's include *Exhibitionism, Fetishism, Frotteurism, Pedophilia, Sexual Masochism/Sexual Sadism* (together known as *S&M), Transvestic Fetishism,* and *Voyeurism*. Some will sound familiar, others will not, but I'ma let you Google em rather than trying to explain some of this sh*t. Of course, there are others. In fact, some sources list as many 547 different paraphilia's. Up until 1973, homosexuality was also

---

[10] If you're a teenage male, you're just letting your hormones think for you, which is pretty common. If you're a teenage female, it's still common to crave sex, but something else had to go wrong in your past for you to pursue it as much as the boys do.

listed as a paraphilia, but was removed due to pressure from gay activists. Albert Eulenburg (1914) noted a commonality across the paraphilia's, using the terminology of his time:

> **All the forms of sexual perversion...have one thing in common: their roots reach down into the matrix of natural and normal sex life; there they are somehow closely connected with the feelings and expressions of our physiological erotism.** They are...hyperbolic intensifications, distortions, monstrous fruits of certain partial and secondary expressions of this erotism which is considered 'normal' or at least within the limits of healthy sex feeling.

Meaning, it's very real and natural for us to have sexual desires and for certain things to become triggers or objects of our attentions. But paraphilia's develop when those things grow beyond our control to become counter-productive to a healthy social/sexual life. Let's face it...its hard enough finding a mate in our communities. Imagine how hard it'll be to find a mate who will let you pee in their mouth.

So what do you do? Depends on how much your, ahem, "interest" affects your life. For some people, they're just preferences. For others, their entire lives have been consumed. If it's caused problems for you, find a self-help group, a therapist, or a healthy outlet for those cravings. There's probably a safe way for you to engage in whatever it is that floats your boat, but bear in mind that whatever's done in the dark will one day come to the light. For the more extreme cases, they've got medications for that kind of stuff, but the jury's still out on whether they work. Again, there's therapy (even holistic therapy) for most disorders. A lot of the time, you're fixated on something that affected you strongly when you were young, while your sexual attitudes where still forming. For example, your dog happened to be in the room "watching" the first time you got some...Now you can't have sex without a dog licking your ass and the Scooby Doo DVD playing on the big screen. Clearly time for some kind of therapy...unless of course, your mate loves you enough to understand. And if you can find a mate who will accept and love THAT, you better thank your lucky stars and NEVER mess things up between yall. Unless, of course, you've got a million dollars for hush money, and enough fame to find someone else who will tolerate your kinky ass.

Don't let your desires turn into lifelong problems. If your "interests" or "preferences" are getting in the way of your sexual and/or overall health, it's time to seek help.

---

3. CHEMICAL GENOCIDE

There's rocket fuel in your tap water. Embalming fluid in cigarettes. Even gasoline in your veggie burger! And of course, these chemicals aren't good for you. The majority of these synthetic additives are linked to cancer and other illnesses one way or the other. But what can you do? With dozens of toxic chemicals in just about everything we encounter, I can understand why some people think you can't do anything to avoid them. But you can. Just as you can avoid bad relationships – even though there are so many toxic people out there – by being more selective with where you meet people, you can change some of your habits and give these toxic elements less of a presence in your life. The foundation is knowledge.

Without an awareness of what's around you (and in you), you can't do anything about it. So at least start by knowing. And the first thing you should know is that – no matter what kind of toxic garbage we're looking at – if you're Black or brown, chances are very high that you're exposed to it more than anyone else. **If you're poor** on top of that, **you're 75% more likely to be exposed to the toxic pollutants that will wreak havoc on your health.**

Considering the centuries-long attack on Black male virility (the ability to make babies), it's "interesting" (to say the least) that the worst health effects are to be found in our reproductive systems. So it's deeper than the acrylamide in potato chips. That's small potatoes (no pun intended) compared to the toxic waste dumps they deliberately place in poor Black and brown communities. While we should certainly work to eliminate toxins in our diets, it's not enough to "change" on an individual level. In fact, all that "personal change" is good for you, but don't believe you're making a dent on the world outside of yourself. As author Derrick Jensen notes in his article, "Forget Shorter Showers: Why Personal Change does not equal Political Change":

> Part of the problem is that we've been victims of a campaign of systematic misdirection. Consumer culture and the capitalist mindset have taught us to substitute acts of personal consumption (or enlightenment) for organized political resistance...I want to be clear. I'm not saying we shouldn't live simply. I live reasonably simply myself, but I don't pretend that not buying much (or not driving much, or not having kids) is a powerful political act, or that it's deeply revolutionary. It's not. Personal change doesn't equal social change...The good news is that there are other options. We can follow the

examples of brave activists who lived through the difficult times I mentioned–Nazi Germany, Tsarist Russia, antebellum United States–who did far more than manifest a form of moral purity; they actively opposed the injustices that surrounded them. We can follow the example of those who remembered that the role of an activist is not to navigate systems of oppressive power with as much integrity as possible, but rather to confront and take down those systems.

So as you read through this chapter, understand that you'll need to take this knowledge and apply it, both to your personal life and, eventually, to the community in which you live. Because YOUR people are suffering. And if you've made it this far, it's your PERSONAL responsibility to start working against that suffering on a larger scale. Don't get overwhelmed though, because even small steps are steps toward a solution.

Toxic chemicals can be found in many household items, including food. Look for safer alternatives (or make your own) or shop organic.

TROPICAL FANTASY MAKES BLACK MEN STERILE!
BY SUPREME UNDERSTANDING

Tropical Fantasy was a Brooklyn-based soda that became an instant hit in hoods everywhere in 1990. It cost less than half of what Pepsi and Coke were charging for their products, and offered the kind of flavors that always seem to be a hit in our communities. You know, flavors like red and purple. Anyway, in April of 1991, rumors began circulating in Black neighborhoods that the beverage was laced with a secret ingredient that would cause sterility in Black men, and that the Ku Klux Klan were the actual bottlers. Demonstrating the power of the Black buyer, sales of the beverage plummeted by a company-crippling 70%.

The rumor didn't spread by word of mouth alone, and this was before the Internet really jumped off. People were actually copying flyers, posting them at stores and passing them out hand-to-hand. The flyers read:

ATTENTION!!! ATTENTION!!! ATTENTION!!!
50 CENT SODAS
BLACKS AND MINORITY GROUPS
DID YOU SEE (T.V. SHOW) 20/20???
PLEASE BE ADVISE, "Top Pop" and "Tropical Fantasy" .50 sodas are being manufactured by the Klu...Klux...Klan.
Sodas contain stimulants to sterilize the black man, and who knows what else!!!!
They are only put in stores in Harlem and minority areas. You won't find them down town... Look around...
YOU HAVE BEEN WARNED
PLEASE SAVE THE CHILDREN

Tropical Fantasy was devastated. Especially because they weren't really down with the Klan, and didn't put any secret genocide chemicals in their sodas. It turned out that the rumors weren't started by the Five Percenters, as the "Save the Children" message suggests (though, in our role as the hood's "conscious news network," we probably did play a role in spreading those rumors). The rumors were actually created and spread by Tropical Fantasy's competitors, Pepsi and Coke. Tropical Fantasy was cutting into their market shares in the hood. And the hood is Pepsi and Coke's biggest market, outside of developing countries like India and Nigeria (See "Selling Coke" in *How to Hustle and Win, Part Two*). After the maker of Tropical Fantasy submitted their products to chemical testing and initiated an expensive PR campaign, they bounced back enough to stay in business, but never really got big enough to "go mainstream." What happened to them wasn't an isolated incident. You may have heard the same kind of rumors about Snapple (I was once told the "K" on the bottle stood for "Klan"), Arizona Iced Tea, Everfresh, and even Church's Chicken.

Why do these rumors spread like wildfire in our communities? According to psychologist Lorraine Hale, the intense historical repression and destruction of Black people in America has led Blacks to become distrustful and suspicious of anything aimed at them. In other words, people of color just "know" that the system is design to "get us" at any opportunity it gets. But this was just another silly rumor, started by big businesses trying to eliminate an upstart company, right?

Kinda. The flyers were frauds, and the KKK link was just hype…but ARE there chemicals in sodas that can really cause sterility? Absolutely. A European study of 2,500 men found that men who regularly drink soft drinks end up with a sperm count nearly 30% lower than those who don't. And that's in Denmark, where the chemical regulations are much tighter than the bullsh*t they throw in the hood! We get the crap no one else will drink! Like those 25 cent colored juices, sometimes called "Quarter-waters," which have also been shown to reduce sperm count. Who else would drink those little anti-freeze lookin things but us? So we have good reason to be paranoid. If only we knew that it's not just the cheapo drinks and foods that have toxic chemicals in them. In fact, the irony of the Tropical Fantasy situation is that no one has ever waged a successful campaign exposing the toxic chemicals in the industry leaders, Pepsi and Coke. Makes you wonder, huh? Just know this, those chemicals we were worried about, they're all around us.

Don't take rumors or marketing on face-value. Get into the habit of looking up what's in the products around you.

MEDICINE MADE JUST FOR BLACK PEOPLE?
BY SUPREME UNDERSTANDING

In June of 2005, BiDil became the first medication approved by the FDA for a specific racial group. The heart medication proved to be better for Blacks than whites due to a difference in genetics. That led to a 2001 clinical trial involving only Black patients – and ultimately to FDA approval to market BiDil specifically to Blacks. While this may be a good thing, since about 750,000 Blacks in America suffer from heart failure, which is what happens when your heart is too weak to pump effectively. But it may also be cause for concern. For one thing, **it shows that chemicals (whether helpful or harmful) can have different results based on a person's genetics. But this has been known for quite a while, and it's why most drugs are tested on America's "preferred" group – middle-age white males...as well as white lab mice, and other animals that are bred (or "grafted") to mimic the recessive traits of white people.** What's deeper though, is now it's clear that drug companies can target specific races – with the FDA's consent. And there's no telling what other companies are doing the same. Then again, maybe there is. As Greg Bishop wrote in the March 2000 issue of the *Konformist*, in an article titled "Ethnic Weapons for Ethnic Cleansing":

> Did You Know?
> Thanks to the Human Genome Project, the genomes of the populations of Estonia, Tonga, and Iceland have been bought and patented by private corporations, with many more lined up for the future. Insurance companies have announced plans to use prospective clients' DNA in deciding whether to grant them health insurance. And a number of political leaders, beginning with NY Mayor Giuliani have demanded that DNA samples be taken from ANYone who is arrested, regardless of how minor their crime. Guess who all that is meant to target?

The Human Genome Project may now open the door to the development and use of genetic weapons targeted at specific ethnic groups. This project is currently being conducted under the auspices of the U.S. Energy Department, which also oversees America's nuclear weapon arsenal.

In October 1997, Dr. Wayne Nathanson, chief of the Science and Ethics Department of the Medical Society of the United Kingdom, warned the annual meeting of the Society that "gene therapy" might possibly be turned into "gene weapons" which could potentially be used to target particular genes possessed by certain groups of people. These weapons, Nathanson warned, could be delivered not only in the forms already seen in warfare such as gas and aerosol, but could also be added to water supplies, causing not only death but sterility and birth defects in targeted groups. Current estimates of the cost of developing a "gene weapon" have been placed at around $50 million, still quite a stretch for an isolated band of neo-Nazis, but well within the capabilities of covert government programs. **On November 15, 1998, the London Times reported that Israel claimed to have successfully developed a genetically specific "ethnic bullet" that targets Arabs**...Some scientists worry that the modified genes that corporations have spliced into fish, fowl, fruit and vegetables have permanently altered the world's food supply. Some may be intended to reduce populations. **The U.S. has a long history of interest in such genetic research. The current home of the Human Genome Project is the Cold Springs Harbor** laboratory on Long Island, NY – the exact site of the notorious Eugenics Research Office that was started in 1910 by the Harriman family. The project's 1910 agenda included governmental imposition of sanctions on such human rights as reproduction, and on U.S. immigration, based on the alleged inferiority of particular ethnic groups. The Eugenics Research Project established medical and psychological conditions that would qualify one for sterilization or euthanasia. Prominent advocates of the program such as the Rockefeller family, Henry Ford, and Margaret Sanger helped smooth the way for the passage of forcible sterilization laws in 25 states. These laws allowed the forcible sterilization of tens of thousands of people, mostly of minority status, during the first half of the 20th century.

> **Did You Know?**
> The herb rosemary minimizes or eliminates carcinogens formed when cooking some foods, say scientists at Kansas State University, who found that seasoning food with rosemary before grilling can reduce cancer-causing substances like Acrylamide by 30 to 100%. "By incorporating one tablespoon of dried rosemary for each pound of flour, we reduced acrylamide by more than 50%," says Leif Skibsted, PhD, a Danish researcher who found the same results. He believes that the antioxidants in tasty rosemary "scavenge" (cleanse) the harmful compounds.

The November 1970 issue of the *Military Review* published an article entitled "Ethnic Weapons" for command-level military personnel. The author of the article was Dr. Carl Larson, head of the Department of Human Genetics at the Institute of Genetics in Lund, Sweden. Dr. Larson wrote of how genetic variations in races are concurrent with differences in tolerances for various substances. For instance, large segments of Southeast Asian populations display a lactose intolerance due to the absence of the enzyme lactase in the digestive system. A biological weapon could conceivably take advantage of this genetic variance and incapacitate or kill an entire population.

So yes, genes matter. And "gene-specific therapy" may be a warning of bigger threats, especially when you consider the long history of biological warfare. The ancient Romans put dead animals in streams to poison their enemies' water supplies, and European settlers gave the Indians blankets infested with smallpox (which was "specifically" more deadly for Indians).

"Advanced forms of biological warfare that can target specific genotypes may transform biological warfare from the realm of terror to a politically useful tool." – Secretary of Defense William S. Cohen, April 28, 1997; Testimony before Congressional Committee

So the only question we should have is not "What if?" but "What now?" For more on this frightening direction in science and medicine, make sure you look out for an upcoming title from Supreme Design Publishing, to be titled *Chemical Genocide.*

TASTY TOXINS
BY SUPREME UNDERSTANDING

Did you know that there are over 14,000 man-made chemicals added to our food supply in our country alone? These additives are not meant to be part of our natural nutrition. Our bodies aren't even designed to handle the accumulation of all these toxins. So I'ma run through a list of some of the biggest offenders and the problems involved with them. Your job is simply to start checking out the ingredients on the stuff you buy.

Acrylamide: Acrylamide, a synthetic chemical used for various industrial purposes, also **appears in french fries, potato chips, and other cooked foods.** Acrylamide is formed in a high heat reaction of chemicals that are naturally present in certain foods such as potatoes and breads. Acrylamide, which is **also found in cigarette smoke, has been shown to cause cancer in animals and damage to reproductive glands.** Frying, roasting, and cooking form acrylamide, but not boiling, steaming, or microwaving. Frying creates the most acrylamide and levels of the toxin increase the higher the heat and the longer the food is in the heat. To avoid it, you can be careful about how you cook your potatoes, avoid frying potatoes, and when you do, stop when they become golden, but not brown. And take your bread lightly toasted rather than Black and brown.

Artificial Sweeteners: See "Is Sugar Bad for You?"

"Keep your sword straight, maintain your weight/ But he ate too much Monosodium Glutamate, and Polysorbate
And drug rate concentrate, with Sodium Benzoate" – Rza "Wu Wear"

Benzene: Benzene can be found in many beverages that contain both ascorbic acid (vitamin C) and sodium benzoate (a preservative). **The reaction between the ascorbic acid and sodium benzoate in beverages can create benzene.** Eating or drinking foods containing high levels of benzene can cause vomiting, irritation of the stomach, dizziness, sleepiness, convulsions, rapid heart rate, and death. **The International Agency for Research on Cancer (IARC) and the EPA have determined that benzene is carcinogenic to humans.** Benzene causes harmful effects on the bone marrow and can cause a decrease in red blood cells leading to anemia. It can also cause excessive bleeding and can affect the immune system, increasing the chance for infection.

BHA/BHT: Butylated hydroxyanisole (BHA) and butylated hydrozyttoluene (BHT) are additional additives to red flag. They are antioxidants used to preserve common household foods by preventing them from oxidizing. Both keep fats and oils from going rancid and are found in cereals, chewing gum, potato chips, and vegetable oils, but there is concern that they may cause cancer. "The structure of BHA and BHT will change during this process [of preserving food], and may form a compound that reacts in the body," says Gerbstadt. "BHA and BHT are not stable or inert. They're not just hanging out and being excreted by the body." Gerbstadt says that they are obviously not added for the purpose of giving people cancer, but for some people, some of the time, there may be that risk (See "Stupid Preservatives").

Food Colorings: Some artificial food colors are made from coal, tar, and petroleum with added antifreeze to hold the color. The human body was not designed to eat petrochemicals and the risk of these ingredients poses to our health is obvious. And although the FDA eliminated many of the most toxic food colorings a while back, there are a few still on the market that give cause for concern. **Blue 1 and 2**, found in beverages, candy, baked goods and pet food, are considered low risk but have been linked to cancer in mice. **Red 3**, used to dye cherries, fruit cocktail, candy, and baked goods, has been shown to cause thyroid tumors in rats. **Red 40**, used in sweets, cakes, biscuits, drinks, condiments, medications, has been linked with cancer. **Green 3**, added to candy and beverages, though rarely used, has been linked to bladder cancer. Studies have linked **Yellow 6**–added to beverages, sausage, gelatin, baked goods, and candy–to tumors of the adrenal gland and kidney. Tartrazine (also known as **Yellow 5**) is a yellow food dye used commonly in children's foods like candies, ice cream, artificially colored drinks, cakes, pasta, certain cereals, and even some alcoholic drinks. Just like sorbic acid and Citrus **Red 2**, it causes hyperactivity in children, exacerbates asthma and respiratory conditions, causes atopic dermatitis and may result, in some instances, to thyroid cancers.

High Fructose Corn Syrup: See "Is Sugar Bad for You?"

Mercury: See "Is Fish Bad for You?" Many products containing high

fructose corn syrup also contain dangerous levels of mercury. In a study published in the journal Environmental Health, former FDA scientist Renee Dufault tested samples of high fructose corn syrup and found mercury in nearly half of the samples. Dufault told the FDA about her findings but the agency "did not follow up." Right. But Dr. David Wallinga, a food safety researcher, did:

> We went and looked at supermarket samples where high fructose corn syrup was the first or second ingredient on the label," he said. These 55 different

foods included barbecue sauce, jam, yogurt and chocolate syrup. We found about one out of three had mercury levels above the detection limit.

MSG: Monosodium Glutamate (MSG) is added to thousands of food and grocery products through a dozen different innocent-sounding ingredients, including: yeast extract, torula yeast, hydrolyzed vegetable protein and autolyzed yeast, textured protein (including TVP), hydrolyzed oat flour, and even corn oil. Thousands of common grocery products contain one or more of these chemical taste enhancers, including nearly all "vegetarian" foods (read labels to check). It imbalances your endocrine system function, which disables your normal appetite regulation and causes you to keep craving and eating more food. **Studies have found that MSG can increase appetite by up to 40%!** So this chemical not only contributes to nationwide obesity, it also helps food companies boost repeat business. **The Mayo Clinic warns that MSG may cause "headache, flushing, sweating, sense of facial pressure, numbness, tingling or burning in or around the mouth, rapid heartbeats, chest pain, bronchospasm, shortness of breath, nausea and weakness."** Animal studies have linked MSG to nerve cell damage in the brains of infant mice. For more, visit www.MSGTruth.org

Nitrites/Nitrates: Food manufacturers add color-fixer chemicals, such as Sodium Nitrate, to preserve meats and also to keep the red color of the meat. Without this, the meat would turn grey, which would obviously keep consumers from buying it. **The USDA tried to ban the chemical Sodium Nitrate in the 1970s, but was unsuccessful due to lobbyists. Researchers actually use Sodium Nitrate to induce cancer in lab animals so that they can research this disease.** So, together with the meat, we are actually eating substances known to cause "cancer."

Olestra: Olestra, a synthetic fat known as the brand name Olean and found in some brands of potato chips, prevents fat from getting absorbed in your digestive system. This often leads to severe diarrhea, abdominal cramps, and gas. Olestra inhibits healthy vitamin absorption from fruits and vegetables.

Propyl gallate: Propyl gallate is a preservative used to prevent fats and oils from spoiling and is often used in conjunction with BHA and BHT. This additive is sometimes found in meat products, chicken soup base, and chewing gum. Animal studies have suggested that it could be linked to cancer, so it's an additive to be concerned about.

White sugar: See "Is Sugar Bad for You?"

What Toxins Do to You

Toxic build-up/exposure has been linked to serious diseases and developmental disorders, including:

- General health problems: Cancer, Cardio-vascular diseases, Immune system diseases, Hormonal imbalances
- Childhood and reproductive health problems: ADHD, hyperactivity, learning disability, autism. May cause reproductive damage.
- Neurological disorders/ brain disease: 25% of the chemicals in the environment are neurotoxins linked to increased incidence of brain disease. Other related symptoms: memory lapses, "brain fog"
- Obesity: "The body naturally manufactures fat in abundance to incarcerate and absorb chemicals and toxins that accumulate over time. As you cleanse the body, one can expect fat and inches to be substantially reduced." – J. K.Paulsen, M.D.
- Miscellaneous Crap: Joint pain and stiff knees, headaches, anemia, nasal congestion and mucus, skin rashes, dark circles under eyes and brown blotches on the face

The very best you can do for your health and longevity is to minimize exposure to toxins in your home and diet. These are factors you have control over.

GASOLINE IN MY VEGGIE BURGER?
BY SUPREME UNDERSTANDING

Let's get a few things clear before we dig into THIS one. First, we all know (or should know by now) that eating a BEEF hamburger (or whatever it's really made out of) is bad for your health. But since they tend to be delicious (although mostly because of the sauce and chemicals), people need alternatives and substitutes when transitioning to a healthier, more plant-based diet. That's why we have veggie burgers, as well as veggie chicken patties, veggie hot dogs, and veggie damn-near-anything-you-can-think-of. I can even tell you where to find veggie intestines. That's right, vegetarian chitlins. Why? These are supposed to be "transition foods," meaning they help you get away from a meat-based diet without suffering from withdrawal! Trust me, that "fake" General Tso's chicken has helped a LOT of aspiring vegetarians make it to the finish line. But just because it's not meat doesn't mean it's good for you.

In fact, a recent study put out by the Cornucopia Institute airs the dirty laundry behind the processed soy products we call health foods. **Many of those delicious veggie burgers are actually made from highly processed soybeans that were treated with hexane, an EPA-registered air pollutant and neurotoxin.** Some people say the report was funded by the meat industry. Knowing how dirty that game can get, I don't doubt it. But it's still worth considering that all that soy might not be the healthiest way to go.

You see, soy is big business right now. But not because soy is going to save your life. Soy is merely a cheap crop that industrial agriculture can grow easily and use in a variety of applications, from livestock feed to biodiesel. Speaking of diesel...I'ma get to it, just give me a second.

Many of us believe fake soy "meat" is healthier than animal meat. And you're right. Just about ANYTHING plant-based is healthier than animal meat! But there are a few reasons why those soy products aren't healthier than, say, a portabella mushroom sandwich or a homemade veggie burger made with actual veggies. First, most brands of non-organic soy burgers use "textured vegetable protein" (TVP) and/or "soy protein isolate", two highly-processed soy products. (See "Processed Foods") In order to meet the demands of health-conscious consumers, manufacturers of soy-based fake meat like to make their products have as little fat as possible. The cheapest way to do this is by submerging soybeans in a bath of hexane to separate the oil from the protein. Says Cornucopia Institute senior researcher Charlotte Valleys, "If a non-organic product contains a soy protein isolate, soy protein concentrate, or texturized vegetable protein, you can be pretty sure it was made using soy beans that were made with hexane."

Just like the Methylene Chloride in my Coffee?

Sounds just like the process to make decaffeinated coffee, where methylene chloride – the solvent used to remove the caffeine from the coffee – is left behind by the process. Methylene chloride is a proven carcinogen that is toxic to lungs, the nervous system, liver, mucous membranes, and central nervous system. Repeated or prolonged exposure to the substance can produce target organs damage. So when you think you're eating or drinking "healthy" (but not "natural" which is just as important), you're actually taking in some of the nastiest chemicals ever.

Hexane-Tainted Products		Hexane-Free Products
Boca Burger, regular		Boca Burgers "Made with organic soy"
Morningstar Farms, regular		Morningstar "Made with organic soy"
Amy's Kitchen	Garden Burger	Helen's Kitchen
Taste Above	Franklin Farms	Superburgers by Turtle Island
Trader Joe's	Yves Veggie Cuisine	Tofurky
President's Choice	It's All Good Lightlife	Wildwood

**Just because it's meatless doesn't mean it's completely healthy for you.
Try to get Hexane-free products when available.**

IS SOY BAD FOR YOU?
BY SUPREME UNDERSTANDING

Meat substitutes can be made from many different ingredients. Some are made from fungus (tastes better than it sounds), like the Quorn brand of "veggie chik'n." Some are made from wheat gluten, sometimes known as "seitan" in supermarkets and restaurants. Other products are made from TVP (textured vegetable protein), which contains wheat gluten and some vegetables. But most meat substitutes are made from soy, in one form or another. And vegetarians who are trying to replace the meat in their diets often eat a lot of "fake meat" to help make the transition easier. When I first became vegetarian, I ate veggie bacon, veggie chicken, veggie hot dogs, veggie everything.

I'm glad it helped me get away from the REAL bad guy (meat), but now I'm moving away from soy products as well. You see, those PROCESSED soy products (like soy protein isolate), which are the kind they use to make most "fake meat" products, are not particularly healthy, even when they are organic. **Processed soy, which is normally "unfermented", contains phytoestrogens that can negatively alter your hormonal levels** (See "Gay Bomb") **and lead to health problems.** Unfermented soy is also difficult to digest and can be rough on the body (but not as rough as meat.

East Asians, who possess some of the enzymes needed to process soy (which many of us don't), typically eat soy in its fermented form (tofu, miso, tempeh, etc.). When soy is fermented, most or all of its toxins are removed, making it safer to consume. When we look at how healthy people are in China, it's not because they eat veggie meat. It's because they eat more vegetables than meat, and even the meat-eaters fast from meat regularly. That's when they eat more tofu. And they've been doing this for thousands of years. Eating the fermented soy products, like tofu, miso and tempeh, that is. All those "other" soy products (like "veggie duck chunks" which are damn good, I got to say) have only popped off in the past 30 years or so. That's thanks to your favorite food-business giants: Archer Daniels Midland, Dow Chemical Company, DuPont, and Monsanto, who are now the largest producers/supporters of the soybean industry. They fund the trade organizations that are now pushing soy products on us like never before.

> **Did You Know?**
> In 2007, grain processors were responsible for two-thirds of our national hexane emissions. Hexane is hazardous in the factory, too: Workers who have been exposed to it have developed both skin and nervous system disorders. And the FDA does not monitor or regulate hexane residue in foods. More worrisome still: "Nearly every major ingredient in conventional soy-based infant formula is hexane extracted."

That's why most conventional soybeans are now genetically modified. **Unless specifically labeled "non-GMO" or "organic," it's almost definite that a soy ingredient is a GMO.** So if you do eat soy, strive to make sure it's organic, non-GMO, and hexane-free. And if possible, choose the fermented kinds over the other versions. Whatever you do, don't overdo it. If you're quitting meat, you should be eating HEALTHIER, which means more vegetables.

WHAT'S WRONG WITH COOKING?

BY SUPREME UNDERSTANDING

"Careful how you season and prepare your foods/ Cause you don't wanna lose vitamins and minerals/ And that's the jewel: Life brings life, it's valuable/ So I eat what comes from the ground, it's natural/ Let your food be your medicine, no Excedrin/ Strictly herb, regenerate in the sun, cause I got melanin" – Dead Prez, "Be Healthy"

In case you didn't know, humans have not only been vegetarian (for the most part) for most of the past 3 million years or so, but we also haven't really done much cooking. For most of our history on this planet, we ate what nature had to offer. And while you know we had to add our own spices and seasonings, we pretty much ate it the way nature served it. Of course, we'll explore that history in more depth in *The Science of Self* (www.TheScienceOfSelf.com), but my point is this: It's only been in the most recent period of our history that we've been "cooking with fire." Does that mean we've gotten smarter? Not necessarily. Fast forward from 20,000 B.C. to 2000 A.D., where we deep-fry, barbecue, or microwave everything.

I'm not saying you should never cook your food. But I do understand why some people are promoting a raw foods diet as a way for us to get healthier. But that kind of lifestyle – where we only eat 100% fresh and prepared fruits, vegetables, nuts and seeds – would be tough for most of us, especially people struggling with getting by from day-to-day.

My queen Mecca did a raw foods "fast" for 30 days, and it wasn't easy. I only made it to day seven. It wasn't hard to make the food (all you really need is a food processor and a recipe book), but I just "had" to have lo mein after a while (maybe it was the MSG calling me).

It's a way for "regular" people like us to live healthier without tons of work, and it's worked for us. Even the author of *The Raw Foods Bible* recommends this approach:

Although I am a big proponent of live, fresh food, I also know from experience that the all raw-food diet is one that only the most disciplined can achieve. It is very hard, for instance, to eat raw dried rice, even after its been soaked for 24 hours. Cooking breaks down the plants cell walls as well the starches and enzymes. Here-in lays the problem. It is those very enzymes that we need for that super energy feeling. **The solution is a balance of raw and cooked foods for most.** If one starts with a 50% goal of raw-live food and adjust it to their own circumstance, they can find the energy, taste and not have to make such a radical dietary change that they cannot adjust, and fall back on old ways. Juice is a super way to start adding raw food to your diet. Not the juice in the bottles and cartons in the supermarket, they are usually long "dead" by the time you buy them. FRESH juice made at the time of consumption, with a home juicer is the kind that really delivers on taste, enzymes and live food goodness…So if you crave more energy and want that veggie glow, try incorporating at least 50% to 75% raw veggies/juice/fruit into your diet. **If you have a hard time leaving that cooked food behind, try "lightly" steaming vegetables (2 to 3 min.) that will keep most of the enzymes and other nutrients in your food. Dried un-sulfured fruit and veggies are also very useful in the winter months to help us retain robust health.** Remember, enzymes are destroyed at 108 degrees so try to keep your fixins cool for good health and good digestion.

> Did You Know?
> Of 40 studies of humans, about 70% have correlated increased cancer risk with high consumption of well-done meat cooked at high temperature.

Nutritional expert Dr. Joe Fuhrman, who doesn't think a 100% raw diet is necessary, also advocates a similar approach:

> **Only small amounts of nutrients are lost with conservative cooking like making a soup, but many more nutrients are made more absorbable.** These nutrients would have been lost if those vegetables had been consumed raw. When we heat, soften and moisturize the vegetables and beans we dramatically increase the potential digestibility and absorption of many beneficial and nutritious compounds. We also increase the plant proteins in the diet, especially important for those eating a plant-based diet with limited or no animal products.
>
> **In many cases, cooking actually destroys some of the harmful anti-nutrients that bind minerals in the gut and interfere with the utilization of nutrients.** Destruction of these anti-nutrients increases absorption. Steaming vegetables and making vegetable soups breaks down cellulose and alters the plants' cell structures so that fewer of your own enzymes are needed to digest the food, not more. On the other hand, the roasting of nuts and the baking of cereals does reduce availability and absorbability of protein.
>
> In conclusion, eating lots of raw foods is a feature of a healthy diet. I always encourage people to eat more raw food. One of my common statements is— the salad is the main dish. Raw food is necessary for digestive efficiency, proper peristalsis and normal bowel function. Certain foods, especially fruit, avocado and nuts undergo significant change with cooking and are best eaten raw. Baking, frying, barbecuing and other high heat cooking methods that brown and damage food form acrylamides, which are carcinogenic. Browning and other high heat cooking methods should be avoided. Cooking techniques like steaming vegetables, stewing foods in a pressure cooker and soup making, do not have these drawbacks. They do not brown foods or form acrylamides.

So no matter what your diet, you probably could use some more fresh (raw) food in your life. Even vegetarians and vegans (especially the new ones) tend to overdo it when it comes to fried foods, processed foods, and microwave meals.

What's Wrong with Barbecuing?

The potential health problems arise from two factors inherent in the barbecuing process: high heat and smoke. Both create chemicals that can cause genetic mutations and unrestricted cell growth that signal cancer.

Barbecue grills get extremely hot, sometimes reaching 600 degrees. When meat is cooked well-done, chemicals known as hetero-cyclic amines or

HCAs are formed in the food. Researchers have found 17 different HCAs that may pose cancer risks. In 1999, a National Cancer Institute study examined the eating habits of cancer patients. It concluded that eating a daily average of 10 grams of **well-done or very-well-done meat** cooked at high temperatures **increased the risk of colorectal cancer by 85%.**

In addition to cooking at high temperatures, grills create smoke when fat from meat drips onto hot coals. The burning fat results in hot flare-ups, and smoke curls around the food. The smoke contains benzopyrene, a potent carcinogen in animals, particularly in the gastrointestinal tract.

A 2001 National Cancer Institute study found levels of benzopyrene to be significantly higher in foods cooked well-done on the barbeque, particularly steaks, chicken with skin, and hamburger. Knowledge about health risks of high temperature cooking began to evolve in 1977, when Japanese scientists showed cooked beef contained "mutagens" – chemicals that change the genetic structure of DNA and cause tumors.

> **Did You Know?**
> Low levels of electrical and magnetic fields can affect the permeability of the barrier surrounding the brain – the Blood-Brain Barrier (BBB). This can significantly affect chemical uptake into the brain, with a predictable effect on the health of some individuals. A book which details the effects of electromagnetic radiation and the practical steps that can be taken in homes and offices is *Warning: The Electricity Around You May Be Hazardous to Your Health* by Ellen Sugarman.

What's Wrong with Frying?

Not only does frying (especially deep-frying) load your food with extra oil and fat, frying food actually damages otherwise healthy oils. **The high temperature makes the oil oxidize so that instead of being good for you, it generates harmful 'free radicals' in the body, which can run amok and cause cancer, heart disease and other health problems.**

Frying also destroys the essential fats in food that your body needs. In fact, frying your food destroys most of the nutrients in your food, especially Vitamins A and E, which would have protected you from those nasty free radicals. Based on what kind of oil you use, how hot you're cooking, and how long you fry, the more damage you can do to your food and to yourself.

When cooking your food, make sure you are not overcooking it to the point where you are losing vital enzymes, vitamin, and minerals.

WHAT'S WRONG WITH THE MICROWAVE?
NOTHIN' SAYS LOVIN' LIKE A HUNGRY MAN MEAL FROM A BOX
BY DIERDRA BAPTISTE

How does Raditation Heat my Food?

It's a common thought that a microwave cooks the food from the inside out but this is wrong. Actually, non-ionizing microwave radiation (yes, radiation) is passed through the food item, and, in a process known as dielectric heating, energy is absorbed by the food molecules that have electric dipoles. This means the molecules have a negative charge at one end and a positive charge at the other. Think magnets. This causes the molecules to rotate with the microwave's alternating electric field. Unlike traditional cooking methods that don't change the molecular structure of your food, microwaves do so in order to "heat" up the food.

If we actually think about radiation, we know if a nuclear bomb were to be dropped 200 miles from us, the radiation would still kill us. Now, that's not to say the amount of radiation in a microwave can be compared to that of a nuke, but damn, why are we eating anything that uses it? Hell, some of us even call it "nuking" our food. If you've ever had to have an x-ray, you'll know that the x-ray tech will put on lead protection to keep them safe from the radiation. According to the FDA, the amount of radiation leaked from a microwave throughout its lifetime is 5 milliwatts per square centimeter at approximately 2 inches from the surface of the oven (whatever the hell that means). This is considered by the FDA to be far below the level "currently" considered harmful to humans. And we believe them…why? No matter how small an amount, butter and radiation just isn't the right flava for my popcorn.

Contamination
Then there's Bacteria! Since the microwave heats the food for such a short period, the food is often cooked unevenly. Heat needs to disperse fully through the food and microwaves only penetrate to a certain depth. Foodborne illness can occur when bacteria in previously cooked food hasn't been heated sufficiently to be killed.

Taste and Nutrition
Microwaves tend to produce food that is bland or just plain nasty-tasting, compared to food cooked in traditional ways. This is because microwaved food tends to be cooked unevenly, or too rapidly, killing essential vitamins and minerals. For example, **a microwave cannot convert Vitamin B12** (which plays a vital role in the normal function of the nervous system and brain), **making approximately 30-40% of the B12 in the food unusable to humans.** (See "Processed Foods")

Burns and Explosions
Why chance your outer beauty with scarring it by scalding or burning from the Box 'o Radiation? Liquid can be superheated to a temperature above its normal boiling point without any visible signs of the normal bubbles we see at boiling. When the liquid is removed from the microwave, or when adding a solid to the liquid, a spontaneous boiling will occur. This is called nucleation and could be volatile enough to cause the liquid to propel from the container.

Do you know how many mothers have unintentionally burned their babies by heating up the bottle in the microwave? (See, "Plastic Poisons.") There's also the danger of explosion from steam pressure in closed container and even certain foods like eggs. Anyone with young children should be watchful of this because they tend to open the microwave before it stops. The result may be burns or other injuries.

Overcooking an item or leaving the microwave unattended can result in fire. Food that is wrapped in metal or dehydrated foods will not absorb the microwave radiation and will produce a standing wave, which will reflect between the cooking chamber and the tube. This will cook the tube and can cause a fire.

There's also the danger of sparks or an electric arc caused by metal objects placed inside. The metal will resonate with the microwave frequency producing high voltage. If you've ever had static electricity and touched someone and felt that shock, you know you don't want to experience this.

Cancer

Berylium oxide, a human carcinogen, is in some magnetrons that have ceramic insulators. These will have a pinkish or purple color to them. If the microwave is damaged from dropping or any other physical injury, the magnetron may be broken, releasing the Berylium oxide. This is a serious danger if handled or ingested by inhaling.

If you still want to use your microwave after considering the pro's vs. the cons, that's fine, so do I. This isn't one of those "Stop or You'll Die" kinds of books. But this information should help you wean yourself from the addiction. You'll feel better, your food will taste better, and for you parents out there, your kids will grow up like we did and remember home-cooked meals.

Learn how to cook your food the old fashion way. Look into getting some iron skillets and pots or eat more raw foods.

DO "SMART" PHONES GIVE YOU BRAIN TUMORS?
BY SUPREME UNDERSTANDING

In 2008, the $148.1 billion wireless industry had over 270 million subscribers in the US (87% of the population) who used over 2.2 trillion minutes of call time. But whenever corporations are making billions of dollars selling you something, there's something they're not telling you. Most cell phones produce a form of radiation known as radio frequency (RF) radiation. And **there are a growing number of scientific studies showing that cell phone use can cause cancer, disrupt pacemakers, decrease fertility, damage DNA, and – of course – increase the risk of traffic accidents.** Not to mention wrecking marriages, but that's another story.

They Denied It Before – It's Pretty Clear Now

While earlier, short-term studies were inconclusive, several recent studies of cell phone use have found an increased risk of developing two types of brain tumors on the ipsilateral side (the side of the brain on which the cell phone is primarily held) among people who used a cell phone for

> **Did You Know?**
> The radiation emitted by a cell phone can penetrate 4-6 cm (1.6-2.4 in) into the human brain. Cordless home phones, television, radio, laptops, and palm held computers all produce radiofrequency (RF) radiation, the same type of radiation that is produced by cell phones.

longer than 10 years. Other recent studies linked cell phone use to an increased risk of salivary gland tumors (Lonn 2006; Sadetzki 2008), an increased risk for neurological symptoms such as migraine and vertigo (Schuz 2009), an increased risk for Alzheimer disease associated with electromagnetic radiation (Huss 2009), and a correlation between prenatal exposure to cell phone radiation and behavioral problems in children (Divan 2008). **One study has shown that children under the age of eight absorb twice the amount of radiation into their brain tissue as adults due to their lower skull thickness.**

Cell Phones and Sperm Counts?

Cell phone storage in front pockets has been linked to poor fertility and an increased chance of miscarriage and childhood cancer. **According to the Cleveland Clinic Center for Reproductive medicine, semen quality "tended to decline as daily cell phone use increased."** Six studies from the U.S., Australia, Japan and Europe reported that

> **Did You Know?**
> Americans send 5 billion texts a day. Your teenage daughter is responsible for 8% of that by herself. But studies have found that too much texting can cause neck back pain from poor posture (which I call "text neck"), elbow or wrist pain (like carpal tunnel syndrome), tendonitis, and even arthritis from repeated pressure on your fingertips. Not to mention straight up death from texting-while-driving.

exposure to cell phone radiation has an adverse effect on sperm counts, motility and vitality (Agarwal 2009; De Iuliis 2009; Erogul 2006; Fejes 2005; Salama 2009; Yan 2007).

The Radiation Limits – See How Your Phone Measures Up

On Aug. 7, 1996, the FCC created guidelines on cell phone radiation (RF) exposure. The guidelines created a measure of the rate that body tissue absorbs radiation energy during cell phone use called the specific absorption rate (SAR). The SAR for cell phone radiation was set at a maximum of 1.6 watts of energy absorbed per kilogram of body weight. The limit was set due to the thermal effects of cell phone radiation (all RF radiation can heat human body tissue at high enough levels) – it was not set to mitigate other biological effects such as DNA damage or cancer.

The FCC SAR limit is based upon a cell phone call that averages 30 minutes when the cell phone is held at the ear. SAR levels for cell phones sold in the US range from a low of .109 to the legal limit of 1.6. The worst phones? Almost always Smartphones/PDAs.

Phone	SAR Level (Watts per Kilogram of Body Weight)
Motorola V365	1.51 W/kg
Blackberry Bold 9000	1.51 W/kg
Blackberry Curve 8300	1.51 W/kg
Motorola MOTO VE240	1.52 W/kg
T-Mobile Shadow	1.53 W/kg
Motorola C290	1.53 W/kg
Motorola Moto Q Global	1.29 - 1.53 W/kg
Blackberry Curve 8330	1.54 W/kg
Motorola W385	1.54 W/kg
Motorola i335	1.53 - 1.55 W/kg
Motorola MOTO VU204	1.55 W/kg
T-Mobile myTouch 3G	1.55 W/kg
Blackberry 8703e	1.44 - 1.55 W/kg
Blackberry Bold 9700	1.39 - 1.55 W/kg
Kyocera Jax S1300	1.55 W/kg
Motorola Moto VE440	1.49 - 1.56 W/kg
Palm Pixi	1.56 W/kg
Motorola i880	1.30 - 1.57 W/kg
Blackberry 8820	1.28 - 1.58 W/kg

For those of you that have Crickets, the radiation levels aren't available on all models, but – since Crickets are marketed to the hood – you can bet the levels are high. You can look up your phone's radiation levels pretty easily at www.ewg.org/cellphone-radiation or (if it's not there) at the online FCC database (using the FCC ID behind your cell phone's battery) at www.fcc.gov/oet/ea/fccid

Other Ways Your Phone Can Kill

Let's not forget that your phone can kill you in other ways as well! According to studies done in England and Utah, a driver on a cell phone is more impaired in function and reaction time than a drunk driver with a Blood Alcohol Content level of 0.08% (past the legal limit). The National Highway Traffic Safety Administration estimates that driving distractions, including the use of cell phones (even on speakerphone), contribute to 25% of all traffic crashes. Don't even get me started on the statistics for my personal vice, texting/emailing/video producing while driving. As if all that wasn't enough, lithium-ion batteries, used in most cell phones, can explode from exposure to high heat, or from overcharging a faulty bootleg battery. These explosions have caused injuries and started fires. And if you're in a dangerous neighborhood (or live a high-risk lifestyle), walking around, looking down, texting away, is not a good look for personal safety!

Tips for Reducing your Exposure to Phone Radiation

1. Buy a Low-Radiation Phone. Consider replacing your phone with one that emits the lowest radiation possible and still meets your needs.

2. Use a Headset or Speaker. Headsets emit much less radiation than phones. Choose either wired or wireless (experts are split on which version is safer). Some wireless headsets emit continuous, low-level radiation, so take yours off your ear when you're not on a call. Using your phone in speaker mode also reduces radiation to the head.

3. Listen More, Talk Less. Your phone emits radiation when you talk or text, but not when you're receiving voicemail messages.

4. Hold Phone Away from your Body. Hold the phone away from your torso when you're talking (with headset or speaker), not against your ear, in a pocket, or on your belt where soft body tissues absorb radiation.

5. Choose Texting over Talking. Phones use less power (less radiation) to send text than voice. Texting also keeps radiation away from your head.

6. Poor Signal? Stay off the Phone. Fewer signal bars on your phone means that it emits more radiation to get the signal to the tower. Make and take calls when your phone has a strong signal.

7. Limit Children's Phone Use. Health agencies in at least 6 countries recommend limits for children's phone use, such as for emergency situations only. For those of you who have babies who love playing with your cellphone (and can tell the difference from a toy version), don't do it. At the very least, turn off the signal/connection on your phone before giving it to them.

8. Lose the "Radiation Shields." Things such as antenna caps or keypad covers reduce connection quality and actually force the phone to transmit at a higher power (with higher radiation).

Come up with your own plan (using the above suggestions) to decrease your exposure to cellphone radiation.

WHAT A WASTE: ENVIRONMENTAL RACISM
BY SUPREME UNDERSTANDING
BASED ON AN EXCERPT FROM HOW TO HUSTLE AND WIN[11]

You may not know it, but you probably live closer to a toxic waste site than you think. You also probably live in an area where air and water

---

[11] Additional content comes from a presentation I did at the 2010 White Privilege Conference (www.uccs.edu/~wpc). The White Privilege Conference is an annual gathering of predominantly white anti-racist, anti-oppression activists, organizers, educators, and sympathizers.

pollution standards are being seriously violated. The chances are good that your environment is making you sicker as we speak.

A confidential memo by the Environmental Protection Agency revealed that even they considered this environmental racism "one of the most politically explosive environmental issues yet to emerge." The EPA planned to spin the issue by pursuing positive publicity in Black and Hispanic-centered publications, until the memo revealing their plan was leaked to the media.

Race is the most significant determinant of the location of hazardous waste facilities. Communities with the highest composition of minority residents had the greatest number of Commercial Hazardous Waste (CHW) facilities.

> **Did You Know?**
> A 1984 report prepared for a California state agency identified Black and Hispanic communities as better candidates for trash-burning power plant sites. A study by the NAACP showed that Blacks are 50% likelier to live near a commercial toxic waste facility. The Commission for Racial Justice has found that three of every five Blacks live in communities with abandoned toxic waste sites.

Sixty percent of the total Black population in the United States (as well as 60% of the Hispanic population) live in communities with one or more uncontrolled toxic waste sites. **A majority of Blacks and Latinos in the U.S. live in areas where two air pollution standards are violated, compared to only one-third of whites.**

According to Michael Novick, "study after study has also shown a clear pattern of hazardous and other waste facilities most commonly being located in existing African American, native and Chicano communities."

For example, in Houston, Texas, all of the municipal landfills and six out of eight incinerators were placed in Black neighborhoods between the 1920s and 1970s. **From 1970 to 1978, three out of four privately-owned landfills were also placed in the Black community. Although the Black community only represented 28% of Houston's population, they had 82% of the trash.**

The community around the nation's largest hazardous waste landfill, in Emelle, Alabama, is 95% Black. The landfill, which operates in the heart of Alabama's "black belt," accepts hazardous wastes from the 48 contiguous states and several foreign countries.

According to a 1983 General Accounting Office study, three of four offsite hazardous waste landfills in EPA Region IV (eight Southern states) were located in mostly Black communities. Today, 100% of the hazardous waste in the region is dumped in the Black community, as reported in "Dumping in Dixie." But Blacks make up only 20% of the region's population.

And what happens? Everywhere you find these toxins, you find all kinds of serious health complications (from cancer to brain damage). From Hunter's Point in San Francisco to "Cancer Alley" in Baton Rouge, people of color have a disproportionately high rate of cancers they blame directly on local plants and dump sites. And it's not just Blacks and Latinos. About half of all Asian/Pacific Islanders and Native Americans live in communities with uncontrolled toxic waste sites.

Is it Just an Accident?

Uh, the title of this chapter IS "Chemical GENOCIDE" you know. So, uh, no it's not an accident. There are countless examples of how governments and huge corporation have worked hand-in-hand to poison minority communities. You can blame it on the fact that poor people are less likely to fight back, but you can't deny that these methods also create a sick form of population control. Considering that the white people in power have historically attempted countless measures to limit the population growth of people of color (from abortion campaigns to forced sterilization), I don't have any problem seeing a "conspiracy" in the details of environmental racism. Especially considering how so much of the toxins directly affect reproduction. If you need proof that our government knows what's going on, here's some:

☐ In 1961, Colorado State Trooper Bill Wilson stopped a milk truck that was spraying liquid on the ground in Denver. According to Wilson, the truck's operator told him he was dumping radioactive wastewater from the Rocky Flats plant and had the government's permission to do it.

☐ Between 1950 and 1980, at the Lowry landfill near Denver, millions of gallons of hazardous industrial wastes were dumped into shallow unlined pits. Levels of plutonium and radioactive americium were 10 to 10,000 times greater than the average levels reported for a nuclear weapons plant in that area. **The polluters included Adolph Coors (who once produced nuclear fuel), Lockheed Martin, Rockwell** (then operator of the U.S. Department of Energy's Rocky Flat's nuclear bomb plant), **Hewlett Packard, IBM, Waste Management, and the Denver Post.** The EPA ITSELF also dumped pesticides and other lab wastes at the site.

☐ "Cancer Alley" is the name given to a 100 mile stretch of land between Baton Rouge and New Orleans, containing seven oil refineries and 175 heavy industrial plants. The EPA reports that the majority of the 23 million pounds of toxic waste released into the air are in two zip code areas, primarily inhabited by Blacks. **A 1992 National Law Journal investigation found that even when the government enforces the environmental regulations against companies in violation, the fines levied in these areas are significantly lower than those levied in white communities.**

☐ In its efforts to locate dump sites on Indian land, Browning-Ferris Industries (BFI) got the listing of tribes through a system of "introductions" provided by the U.S. Bureau of Indian Affairs. Because of massive waste dumping in Native American communities, reproductive cancer among Navajo teenagers is 17 times the national average.

Historically, polluting industries have been placed near poor areas and the pollutants were considered trade-offs for economic development. For example, a paper mill spewing its stench in one of Alabama's poverty-ridden black belt counties led Governor George Wallace to declare: "Yeah, that's the smell of prosperity. Sho' does smell sweet, don't it?"

And incentives have been used to lull unknowing residents into accepting toxic dumping. For example, the Los Angeles Bureau of Sanitation offered Gilbert Lindsay, a Black city councilman, a $10 million "Community Betterment Fund" if his district would host a hazardous waste incinerator.

According to author and Radioactive Waste Project director, Diane D'Arrigo:

> People around regular trash landfills will be shocked to learn that radioactive contamination from nuclear weapons production is ending up there, either directly released by DOE or via brokers and processors.

In fact, since most story ideas for shows like *Law and Order* are "ripped from the headlines," there's actually a 2007 episode of *Special Victims Unit* called "Loophole" that covers ALL this.

What Can We Do?

You've got two options (actually three, if you include the approach of radical environmentalists like Helen Woodson).

A. Judiciary action, employing the Equal Protection Clause. A number of successful court battles have led to changes in communities just like yours.

B. Political Action and Grassroots Action. For example, almost a thousand people, primarily Hispanics from all over California, marched a mile and a half to the gates of a proposed hazardous waste incinerator chanting "el pueblo parara el incinerador" (the people will stop the incinerator). In 1987, the organizers of this protest had helped elect a local woman, Lucille Roybal-Allard, as the district's state assemblywoman. "They think that if they pick a poor community, they won't have any resistance... We are here to prove that they are wrong," she warned.

List ways in which you can get involved to reduce chemical and environmental waste in your community.

PLASTIC POISONS
BY SUPREME UNDERSTANDING

Besides the fact that most plastics are made from petroleum, a non-renewable resource, and are not biodegradable, using plastics in cooking and food storage can carry some serious health risks. A whole bunch of petroleum-based chemicals go into the manufacture of plastics. Some can leach into food and drinks and possibly impact human health. Leaching increases when plastic comes in contact with oily or fatty foods, during heating and from old or scratched plastic. The types of plastics shown to leach the most toxic chemicals are polycarbonate, PVC and styrene. This doesn't mean that other plastics are entirely safe. These plastics have just been studied more.

If you have to use plastic in cooking and heating your food or beverage, use only the ones coded PETE, HDPE, LDPE, and PP. Avoid all the rest, especially those coded PVC, V, PS, and OTHER. Plastic codes can be found on bottom of plastic containers.

What the Codes Mean

PETE: Polyethylene terephthalate ethylene used for soft drink, juice, water, detergent, cleaner and peanut butter containers.

HDPE: High-density polyethylene, used in opaque plastic milk and water jugs, bleach, detergent and shampoo bottles and some plastic bags.

PVC or V: Polyvinyl chloride, used for cling wrap, some plastic squeeze bottles, cooking oil and peanut butter jars, detergent and window cleaner bottles.

LDPE: Low density polyethylene, used in grocery store bags, most plastic wraps and some bottles.

PP: Polypropylene, used in most Rubbermaid, deli soup, syrup and yogurt containers, straws and other clouded plastic containers, including baby bottles.

PS: Polystyrene, used in Styrofoam food trays, egg cartons, disposable cups and bowls, carryout containers and opaque plastic cutlery.

Other: Usually polycarbonate, used in most plastic baby bottles, 5-gallon water bottles, "sport" water bottles, metal food can liners, clear plastic "sippy" cups and some clear plastic cutlery. New bio-based plastics may also be labeled #7.

And if you're going to use plastic to store or cook your food, follow the advice below:

☐ **Avoid using plastic containers in the microwave.** Since chemicals are released from plastic when heated, it's safest not to microwave food and drinks in plastic containers. Instead use glass containers. If you do microwave in plastic, use only plastic labeled "microwave safe." Note that "microwave safe" does not mean that there is no leaching of chemicals. Avoid using for fatty foods.

☐ **Beware of cling wraps, especially for microwave use.** Instead use waxed paper or paper towel for covering foods. If you do use plastic, don't let the plastic touch the food. For plastic-wrapped deli foods, slice off a thin layer where the food came in contact with the plastic and rewrap in non-PVC plastic wrap or place in a container.

☐ **Use alternatives to plastic packaging whenever possible.** Use refillable containers at your local food cooperative. Bring your own take-home containers to restaurants. Bring reusable bags or cardboard boxes to the grocery store.

☐ **With plastic water bottles, take precautions.** If you use a polycarbonate water bottle, to reduce leaching of BPA, don't use for warm or hot liquids and discard old or scratched bottles. Water bottles from #1 or #2 plastics are recommended for single use only. For all types of plastic, you can reduce bacterial contamination by thoroughly washing daily. However, avoid using harsh detergents that can break down plastic and increase chemical leaching.

☐ **Replace baby bottles.** Discard old, scratched polycarbonate baby bottles and "sippy" cups. Heat foods and drinks outside of the plastic and then transfer into the plastic only after they are cool enough to eat or drink.

In fact, ANY PLASTIC that shows signs of wear–such as scratches or a cloudy, crackled appearance–more readily leaches chemicals and needs to be discarded right away. Scratches can also harbor bacteria.

Familiarizing yourself with plastic codes like PETE, HDPE, PVC, PP, and PS can help reduce your exposure to harmful plastics.

BPA CAN MAKE YOU A NEW MAN
BY MARCEL MALEKEBU

BPA (or Bisphenol A) is an organic chemical compound that is utilized in the synthesis of polycarbonate plastics and epoxy resins (usually used to make composite materials like fiberglass and carbon fibers). BPA is actually a toxin, or poisonous substance. **Since as far back as the 1930s, BPA has encountered much controversy because of its detrimental psychological effects on children. Studies have shown that the amount of exposure one has to BPA is increased heavily when eating or drinking from canned foods or epoxy lined boxes (which is essentially everything).** Examples of foods with very high concentrations of the toxin are; chicken soup cans, infant formula, and ravioli. Actually, nearly all infant formulas have BPA in their packaging. Over 130 studies have shown that low doses of the BPA compound have proven to cause a number of health problems, including; behavioral development issues, decreased maternal behavior, different socio-sexual behaviors, Down Syndrome, insulin resistance (which leads to Type II diabetes), reduced sperm count in males, increase in risk of prostate, breast, and ovarian cancer, and changes in brain chemistry. These changes can be drastic, leading to imbalances that can potentially alter normative hormonal processes, including those associated with sexuality.

Does this mean that BPA can cause homosexuality?

No. At least, not necessarily...However, BPA is, in fact, estrogenic, meaning that it's loaded with the female sex hormone. This can have very astonishing effects on fetuses, infants and children because of the unnatural hormonal levels that cause imbalances in the brain.

It doesn't take a long time for the BPA to break its bond from the lining and seep into the actual food. And heat can speed up this process.

Recent studies report that approximately 93% of the population has been exposed to and still has these low doses of BPA in their system. Black people have experienced exponentially more negative effects from BPA than whites. In fact, **by the age of eight, 48.3% of "African-American" girls hit puberty, while only 14.7% of their white counterparts do.** This is most likely due to the amount of poverty in the Black community and the lack of information about nutrition in low-income neighborhoods and communities.

There are a number of ways you can reduce your BPA intake on a daily basis by purchasing glass jars of tomato sauces and such products instead of canned foods, buy frozen or fresh vegetables and fruits, and beverages in glass and/or plastic bottles. The plastic bottles are most often not made with BPA anymore, and are better than canned soda or boxed juices.

And there's more than just BPA. In "Gay Bomb," an article in *How to Hustle and Win Part Two*, Supreme Understanding writes:

> **There are other chemicals, known as NPEs (Nonylphenol ethoxylates), which are found in cosmetic products.** Usually they are in those fruity-ass shampoos and hair products some of you pretty boys wear. **Those NPEs are also endocrine disruptors, and they have been shown to change the sex of fish in affected water.** It also increases estrogen, and has been shown to cause the growth of breasts in boys. According to an article in *New Scientist Magazine*, "Slight anatomical oddities in infant boys are being heralded as the first evidence that gender-bending chemicals are affecting humans."
>
> There are other chemicals in the food we eat. **We now use about 10 lbs. of pesticides per year for every man, woman and child in the U.S. Many of these chemicals are affecting us to the point where we are in danger of not being able to reproduce within 50 years. Many** cheaply produced foods average over 10 different pesticides in one sample. Depending on where you live, there are even herbicides and insecticides in your glass of water. These chemicals are not removed by water treatment such as chlorination. Endocrine interrupting pesticides can alter the sex of a child during the first 6 weeks of pregnancy, and in some cases, cause a person to have traits of the opposite sex.
>
> **Phthlates. BPA. NPEs. And dozens of others. And studies show that poor communities, especially Black and Hispanic ones, get most of this sh*t sent straight to them.** That sh*t is in you right now. And if you have a child, your child has 20 times more in their system than you do. What does that tell you? Do you still think its all natural?

Take steps to limit the use of harmful BPA products in your home.

TOXINS IN YOUR HOME
BY SUPREME UNDERSTANDING

When the Environmental Working Group did studies of toxins in children, their tests found as many as 232 chemicals in the 10 newborns, all of minority descent. And children actually suffer the most from such chemicals because they are exposed to these substances from an early age, when they don't have the natural "detox" processes developed enough in their bodies to handle them.

Note: Before you start reading and start freaking out (or shutting down), we need to say this: "Chronic Toxicity" refers to regular exposure. An occasional exposure to some hazards is not something to worry about. For example, regular, day-long exposure to fluorescent lighting (school, work) can lead to a number of health problems including behavioral problems in children. Obviously, working occasionally under fluorescent lighting is not something for most people to worry about. I may use an unhealthy household product an occasion (and don't worry about it), but I try to stick to the non-toxic ones when they are available for purchase.

Aluminum: Aluminum is toxic even in small amounts if it's deposited in the brain. Aluminum toxicity has been linked to Alzheimer's disease, osteoporosis, colic, rickets, gastrointestinal problems, extreme nervousness, anemia, headaches, decreased liver and kidney function, memory loss, speech problems, softening of the bones, and aching muscles. Research has shown that the longer you cook food in aluminum pots, the more they corrode, and the more aluminum is absorbed into the food and your body. Replace the aluminum pots and pans with some stainless steel cookware, and not the non-stick kind either.

Arsenic: Arsenic has been used as a poison for thousands of years. That didn't stop companies from trying to use it in household products. In 1980, inorganic arsenic compounds were finally declared carcinogens and banned. By 1985, the U.S. had stopped producing arsenic, but remained the world's leading arsenic consumer. Most of the imported arsenic was being made into chromated copper arsenate (CCA), a wood preservative for "pressure-treated" decking, landscaping, walkways, picnic tables and playground equipment. It took consumers until 2002 to pressure the wood industry to stop. While only older wood structures now contain arsenic, since they're older, they're "leeching" (giving off) the chemical in playgrounds and backyards around you. **If you've got some old wooden stuff in your yard, get it checked. If you let your kids play at an old ghetto playground, find out what they hell they're licking and sliding down.**

Asbestos: Asbestos is valued for its fire-resistant insulating properties. But inhaling those short, sharp fibers can lead to lung cancer, mesothelioma (cancer of the lung or abdominal lining) and asbestosis, an irreversible respiratory disease. **Studies by the Environmental Working Group (www.ewg.org) show that 10,000 people die of asbestos-related diseases annually.** EWG calculated that this may be a low estimate, since symptoms may not appear for 20-50 years after exposure. **EWG also dug up documents dating back to the 1930s showing that corporate executives knew and concealed the dangers from workers making or handling asbestos-laden building materials and car parts, as well as from the consumers who would be receiving them.** For more info, call the Consumer Product Safety Commission at 1 (800) 638-CPSC.

BPA: Bisphenol A is a toxic chemical is used to make plastic. See "Gay Bomb."

Carbon Monoxide: At low levels, it can case fatigue and chest pain. In higher concentrations, it can cause impaired vision and coordination; headaches; dizziness; confusion; nausea; and flu-like symptoms. It's fatal at very high concentrations. You can get an inexpensive Carbon Monoxide monitor to check your home's levels.

Chromium 6: A strong carcinogen, found in drinking water and pressure-treated wood used in your home, park, or daycare center.

Flame Retardants: A study of more than 150 U.S. children conducted over 7 years associates prenatal exposure to higher concentrations of polybrominated diphenyl ether (PBDE) flame retardants with lower brain development in infants. PBDE flame retardants have been used for decades in a wide variety of goods, including automobile and airplane components, electronics, and home and office furnishings.

Fluoride: In your water supply. (See "Rocket Fuel in My Tap Water?")

Lead: See "Dying to Learn."

Radon: Radon is a radioactive gas given off by soil or rock with trace amounts of uranium or radium, so it normally enters homes through cracks in the foundation floor and walls, drains, joints or other openings. Radon can increase the risk of lung cancer. While there's much less radon in American homes these days, nearly 8 million US homes, or 1 out of every 15, still have Radon levels above the EPA "safe limit." Granite countertops, especially those from Brazil, can also give off Radon and radiation. But Radon tests aren't expensive. For more info, call the National Radon Hotline at (800) SOS-RADON. If high levels are found, hire a state-certified or EPA-certified contractor to fix the problem.

Teflon: Teflon is an example of a Perfluorinated compound (PFC). Any product that is grease-resistant is probably coated with this stuff, including non-stick cookware, microwave popcorn bags, dental floss, and carpets. EWG recently did a study of cookware coated with Teflon and other nonstick type surfaces. They found that these surfaces break apart under high temperatures and emit several toxic gases, carcinogens, environmental pollutants, and MFA, which is a chemical that is lethal to humans even at low doses. **In a UCLA study, women who had higher levels of these compounds in their blood had fertility problems.** Eliminate the nonstick stuff and replace it with regular stainless steel cookware, or – if you can afford it – cast iron.

VOCs: Volatile Organic Compounds are toxic gases that pollute your air. The most common VOC sources are carpets, flooring, paints, some plastics, and household cleaners. Look specifically for the product to be labeled with zero or low VOCs – of course, zero is best. VOCs are often found in new buildings and new cars. In fact, that "new car smell" comes mostly from the 30 to 40 different VOCs emitted from the glues, paints, plastic, and vinyl inside the car. Some people experience sore throats, nausea, headaches, and drowsiness from breathing them and long-term exposure can be more serious. **An Australian study done in 2001 found that new car riders are subject to toxic emissions several times higher than the limit deemed "safe" for humans.** What can you do? Don't buy your car new (a smart financial decision also), because VOC levels drop significantly after a few months. If you must buy a new car (why?), then buy Japanese (they're the only ones working to limit VOCs in their cars). Oh, and roll your windows down and let that fresh air circulate!

> **Did You Know?**
> Microwaved popcorn is worse for you than you think. A report from the FDA indicates that a chemical coating used in microwave popcorn bags breaks down when heated into a carcinogenic substance called perfluorooctanoic (PFOA). A second potential danger in microwave popcorn is diacetyl, an FDA-approved, but possibly dangerous, chemical found in the fake butter flavoring.

Proof search your home and read the labels on some of the products you always buy for some of these harmful chemicals.

ROCKET FUEL IN MY TAP WATER?

BY YVETTE GZ

In efforts to make our water more clean and drinkable, companies have added ridiculous amounts of cleansers and disinfectants that end up acting like human pesticides. To top it off they don't even kill all the bacteria or parasites in the water. But that's not even scarier than the number of chemicals we drink daily and what they do to our bodies. Here's a short list (there's more) of the main chemical compounds in tap water. However keep in mind that these vary from region to region. **To check** your tap water, visit www.ewg.org/tap-water or call the EPA's Drinking Water Hotline at (800) 246-4791

Chlorine: Although it's used to disinfect anything from water to clothes and hard surfaces, chlorine doesn't guarantee a 100% bacteria/parasite-free cleansing. What's worse is that it increases your risk of getting cancer. The U.S Council of Environmental Quality reported that people who drank chlorinated water had a 93% higher risk than those who didn't. You absorb more chlorine through your skin while taking a shower than you do drinking 6 glasses of water! Then your skin and hair are stripped of their natural oils and left dry and unnourished. You also breathe chlorine from the vapor, which can damage membranes in your lungs. Your best protection is a shower filter you can order while getting a water filter system installed.

"I am appalled at the prospect of using water as a vehicle for drugs. Fluoride is a corrosive poison that will produce serious effects on a long range basis. Any attempt to use water this way is deplorable."
- Dr. Charles Gordon Heyd, Past President of the American Medical Association

Fluoride: It's allegedly supposed to help your teeth from decaying, but too much of it's actually toxic and can damage your tooth enamel and cause joint pains and bone fractures. Some studies even link it to osteosarcoma (bone cancer) since 90% of fluoride stored by your body goes to your bones and your body stores half the fluoride you consume. That fluoride also accumulates in your pineal gland, which is located in the center of your brain and is crucial to your mind and development. **Fluoride can stunt growth and change behavior.** The National Research Council also found that fluoride presents risks to the thyroid gland, which regulates many functions in your body including your metabolism. This can increase the risk of cardiac disease, high cholesterol, depression, fatigue, weight gain, constipation, fuzzy thinking, slow reflexes, low blood pressure, fluid retention, body pain, and, in pregnant woman, decreased intelligence of offspring. Fluoride is present in 2/3 of U.S public water supplies.

Ammonium Perchlorate: This is an oxidant found in solid rocket fuel, military explosives, bottle rockets, fireworks, highway flares, automobile airbags and black powder. And it's in your water (and your food). A 2003 EWG analysis of government data, "Rocket Fuel in Drinking Water," determined that perchlorate had been found in drinking water, groundwater or soil in at least 43 states. When EWG looked at lettuce grown in some of those states, 18% of the samples contained perchlorates. Another study found that 31 of 32 samples of supermarket milk contained perchlorates. **Scientific research has established that perchlorate in significant amounts disrupts production of thyroid hormones, and adequate thyroid hormones are crucial to normal brain development and growth in the fetus, infants and young**

children. CDC studies have found perchlorate in the urine of every person tested and have discovered that children between 6 and 11 had perchlorate levels 1.6 times higher than adults. A EWG analysis of data from the U.S. Food and Drug Administration (FDA), published in January 2008, found that 75% of nearly 300 commonly consumed foods and beverages were contaminated with perchlorate.

Sewage and Parasites: Throughout the world, municipal and industrial waste is routinely dumped into local waters. And plenty of cities in the US are routine dumpers. The largest water-contamination disease outbreak in US history occurred in 1993, when Milwaukee's water supply was infected with the parasite *Cryptosporidium*. 400,000 people got sick. 100 died. The cause? Raw sewage that was being regularly dumped into Lake Michigan - and still is.

Pharmaceuticals: Other pharmaceuticals (compounds used in pharmacy drugs) found in low-levels in drinking water include:

❏ Atenolol: used to treat cardiovascular disease
❏ Atrazine: an organic herbicide banned in Europe but still used in the US. It's implicated in the decline of fish stocks and in changes in animal behavior.
❏ Carbamazepine: a mood-stabilizing drug used to treat bipolar disorder.
❏ Estrone: an oestrogen hormone secreted by the ovaries and blamed for causing gender-bending changes in fish.
❏ Gemfibrozil: an anti-cholesterol drug
❏ Meprobamate: a tranquilizer widely used in psychiatric treatment
❏ Naproxen: a painkiller and anti-inflammatory linked to increases in asthma attacks.
❏ Phenytoin: an anticonvulsant that has been used to treat epilepsy
❏ Sulfamethoxazole: an antibiotic used against the Streptococcus bacteria, which is responsible for tonsillitis and other diseases
❏ TCEP: a reducing agent used in molecular biology
❏ Trimethoprim: another antibiotic

They also found America's favorite drug, cocaine (also found on 85-95% of US paper money, according to a 2009 study), morphine, cooking spices, fragrances, and even sunscreen.

Purifying your own water is a healthy alternative to dirty tap water.

NO GENIE IN THE BOTTLE
BY YVETTE GZ

If you're scared about drinking tap water again, hold your horses before running to bottled water. In reality it isn't even guaranteed that it's safer or healthier than tap water. Here's why.

1. Bottled water is less regulated than tap water

We're programmed to think the opposite, but in reality the bottled water industry has less pressure to ensure the best quality in their products.

Some companies even use tap water to fill up plastic bottles and sell them at 10 times the price! Why? Because bottled water is considered a food product and is regulated by the Food and Drug Administration (FDA) whereas tap water is regulated by the Environmental Protection Agency (EPA), which has a higher standard when it comes to drinkable water.

The EPA demands no confirmed E. coli or bacteria contamination allowed in tap water and requires specific treatments of tap water sources like disinfection and regular testing. Even though perfect results are not 100% guaranteed, the EPA makes sure any violations against its policy are dealt with. The FDA on the other hand, only sets a minimum level for contaminants and E. coli presence in bottled water and it doesn't even consider exceeded amounts a violation if the company openly says so on the label. The FDA also requires inspection, sampling and approval of water sources.

However, a federal review revealed that 25% of water bottlers have no record of FDA approval and that the FDA doesn't even have one full-time staff to monitor or regulate bottled water. So for the most part, bottled water companies are self-regulated and can do whatever they want with their product as long as it's not ridiculously contaminated or poisonous. With that said, bottled water is not worse or better than tap water because its quality depends on the brand's policy of treatment.

> Did You Know?
> Dasani and Aquafina, two top-selling water brands, have admitted that their products are nothing but tap water in a bottle?

Some brands treat their water better than tap water standards while others treat it worse.

2. They contain contaminants too

The Natural Resources Defense Council (NRDC) ran a research on 103 water bottle brands and found that "at least 25% of the brands tested contained chemical contaminants at levels above the strict, health-protective limits of California, the bottled water industry code, or other states" and many of them exceeded federal safety levels for chemicals in drinking water.

Another investigation by the Environmental Working Group (EWG) tested 10 major brands and found 38 pollutants. It concluded that Walmart's Sam's Choice and Giant's Acadia are no different than tap water and also exceed safety limits. Out of the 10 brands, 4 had high levels of THMs, 5 had fluoride like tap water, 6 had nitrates, 1 had ammonia, 2 had pharmaceuticals, and 9 had an average of 2.5 synthetic chemicals (3 of those brands had about 8 chemicals in them). Bacteria contamination was also found in 4 brands, and the most shocking, radioactivity contamination in 7 brands!

3. Deceptive advertisement

Bottled water brands use misleading images to tap into the subliminal mind, like most companies do. They'll use pictures of mountains, volcanic plains, glaciers, fresh springs or waterfalls with flowers growing on the river banks and sunshine in the background. But none of those are guarantees that the water actually comes from a fresh and clean source. **For example, a brand called "Spring Water" has a picture of a mountain and lake on the label, but their water source is actually from a well located near an industrial waste site and right in the middle of a warehouse facility in Mills, Massachusetts.** Another one named "Aliska" says "Alaska Premium Glacier Drinking Water: Pure Glacier Water from the Last Unpolluted Frontier, Bacteria-free," but was found to be from a public water supply.

Words like "pure," "glacier," "premium," "natural," "mountain water," "clean" or "healthy" mean nothing but false advertisement most of the time.

4. It's expensive

Drinking 8 glasses of tap water a day for a year is equivalent to 49 cents, whereas bottled water sells for about $1 per 16 ounces! Which is what, 2 glasses? **One bottle of Evian costs about the same as 1000 gallons of tap water.** At this rate, bottled water is more expensive than gasoline. If that isn't a rip off then I don't know what is.

5. Its garbage

The world consumes over 41 billion gallons of bottled water per year and America alone consumes 7 billion of it. But check this; it takes 1.5 million barrels of crude oil to make enough bottles to meet America's demand every year. That's enough to fuel 100,000 cars in the same amount of time and just think about how much energy (fuel) it takes to produce and transport them nationwide and worldwide.

Most importantly, less than 20% of water bottles get recycled, which leaves about 86% to become garbage or litter. When plastic is burnt up with other trash in landfills, toxic chlorine and other chemicals are released in the atmosphere while more toxins are deposited in the ground potentially increasing water contamination. Also, plastic takes between 400 to 1000 years to decompose, and we're throwing away over 30 million plastic bottles a day!

Still want to consume bottled water?

Though drinking bottled water is better than drinking no water, try adopting the habit of recycling. You can easily find sources online that can tell you where and how to do it. Environmentalists are so big on recycling that some will even pay you for it.

Invest in 1 or 2 large, BPA-free, water jugs. These can last a family of four 3 to 5 days.

DYING TO LEARN: LEAD POISONING AND ENVIRONMENTAL RACISM

BY WISE INTELLIGENT

According to a September 23, 2008 *Trenton Times* newspaper article by Lisa Rich, titled "Unsafe Lead Levels Found in 8 Schools," Trenton's public-school children are exposed to lead poisoning, which can cause *permanent* learning and behavioral problems, seizures, coma and death. Could this be the cause of some of the behavioral issues we hear inner-city school teachers complaining about so often?

According to the report, only 10 public schools were tested for lead contamination, 8 of which had lead levels in the water as high as 220 parts per billion. In schools where lead levels were well over the 20 parts per billion standard, water fountains and sinks were shut off but could not be replaced due to lack of funds and/or personnel.

Now, let me spin the lens just a little. The U.S. government came quickly to the aid of Bear Stern to the tune of $300 million, Fannie Mae and Freddie Mac $85 billion, all without what can be considered protest from the majority white population. But, whenever a measure is proposed to spend tax payers' dollars to give non-white children in America an education equal to that given their white (or politically correct "suburban") counterparts these same white people fight such attempts all the way to the Supreme Court.

Many of us are well aware that the deplorable state of affairs in predominately Black communities and their school districts – apartheid schooling as well as environmental racism – are "intentional and calculated." This intent cannot be demonstrated any clearer than in the Lead-Paint study conducted in the 1990's on infants and children in a Baltimore low-income housing project by researchers at the Kennedy Krieger Institute (which is an affiliate of John Hopkins University).[12]

In the study, the blood lead levels of children entering the program were documented as "at a safe level." However, after just one month, some of the children's blood contained "excessive lead," and that they "had since had neurological problems." One month!

---

[12] Keep in mind how universities have always played a major role in genocidal experimentation carried out on African Americans, while being sponsored by private "philanthropic" institutions. It was Wake Forest and the University of North Carolina at Chapel Hill that supported the eugenics movement carrying out tens of thousands of sterilizations on defenseless African Americans.

The mothers of two of the children filed negligence lawsuits against the Kennedy Krieger Institute, lamenting that the researchers had failed to warn them about the risks of the study and the danger that their children could be poisoned by lead in the houses. Only low-income children were used for the study and their parents were reportedly "enticed" by food stamps, money or other incentives. The Maryland Court of Appeals eventually overturned lower court decisions dismissing those cases and sharply criticized the researchers and their institutions for failing to see the basic ethical violations of enlisting healthy children to live in potentially dangerous housing.

Yet *The Washington Post* soon reported, "Since the court issued its ruling regarding the lead paint study, the institute has continued its research with two studies related to lead paint." For beginners, there is plenty of lead saturating the hood:

❑ high levels of lead in inner-city drinking water due to lead-based piping in homes built before 1978 (the majority in most hoods),

❑ lead-based paint in homes built before 1978,

❑ lead in urban soil due to the many factories and plants operating in urban areas during America's Industrial era,

❑ and lead throughout the overall environment due to high-traffic areas and lead-based fuel emissions from vehicles

At the same time, we also face direct assaults from scientists, government agencies, and "researchers" who have continually found no foul in using us as human guinea pigs in the spirit-depleting experiment America has been for many African Americans.

Research, like findings published by Deborah W. Denno in *Biology and Violence: From Birth to Adulthood,* has demonstrated why, in light of recent studies, the entire criminal justice system may need to be recalibrated because some violent crime can be linked to heavy metal uptake and is therefore a health issue and should be diagnosed and treated as such.

Musician/activist Bono said on CNN that with $25 billion you could put most kids in school, eradicate diseases like Malaria and change the water supplies for children in the whole world. For $25 billion, you could put every kid who's out of school *in the world* into school! I think this is a small price to pay to change the face of poverty. The return on the investment is unmatched. However, the majority of the white population is more active and visible participants in people's movements for "equal treatment" of animals than they are visibly active in a people's movement for equal treatment of African American and/or Hispanic children.

Unless rappers, DJ's, graffiti artists, breakers, producers, and other Hip Hop adherents (who themselves were victims of these same appalling conditions) become community activists and organizers, starting (or at least attaching their image, name, and/or resources to) programs in urban communities that deal with youth empowerment issues, I'm afraid the current trend towards disenfranchisement, poverty, ignorance and violence will continue unfettered!

We can, we should, and we must support and establish organizations like United Parents Against Lead (UPAL), an organization whose mission is to abate the presence of *criminal-behavior-facilitating variables* like lead poisoning and other environmental hazards "through education; advocacy; and resource referral." (www.upal.org)

UPAL chapters (with the continued support of the Hip Hop community) should be established in every urban community in the country as the premiere organization for community awareness and abatement of environmental hazards. This organization would serve as the mouthpiece of the community while working in conjunction with local, state and federal environmental agencies like the EPA, DEP, HUD, CDC, and EJA, to rid our communities of the environmental hazards that have contributed to everything the hood is plagued with, from school failure to violent and criminal behavior.

Get involved with organizations like UPAL to educate yourself and others on ways to prevent lead poisoning in our public schools.

GETTING THE LEAD OUT...OF YOUR HOME
BY SUPREME UNDERSTANDING

Lead affects the nervous system. That means brain damage. Reduction in IQ begins with lead levels as low as 7 ug/dl (micrograms per deciliter of blood). Guess how much lead that means? Very little. It doesn't take much at all.

Beyond intellectual impairment, researchers have also found that lead can stunt physical growth (at 1 ug/dL), contribute to ADHD symptoms (at 2 ug/dL), and even cause cavities (at 3 ug/dL). At higher levels, slow lead poisoning causes memory loss, mood swings, infertility, nerve, joint and muscle disorders, cardiovascular, skeletal, kidney and renal problems and possibly cancer.

Are my children at risk?
If you're Black and poor, most definitely.

More than 40% of American homes still have lead-based paint in them. But Black children are five times more likely than white children to suffer from lead poisoning, according to the CDC. Lead poisoning endangers the health of nearly 8 million inner-city children, mostly Black and Hispanic. **As of 2003, nearly half (47%) of Black children ages 1 to 5 had blood lead levels in the range of 5 to 10 ug/dL, which corresponds to a loss of 4 to 7 IQ points.** 19% of white children and 28% of Hispanic children fell in the same range. Among Black children in large cities, 36.7% have blood lead levels of above 10 ug/dl.

To minimize the risk of lead in your walls you should:

☐ If you live in or are planning to buy a house built before 1978 have an inspector check it.

☐ If you discover lead in your home, consider covering over paint with wallpaper, paneling or a thick coat of new paint (make sure it's non-toxic paint!).

Your chances of having lead in your drinking water are high if:

☐ Your home has faucets or fittings made of brass which contains some lead

☐ Your home or water system has lead pipes, or your home has copper pipes with lead solder AND the home is less than 5 years old

☐ You have naturally soft water

☐ Water often sits in the pipes for several hours

To minimize the risk of lead in drinking water you should:

☐ Use a water filtration system to remove pollutants.

☐ Flush your pipes. Don't use water that has been sitting in your pipes over six hours. Only use water thoroughly flushed from the cold water tap. Flush until the water becomes as cold as it will get (this can take up to 2 minutes or longer). Once you've flushed a tap, fill a container and put it in the refrigerator for later use.

☐ Use only cold water for drinking, and especially for making baby formula.

☐ Never cook with or consume water from the hot-water tap. (Hot water dissolves lead more easily and is therefore likely to contain higher levels.

☐ Have your water tested by a competent laboratory approved by your state or the EPA. (Your local or state department of environment or health should be able to tell you which labs are qualified.)

☐ If you want to test the water yourself, you can buy a test kit online for less than 15 bucks. Isn't that worth the price of avoiding brain damage?

If you have a young child at home who is at risk for lead exposure, talk to your physician about having the child's blood tested for lead levels.

For more information on lead toxicity, check out UPAL.org, visit the EPA website, or call the National Lead Information Center at 1(800) 424-LEAD

Get the Lead Out

You can remove toxic minerals from your body, and protect against taking them in by:

☐ **Saturation.** Eating a diet with a high level of a wide range of minerals, so your cells become saturated with minerals. Toxic minerals are then likely to be excreted rather than taken up.

☐ **Chelation.** Certain foods and drinks such as kombucha, coriander (cilantro) and seaweed actively draw a range of minerals to them, and pull them out of the body via excrement. Clay baths also have this effect.

☐ **Antioxidants.** A diet high in antioxidant nutrients and enzymes protects you from toxic minerals.

VACCINES AND POPULATION CONTROL?

BY SUPREME UNDERSTANDING

The Bill and Melinda Gates Foundation recently hosted a presentation on how ultrasonic frequencies could be used to sterilize men from a distance. Yes, you read that right. I can only imagine how they would use that…and who they'd use that against. Doesn't sound like something "good guy" Bill Gates would be into? You have no idea.

In addition to this sterilization program (which would use sharp blasts of ultrasound directed against a man's scrotum to render him infertile as a sort of "temporary castration"), the foundation also funded a new "sweat-triggered vaccine delivery" program based on "nanoparticles that penetrate the skin through hair follicles and burst upon contact with human sweat to release vaccines." According to Gates, he's raising money to develop vaccine programs "designed to protect children in developing countries from various diseases, including tetanus."

But the Gates tetanus program bears striking resemblance to another tetanus program that sterilized thousands of women and caused abortions in many others in the Philippines. (As reported by the BBC in conjunction with the Philippine Department of Health and the Philippine Medical Association, women in child-bearing years were given a vaccine that was combined with a chemical known as Human Chorionic Gonadotropin (HCG), an anti-pregnancy agent.). But why sterilize people? At a February 2010 TED conference, Gates talked about reducing CO_2 emissions worldwide, by limiting population growth. He said:

> The world today has 6.8 billion people. That's headed up to about nine billion. Now if we do a really great job on new vaccines, health care, reproductive health services, we could lower that by perhaps 10 or 15 percent!

This "population elimination" idea may sound similar to the "conspiracy theories" about the spread of HIV in Africa (which led Nobel Peace Prize laureate and environmental activist Wangari Maathai to charge that "AIDS is a biological weapon manufactured by the developed world to wipe out the Black race" although he later denied such sentiments), but the connections between the spread of smallpox vaccines and HIV in Africa were just one of many cases where Western vaccines (or other medicine) brought hidden problems with them.

As recently as 2004, pharmaceutical scientist Dr. Haruna Kaita was contracted by an Islamic body to check out polio vaccines being administered by the WHO in Nigeria. After extensive and repeated tests carried out using state-of-the-art facilities in India, a shocked Dr. Kaita reported that the vaccines were laced with contaminants, some toxic and some having "direct effect on human reproductive system."

But why sterilize people in poor countries?

Sterilization, eugenics, and population control all go hand-in-hand. It's all about controlling who is here in 100 years. And it's been going on for quite some time. In 1798, Thomas Malthus published *An Essay on the Principle of Population*, describing his theory on how population growth will exceed earthly resources to provide food for all people. We now know that there is certainly enough food (and land) on the planet to feed everyone, and that hunger is a result of poverty and other forms of social inequity, not simply "too many people."

In fact, many European nations have 10 times more people than your average African nation with twice the land. Also, when you factor in the amount of resources it takes (fossil fuels, land, water, etc.) to feed people on a meat-heavy over-indulgent Western diet, that's very different from what the rest of the world needs to survive.

Soon after the US State Department published the Global 2000 Report for the President in 1980 advising that the world population must be reduced by 2 billion people by the year 2000, Thomas Ferguson of the State Department Office of Population Affairs, Latin American Desk, elaborated:

> **There is a single theme behind all our work – we must reduce population levels.** Either governments do it our way, through nice clean methods, or they will get the kinds of mess that we have in El Salvador, or in Iran or in Beirut. Population is a political problem. **Once population is out of control, it requires authoritarian government, even fascism, to reduce it**...Our program in El Salvador didn't work. The infrastructure was not there to support it. There were just too goddamned many people...**To really reduce population, quickly, you have to pull all the males into the fighting and you have to kill significant numbers of fertile age females**...The quickest way to reduce population is through famine, like in Africa, or through disease like the Black Death.

Does this put everything in perspective for you?

Does it help you understand why Gates would fund something like the programs above?

Does it change the way you see all those wonderful agencies doing "healthcare" in developing countries? (Not all, of course, because there are many smaller groups that have good intentions)

Does it make you think about what similar agencies are doing (and have already done) with the Black and brown communities of THIS country?

Does it make you take a fresh look at why they push birth control and abortion so hard in the hood, while putting fertility clinics and sperm banks in white neighborhoods?

Does it make you wonder what this rush to "stop global warming" is really about, since they're trying to "save the planet" while getting rid of most of the people on it?

As we'll explain in depth in *Chemical Genocide*, this new wave of environmentalism is NOT centered on the interests of Original people. In fact, most of its strongest advocates are all FOR wiping YOU off the planet. Here are a few more quotes to think about:

> "Malthus has been vindicated, reality is finally catching up with Malthus. The Third World is overpopulated, it's an economic mess, and there's no way they could get out of it with this fast-growing population. Our philosophy is: back to the village." – Dr. Arne Schiotz, World Wildlife Fund Director of Conservation, 1984

> **"The biggest problems are the damn national sectors of these developing countries. These countries think that they have the right to develop their resources as they see fit. They want to become powers."** – Thomas Lovejoy, vice president, World Wildlife Fund U.S.A., 1984

> "If we look at things causally, the bigger problem in the world is population. We must set a ceiling to human numbers. All development aid should be made dependent on the existence of strong family planning programs." – Sir Peter Scott, chairman, World Wildlife Fund U.K., 1984

I used to get mad about those commercials pushing the plight of the polar bear, and after seeing the quotes above, I understand why. There's more:

> "It will be impossible to feel that the world is in a satisfactory state until there is a certain degree of equality, and a certain acquiescence everywhere in the power of the World Government, and this will not be possible until the poorer nations of the world have become...more or less stationary in population...If there is not to be an endless succession of wars...this will probably have to be done, in many countries, as a result of governmental measures. This will require an extension of scientific technique into very intimate matters." – Bertrand Russell, *The Impact of Science on Society*, 1952

> "What would it take to accelerate fertility decline in the least developed countries?" – March 2009 U.N. Population Division policy brief

> "Frankly, I had thought that at the time Roe was decided, there was concern about population growth and particularly growth in populations that we don't want to have too many of." – U.S. Supreme Court Justice Ruth Bader Ginsburg

> "It now remains for the U.S. government to set a sensible example to the world by offering a bonus or yearly pension to all obviously unfit parents who allow themselves to be sterilized by harmless and scientific means. In this way the moron and the diseased would have no posterity to inherit their unhappy condition. **The number of the feeble-minded would decrease and a heavy burden would be lifted from the shoulders of the fit.**" – Margaret Sanger, Founder of Planned Parenthood, 1926

> **"All children who are born, beyond what would be required to keep up the population to a desired level, must necessarily perish**...Therefore...we should facilitate...the operations of nature in producing this mortality; and if we dread the too frequent visitation of the horrid form of famine, we should sedulously encourage the other forms of destruction, which we compel nature to use. **Instead of recommending cleanliness to the poor, we should encourage contrary habits. In our**

towns we should make the streets narrower, crowd more people into the houses, and court the return of the plague. In the country, we should build our villages near stagnant pools, and particularly encourage settlement in all marshy and unwholesome situations. But above all we should reprobate specific remedies for ravaging diseases; and restrain those benevolent, but much mistaken men, who have thought they are doing a service to mankind by protecting schemes for the total extirpation of particular disorders." – Malthus, *An Essay on the Principle of Population*, 1798

And one more, in case you're unclear as to whom these *undesirable* people are:

"**The white population of the world will soon cease to increase. The Asiatic races will be longer, and the negroes still longer,** before their birth rate falls sufficiently to make their numbers stable without help of war and pestilence. Until that happens, the benefits aimed at by socialism can only be partially realized, **and the less prolific** (child-bearing) **races will have to defend themselves by methods which are disgusting even if they are necessary.**" – Bertrand Russell, *The Impact of Science on Society*, 1952

Be less trusting of what organizations, corporations, and even some doctors about what you should put in your body.

WHAT CAN I DO ABOUT ALL THIS?

You may have never heard of it, but the President's Cancer Panel, which reports directly to the president – just released a new report on these chemical toxins we've been describing in this chapter. The landmark report[13] evaluates current scientific evidence and the positions of over 40 experts, and concludes that public health officials have "grossly underestimated" the role environmental contaminants may be playing in the 1.5 million Americans who are diagnosed with cancer each year. The report called for stricter regulations on chemicals and safer alternatives, especially noting that these toxins are most dangerous to young children and unborn babies.

In this government-issued report, they actually admit that today's babies are "pre-polluted" with over 300 different chemical contaminants found in the umbilical cord blood of newborn babies!

Let me repeat: These were not weirdoes and conspiracy theorists. These are mainstream, highly-respected scientists (the head of the panel is a Black man!) saying this. I hope that's not what you needed to hear to take us seriously, but if you did, there you go. So what do you do?

Here are the President's Cancer Panel's recommendations (from pages 145-147 of the report) for what you can do to protect yourself and your family.

❑ Choose foods, house and garden products, play spaces, toys, medical tests, and medicines that will minimize your kids' exposure to toxic

---

[13] http://deainfo.nci.nih.gov/advisory/pcp/pcp08-09rpt/PCP_Report_08-09_508.pdf

chemicals. (This means eating organic as much as possible and buying products that you know to be free of BPA, phthalates and other endocrine disruptors.)

☐ Eat meat produced without antibiotics and added growth hormones. Avoid or minimize consumption of processed, charred, and well-done meats to reduce exposure to carcinogenic heterocyclic amines and polyaromatic hydrocarbons.

☐ If you're pregnant or thinking about it: Both mothers and fathers should avoid exposure to endocrine-disrupting chemicals and known or suspected carcinogens prior to a child's conception and throughout pregnancy and early life, when risk of damage is greatest.

☐ Take off your shoes when you enter your home, especially if you work with or around chemicals. (Wash work clothes separately from other laundry.)

☐ Filter your tap water. And continue to choose tap water over commercially bottled water. (See, "BPA Can Make You A New Man.")

☐ Store food and water in containers made from stainless steel, glass, or BPA- and phthalate-free plastic.

☐ Don't microwave in plastic, since chemicals can leach into food when it's heated. (See, "Plastic Poisons.")

☐ Stop using chemical fertilizers and pesticides on your garden to keep these chemicals from contaminating drinking water supplies.

☐ Properly dispose of medications, household chemicals, paints and other materials to minimize drinking water and soil contamination.

☐ Turn off lights and electrical devices when not in use to reduce your exposure to petroleum combustion by-products.

☐ Drive a fuel-efficient car, bike or walk when possible, or use public transportation to cut the amount of toxic auto exhaust in the air.

☐ Wear a headset when you use your cell phone, keep calls brief, and text instead of calling when possible to reduce your exposure to electromagnetic energy.

☐ Have your home's radon levels tested periodically.

☐ Avoid second-hand smoke. (And don't smoke yourself. Duh.)

☐ Talk to your doctor about the need for tests or procedures that involve radiation exposure and keep a record of all imaging or nuclear medicine tests received and if known, the estimated radiation dose for each test.

☐ Wear sunscreen and UV-protective clothing. (See "Skin Cancer is NOT Prejudiced")

☐ Tell your Congressperson to support the Safe Chemicals Act of 2010, which would overhaul the riddled-with-loopholes Toxic Substances Control Act of 1976.

☐ Organize and educate people in your community about what's happening.

Add many of these steps to your daily routine. Convince the people in your household of how important this is.

4. Having Healthy Children

Birthing Babies in the Hood
BY SCIHONOR DEVOTION

I work as a Labor Doula, which means I care for the pregnant mother before, during, and after her labor process. I'm also a Homebirth Midwife assistant, so I've helped women have babies in hospitals, in birthing centers, and at home. I can tell you from firsthand experience that hospital staff tends to treat young, "urban" women with less respect than those who, ahem "look differently" or are in a different financial class. So if you're having a hospital birth, go in prepared, as if you were a soldier going to war. Be knowledgeable about the labor process and the hospital's techniques for dealing with pregnancy, labor, and birth.

Many women are now realizing that, if they are having "normal" pregnancies, they can do something about being uncomfortable during childbirth. Many women are now choosing to have homebirths or birthing center births with midwives. This way, they can be more relaxed, in a warm environment, instead of being in labor, strapped down to a bed against their body's natural instincts.

Yes, I said HOME birth. It's more common than you think, even in the hood. And yes, homebirth is safe. Midwives don't come to births with white aprons, hot water and shoe strings the way the old movies show you. They are highly trained and equipped with medical equipment such as oxygen as well as herbs and other formulas and advice to help women during their out-of-hospital birthing process.

One of the main things that you get with midwifery care is time and attention from a care provider as opposed to the 5 minute office visit, rushed by patients needing to get in behind you. As a matter of fact, homebirth midwives will even visit you at home, so you don't even have to go anywhere as you get closer to your delivery. **Using a midwife increases the chances that you will have a medication** (epidural) **free birth which in turn decreases your risk of having to have a cesarean section** (C-section). (See, "What Is A Birthing Center?")

Make sure you ask these questions about what your birthing process will be like and the procedures and drugs that you are given.

Questions To Ask Your Hospital/ Midwife/ Birthing Center

- ☐ Will I know which doctor/midwife will be at my labor ahead of time? How much time will I have during pregnancy to get to know them?
- ☐ Am I allowed to bring labor support, or does the hospital provide uninterrupted Doula support during my labor and just after delivery?
- ☐ Will my husband/partner, family be allowed in the labor and delivery room with me?
- ☐ If I chose a drug free birth, will my request be honored?
- ☐ Will I be allowed to walk the halls during labor?
- ☐ Am I encouraged to move freely during labor?
- ☐ Will I be attached to an electronic fetal monitor continuously?
- ☐ Does this hospital have mandatory procedures such as (enema, A.R.O.M. (Artificial Rupture Of Membrane, Shaving, I.V., etc.)?
- ☐ Is laboring out of a bed a problem for the hospital staff here?
- ☐ Will I be allowed to deliver my baby in any position that I chose to?
- ☐ Am I allowed to eat and drink during labor to stay well hydrated?
- ☐ Do you have any non-medical alternatives for pain relief?
- ☐ Who cuts the cord?
- ☐ How long will my postpartum stay be?
- ☐ How often do I feed my baby? Am I allowed to feed the baby on demand, or will he/she be put on a schedule?
- ☐ What circumstances require an episiotomy, and are a warm compress and/or oil used as an alternative to cutting my perineum? What is the hospital percentage of giving episiotomies? How often does my doctor cut women's vaginas during labor?
- ☐ Can I nurse my baby immediately after birth if I choose to? Do you have consultant to help me if I need assistance?
- ☐ Does the staff here use forceps and/or vacuum routinely? What are the dangers?
- ☐ How often will I be allowed to see my baby?
- ☐ What is the hospital percentage of cesarean section? What is my doctor's percentage?
- ☐ Can my baby stay with me from birth to discharge? If not, Why?
- ☐ If cesarean section is necessary, who can be with me? Can I replace unnecessary students with my support team?
- ☐ When can my other children come to visit the baby and me?
- ☐ Are the labor, delivery, and recovery all in one room?
- ☐ If my water breaks before contractions begin, can I stay at home until labor begins on its own?

Questions to Ask About Drugs and Procedures

Participate in your care and get the answers you need to make a decision.

- ☐ Why do I need this drug/procedure? What problem are we looking for?
- ☐ Will my baby be safer after taking this drug or going through this procedure?
- ☐ Will I be safer after taking this drug or procedure?
- ☐ What are its known side effects?
- ☐ Will the benefits outweigh the side effects?

- What are the risks to the baby and me, if I don't do this procedure or take this drug?
- Are there alternatives that I can try before taking these drugs or doing this procedure?
- What will it tell us? How accurate and reliable are the results?
- If the test detects a problem, then what will happen next? What decisions will I have to make?
- If the test does not detect a problem, then what will happen next?
- Describe the treatment. How is it done? How likely is it to solve/detect the problem?
- How can I get a second opinion?

> **Did You Know?**
> Folic acid not only helps blood cell and hemoglobin formation, but alleviates heavy menstrual bleeding, hemorrhaging in childbirth, and improves lactation. A deficiency can cause neural tube defects including spina bifida, anencephaly, and encephalocele. An expectant mother needs double the required iron levels of a non-pregnant woman because her baby needs enough stored iron to last for their first six months of life!

If you are interested in looking into out-of-hospital birth options, search the internet for homebirth midwives, birthing centers and labor or postpartum doulas in your area.

Know about your hospital/midwife/birthing center, and be aware of the drugs and procedures involved during child birth.

NOURISHMENT AND NUTRITION DURING PREGNANCY
BY SCIHONOR DEVOTION

What is Nutrition?
1. The process of nourishing or being nourished, especially the process by which a living thing takes in and uses food. 2. Nourishment. 3. The study of food and nourishment.

What does it mean to Nourish?
1. To provide a living thing with the food or other substances necessary for life and growth. 2. To promote the growth or development of; sustain 3. To keep alive; harbor

Both words have their root in *nourir*, which literally means "to suckle." They are also similar to Nurture.

What does Nurture mean?
1. To feed, protect, and nourish. 2. To educate or train. 3. To help grow and develop.

Based on the relationships of these words along, it's quite evident that both Nourishment and Nutrition during pregnancy entail more than just providing the body with physical foods. Beneficial mental foods are also required. To be able to grow, develop, and sustain a healthy life, a mother must be mentally and physically fed and nurtured. So often, we tend to forget that the unborn baby in utero is not cut off from the physical world. The child is affected by all that its mother experiences, eats, dreams, sees, smells, reads, etc. This conscious being is totally capable of responding to all within his immediate home (uterus/womb) and abroad (the outside world). Overall, a mother's mental and physical well-being or lack thereof has a major effect on the unborn child, and nourishment and nutrition are holistic experiences that go far beyond just eating what some may call a meal.

Good health during pregnancy helps to ensure that your baby is healthy, intelligent, and resistant to infection. it's known that a well-nourished mother is likely to result in a healthy baby, while a poorly nourished mother is likely to experience complications during labor and delivery, and her baby is

also likely to have problems as well, sometimes well into childhood and adulthood.

People with limited incomes usually tend to cut back on nutritious foods in an effort to save money for other things. Unfortunately, they are doing themselves, their families and society as a whole a disservice since they are more likely to produce children with illness and even higher mortality, morbidity and congenital problems.

The first thing that a pregnant woman or a woman planning to conceive can do to be healthy is to actually commit to doing so. The ideal preparation time prior to pregnancy is at least 1 year; however it's never too late to get your body in a better state for conception. Every partner should commit to support his woman with her transition. it's **not suggested for women to make major changes in their diets during their pregnancies.** For example, you wouldn't go from eating a meat-dominated diet to eating a raw food diet and vice versa. Incorporating better food choices and gradually weaning out the "poor" choices is a good way to go. Every pregnant woman deserves to eat without worrying about too much weight gain. However, choosing the optimal foods is the key. If we eat what we should be eating, then we probably won't gain too much weight during pregnancy. Study the foods that you crave for.

Food Sources for Needed Nutrients

This chart will show the nutrient needed and the foods and herbal sources from which these foods can be obtained.

Nutrient	Non-pregnant/ Pregnant/ Lactating Women	Food and Herbal Sources
Kilo-calories	2200/ 2500/ 2600	Non-pregnant women need an average of 2200 Kilocalories (commonly known simply as "Calories") daily, but pregnant women need more (2500), and lactating women need even slightly more (2600).

Vitamin A (mcg*)	800/ 800/ 1300	Orange fruits/vegetables (carrots, sweet potatoes, apricot, cherry, mango, peach, papaya, pumpkin, squash), dark green vegetables, seaweed, dairy, fish liver oil, eggs, liver, alfalfa, watercress, nettle, red raspberry leaves, dandelion, comfrey, nori, yellow dock, lamb.
Vitamin B6 (mg*)	1.6/ 2.2/ 2.1	Egg yolk, soybeans, beans, peanuts, walnuts, banana, cabbage, cauliflower, potatoes, prunes, avocados, brown rice, wheat bran/germ, molasses, nutritional yeast, salmon, and organ meats. 1 banana (90 mg) has more than 3 oz. of beef (71 mg) or chicken (45 mg).
Vitamin B12 (mcg)	2.0/ 2.2/ 2.6	tempeh, miso, fortified nutritional yeast, dairy products (except butter), some sprouts may have B12 producing bacteria on their surface, foods fortified with B12 such as cereals, vegetarian meat substitutes, eggs, cheese
Vitamin C (mg)	60/ 70/ 95	Cantaloupe, kiwi, red pepper, strawberries, cauliflower, broccoli, green bell pepper, tomato, cabbage, green leafy vegetables, alfalfa sprouts, rose hips, watercress, dandelion greens, red clover, burdock, nettle
Vitamin D (mcg)	10/ 10/ 12	Type 1 –animal derived Type 2 – made in the skin when you come into contact with ultraviolet rays of the suns. Type 3 – Synthetic form used to fortify milk, some breakfast cereals, and other foods.
Vitamin E (mg)	8/ 10/ 12	Vegetable oil, wheat germ oil, legumes, green leafy vegetables, nut butter, butter, egg yolks, milk
Vitamin K (mcg)	55/ 65/ 65	Most Vitamin K is found in plants. Like Vitamin B12, Vitamin K is also made in the body. Type 1 – comes from plant and animal sources Type 2 – (the best source) comes from good bacteria living in the intestines.
Calcium (mg)	1200/ 1200/ 1200	Soybeans, tofu, blackstrap molasses, all-bran cereal, broccoli, yogurt, cow milk, hard cheese, salmon, chicken breast, almonds, sea vegetables, alfalfa, red clover, red raspberry leaves, nettle, chamomile, dandelion, kelp, dulse. ½ cup firm tofu (258 mg) has more than 3 oz. salmon (203 mg)
Folate (Vitamin B9) (mcg)	180/ 250/ 280	Green leafy vegetables, wheat germ, nutritional yeast, whole grains, lentils, nuts, eggs, navy beans, banana, enriched cereal, milk, almonds, chicory greens, romaine lettuce, spinach, Brussels sprouts, chicken. ½ cup almonds (78 mcg) has more than 3 oz. chicken (3 mcg)

Nutrient	Amount	Sources
Iodine (mcg)	150/ 200/ 200	Kelp, seaweed, watercress, dulse, Irish moss, all plants, saltine crackers, lima beans, eggs, cow milk, iodized table salt, saltwater fish. 3 oz. salt water fish (250 mcg) has more than 6 saltine crackers (200 mcg) but less than 3 oz. wakame seaweed (500+ mcg)
Iron (mg)	15/ 15/ 15	Green leafy vegetables, dried fruits (raisins, apricots, figs, prunes, currants, and cherries), blackstrap molasses, sea vegetables, legumes, whole grains, eggs, lentil, chickpeas, all-bran cereal, lima beans, prunes, broccoli, avocado, asparagus, chicken. 1 cup of lentils (6.6 mg) has more than 4 oz. of chicken (1.2 mg) or beef (3.5 mg)
Magnesium (mg)	280/ 355/ 355	Green vegetables, nuts, seeds, soy products, mineral water, okra, brazil nuts, almonds, wheat germ, dates, dried figs, prune juice, corn, milk, beef, salmon. 1 ear of corn (28 mg) has more than 3 oz. of beef (28 mg)
Niacin (mg)	15/ 20/ 20	Peanuts, dry beans, peas, wheat germ, whole grains, enriched breads, avocados, dates, figs, prunes, cow milk, eggs (the body changes the tryptophan in eggs to niacin)
Potassium		Sweet potatoes, lima beans, bananas, figs, cantaloupe, prunes, squash, raisins, apricots, beets, peas, watermelon, oranges, grapefruit, turkey and fish.
Phosphorous (mg)	1200/ 1200/ 1200	Alfalfa, red raspberry leaves, dandelion leaves, watercress, caraway seeds, comfrey, seeds, nuts, grains, yeast, wheat germ, bran, hummus, baked beans, firm tofu, cashew butter, beef, chicken, most fruits and vegetables. ½ cup all-bran cereal (294 mg) has about the same amount of phosphorus as 3 oz. beef (298 mg)
Protein (g)	55/ 65/ 65	Tofu, soybeans, lentils, chickpeas, peanut butter, wheat germ, carob, oat bran, tempeh, lima beans, white beans, whole grains, beef, chicken. 1 cup of firm tofu (40 g) has the same amount of protein as 4 oz. roasted chicken.
Riboflavin (Vitamin B2) (mg)	1.3/ 1.5/ 1.5	Brewer's yeast, seaweed, wild rice, dried peas, beans, peanuts, sunflower seeds, dark leafy green vegetables, asparagus, broccoli, mushrooms, avocado, miso soup, eggs, cottage cheese, cow milk, organ meats
Thiamin (Vitamin B1) (mg)	1.1/ 1.5/ 1.6	Wheat germ, whole wheat, enriched flour, brown rice, spinach, cauliflower, nuts, sunflower seeds, beans, peanuts, peas, avocado, many dried fruit, blackstrap molasses, oatmeal, seminola, walnuts, pistachio nuts, green peas, soy milk, soybeans, salmon (½ cup sunflower seeds .65 mg has more B1 than 4 oz. salmon .31 mg)

Zinc (mg)	12/ 19/ 19	Pumpkin seeds, tofu, beans, brazil nuts, green peas, peanuts, beets, beef, chicken (4 oz. pumpkin seeds 4.5 mg. has more than 4 oz. chicken 2.3 mg)

Changing your diet drastically is unhealthy and can be dangerous. Make a list of some immediate changes suggested in this chapter you can implement to make the transition easier.

WHAT IS A BIRTHING CENTER?

BY SCIHONOR DEVOTION

A birthing center is a facility that offers prenatal and postnatal care as well as delivery. While hospitals focus on illness and high-risk pregnancies. Pregnancy is considered a natural and healthy process in a birthing center. The mother is encouraged to have input in her birthing experience. A birthing center provides personalized care with certified nurse-midwives, labor coaches, doulas, breastfeeding instructions and more.

Some Qualities of a Birthing Center

❏ The mother and her baby are *never* separated

❏ The episiotomy rate (cutting of the perineum [*tissue*] between the vagina and the anus) is less than 12%. Hospitals have a rate of over 90%. Warm olive oil and warm compresses are used to help stretch the woman as opposed to cutting her.

❏ The mother is encouraged to eat and drink during her labor if she pleases, to give her energy. This is not allowed in most hospitals.

❏ As opposed to having strangers and interns in your birthing room, you can be surrounded by familiar faces of family and friends. As many or as little as you like.

❏ The birthing center is equipped with a living room area and kitchen for family and friends

❏ The birthing center usually has a rocking chair, birthing balls, birthing stools, massage showers, and Jacuzzis to help make the mother comfortable and relaxed.

❏ Compared to the expense of giving birth in a hospital, it's cheap and most accept insurance.

❏ The mother is encouraged to meet with all staff members before her birth, so that she is familiar with the staff that is there.

❏ Classes such as breastfeeding, newborn care, childbirth preparation, yoga, massage, etc. are offered: usually at little or no cost.

❏ Meetings are also available such as groups for single mothers, toddlers, fathers, etc.

❏ Only about 12% of all births are transferred to the hospitals. Sometimes, the laboring mother decides that she wants drugs. Only about 2% are emergency transfers.

❏ The woman has the freedom to choose her positions while birthing.

❏ Water birth is an option.

❏ The woman is not strapped in stirrups and fetal monitors.

- ❏ A Doppler is used in between contractions to check and monitor the baby's heart rate.
- ❏ There is no routine enema or I.V.
- ❏ U can burn incense, oil, etc. to make the room how you want it. You can bring things that will make you comfortable such as pictures, bed sheets, etc.
- ❏ You are free to take pictures and video tape your birth.
- ❏ You leave usually within 24 hours after birth and most of the time a nurse will visit you at home the next day to check on you and the baby.
- ❏ Families are encouraged to keep in touch with any questions that they may have before and after delivery

Look for Birthing Centers in your city, read some reviews on them, and consider if you'd prefer one over a hospital.

THE EPIDURAL AND ITS EFFECTS
BY SCIHONOR DEVOTION
ORIGINALLY PUBLISHED IN THE 14TH DEGREE AND BEYOND

Many women have succumbed to the fear of childbirth and have made up their minds before labor and sometimes even before pregnancy that they are going to get "drugs" so that that they cannot feel the pain of labor. Some women even think that "Walking Epidurals" will allow them to actually walk. Walking epidurals are a mix of narcotic and local anesthesia. it's thought that epidurals are completely harmless and don't cross the placental barrier but new research is suggesting that there could be a possible link between epidurals given during labor and long term behavioral problems and learning in children. Along with this new research, there are other disadvantages that have already been tested and proven. Here are some things to consider.

I Understand that an Epidural...
- ❏ Will require an I.V. to be inserted prior to receiving the epidural.
- ❏ May increase the possibility of a cesarean instead of a vaginal birth.
- ❏ May increase the possibility of a urinary catheter because I may not be able to urinate with the epidural. I also understand that the catheter may increase my risk of a bladder or urinary tract infection, requiring antibiotics, which may, in turn, cause me to have a yeast infection and cause my baby to have thrush.
- ❏ May increase the possibility of a vacuum or forceps delivery because I may not be able to push the baby out.
- ❏ May increase the possibility of an episiotomy because the I.V. may cause my perineum to be engorged and therefore not able to stretch to allow the baby to be delivered easily.
- ❏ May lower my blood pressure possibly requiring additional medical intervention.
- ❏ May slow down my contractions, usually requiring additional medical intervention (Pitocin).

- ☐ Will severely restrict my mobility during labor.
- ☐ May cause itching, requiring additional medical intervention, which, in turn, may cause additional discomforts.
- ☐ May provide uneven or incomplete pain relief.
- ☐ May cause spinal headaches or spinal fluid leaks, requiring additional medical intervention after the birth.
- ☐ May reduce the natural production of endorphins, which, in turn, will reduce endorphin response associated with pleasure and joy.
- ☐ May cause disturbances of the fetal heart rate requiring additional medical intervention for my baby.
- ☐ May cause my baby to have drowsiness at birth and poor sucking reflex, requiring additional medical intervention, which decreases the chance of breastfeeding.
- ☐ May cause maternal fever, which can lead to hypothermia and require additional medical intervention, including neonatal NICU workup, such as a spinal tap.
- ☐ May cause decreased muscle strength and tone in the first hours of my baby's life.
- ☐ May cause decreased maternal/infant bonding.
- ☐ May prompt prolonged / lifelong back pain

Did You Know?
The stress of racism can cause premature births for Black mothers. Black women at every socioeconomic level have higher rates of preterm birth and infant mortality. Incredibly, these rates exceed those of white women who have not even finished high school and those of Black women who emigrated to the U.S. from other countries. For example, infant mortality in white women with a college degree or higher is 4 per 1000, while for similarly educated Black women, the rate is 12 per 1000 births. According to the Institute of Medicine, preterm births and complications (breathing problems, cerebral palsy, mental retardation) account for health care expenses in excess of $26 billion a year. Researchers have found that the physiological side effects of stress caused by chronic racism may increase the risk of premature infants in Black women.

An epidural is given only when a woman is in active labor. Before it's given, an IV is given with 1-2 liters of fluids. This IV will be kept in place during the duration of the labor. Your back is wiped with an antiseptic solution so that there is less of a chance to be infected by bacteria on your skin. A small area of skin in numbed with a local anesthetic. Then, a larger needle is injected into the small area and into the epidural space of your spine. A catheter is threaded into the needle until the tip reaches the space around the spinal cord, which is called the epidural space.

The anesthesiologist will test the area to make sure the injection site is correct. If so, a dose of medication is given. The catheter will be taped to the mother's back so that additional medication can be given later on. If the epidural is effective, the uterine nerves begin to numb. After 10 minutes, it should be active. This will be repeated throughout the labor.

It is important to make sure that it wears off before it's time to push or the mother may not be able to push her baby out on her own. Tools such as forceps and vacuums may need to be used and if that is unsuccessful, a cesarean section will be necessary. When the drugs wear off, the pain may be more difficult to deal with since there is no time to climb the mountain of pain and suddenly end up at the peak of it.

The Purpose for the Pain

The "pain" will guide you. When a woman is feeling this, she will probably move to help deal with it. Most often, the positions that she chooses to assume for comfort are also for the benefit of the labor process. The positioning helps to rotate the baby and allow the baby to descend as labor progresses.

The stress hormones that are produced in response to "labor pain" help to protect the baby against insufficient oxygen and help to prepare their lungs for breathing on their own.

There are nerves in a woman's cervix, pelvic floor muscles and vagina that cause not only pain but stretching sensations as well. The stretch receptors in these areas send signals to the pituitary gland telling it to make more oxytocin which is needed to cause contractions, dilation and the urge to push. If you get rid of this pain, you wipe out your body's ability to continue to function on its own.

Find some natural ways to help you cope with the pain. Ask your doctor for alternatives to an epidural.

C -Sections - Why, When and What can Happen
BY SCIHONOR DEVOTION

A cesarean section (or C-section) is a form of birth in which the mother's abdomen and uterus are cut open. It used to be done when a mother's or baby's life was in danger, but recently it's also been done for convenience, even if the birth would have been a normal, natural birth. Here in the U.S., C-sections become the most common major operation performed, even though The World Health Organization (WHO) states that no region in the world is justified in having a C-section rate greater than 10%-15%.

Why are there so Many C-Sections in the US?

Continuous Electronic Fetal Monitoring (EFM) has its downside since it doesn't allow women the freedom to move around. Moving helps to aid in labor progression. Studies have shown that EFM is not more accurate than period checking through other means...it's just easier. Dr. Edward Hon and Dr. Orvann Hess invented the electronic fetal monitor in 1957 to treat women with high-risk pregnancies. Almost 30 years later, Dr. Hon said at a conference on "Crisis in Obstetrics: The Management of Labor:

> If you mess around with a process that works well 98% of the time, there is much potential for harm... [most women in labor may be] much better off at home [than in the hospital with the electronic fetal monitor].

Labor Inductions. Overstimulation of the uterus limits the blood flow to the placenta and baby. The mother's mobility is also limited when induction take place. When the mother doesn't get the contractions that she was expected to get after being induced, the staff may claim a need for a C-section. Or, the contractions may be so painful that the mother asks or an epidural, which increases her risk of C-section. If you want to avoid an unnecessary cesarean, avoid induction of labor. In many hospitals, pitocin or cytotec are used to induce labor.

Liability. Many care providers are worried about malpractice and they have good reason to be. Each year doctors are getting sued left and right, so they don't take the time to be patient and allow a mother to labor normally and naturally even when she and the baby are not in danger.

Breech Babies. Doctors used to be trained to handle breech babies vaginally. Now, almost 97% of breech babies are delivered by cesarean. There are only a small handful of Obstetricians and Midwives who are skilled in handling breech vaginal births.

Money, Money, Money. A vaginal birth can cost anywhere between $9,000 and $17,000 while a cesarean section can cost anywhere between $14,000 and $25,000. So, looking at these numbers, which one do you think your doctor would prefer to take home?

Elective Cesareans. Many women are choosing to have a C-section for their own reasons. The most common reasons are that mothers are afraid of the pain of vaginal birth and they want to be in control of when the baby is born. Some are also afraid of the vaginal damage myth. Trust me, there's no need to worry – it does go back to normal. As Dr. Roshini Raj has written:

> **With every C-section you have, your chance of serious complications – such as uterine rupture, placenta abnormalities, and postpartum hemorrhage – go up.** These problems can be very dangerous for you and your baby. But…every woman heals differently, and while one woman may be able to have three C-sections safely, another may be advised to stop after just one Cesarean because of significant scar tissue or poor healing. But even one Cesarean sections carries some risk…Subsequent C's are riskier than the first one, so the decision to have an initial one shouldn't be taken lightly. I've heard of women (even some physicians) who schedule a C-section for a first baby for the sake of convenience. This is major surgery, people! So unless it's medically necessary, you should take the vaginal route.

When is a C-Section a Reasonable Choice?

There are several situations that can be considered indications for cesarean, an ethical doctor may recommend a C-section if…

☐ The child is in distress showing that the baby isn't getting enough oxygen.

- ❑ There is a "failure to progress" or they feel that your labor is taking too long to progress.
- ❑ The mother is having health issues such as preeclampsia, gestational diabetes or has an injured pelvis.
- ❑ There are placental complications such as an umbilical cord prolapse or uterine rupture.
- ❑ There is more than one child.
- ❑ There is the rare chance that the baby is too large for the birth canal (CPD).
- ❑ Rare umbilical cord abnormalities.
- ❑ STD's such as herpes is active and can be passed to the baby if born vaginally.
- ❑ Previous C-section - This is highly debated since it has been shown that mothers have given birth to healthy babies after they've had a previous cesarean safely.[14]
- ❑ An issue with the perineum's healing from a previous birth or Crohn's disease.

> Did You Know?
> Indigenous healers in Uganda performed a successful cesarean section...in 1879. Cesarean sections are much older than Julius Caesar (who they're named after). Indigenous people have been recording as performing such surgeries since ancient India and Egypt. However, these procedures were only done when the mother's life was in danger.

What are the Risks?

A cesarean birth is major abdominal surgery. The health risks far outweigh a vaginal birth even if the mother has had a previous cesarean.

- ❑ Higher risk of infection in mother during surgery than with a vaginal birth.
- ❑ Longer hospital stay for cesarean mothers and extended recovery time.
- ❑ Cesarean babies do not breastfeed as easily as vaginally born babies.
- ❑ Long-term effects on mothers can include future ectopic pregnancies.
- ❑ Increased risk of hemorrhage, which may lead to transfusion.
- ❑ Hysterectomy to control hemorrhage, which sterilizes the mother.
- ❑ Trauma to bladder, uterus, bowel, or other organs from cutting during surgery
- ❑ Problems with anesthesia leading to paralysis or even death.
- ❑ Babies born by cesarean have a higher rate of developing breathing problems, since the fluid in the baby's lungs was not released as they would have been in a natural birth (the baby gets a natural massage from the contractions while traveling down the vaginal canal), which often results in pneumonia or other respiratory issues.

Women who have cesareans are at least 5 times more likely to die as a result of childbirth than women who have vaginal births. And it doesn't stop there. C-sections have been linked to lower fertility, placental complications with subsequent pregnancies, future babies born with abnormalities or injuries to their brains or spinal cords due to placental

---

[14] Vaginal Birth After Cesarean (VBAC) - Current evidence shows that most women can have safe vaginal births after a prior cesarean. Uterine rupture is a common fear among women who have had a previous cesarean but a complete rupture occurs in much less than 1% of women attempting a VBAC.

insufficiencies, premature babies, pain in the incision area long after the surgery, painful sex, problems with bowel movements, and more.

Educate yourself on why and when a C-section birth is needed and don't get intimidated or coerced by medical practitioners who are only concerned about money and convenience.

SERIOUS PREGNANCY ISSUES
BY SCIHONOR DEVOTION

Let's look at some serious symptoms that women experience during pregnancy. Although we can't discuss all problems that can occur, these go beyond the regular uncomfortable symptoms of pregnancy like hemorrhoids, heartburn, nausea and back aches.

All of the issues that are mentioned in this article will require some sort of attention if not medical attention unless you have a home birth midwife or holistic healer who is willing to deal with at least some of these issues holistically. Talk to your care providers about your options.

Your pregnancy may be complicated if...

- ☐ You are either younger than 17 or older than 35
- ☐ You have a history of miscarriage
- ☐ You have an incompetent cervix
- ☐ You tested positive for Group B Strep
- ☐ You had High Blood Pressure (HBP) prior to getting pregnant
- ☐ You develop HBP (Preeclampsia/Toxemia) during pregnancy
- ☐ You had diabetes prior to getting pregnant
- ☐ You develop gestational diabetes during your pregnancy
- ☐ You have a breech baby at the end of your pregnancy
- ☐ You are carrying more than 1 baby
- ☐ You are Rh- while your baby is Rh+
- ☐ You have Sickle Cell or another serious disease such as lupus, cancer, thyroid disease, rheumatoid arthritis, or epilepsy
- ☐ You contract a childhood disease like chicken pox, mumps, fifth disease or rubella during pregnancy. *If you have been vaccinated for any childhood disease, it's recommended that you wait 3 months before getting pregnant
- ☐ You've contracted cytomegalovirus (usually from sick children).
- ☐ Your water breaks before 37 weeks of pregnancy
- ☐ You have Anemia of Iron, Folic Acid or B12 deficiency
- ☐ Your pregnancy goes beyond 42 weeks
- ☐ Your mother took the drug DES during her pregnancy with you
- ☐ You have placental problems like placenta abruption or placenta previa
- ☐ You use alcohol, drugs or smoke cigarettes
- ☐ You have asthma
- ☐ Your baby has a genetic condition like Down syndrome or a problem in organs like the liver, kidney, heart, etc.

- ❏ You have an infection like Hepatitis C or Toxoplasmosis
- ❏ You're taking prescription drugs that are unsafe during pregnancy.
- ❏ You are obese
- ❏ You suffer from depression or other mood or emotional disorders
- ❏ You have heart disease or a disease of another major organ
- ❏ Your baby is suffering from Intra Uterine Growth Retardation (IUGR)

Signs to look out for...

- ❏ Bleeding during pregnancy
- ❏ Abdominal Cramping
- ❏ Pain in the pelvis
- ❏ Water leaking or gushing
- ❏ Headaches
- ❏ Swelling hands and face
- ❏ Blurry eyesight
- ❏ Weight gain of about 1 pound a day
- ❏ Painful urination
- ❏ Dizziness
- ❏ Hot flashes followed by feeling cold
- ❏ Rashes
- ❏ STD outbreaks or discharge
- ❏ Urinary Tract Infections
- ❏ Severe vomiting
- ❏ Weight loss
- ❏ Vaginal infections
- ❏ Absence of fetal movements
- ❏ Diarrhea
- ❏ Itchy soles of feet, palms, legs or whole body
- ❏ Cravings for strange things that are mostly not food items, like dirt, chalk, ice, clay, etc.
- ❏ Persistent back pain
- ❏ Regular contractions before 37 weeks

Things to AVOID as much as Possible

Stress - Babies can be born prematurely or with low birth weights. More tests are being done to see what the effects of stress are on babies but some believe that babies born to women who are stress are more likely to have birth defects.

Cat Litter - Toxoplasmosis is a parasite found in cat litter that can be passed from a mother to her unborn baby. It can lead to intrauterine growth retardation, preterm labor and miscarriage.

Sick Children - Childhood diseases can cause cataracts, heart disease, deafness, premature labor, miscarriage and more. CMV is usually contracted when dealing with small children who can pass it. It can affect babies by causing enlarged spleens, rashes, liver problems, seizures and jaundice. .

Artificial Sweeteners (like Equal, NutraSweet, Sweet N' Low and Cyclamate) can cross the placenta and remain in the baby's tissue.

Caffeine increases blood pressure and heart rate and is a diuretic which means it make you pee al lot which can lead to dehydration. Coffee is not the only beverage with caffeine in it. Teas, Soda and even some Vitamin Water have caffeine.

Smoking anything with tobacco or nicotine can be a serious problem but many people don't take it as seriously as they should. When you smoke or are around smokers, you are providing your baby with less oxygen than if you were smoke free. This can have negative results. Babies can be born too early, have frequent colds, lung problems, learning disabilities, and they may not even grow physically as they would if they were healthier.

Alcohol - Consuming alcohol during pregnancy can result in a child with physical, mental or neurobehavioral birth defects. The baby can even be born with withdrawal symptoms.

Fish (due to its mercury content) - Mercury is a contaminant and is found in fish. It can be harmful to the baby's brain development and nervous system.

Certain Teas - Non-herbal teas like Black, Green and Oolong are naturally caffeinated and can complicate your pregnancy. Some safe herbal teas to drink are red raspberry, peppermint, chamomile, ginger root and lemon balm. In moderation, alfalfa and yellow dock can be used for their beneficial properties. You can check your local health food store and look for pregnancy teas already packaged for you. DO NOT consume Black Cohosh or Blue Cohosh if you are not beyond your 37th week of pregnancy. These herbs induce labor and must be taken with caution.

> **Did You Know?**
> It is not known how continued use of ultrasound will affect babies in the future, but it's now being discussed that they could suffer from some hearing disabilities after birth or even later in life. So, if you don't need the procedure done, think twice before getting it.

Raw/unclean foods - Raw meat, raw eggs, unpasteurized dairy, soft cheeses, deli meat, and unwashed vegetables can be contaminated with salmonella, e-coli, toxoplasmosis or listeria which can complicate pregnancy by increasing the risk of having a low birth weight baby, having a premature baby or even having a miscarriage.

Cleaning Chemicals can be very dangerous to inhale. Be sure to protect yourself by using gloves, opening a window or even wearing a mask if you must. NEVER mix bleach and ammonia! it's very dangerous!

Pesticides can be dangerous and can cause a problem with a baby's development by causing cleft lips, neurotube defects, heart problems, limb defects or miscarriage.

Recreational Drugs can cause a host of complications in an unborn baby, most of which are long lasting well after birth. Most of these drugs cross the placenta and can cause the placenta to detach from the mothers uterus too soon causing miscarriage or preterm labor, birth defects of the major organs like the brain or even the genitals, feeding problems when baby is born, withdrawal symptoms, low blood sugar, poor muscle control and a whole lot of other complications that are not easy to deal with.

Other things to avoid are roller coasters and thrill rides, perfumes, paint fumes, tanning machines, x-rays, hot tubs, saunas and CAT scans.

Be on the lookout for potential complications. Get a doctors opinion whenever you want to.

EMERGENCY CHILDBIRTH
BY SCIHONOR DREEVOTION
ORIGINALLY PUBLISHED IN THE 14TH DEGREE AND BEYOND

If you are pregnant or know someone who is pregnant, now is a good time to start thinking about what you'd do in case of an emergency and can't get to any outside help. If you planned to have your baby in a hospital or birthing center, you may feel uncomfortable not being able to get there, but remember that we have been birthing before hospitals were even around. Stay calm. If you planned to have a home birth, you may also be uncomfortable, but that is natural for childbirth.

If you are with the mother when she goes into labor, you can most likely tell by her attitude if she is in active labor. Communicate with her and this will help you to determine if you will need to take action soon.

You will have to ask yourself a few questions.

❑ Has the mother had babies before? Usually, the mother's first birth will be longer. This may give you some time to get some help. If the baby is crowning, then you are about to deliver a child.

❑ How frequent are the contractions? If the contractions are more than 5 minutes apart, then you may be able to get help. If they are less than 2 minutes apart, again, you are about to deliver a baby. To time contractions, you should begin looking at your clock from the beginning of one contraction to the beginning of the next. If the contractions begin in the abdomen area, then they are real labor contractions. If they are confined to the abdomen area, they may be false labor contractions.

❑ Has the water broken? If the mother's water has broken, check or ask her what color it was. If it had a yellow/green tint, there may be some meconium in it. That is the baby's bowel movement. This can cause infection if the baby is not delivered in a timely matter.

❑ Does the mother feel like she has to move her bowels? This feeling is the baby's head pushing on the rectum on the way out of the vagina. She may also have a strong urge to push. Pushing too early in labor can cause her cervix to swell which will not help the delivery. She will know when to push.

If you have access to supplies get them or have someone else get them as soon as possible.

You will need...

❑ Pillows, clean sheets, clean towels
❑ Rubber gloves
❑ Container for placenta
❑ Clean scissors

❑ Clean cord ties
❑ Boiling water and hot water
❑ Baby blanket, caps, and socks (babies lose most of their body heat through their heads)

❏ Bulb syringe (not a needle) |❏ Olive oil (warm if possible)

Wash your hands and wear gloves if possible. (This will probably be all that you have time for).

What you will do...

Stay calm and try to calm the mother. Don't try to delay the birth. Keeping or pushing the baby in when the baby is coming out can cause damage to the child.

Choose a birthing area (bed, table, and chair, whatever makes the mother feel comfortable). Remember this is her birth. She needs to be free to move as her body tells her. Cover the birthing area with clean sheets, towels, or even newspaper can be used if you have to.

Suggest she use the bathroom to urinate. A full bladder may be in the baby's path. Go with her to make sure the baby doesn't "fall out."

Let the mother choose her position to give birth in and watch her for cues for help. Encourage her to rest in between her contractions. She may also want some ice chips or something to sip on. She needs the energy. Allow her to stay hydrated. If she spits up, that is fine. This will not hurt her or the baby. She will be able to feel when the baby is coming. She will probably say, "It's coming!!!" or something like that. She is serious.

You may see the baby's head showing (crowning). Tell her to push with her contractions and rest in between. Apply warm olive oil or warm water to the perineum (the area between the vagina and anus). This will prevent her from ripping and tearing.

She may have a bowel movement due to pushing. Just wipe it away from front to back and keep your attention on her. You'll be surprised what you can do (without flinching) in times like this. Just try not to get anything on your hands.

As the baby's head is delivered, ask her to relax. When the head is delivered, the baby will naturally turn to either the left or right side to face the mother's thigh. If the umbilical cord is around the baby's neck, slip two fingers between the cord and the baby's neck and pull it around the baby's head. If the bag of water has not broken, you can tear it gently.

Support the baby's head and get the bulb syringe. Squeeze the syringe and then place it in the baby's mouth about 1 to 1.5 inches. Then release the bulb slowly. This will draw the mucus and water into the syringe. Dispose of the syringe contents. Suction the little nose as well. You may have to repeat a few times. Do NOT suction vigorously. This may stimulate laryngeal spasm.

The mother may only have to give a few more pushes and the baby should come out. She may need help though. Support the head in an upright position and this will help the lower shoulder out. **Once the**

shoulder is out the rest of the body will slide out. Be prepared.

As the baby slides out, support the baby with one hand under the head and the other hand under the body. The baby will be bluish and covered with a white, slippery, soft film called vernix. This helped to protect the baby from the liquids in the mother's womb.

Use a towel to cover the baby and record the time of birth if possible. Place the baby on the mother's stomach and breast on its side. Don't pull on the cord when picking the baby up.

While the baby is on the mother, raise the hips a little higher than the head to allow the liquid to drain. While the mother holds the baby, suction the baby's nose and mouth. **If the baby is not breathing on its own, slap the bottom of the feet and massage the baby's back.**

Keep the body wrapped up very warm. Babies are used to a warm womb. The umbilical cord will stop pulsing because the baby no longer needs it. When the cord has stopped pulsing, you can tie and cut the cord. **To cut the cord, the area must be clean.**

Place the clamps or tie with a thick shoestring on the cord about 1-3 inches apart, about 8 to 10 inches and then the other about 4-6 inches from the baby's navel. At about 1 inch from the clamp that is closest to the baby's body, cut the cord. Make sure the scissors or knives are sterile.

If you cannot get anything sterile, there is no need to cut the cord. The baby will not be hurt if the cord is not cut. You have to cut the cord with something clean. You don't want to get it infected. Just tie it once and let it be delivered. The cord may bleed, but this is fine. Cover the stump with a clean gauze or cloth since it's vulnerable to infection.

The mother may feel cramps in her belly. Now it's time to deliver the placenta. The placenta should be delivered within the next 20 minutes after the baby. This does not hurt.

Encourage the mother to nurse her new baby. The nipple stimulation will help to release a hormone called oxytocin (This hormone causes contractions). This will also control the bleeding. Place your hand on her belly and check for a grapefruit sized ball. This is her uterus.

Massage the area using circular motions. You will continue to knead this area for about two hours after birth on and off. Encourage her to bear down to deliver the placenta. There may be bleeding. This is fine. When the placenta is visible, grab it and turn it gently. Don't pull it. Slowly guide it out of the vagina. Check the placenta to see if it looks whole. If pieces of the placenta are left in the mother, much bleeding may continue. Wrap the placenta in a container or bag.

There should not be much bleeding. About 1-2 cups is fine. If there is a lot of bleeding, the mother may be torn. Check her skin for tears and when you find the tear, place direct pressure on it with a clean towel or sanitary napkin. Keep both of them warm.

In some cases, there may be complications. The birthing mother may go into convulsions or have other complications. There may also be problems with the baby's birth such as Shoulder Dystocia (wedged shoulders), Breech Delivery, a prolapsed umbilical cord, placenta previa, abruption placenta, or a ruptured uterus.[15]

Taking the necessary precautions ahead of time will make the birthing process easier once you are pressed for time.

FINDING A PEDIATRICIAN
BY SCIHONOR DEVOTION

Before your baby is born, you should have already interviewed and decided on a pediatrician. Call your health insurance and get the names and numbers of pediatricians that they cover in the area in which you are willing to travel. Remember, you don't want the doctor to be too far in case you have an emergency. You also don't want to settle on a doctor just because they are close to home. You want to be sure that they share your health care philosophy and are willing and able to answer and address your questions, concerns and needs. You can also go to the health insurances web site to search for names and locations there. If you are looking for a more natural or holistic doctor, you can use natural magazines as a resource, ask other parents who that use, or you can do an internet search. **Some insurance companies will even cover the costs for some holistic practitioners.** Did you know that Medicaid in New York covers homebirth? You never know what you'll find unless you ask.

Some things to consider when deciding on a pediatrician are...

❏ What insurance do you accept?
❏ What are your standard fees if I have no insurance?
❏ Which medical school did you attend?
❏ Where did you do your residency?
❏ Are you board certified or board eligible?
❏ How long have you been in practice?
❏ Which undergraduate school did you attend?
❏ Are you a member of the American Academy of Pediatrics?
❏ What hospital are you affiliated with?
❏ Can I call you 24 hours a day?
❏ Do you have an answering service/paging service?
❏ What are your office locations and hours?
❏ What would I do if there is an emergency?

---

[15] These websites will help you further prepare: www.yalad.com www.midwifery2000.com www.homedelivery.org www.homebirthsupplies.com www.storkhelper.com

- Do you have a backup doctor? Where is he/she located? Do they follow your idea of good practice?
- When do you think prescription drugs are necessary?
- How do you feel about childhood vaccines and will you explain each vaccine and their adverse reactions before giving them? If I choose not to have my child vaccinated, will you continue to care for them? Do you offer exemptions?
- What tests do you do routinely after birth?
- Do you consider circumcision to be medically necessary (even though the American Academy of Pediatrics does not)? If I decide not to have the procedure done, what must I do? If I decide to have the procedure done, what must I do?
- Do you recommend cloth or disposable diapers and what are the pro's and cons of each?
- I have a particular diet (vegetarian, vegan, raw foodist). How do you feel about this type of diet and have you cared for children with this type of diet in the past?
- What are your thoughts on breastfeeding and how long do you recommend I do it for? Do you have a list of lactation consultants or someone I can call if I need assistance or have questions?
- What type of infant formula do you recommend?

Notice during your interview...
- Was the doctor and his staff respectful of you and did you feel comfortable?
- Do you know anyone who has used this doctor before successfully or unsuccessfully?
- Were there age appropriate toys and books for the children?
- What did you notice about the office decoration?
- Are both the office and restroom clean?
- Is the doctor patient?
- Were all of you questions answered?
- How does the doctor interact with children?
- How long did you wait to meet with the doctor?
- Did you hear or see anyone complaining about their care or experience?

Make a checklist of questions you would like to ask your prospective pediatrician before your first visit.

HOLISTIC PRENATAL HEALTH, LABOR AND DELIVERY
BY EBONI JOY ASIATIC
ORIGINALLY PUBLISHED IN THE 14TH DEGREE AND BEYOND

Holistic health pertains to the *all* in all of us, prenatal health begins before conception; just as labor and delivery preparation begins way before the contractions ever start.

The Baby Weight. To gain weight slowly, yet steadily, keep in mind that it's recommended that women **consume an extra 200 calories a day**

during their first trimesters, and in addition to their normal caloric intake will need **300-500 extra calories a day during the second and third trimesters.** These calories are necessary to ensure the constant growth and development of your baby. These measurements are approximate, but typically by the end of your pregnancy 6-9 of the pounds you gain will be your infant's, 1½ pounds will go to the placenta, amniotic fluid will accumulate to 2 pounds, your breasts will enlarge by 1-3 pounds, your uterus will enlarge by approximately 2 pounds, fat stores and muscle development consists of 4-8 pounds, increased blood volume will be 3-4 pounds, and increased volume in other bodily fluids will add 2-3 pounds. Depending on the size of your baby and the amount of fat and muscle you store during pregnancy, an expectant mother should gain anywhere between 22-35 healthy pounds during her pregnancy.

The Baby's Weight. The weight that a baby will be at birth is partially determined by the amount of weight the mother gains during pregnancy. A desirable weight for full-term newborns is between 6½-9 pounds, because babies born within this weight class usually have a lower rate of sudden infant deaths, fewer mental and physical handicaps, fewer childhood illnesses, and are generally better mentally and physically able than smaller, premature infants.

Herbs

Herbs were the essential "medicines" in any healer's repertoire long before "western medicine" was ever thought of. The use of herbs to cure disease, treat ailments, and attain optimal health is a primary aspect of holistic approaches to health. Herbalism is a traditional medicinal characterized by the use of plants, roots or extracts as medicines; and the herb is the plant or plant part used for these medicinal means.

What People DON'T Take: Many of the herbs that have helped keep your immune system functioning in tip-top condition prior to pregnancy are no longer safe to take during pregnancy.

☐ Herbs such as aloe vera, angelica, autumn crocus, barberry, black cohosh, celery seed, cinnamon, devil's claw, golden seal, hyssop, juniper, male fern, mandrake, parsley seed, pennyroyal, pokeweed, rosemary, rue, sage, southernwood, tansy, thuja, wormwood and yarrow have all been known to stimulate the uterus and cause pre-term labor contractions and even result in miscarriage and should thus be avoided.

☐ Pennyroyal has been known to be used as a "natural" method of abortion because it's so effective at causing miscarriages.

☐ Goldenseal has been used by midwives to assist with uterine contractions in slow labor, but it should not be taken without the guidance of a professional, and should never be taken throughout one's pregnancy.

What People Take: Other herbs are safer and can help ward off morning sickness (like chamomile, ginger, peppermint and black horehound) or other problems, and can be taken as teas, smoothies, made into compresses, or the mother-to-be can soak in a bath of them.

❏ Some herbs are also recognized as promoting female reproductive health, the strengthening of uterine muscles, enhancing lactation, and general womb/women's wellness include alfalfa, dandelion root, kelp, nettle leaves, oat straw, and yellow dock.

❏ Olive oil is often used to massage the perineum – the area of tissue between the opening of the vagina and opening of the anus – massaging this area with two fingers stroking downward from the vaginal opening with olive oil in the last month of pregnancy is said to help prepare the perineum for stretching and helps prevent tears and the need for episiotomies.

❏ Alfalfa and kelp are good sources of many vitamins and minerals; alfalfa has vitamin K, which is essential for normal blood clotting, and kelp has calcium, which is essential for proper bone and teeth development in the baby and maintenance of bone density, teeth and gums in the mother.

❏ St. John's wort and shepherd's purse help uterine contractions at birth.

❏ In the last four weeks of pregnancy, blessed thistle, blue cohosh, false unicorn root and squawvine may be taken to prepare the uterus for an easier birth by aiding contractions – but they should not be taken in the first two trimesters of pregnancy.

❏ To enrich the production of milk – burdock root, dandelion, ginger, and nettle may be taken, as well as red raspberry leaf – which is quite possibly the most popular and widely used among these herbs to ensure pregnancy health.

❏ Raspberry or red raspberry leaf is commonly used to soothe and prevent bleeding gums (which many pregnant women experience due to loss of calcium reserves), relax the muscles of the uterus during contractions and therefore aiding the birth of the baby and placenta, eases cramping, and is a source of iron, calcium, manganese, magnesium, vitamins B1, B3 and E. it's also considered to be a fertility aid, and is used to prepare the womb for pregnancy.

Sitz Bath

Sitz baths have been known to relieve discomfort from infections of the bladder, prostate or vagina; menstrual cramps; uterine cramping after birth; genital sores; inflammation of the prostate gland or prostate infections; surgery in the rectal area; and inflammatory bowel disorders. Most sitz baths are comprised of a person simply sitting in warm water for about 20 minutes; sometimes Epsom salt or baking soda is added. To ease the discomfort of yeast infections, women can take a warm saline sitz bath with sea salt or Epsom salt and vinegar – the vinegar balances the vaginal pH (acidity and alkalinity).

An herbal sitz bath after delivery can help to ease the muscles and tissues around a woman's vagina, relieve uterine cramps and the pain of an episiotomy or perineum tearing, as well as speed healing in that area. The bath can be taken by sitting in a small basin or plastic tub placed inside your bathtub, sitz bathtubs may also be purchased that fit on top of your toilet seat.

A sitz bath recipe (from Dandelion Botanical Company in Seattle):

❏ 1 oz. each of chamomile, chickweed, marshmallow root, plantain, lavender flowers, and calendula

❏ 2 oz. of rosemary and uva ursi

❏ 2 oz. sea salt.

To prepare the bath, pour boiling water over 4 ounces of the herbal blend. Let it steep for at least 4 hours. Strain the infusion into a bowl or directly into your sitz bath basin, then sit with your vaginal area in the bath for about 15 minutes. This process can be repeated several times a day if you don't have stitches. If you do have stitches, a sitz bath should only be taken once a day.

Exercise

The strengthening of one's muscles and heart health allows them to better cope with labor and delivery. Exercise also helps you to regulate your breathing which helps manage pain, and exercise decreases the sheer fat weight gained during pregnancy enabling a woman to lose her pregnancy weight more quickly after delivery (losing weight should NOT be a concern during pregnancy). Various exercises can be done during pregnancy as long as the mother is not straining herself – including swimming, brisk walking, aerobics, yoga (See "Prenatal Yoga"), and dance (the hip and waist movements used in salsa and belly dancing specifically help to widen a woman's pelvic opening and strengthen her pelvic muscles). (See, "Keep It Tight…Aight?" for Kegal Exercises.)

Create your own "Holistic Prenatal Health Regiment." Know what to do, and what not to do. Incorporate the right foods and exercises.

PRENATAL YOGA

BY EBONI JOY ASIATIC

Other than Kegel exercises, one of the most highly recommended exercises during pregnancy is yoga. Yoga is a combination of posturing, breath control, meditation, and visualization techniques in order to bring awareness and syncopation to the mind, body and spirit (breath). It helps us reconnect and stay in tune with the process of childbirth so that we can better recall how to ease the process along with our own conscious, meditative efforts.

During pregnancy the spine has a tendency to curve more than it naturally does which hunches the shoulders and upper back forward and collapses our ribcage. So not only is your growing baby taking up space from your internal organs, but your changes in posture are compressing your lungs and diaphragm resulting in shortness of breath. This is also a primary cause of heartburn – the stomach gets compressed and its acids regurgitate up the esophagus. Many prenatal poses help to cease this problem by opening the chest; prenatal poses also facilitate the opening of the pelvis to prepare for the baby's descent through the birth canal, and increase the flexibility of the uterine and pelvic muscles.

An important guideline for exercise during pregnancy is to know your limitations and practicing stances that make your body feel as though it's being strengthened. **Avoid activities that endanger the abdomen, have quick jarring, bouncing, or twisting motions, rapid starts and stops, and avoid exercises that require you to lay flat on your back once you have entered the second trimester** (4th month of pregnancy) – as it decreases blood to your baby and placenta. If you feel any pain in your back, knees or abdomen area you should come out of that pose; and if you experience any cramping or overheating you should take a rest from exercising altogether. Honoring the health of your unborn child is always primary and should remain part of your conscious thoughts.

Keep in mind that there are poses that pregnant women, especially after their first trimester, should not attempt (like the cobra pose) and some that should be altered to prevent over-stretching (like the extended triangle pose) – **please contact a professional yoga instructor or purchase a prenatal DVD to ensure that you are practicing yoga as it should be done during pregnancy.** Below, I have provided photographs of myself performing, at nearly 30-weeks pregnant, just a few of the most highly recommended prenatal yoga poses:

Butterfly pose (baddha konasana): A sitting pose that helps open the

pelvis, stretch the spine and open the rib cage. Gently sit balanced on your sit bones, sit up straight, and pull your legs in by touching heel to heel. If your knees feel any discomfort, place rolled towels or blankets underneath them. Gently press the knees down and away from each other. Stay in this pose for a few breaths, and then from this position lean back on your right palm, bending your elbow, and reach for the sky leaning to the right by stretching your left arm and shoulder over your head. Repeat on the other side by stretching the right arm and leaning back on the left palm.

Cat pose (bidalasana) and Cow pose (bitilasana): These positions help relieve back pain, increases spinal flexibility and abdominal strength. Come to a neutral tabletop position aligning hips over knees and shoulders over wrists. Keep knees hip distance apart and arms straight. For the cat pose – arch your back while gently tilting the pelvis up and out as you roll the head, neck and shoulders back, inhaling. For the cow pose

– exhale and curl the tailbone under and in, rounding the back, tucking chin to chest. Follow the breath

for a few cycles through these poses.

Squatting (malasana): This pose relaxes and opens the pelvis, and strengthens the calves, thighs and hamstrings, as well as elongates your spine. Stand against a wall for support with your feet wider than your hips, with your feet parallel to each other (or turn them slightly out if it's more comfortable). Bend your knees and ease your way down into a squat, bringing hands together at heart. Open through the chest as you gently press your knees wider. If you are past 34 weeks and your baby is in the breech position, only squat halfway. If you need to, use props such as yoga blocks or a few stacked books on which to rest your bottom (as done in the picture). Focus on relaxing and letting your breath drop deeply into your belly.

Warrior II (virabhadrasana II): This pose strengthens the legs, knee muscles, shoulders and arms; it also increases pelvic and spine flexibility. Bring the legs about a legs length apart. Align the front heel with the arch of the back foot. Bend the front leg to a depth of 90 degrees if you can, positioning the knee over the ankle. Press firmly through the outside edge of the back foot. Bring both arms up reaching to opposite sides of the room. Gaze softly over the front foot. As you get larger and heavier, you may need the use of a chair for support under the pelvis. Repeat this pose on the other side. (FYI, in the picture my arms are tilted a bit too much and my right knee should be bent a bit more to achieve the 90 degree angle.)

Resting Pose (savasana): Usually the resting pose is done on the back, however after the fourth month of pregnancy it should be adjusted and done on the side. Resting pose gives your body time to process the information it has gained during its exercise, and relax the mind, body and breath to bring them back into a harmonious flow. Use any number of

blocks, pillows or rolled-up towels for cushioning and comfort. Relaxation postures like the resting pose oppose the effects of stress. Rest here and remain in this pose as long as you like. When you come out, use arms for support and come to a comfortable seated position, hands at heart center. Find gratitude for your practice and your unborn baby.[16]

Meditation

Meditation is an essential aspect of yoga because it helps you clear your mind and just be still, aware of the present, and equally able to visualize the outcome you seek to achieve. Yoga is a physical discipline, and meditation is a mental discipline, one that enables its practitioners to gain awareness and relaxation at will. When meditation techniques are put to practice by expectant mothers it can help them plan a stress-free labor and delivery by disciplining them to clear their minds, focus, visualize and manifest. In her book *Holistic Parenting from the Pan-Afrikan Perspective*, Iya Raet mentioned how meditating on your baby's birth can begin as soon as conception is confirmed; she said: (See, "Mediation: A Path To Inner Freedom.")

> I talked to my son, guided him through our birth experience... I reassured him that it would be safe to leave the womb when it was time. I visualized him leaving my womb in a peaceful manner. I visualized my cervix opening slowly like a lotus flower, allowing his head to enter the birth canal. I envisioned him crowning slowly, and then pulling him up with my own hands onto my belly.

Breathing Techniques

"Breath is life" and therefore with concentrated breath circulating through our bodies, being shared with our unborn babies, we feed our children with the breath of life for the duration of their lives during pregnancy. Breath techniques are meant to build mastery over the mind and body. In Zazen, the meditation of the Buddha, the practitioner sits comfortably and stills their mind by counting the flow of their breath – counting alternately each inhalation (1) and exhalation (2) from one to ten. This count is repeated every time you reach 10. This is a practice that helps prevent your thoughts from drifting. Once your count is steady, start counting each breath cycle – inhale, exhale (1) – inhale, exhale (2) – and so on and so forth until you reach ten, at which time you repeat the meditation. As you become more knowledgeable about your breathing patterns, you should be able to be aware of the count without counting. Zazen breath meditation helps its practitioners develop the power of focused concentration and create a serene, peaceful mind-set for themselves regardless of environment – this ability will come in handy

---

[16] On sites like www.yogajournal.com and www.squidoo.com/yogaduringpregnancy you can find excellent recommendations for prenatal poses with a brief explanation of how each pose helps maintain the overall holistic well-being of mind, body and breath.

during labor, especially if you are delivering in a hectic environment like a hospital.

Another breath meditation is Vipassana, meaning "to see things as they really are", and serves the purpose of helping its practitioners develop insight into the true nature of things through self-observation by being aware of one's breath, how it enlivens the body, and recognizing the sensations caused by this repetition. Vipassana meditation classes are an extremely intense 10-day all-day course that aims to first calm the mind by instituting a basic moral code upon its students, and from there completely eradicate mental "devils" (or impurities) so that its practitioner can achieve happiness in their acquisition of mental freedom. Again, this technique is another means of teaching an expectant mother to:

❒ transfer only positive thoughts and emotions upon her unborn child,
❒ think and act optimistically so that the energy she puts out comes back to her in the form of optimal success, and
❒ heal herself from suffering – whether mental worries or labor and delivery pains

This technique's focus on the interconnectedness between mind and body causes its practitioners to embrace their physical sensations by understanding the cause and effects of them. This discipline teaches that self-transformation can be achieved through self-observation, increased awareness, non-delusion, self-control and peace.

In the disciplines of meditation and breath control, you are channeling energy – the energy you choose that will best aide you in achieving your meditative goal – and this energy is proven to bring its practitioners self-knowledge, emotional balance, and psychological well-being. Mental peace and happiness must be a primary acquisition before we can achieve well-rounded holistic health that branches to our physical health as well. Meditating on the gift that will be received once labor is complete allows women to channel the truth of the mantra that labor pain is "pain with a purpose." Alleviating some of the suffering of labor by visualizing the outcome of the experience of delivery is an act of mind over matter. And so it's important to visualize your birth and meditate on what steps need to be taken in order to create this heavenly experience for yourself and your unborn child.[17]

Take at least 15-30 minutes a day to attempt some yoga exercises and breathing techniques during your pregnancy. To keep it fresh, mix it up and try a new pose every day.

---

[17] *The Yogi Science of Breath* by Yogi Ramacharaka goes much deeper into this matter. You can now find this work at www.SupremeDesignOnline.com

FORMULA: THE BEST MILK SINCE BREAST MILK?

BY RODNEY JONES

For years I wondered, what exactly is this "formula" that almost everyone is pumping into their babies' mouths before the baby can say "Stop bullsh*ttin and pull out that tatty!" I mean is it "baby brain growth" formula? Is it "baby talk faster" formula? Is it "make sure baby hits puberty at 7 years old" formula? (I'd put money on that one) What the hell was in that formula? So I took the time one day to sit down and look up the ingredients in this magical "formula", and what I found was just unbelievable (well not to me). Keep in mind that the baby formula industry brings in $8 billion annually and we all know, in America, big business comes before your health any day. Of course I'm not going to keep you in the dark about what's in it so on to the next paragraph.

> **Did You Know?**
> The US was ranked 12th in the world in infant mortality in 1960. It slipped down to 23rd in 1990, and was 29th by 2004, tied with Slovakia! And that's not even factoring for racial disparities. Infant mortality among whites in 2005 was 5.76 per 1,000 births, 8.06 among Native Americans, 8.3 among Puerto Ricans, and 13.68 among Blacks. And depending on where you live, there's even more disparity. In 2006, Tennessee reported infant mortality rates that surpassed the national average by over 31%, with the rate for Black babies twice that of whites.

A list of baby formula ingredients I found contained the following: Fluoride, Perchlorate, Hexane, Melamine, Cyanuric Acid, Mercury, Formaldehyde, BPA's and all sort of other things you wouldn't feed to your family pitbull named "overkill", let alone your own child had you known better.

Everyone knows, or should know what mercury is by now. It's that silver stuff that was in your big mama's thermometer. You know that stuff that gets in the water and makes fish born with 3 eyes and 11 fins (and two of those fins have human toes). That same mercury laced formula that you are forcing down your kids throat is causing rashes, constipation, diarrhea, lethargy and autism just to name a few symptoms. **So when you see your kid looking spaced out at 5 months old, or you have to get them a prescription for eczema cream every two months, now you know why (Mercury is also found in High Fructose Corn Syrup, which is in about half of the products in your local grocery store from soda to Oreos, to...just about anything you can name).**

Another substance in baby formula is Melamine. When Melamine is consumed in grown humans it's known to produce kidney stones. Kidney stones are known to block urinary flow and make urination painful, cause kidney failure and in some cases, even death. That's what it can do to a "Grown ass man", **so just imagine the harmful potential it has to an infant forced to drink baby poison, I mean formula.**

This next one is my favorite; Cyanuric Acid. Cyanuric Acid is a white odorless substance used as a component in different bleaches, disinfectants, and herbicides. When too much Cyanuric acid was put into a Chinese manufacturer's batch of baby formula, infants were turning up sick left and right all over China. Eventually, the Chinese version of the FDA recalled all of the formula from this company; liquid and powdered forms.

We may never be able to get this stuff off of the shelves of the grocery store but we can refuse to buy into this pipe dream that formula is any type of healthy for your child. So with this information exposed, I advise you to look up the ingredients that I mentioned above.

Limit your baby's exposure to formulas when possible. Instruct any baby sitters, guardians, and relatives, to do the same.

BREASTFEED YOUR BABIES!
BY SCIHONOR DEVOTION

The American Academy of Pediatrics recommends breastfeeding your child for at least 12 months with breast milk being the only food for the first 6 months. That means no meat and potatoes, no cereal in the bottle at night, no formula, no nothing except for breast milk.

A study was done at the Brigham Young University in 2001. The study found that while 65% of white women breastfed their babies, only 30% of Black women breastfed their babies. **The rate of infant mortality among Black babies is 1.3 times higher than the rate for white babies largely due to Black mothers not breastfeeding.** In other words, our babies are dying at an alarming rate, which can be associated with the lack of breastfeeding.

The *Journal of the American Medical Association* says that "Breastfed infants are 80% less likely to die before age 1 than those never breastfed." College educated women are almost twice as likely to breastfeed their children than those who don't extend beyond high school. Foreign-born women are 75% more likely to breastfeed their babies than American born women.

Ross Formula Company did a survey that showed that at 6 months after birth, only 14.5% of women in this country were still breastfeeding. Why is this happening in the United States? Around the world, women are breastfeeding their children until the ages of 3, 4, 5 and up. Of course this sounds crazy to those of us living in this country.

If more women would support breastfeeding, employers would have to make changes to their policies on taking breaks for mothers to pump their milk, mothers working at home, mothers having longer paid maternity leaves, mothers bringing their babies to work, and many other accommodations. Many of them already have. After all, this is how it's done in other countries. But if it appears that women don't even want what's best, why should the government care?

Many Black women don't get the breastfeeding education during prenatal visits that we need, nor do most of us educate ourselves about breastfeeding before we have a baby or even get pregnant. As a matter of fact, many of us are not even taught what our breasts are for. But that's a whole notha story. We have a lack of confidence partially due to the fact that many of us have never even seen a woman breastfeeding her child. Since many of us are not around other women who breastfeed, we are not getting the support that we need to feed our children properly. We don't get the support and information from our families, peers, community or medical community. There are/ however, organizations, lactation consultants, midwives, doulas, OB/GYN's, and new mothers groups that can help women learn about breastfeeding and support her while she does.

Every mammal makes milk to feed his or her young. Why are we feeding our young cow's milk? Do you see a cow drinking a monkey's milk? Of course not, because nature has made it so that each of us make milk to feed our own children. **The composition of our breast milk changes with the needs of the child. Breast milk provides immunity to disease and infection. It gives the child just the right combination** of vitamins, minerals, sugars, enzymes, and fats for your child's growth and development. Formula cannot duplicate this. Formula and cow's milk both lack many things that breast milk provides, including brain-developing substances. They cannot compete with a mother's milk, which is **custom made** for her child.

Babies who are fed **colostrum**, which is the **"pre-milk,"** often called **"Liquid Gold"** because of its value, are less likely to suffer from ear infections, milk allergies, jaundice and more. This saves the parent's time from hospitalization or doctor visits, money, time away from work, and heartache. **Breastfed babies are also less likely to suffer from constipation, diarrhea, tooth decay, childhood diabetes and more. They are also said to be smarter than their formula-fed counterparts.** Breastfeeding prevents obesity, lowers the risk of heart disease, lowers the risk of juvenile diabetes, lowers the risk of multiple sclerosis, lowers the risk of allergies and asthma, and prevents digestive diseases. Breastfeeding your baby as a child will benefit him or her as an adult. Breastfed babies also smell better than formula fed babies, their stool smells are easier to handle, they have clearer skin, better vision, respiratory systems, and endocrine systems which reduces the risk of getting diabetes, and more.

> Did You Know?
> Perchlorate is an ingredient found in Rocket fuel (I would tell you which brands of formula Perchlorate is in but the FDA won't reveal the names).

Breastfeeding also has many benefits for the mother. Mothers reduce their chances of uterine cancer, ovarian cancer, and breast cancer. They lose weight after birth faster, have less risk of osteoporosis and postpartum depression, save money from buying formula, have a faster recovery (since breastfeeding encourages your uterus to return to its pre-pregnancy state), and more.

There are many myths around breastfeeding that I personally have heard including…

Breastfeeding hurts: If the baby is latched on properly, it won't hurt. Practice! Not all babies' latch on correctly the first time. Get help from a lactation consultant or a Postpartum Doula. The nipple should be as far back into the roof of the baby's mouth as possible. Don't worry, you won't choke them.

The baby does not get enough. – Breasts work like supply and demand. The more you feed the baby, the more they make. If the baby is soiling diapers, and gaining weight, then they are fine.

Breastfeeding is not possible for a woman with small breast. – Breast size has nothing to do with it. You breasts prepare to nourish your child when pregnancy begins.

My breasts will sag if I breastfeed. – Pregnancy, age, and gravity make your breasts sag. Not feeding your baby! Lame excuse.

The baby will become too attached – Nah. Listen to Erykah Badu:

> When I first had the baby, I was breastfeeding for two years straight, so we were together for two years of his life – every day, all hours of the day. So I was two people, and I eventually morphed back into one. Now he's part of me. He's very independent as a result of it. I thought it was going to be the opposite…I was very worried that he was going to be attached since we were together every day, but I guess it made him feel comfortable: 'I know she's around. She'll be there.' It made me feel like a very responsible person and tidy, and my health was better because I'm now responsible for someone's whole reason for being.

> Check www.blackmothersbreastfeeding.org

Pregnancy Tea

This tea is full of nourishment. It contains iron, calcium and many more vitamins and minerals. Many people like to drink this tea warm, however, it can be taken cooled. This tea is also great for the postpartum period as it aids in milk production.

- ❏ 4 tsp. Red Raspberry Leaf – Vitamin and mineral rich, tones uterine muscles, high in iron so it's said to prevent hemorrhage
- ❏ 4 tsp. Nettles – High in protein, vitamins A, D, E, B6, K, calcium, iron, magnesium, phosphorus, trace minerals, and digestive enzymes. High in chlorophyll and carotenes.
- ❏ 2 tsp. Oat straw – Rich in calcium and magnesium. Relaxes nerves, helps manage pregnancy discomforts
- ❏ 1 tsp. Alfalfa – High in protein, vitamins A, D, E, B6, K, calcium, iron, magnesium, phosphorus, trace minerals, and digestive enzymes. High in chlorophyll and carotenes.
- ❏ 1 tsp. Rose Hips – High in vitamin C, boosts immunity and circulatory system
- ❏ 1 tsp. Red Clover – Red Clover also contains vitamin A, vitamin C, B-complex, calcium, chromium, iron, and magnesium.
- ❏ 1 tsp. Spearmint Leaf – gives relief to your digestive system and eliminates gas from the system. Also, it tastes good.

If you are not going to use the dried herbs immediately, mix all of them in a large airtight container and store it in an area that is away from heat and light. If you are ready to enjoy your tea, mix the herbs in a quart sized jar full of boiling water, cover and let it steep for at least 30 minutes but no more than 2 hours. Strain the herbs, sweeten if desired using agave, honey, or other natural sweeteners and sip during the day. If you find the infusion to be too strong for your liking, add more water. Enjoy!

There is nothing option better than breast mil during your baby's first six months. Pump and freeze your milk to make breast feeding more convenient.

HOMEMADE BABY FOOD

BY SATORI ANANDA

In 1995, I was 19 years old with two children, a boy 3 years old and a new born daughter. I was on food stamps and WIC giving my babies what I thought was the most nutritional food available. I had quit school in the 9th grade and was basically uneducated in many subjects, especially nutrition. I wasn't breastfeeding and was actually under the impression that the baby formula I was giving my children was better than the milk I produced naturally. False advertising, lack of information and no access to nutritional education except TV commercials found me giving my children fake juices, sugar cereals, cow milk, cookies, candies, fast food and everything else that claimed to be healthy.

Naturally, today those two suffer from a variety of side effects of those early choices. Asthma, allergies, ear infections, and eczema to name a few of the issues we have dealt with over the years.

The People's Lunch Counter in Dallas is a nonprofit dedicated to providing healthy food to better the lives of the people. One of the programs we are developing focuses directly on educating teen mothers in low income environments on how to feed their babies with natural food. it's cost effective and has long term benefits to the children. Access to and the consumption of healthy food is a proven link to higher test scores and educational success.

By making the food we give our children we control the energy that is put into the preparation of the food. The love and desire for success for babies is then transferred to them directly along with the nutritional benefits of the right foods. Knowing what ingredients are in your babies' food provides a level of satisfaction for the parent and making baby food at home is economic and cost effective as well.

To make many of the baby foods I am listing requires only a fork or blender in some cases. Our program encourages mothers to participate in our community gardening. By growing your own fruits and vegetables making your own baby food is very cheap! The best fruits and veggies to start with are apples, apricots, bananas, blueberries, mangoes, peaches, pears, plums, prunes, asparagus tips, avocados, carrots, peas, potatoes, sweet peppers, sweet potatoes, and winter squash. Fresh fruits and vegetables are the best of course but if access to those are not available canned fruits and frozen can be used.

Proper storage and washing of the produce is important. Some fruits and vegetables will require cooking to soften them. Like apples, for instance. Boiling is what we recommend and using just enough water to cover the produce is best. You can use the leftover water during the rest of the process. Next, just peel and remove any pits if necessary and take out any seeds.

Some fruits and vegetables won't need any liquid. Just use the fork to mash, add a seasoning or two, and serve. For some, you may need to add a little liquid like breast milk or the leftover cooking water. The more your baby starts to get used to solid foods the less liquid you will need.

Never sweeten the food. Babies don't need the extra sugar, but seasonings are fine when used lightly. Remember to try one new food at a time to see if your baby has any allergy to the new item. Also foods like bananas and kiwi don't require cooking to mash up.

Freezing extra portions of the baby food is okay before you feed the baby, but remember that saliva breaks down the food so once you start to feed the baby from the container it can't be restored. Microwaving baby food is not recommended, if you are not aware of the concerns regarding microwaves and plastics please research that.

Recipes for more advanced food are available on the net or in bookstores but the basic food preparation information above will work for children up to about 14 months.

Easy first-time baby food preparation

- ❏ Remove the banana peel and just mash it with a fork. Adding some breast milk or formula will help with the consistency.
- ❏ Prepare melons the same way by mashing and serving or adding to baby cereal.
- ❏ Bake a sweet potato on 375 degrees in its skin and then remove the inside and mash with a fork.
- ❏ Additional home prepared baby food can be found online at: www.homemade-baby-food-recipes.com

Making and preparing your baby meals at home is the best way for them avoid high modified sugars and unhealthy preservatives.

MY BABY'S BOTTOM: DISPOSABLE VS. CLOTH
BY SCIHONOR DEVOTION

From the time our babies are born, most of us will just do what's popular and use those cute little newborn diapers with the belly buttons cut out and go through the stages of diapers until they are potty trained. However, it's important for us to keep our baby's bottoms protected and safe. Did you know that there are dangers to using those commercial disposable diapers? Better yet, did you know that there were alternatives to using them? Well, there are. Here are some of the dangers of using disposable diapers and some benefits of going with alternatives.

Some Dangers of Disposables

☐ Gel Beads in disposables that make them more absorbent are made of Sodium Polyacrylate which was banned from being used in tampons due to its relationship with causing Toxic Shock Syndrome (TSS) in women.

☐ There is an increase in testicular temperature in boys which is associated with infertility. In other words, if the male testicle temperature is high when they are babies it kind of messes up their internal testicular cooling systems for life.

☐ Disposable Diapers contain Dioxins which are chemicals linked to cancers. In lab animals dioxins have proven to cause liver problems, birth defects and genetic damage. We don't know how this chemical will effect babies as adults.

☐ Higher incidence of diaper rash is reported. Since the diapers are supposed to be able to hold more waste, parents don't change their baby as often which means that this waste is sitting on the baby's bootie for long periods of time and can cause irritations.

☐ Disposables are not biodegradable, so each year, we fill landfills with tons of urine and feces along with paper and plastic and other stuff, polluting the water and soil that we use. The packages actually tell you to flush the feces before tossing the diaper but you probably didn't even notice the fine print.

☐ Disposables can cost about $1,000 a year.

Some Benefits of Cloth Diapers

Before I go in, I want to be sure that you don't have the impression of a piece of cloth tied around a baby's bottom and maybe sealed with a safety pin on the side. Although, that too will work, modern cloth diapers are advanced and equipped with Velcro and all that good stuff for convenience, which is what many parents are concerned with.

☐ Cloth diapers contain no dioxins produced by chlorine bleach or sodium polyacrylate.

☐ Baby's skin can breathe and not be smothered reducing diaper rash incidents.

☐ Cloth is better for our planet and is economically cheaper than disposables.

☐ They can be washed and even reused for subsequent children.

Some Benefits of Chlorine Free Diapers

☐ There are no dioxins involved, which are cancer causing agents.

☐ There is less harm to our planet since these diapers will not pollute the water and soil supply.

Make the switch to cloth or chlorine-free diapers. They're safer, more environmentally friendly and economical!

PUTTING YOUR BABY TO REST
BY SCIHONOR DEVOTION

Many people have heard about Sudden Infant Death Syndrome, also known as SIDS. SIDS is an unexpected and sudden death of an infant between the time of birth and one year, who is seemingly healthy after an autopsy is done, an investigation of the place of death and a review of medical history have all been completed. it's **reported that almost 3,000 – 4,000 infants die from SIDS each year. Approximately 85% of SIDS deaths usually occur between the 2nd and 4th month after birth. Ironically, the DPT vaccine is given at 2 months, 4 months and 6 months.** Is this a coincidence? Hmmmm…

Researchers have not been able to tell us what exactly causes SIDS but there is concern about the baby's mattress itself. **Mattresses tend to emit gases from chemical treatments.** There is also the idea that **when babies sweat, drool, stool or urinate on their mattress, natural fungus will be produced.** It's said that these can contribute to the SIDS risk when babies breathe in the emissions. This may be why children who get vaccinated are more likely to die from SIDS as their body temperatures are raised after they are vaccinated and maybe the vaccines trigger sensitivities to the fumes being emitted.

It's suggested that you **never reuse a mattress that has been used by another child, as their sweat, drool, stool, or urine may cause fungus to grow on the mattress.** It's also suggested **that all baby mattresses be covered with a thick, clear polyethylene sheeting which can be found in a hardware store.** The sheet must be at least 125 microns or 5 mil. This can prevent the mattress emissions to be released. It can prevent fungus from growing. And, it can be easily wiped down when changing baby's bedding. We may not know exactly what causes SIDS, but we do know what does not cause it. SIDS is not caused by suffocation, vomiting or choking. it's not contagious, hereditary or the result of child abuse.

Some say that putting your baby to bed with you can contribute to SIDS but other studies have shown that "co-sleeping" can actually reduce the risk of SIDS. **Some co-sleeping benefits are that babies are content when they are close to their parents and cry less at night which keeps their adrenaline levels lower, their heart rates steady and the blood pressure regular.** Their body temperatures are regular as well and they take fewer pauses while sleeping close to their parents. They usually sleep for longer periods during the night which is a big plus and if you are breastfeeding, there is nothing like not having to get up to make and warm a bottle, but instead to just roll over and pop it in. Other countries around the world co-sleep with ease and think we are crazy here for putting our babies to sleep in a crib as if it's a jail. If you've ever had a sick child want to rest with you or a child crawl in your bed at night and you wake up with a knee in your neck, then you know that it's just instinctual for babies to want to be close to their parents and be content.

As strange as it may sound, it could be deadly to place your baby to rest in your bed too, so there are some precautions that you should take:

- ☐ Don't put babies to sleep on really soft mattresses, especially pillow tops.
- ☐ Be sure that there are no gaps between the mattress and the bed frame and the bed and the wall.
- ☐ Never put baby to co-sleep on a couch
- ☐ Never put baby to sleep on a waterbed or pillow top mattress. They may not be able to turn if they have a hard time breathing.
- ☐ Remove all extra bedding and soft stuff like teddy bears from the bed while they are sleeping.
- ☐ Never co-sleep if you are obese, taking illegal drugs, drinking alcohol, extremely exhausted, on medical sedatives or mind-altering drugs or have sleep disorders.
- ☐ Don't overdress your babies when they rest. Their temperatures could rise which contributes to SIDS risk.
- ☐ Don't put infants to rest with other children or pets. I heard of an incident of a cat sitting on a baby and smothering the child.
- ☐ Be sure to remove all strings like curtain cords, extra clothing or bedding, strings on clothing or even your hair.
- ☐ Putting your baby to rest on their back will help them to breathe and will avoid direct contact with any fumes from the mattress.
- ☐ Cover mattresses with a thick, clear polyethylene sheeting which can be found in a hardware store to keep fumes from being emitted into the air.

Sleeping with your baby improves their physical, mental and emotional health. Take the necessary precautions to make sure your baby is safe when sleeping with you.

HOW TO KEEP YOUR BABY'S TEETH HEALTHY
BY SCIHONOR DEVOTION

Many people don't realize that when they put their children to rest with a bottle; they can cause major damage to the child. Their teeth could rot. **If the bottle has milk, formula, or juice in it when they are put to bed, these drinks can sit in the baby's mouth overnight and eat away at their teeth.** This process is called "Baby Bottle Tooth Decay (BBTD)." This can be very painful for the child, and very expensive for the parents who have to pay for the treatment. Sometimes, children with BBTD have to be hospitalized so that their teeth can be pulled.

To prevent this...

- ☐ Put your baby to bed without a bottle. Don't let the rest with a bottle in their mouth. If you do decide to give them a bottle, make sure it's pure water with no sweeteners (honey, sugar, or syrup).
- ☐ Make strong efforts not to always soothe your baby with a bottle. Try other alternatives, such as cuddling, reading, talking, singing, and playing so that he/she does not get used to always having it.
- ☐ Don't dip their pacifiers in sugar, honey, syrup, or anything sweet. These can cause their teeth to rot. Also, giving babies honey before they are at least one year old can cause Infant Botulism.
- ☐ Be sure to brush their teeth until they can properly do it themselves.

Finally, do your research on fluoride. You may have been told that fluoride is necessary in keeping your baby's teeth and even your teeth strong; however, studies have shown that there is no dental difference in areas that have fluoridated water and those without. Also, before 1945, fluoride was considered to be an environmental pollutant.

Look in your local supermarket for fluoride-free alternatives to keep your baby's teeth healthy.

OMG! MY BABY IS SICK!
BY SCIHONOR DEVOTION

Caring for a sick baby is not an easy task. Sometimes just finding out what is bothering them is a challenge in itself, since they often cannot talk to let you know what is going on, what they may be feeling, and what they think they need. With time, you will know your baby better than anyone else and will be able to notice that they've had changes is sleep patterns, fussiness, eating, and even moving their bowels and urinating.

If you feel like something may be wrong, watch them. Also, talk to other parents and describe what you are noticing. If you have a pediatrician that you trust, call them. But know that doctors do not always have all the answers either. All in all, your child's health care team consists of a whole community. Parents, family, friends, doctors, midwives and even babysitters, teachers and coaches should all play a role in a child's wellbeing. However, trusting your own instincts is probably the best thing you can ever do as a parent.

The three most common symptoms in a "sick" child are fever, diarrhea and vomiting. I say sick like that because they may not be REALLY sick. They just may not be in the best of health and therefore may need a little attention. In other words, a slight fever does not mean your child is "sick." Let me explain.

Fever

A baby's temperature can vary throughout the day depending on what they are wearing and the temperature outside if they are out and even the temperature inside if they are in. So, don't be alarmed if your baby is a little warmer or cooler than usual. You may have to change their environment or dress or undress them slightly. When my children were infants, I almost never checked their temperature because I had a pediatrician who made me comfortable with being able to watch and judge their behavior and even feel for high fevers. However, if you do take temperatures, it's now recommended that an underarm reading be taken. A normal reading for an underarm temp is between 95-99°F and a mild fever is between 99.4-101°F. Anything higher than that is considered a fever. If you take a good ol' rectal temperature, a normal reading would be between 98.2-100.4°F. A mild fever would be considered 100.6-101°F. Anything above that would be considered a fever. Usually when a baby has a fever, it's a sign of an infection. Don't worry. If your baby has a mild temperature, it's not usually associated with an infection like a higher reading would be. I recommend though taking the reading again after the thermometer has cooled off, just to be sure your reading is accurate. The fever means that their immune systems are hard at work. Pay attention and look out for other changes like exhaustion, loss of appetite, vomiting, diarrhea and irritability. You may be able to narrow down and figure out what may be bothering them. Don't forget that if your child has recently been vaccinated it's highly likely that they will be irritable, in pain and will have a fever.

I've heard of parents tell how afraid they are of febrile seizures/convulsions, so they give their babies some sort of over-the-counter fever reducer as soon as they suspect a fever or when fever begins. The problem with this is that when "medicating" your child with fever reducers, their immune system will not have a chance to do its thing and fight whatever it's that may be ailing them. Febrile seizures are rare and only occur is about 4% of children between 6 months and 4 years. They are usually the result of a fever either rising or falling really quickly. But the fever itself is not very likely to be the cause of a problem such as brain damage. If a baby's temperature is more than 106°F, then injuries can occur but they are still not very common. If your baby is seizing though, do not put anything into their mouths or try to stop the seizure. You can turn the baby on the side and call 911 or your pediatrician if you think 911 is a joke. The baby should be evaluated just to see if the reason the seizure occurred can be determined.

Some Things That May Help

Give them a sponge bath in lukewarm water. Not hot. Not cold. It may or may not bring their fever down but it may calm them and make them a little more comfortable. Add a few drops of lemon, peppermint, eucalyptus or catnip essential oils to the water to help reduce the fever, if that is your goal. And when they get out and you want to pamper them, give them a nice massage with oil but do not use talcum powder (baby powder). It is made from mineral talc, so it may be considered natural without all of the added fragrance and stuff but it can do lots of damage to their lungs. If you want to use a powder, you can make your own. Use about 1 cup cornstarch and add about 20 drops of lavender essential oil to it and there you go...baby powder.

Give them lots of fluids, especially breast milk if they are breastfed. Don't force them to eat though. Their bodies will tell you when they are ready for food. I used a homeopathic remedy called belladonna to reduce my children's fevers successfully. I also used catnip tea and feverfew tea diluted with water really well.

When to Call For Help

- ☐ Baby has temperature of 101°F and is less than three months old.
- ☐ Baby has a fever of 103°F and has a change in behavior.
- ☐ Baby seems dehydrated and has not urinated in six hours, has little to no tears and has a dry mouth
- ☐ Baby can't be calmed down and is very irritable.
- ☐ Baby has difficulty breathing or is breathing really fast or really slow.
- ☐ Baby can't swallow or it's very painful to swallow.
- ☐ Baby has a skin rash or inside of their mouth is looks unusual.
- ☐ Baby has sunken eyes.
- ☐ Baby has a stomach ache
- ☐ Baby has had a fever for more than 3 days

Diarrhea

Breastfed babies usually have a yellowish-greenish stool but all babies stools are usually consistent in color unless they've eaten something that they do not usually eat or they are not well. With diarrhea, a baby's stool will become runnier. If you see blood in their stool, there may be a problem, although, their anus may just be irritated, especially if they are constipated. **Diarrhea can lead to dehydration. If your child has been vomiting, there is an even greater risk that they can become dehydrated.** Remember, their bodies are small and have a lot less body fluid than we do. Green stool means that food is going through their digestive tract very quickly and may not necessarily mean that there is an infection. Diarrhea can be caused by a few things like, increased juice intake, introduced new foods into their diet, an allergic reaction to a food or drink, bacteria or parasites, a viral infection (usually gastroenteritis) or even antibiotics.

Some Things That May Help

Doctors may suggest a rehydration drink like Pedialyte to replace fluid loss. If you are breastfeeding, keep on nursing. That is the BEST thing to give them for replenishing. You can also try products similar to Pedialyte like Recharge or Ultima Replenisher or even coconut water, which is amazing when it comes to rehydration due to its electrolytes. When they are ready to eat, offer small amounts of food. Don't try to stuff em'

When to Call For Help

- ☐ If they pass stool more than six times in eight hours
- ☐ If they have bloody stools
- ☐ Lethargic/tired, sleepy, weak
- ☐ Stomach ache
- ☐ Can't keep fluids or food down / Vomiting
- ☐ Isn't urinating, no tears, dry mouth

Vomiting

Infants often "spit up," which is normal. Vomiting, though, is when it's forceful and the baby expels a large amount of whatever it is that is in their stomachs. Sometimes it even comes out of their noses. Vomiting can be caused by a few different things like a viral infections called gastroenteritis, fever, stomach disorders, food poisoning, meningitis, medications, or feeding them food they have no business eating at their age like fast food, pizza, burgers, fried foods, etc.

Some Things That May Help

Wait about 30 minutes after they've vomited so that their stomach can settle before you try to feed them something else.

If you are breastfeeding, keep breastfeeding when they are ready. Breast milk is easy to digest.

You can try to give them a teaspoon of a rehydration liquid like Pedialyte or coconut water for non-breastfed babies and see if that stays down before giving them more.

Ginger tea is good for calming an uneasy stomach too but it must be very well diluted. Do not give infants honey.

When to Call For Help

❏ They have not urinated, has a dry mouth and barely no tears

❏ Forceful vomiting for more than 8 hours

❏ Diarrhea along with the vomiting

❏ Lethargic / Tired, Sleepy, Drained, Weak

❏ Bloody Stool

❏ Abdominal pain

❏ Isn't showing signs of improvement after 12 hours

❏ Fever

❏ Headache

Ear Infection

An ear infection is caused by bacteria in the middle ear which is the space behind the ear drum. Ear infections are very common but less likely to occur in breastfed babies. **Children often get ear infections after getting a cold since colds cause congestion which can block the passage between the middle ear and the throat.** It's called the Eustachian tube. You can recognize this tube when your ears "pop". It brings balance to when there is an air pressure change. If it's blocked, bacteria can grow here.

As your child grows older, this space grows also allowing easier drainage and therefore less bacterial growth. The direction of this tube changes with age. Being around many other children like in day care can also increase their risk of ear infection since colds are passed around often. Being around smokers is also a risk factor. Ear infections can cause hearing loss if it's not treated.

Your pediatrician may prescribe an antibiotic and suggest an acetaminophen like Tylenol or ear drops. Ask an elder what they used to do to treat ear infections back in their day. They may tell you that they used to put a few drops of warm oil like olive oil, Vitamin E, almond oil or even vegetable oil in the ear a few times a day like my grandfather did. I've used olive oil with a few drops of lavender essential oil successfully.

Some things that you should be on the lookout for:

❑ Liquid leaking from ear	❑ Fever
❑ No appetite or irritable while eating or drinking	❑ Pain in the ear area – They may reach for their ear or pull at it
❑ Sleeps better in an upright position since laying down is uncomfortable	❑ Nausea and Vomiting

Oral Thrush

Thrush is a form of a yeast infection that looks like cottage cheese inside of your baby's mouth on the roof, tongue or sides. Their mouths may have white patches that are not easy to wipe off like milk would be. It may also hurt when the baby is nursing or drinking from a bottle. Yeast in part of everyone's digestive system but can sometimes become unbalanced. When this happens, an infection arises. Since it's related to the digestive system, it can also lead to diaper rash. Medications like antibiotics can easily cause a bacterial imbalance since it kills the "good bacteria" which keep yeast under control along with the "bad bacteria". And, if you are nursing, medicines that you may be taking can affect their systems as well.

Some Things that May Help

❑ A doctor may prescribe an oral medicine to kill the bacteria

❑ Allow your nipples to dry between feedings if you are nursing

❑ Clean all bottles and nipples properly. Also clean baby's sucking toys, pacifiers, breast pumps, towels, burp cloths and anything else that may come in contact with their mouths (or diaper area if they have diaper rash)

❑ Take probiotics which will bring some "good bacteria" back to bring a balance to the unbalanced system. Nursing babies will benefit.

❑ Apple cider vinegar on the nipples will also help. Rinse nipples well before feeding.

❑ Wear cotton bras and wash them in hot water after each wear.

Learning these indicators will assist you in dealing with your child's "sickness" more effectively, as well as knowing when to seek additional help.

FIRST AID FOR COMMON CHILDHOOD INJURIES
BY POWERDISE CEEMECCA EARTH

Rules to Remembering Before Administering First Aid

Regardless of the nature of an accident or injury, certain rules for treatment and care apply. Here are the most important:

❑ Don't get hurt yourself. You'll be valueless to the victim if you're injured in a foolhardy attempt to help. If you cannot reach the victim without risking injury, wait for assistance.

- If the child is in danger of further injury and you can safely move him or her, do so but always try to keep movement to a minimum.
- If there appears to be an injury to the head or neck, don't move the child unless it's absolutely necessary; then try to move the head and neck as a unit. Cushion head and neck with pillows when moving.
- Cover the child with a light blanket.
- Give fluids by mouth only if the child is awake. A good rule is to allow the child to drink only if he or she can hold a glass. If in doubt, don't because the child may require an anesthetic or surgery later.
- Avoid stimulants and painkillers. Minor medications, such as aspirin or an aspirin substitute, may be given in dosages appropriate for size and weight; they're usually listed on the container.
- Remain with the child; send others for help. If you are alone and must go for help, make sure an unconscious child is breathing and that the airway is open. Make sure the head is turned to the side, or tilt back the head to make sure the airways is open.

Animal Bites

Wash the wound thoroughly with soap and water to remove the saliva; hold the wounded area under running water to rinse it well. Dry with clean gauze. The wound should be examined by a physician. A tetanus shot may be recommended. Although rabies is rare among urban pets, the animal should be identified and observed for a period of ten days to see if it develops symptoms of the disease. If the bite is the result of an unprovoked accident by a wild animal, such as a skunk, bat, squirrel, or chipmunk, an attempt should be made to capture the animal; if it cannot be caught, a rabies shot may be necessary. In some communities, you're required to report all animal bites to health authorities. Your own domestic pets should be inoculated against rabies, and the inoculations should be kept current.

Human Bites

If the skin is not broken, wash the area with mild soap and water, and dry with clean gauze. An antiseptic or dressing is not necessary. Ask your physician about any human bite that breaks the skin, because such bites frequently become infected.

Bee, Wasp and Hornet Stings

A cold compress or calamine lotion will relieve itching; diluted household ammonia or rubbing alcohol applied to the sting and surrounding area also may help. If the stinger-seen as a small dark object in the center of the wound-remains in place, scrape or flick it out with a fingernail; don't attempt to remove it with tweezers. The movement may inject more venom into the wound. For intense itching or multiple stings, give the child a cool bath to break the itching cycle, and apply a soothing bath lotion. Oral antihistamines may also be given. In severe cases, a physician may prescribe an ointment to be applied to the sting.

Some children have a severe reaction to only a single sting. If the child's throat or the interior of the mouth swells, if breathing becomes difficult, or if the child becomes drowsy or unconscious, immediate medical attention is called for. Phone your physician and take the child to the emergency room or a hospital. Discuss with the doctor what to do in the event of a repeat sting.

Infected Wounds

Signs of infection around a cut or scrape are redness and swelling, often accompanied by a feeling of heat and throbbing pain. If possible, immerse the infection in warm water. Repeat three times daily. If the area is not easily immersed, apply a bulky bandage made from a small towel or sanitary napkin (yuck), and pour the solution over it, repeating the treatment until the inflammation has disappeared. Consult a physician if the area is large or seems to be spreading.

Broken Bones

Don't attempt to move a child who may have a broken bone. Speed seldom is important in the treatment of broken bones. Keep the child covered and lying down while waiting for the emergency squad or ambulance. Give nothing by mouth in case the child requires anesthetic or surgery later. Don't attempt to set broken bones. If the child must be moved from an exposed or dangerous place, apply an emergency splint fashioned from any rigid material, including boards, sticks, rolled newspapers, or even a folded pillow. The splint should be on both sides of the affected limb and should extend above or below the adjacent joints. To immobilize the area of the break, tie the splint with bandages above and below it, if the spine may be fractured, don't attempt to move the child under any circumstances. Wait for emergency help.

Bruises

Most require no treatment. For major bumps, apply ice or cold cloths immediately to keep down the swelling. Elevating the bruised limb also will lessen the swelling. If the skin is broken treat the bruise as an open wound.

Burns

If the area is small, immerse the burned part in water or hold directly under a faucet, to relieve pain and reduce local reaction to the burn. Wash with a mild soap. Burn ointments are not necessary for minor burns, and never use butter. A dry, sterile dressing will keep out air and provide relief from pain. Don't attempt to treat major burns, especially those in which the skin is broken. Never deliberately break blisters. Blisters develop naturally to heal the burn. Cover the child immediately with a clean sheet, and take him or her to a hospital or summon an ambulance.

Chemical Burns

When lye, caustic soda, or any other corrosive substance causes the burn, you must flood the burned area immediately with cold water; strip off all clothing that may have come in contact with the chemical, and quickly place the child under a shower. Acid burns also should be flooded, and then rinsed with a neutralizing solution of baking soda. After washing the area, you should phone a physician or the local rescue squad. Medical personnel always should examine chemical burns, especially if the corrosive substance has dried.

Choking

When a child chokes on a piece of food or other object, coughing usually will expel the object. If the child is unable to cough, or coughing produces no results, turn a small child over your knee and give four sharp blows between the shoulder blades with the heel of the hand. If the airways remain obstructed, turn the child on his or her back and give four sharp thrusts on the breastbone as if giving cardiopulmonary resuscitation (CPR). Don't apply pressure to a child's abdomen.

Swallowed Object

Most small objects swallowed by a child will pass through the system harmlessly. This is especially true of buttons or other round items, but even open safety pins, tacks, and similar sharp objects usually don't harm the stomach or bowel. Don't give the child a laxative, and don't induce vomiting. Notify a physician, who may follow the objects progress by X-ray. If the physician considers the object dangerous-and particularly if it has been ingested into the lungs-it may be extracted by inserting a flexible instrument down the pipe hole.

Fainting

Rare in children, fainting is caused by a temporary deficiency in the blood supply to the brain. The child usually is pale and may crumple to the ground. Keep the victim lying down until the head or elevating the feet to hasten the return of blood to the brain. Make the child more comfortable by loosening tight clothing. Sprinkling water on the fact to revive the victim isn't necessary.

Unconsciousness

Serious accidents, such as a severe injury or burn, poisoning, gas inhalation, or electric shock, may cause unconsciousness. Sunstroke or heat exhaustion also may cause unconsciousness, but rarely in children. Sunstroke or heat exhaustion also may cause unconsciousness, but rarely in children, if breathing has stopped, begin mouth-to-mouth resuscitation at once. If the child is unconsciousness from a fall, avoid turning the head and neck, if breathing appears adequate; keep the patient lying on the back, with head turned to the side to keep the airway open. Remove constricting clothing, and cover lightly. Summon emergency help; don't wait for the child to revive. Take care in moving an unconscious child because of the possibility of head injury. Don't give water or other substances by mouth to an unconscious child, and don't shake him or her in an attempt at revival.

Falls

In any fall from a high place or when the child is unconscious or seems to have suffered a severe impact, take him or her immediately for emergency treatment. Or phone the physician and report the symptoms. For infants, immediate evaluation is very important. Even if the fall seems slight, a physician should be consulted if the child appears drowsy, acts dazed, turns pale, has memory lapse, or vomits after the accident.

Poisoning

Drugs, medicines, cleaning fluids, and other such substances are the most common causes of childhood poisoning. If you see evidence that a child has swallowed any of these, act fast. Telephone the poison control center in your community, if one exists, or your physician or hospital, and be prepared to give immediate first-aid treatment. First, try to determine what is swallowed, because treatment differs according to the substance. Don't waste time looking for the container for an antidote; information on bottles and cans may be out of date. For many poisons, the doctor or poison control center may recommend syrup of ipecac to induce vomiting. Have some available–it can be purchased without prescription. The usual dose is one tablespoon of syrup of ipecac for one-year-olds and above, two teaspoons for children under one year. If vomiting has not occurred within 20 minutes the dose may be repeated. Do not give ipecac unless instructed. When the child vomits, hold him or her face downward in your lap so the vomited material clears the throat and is not swallowed.

If ipecac is not available, feeding the child warm milk and then tickling the back of the throat with a tongue depressor or spoon may induce vomiting sometimes. Unless you're told otherwise, don't wait for vomiting to occur before getting medical help. If possible retrieve the poisonous substance and take it with you.

List and discuss First Aid procedures and protocol with everyone in your home. "Acting out" a drill may also help in remembering what to do in case of an emergency.

Your Kid Is Not Chunky, Thick, or Big-Boned...They're Fat

BY C'BS ALIFE ALLAH

Listen. That's not baby fat on your child. Those are pounds of a burden that your son or daughter will pay for in spades later on in their life. That child does not have a thyroid problem (Do the people saying that even know what and where the thyroid is?). Also, how is their fatness genetic when we know that slave masters weren't bringing over any fat-ass slaves? And though we realize that people of color worldwide (in general) love a woman with a little thickness on her, there is a huge difference between thickness and when you're so fat that you wheeze when you walk. Let's deal with some straight-up facts.

Between 1986 and 1998, a national survey showed that obesity doubled in children between the ages of four and twelve. A more recent study found that 46% of Black and Latino children are overweight by the age of 3! Incidents of obesity have increased with the spreading of fast food joints and a sedentary lifestyle among the youth. This issue is growing so fast that the government has a Childhood Obesity Task Force! Michelle Obama adopted this as one of her major causes. The government realizes that the wealth of any Nation is the youth. One reason why childhood obesity is such an issue is because it's the foundation for a host of health problems that can and will afflict a person for the rest of their life. From a government standpoint it hits them two fold. First they won't be able to be a full, productive member of society, and secondly they will become a drain on government financial resources in terms of health care.

> **Did You Know?**
> Food allergies in American children are on the rise, now affecting about 3 million kids, according to the first national study of the problem. About 1 in 26 children had food allergies in 2008, up from 1 in 29 kids in 1997. And nobody knows what caused the 18% increase.

What are the Results of Being Fat Albert?

Well, one thing is, you won't have a cool group of children who hang around you and occasionally burst into spontaneous song. Anyone who went through school knows that the fat kid is most likely going to be the one who gets picked on, which will hit them with low self-esteem and depression. This sets a cycle in motion, of feeling bad and indulging in food (or worse) to feel better, and then feeling bad all over again. it's your job as the parent to prevent or break this cycle from making it to the point where it's hardwired into your child's brain.

Type 2 Diabetes in children, once unheard of, has risen 45% in this country in the last 10 years, largely due to childhood obesity. An obese child is more likely to develop heart disease (via high cholesterol and/or high blood pressure), asthma, and/or sleep apnea. They have a higher risk for CVD or Cardiovascular Disease. They also have a higher rate of developing Hepatic Steatosis, which is a fatty degeneration of the liver. Oh wait, I forgot the most obvious element we tend to overlook. Obese children and teens are more likely to become obese as adults...if they make it.

What Can I Do?

Don't starve your child. It is not all about how much they are eating anyway. It is more about WHAT they are eating. They are growing and developing, so they need the right nutrients/calories for them to progress as they should.

Focus on reforming the eating habits of the whole family. Go with the 'all for one and one for all' motto. Don't make it about just the obese child. Everyone in the family can benefit from cleaning up their eating habits. Try to eat together as much as possible.

Look for ways to remix the meals you already eat. Cut back on salt. Use lower fat milk in cooking. Choose leaner meats, fish and poultry. Add more fruits and vegetables to your general meals. Don't fry as much.

Get your child from up in front of the TV. Take a walk WITH them. Make up an exercise routine to do WITH them. Get them into a dance class. Martial arts. Jump rope. Something.

Make some healthy snacks yourself to have around the house. Dried fruit. Granola mixes. Cut down eating stuff with refined sugar.

Get the focus on health and not weight.

Cut back on those empty calories of fruit drinks, sodas, etc. Get some 100% juice up in that house and make sure that everyone is drinking enough water.

Finally BE the example. Eat right. Keep physically active. Be the parent that your child needs you to BE.

Focus on introducing a healthier lifestyle in the home instead of having your child lose weight.

IS YOUR CHILD HYPERACTIVE?

The diagnosis that appears to work best is called a Connor's score. This is a very simple checklist which works well in clinical practice and has been used for research purposes. If the parents do the scoring, then they make the diagnosis, and are more trusting of the result. In evaluating your child's behavior, Score 0 for not at all, Score 1 for sometimes, Score 2 for quite often, and Score 3 for a lot.

Trait	Score
Restless or overactive	
Excitable or impulsive	
Disturbs other children	
Fails to finish things	
Short attention span	
Constantly fidgeting	
Inattentive, easily distracted	
Makes demands that must be met right away	
Easily frustrated	
Cries often and without provocation	
Mood changes quickly and dramatically	
Temper outbursts	
Explosive and unpredictable behavior	
TOTAL	

A score of 15 or more suggests that hyperactivity is likely. The question, however, is what does *that* mean?

Take the above survey. Make sure your child has a safe place to spend their energy. Put them in basketball or boxing programs.

BEAVER BUTT JUICE

BY SUPREME UNDERSTANDING

We couldn't do a chapter on children without talking about candy. Now, I'm sure you're wondering why this article is titled "Beaver Butt Juice" if it's about candy. Don't worry. We'll get to that in a minute. Let's start with the basics though. You're a grown-ass man or woman. Why are you eating candy? Okay, maybe I shouldn't ask that, considering that many of us never grew up, and the rest of us are chemically-addicted to sugar. So I guess it's not a fair question. After all, I was still eating candy until I began work on this book, and I'm still having a hard time letting go of my chocolatey snacks. But it's a reasonable question, and it should at least get you thinking about the nature of what you put in your system. Indigenous people have sweets and snacks, but nothing of the "pure sugar + color" variety, like we have in the West. Instead of eating a fake, gummy version of a strawberry, we'd just eat the strawberries! Or we'd have dried fruits if we were goin for the gummy taste. But now, you're only getting that "gummy" taste thanks to an incredient called gelatin, which is a perfect reference point to illustrate what's wrong with most of the crap we eat.

As Marni, author of the "La Vegan Loca" blog writes:

I am often surprised when I'm having a conversation with someone about being vegan and despite starting with lots of questions for me, we quickly get to a point where they ask me to stop telling them the truth about what they eat. When I realized what was really happening in the meat and animal byproduct industry, I was horrified. I was disgusted. I was flaming pissed. I was eating that stuff! Why didn't I know sooner? Why doesn't everyone know?

Gelatin is a great example. Mmmm...who doesn't love jello? Harmless, wiggledy jiggledy jello. It's fun. It's colorful. Adored by kids everywhere. They even give it to you in the hospital when you are at your most vulnerable. What could be wrong with it?

How 'bout the fact that gelatin is manufactured from the boiled hooves, bones, and skins of animals, for starters. That's just wrong. Do you think kids (or anyone for that matter) would be so excited about eating jello if they knew it was really manufactured from some demented witch's brew of slaughter house dregs? Yum! Appetizing, right? Who comes up with this stuff, anyway?

And it doesn't stop at gelatin. Food and candy manufacturers use crushed bugs as red food coloring (listed in the ingredients as carmine or carminic acid, but sometimes listed only as "natural color"). They use beetle secretions in sprinkles and candies (listed as shellac, which is also used in wood varnish). That's some real "Beetle Juice" for ya! There's sheep secretions in bubble gum (lanolin), beef fat in ALL Hostess snacks, and even COAL TAR in many red-colored candies. Just so you understand, coal tar is listed as #199 on the United Nations list of "dangerous goods," but that doesn't stop people from using it as "Allura Red AC" in red-colored candies, sodas and other sweets. You've already read about the pig intestines used to make malt liquor and the pig blood in cigarette filters, but don't think your snooty red wine is safe. "Fining" is a process used by wineries to remove particles and impurities from wine. Fining agents include isinglass (from sturgeon bladders), gelatin (from pig bones), and ox blood. And when grapes are gathered for wine, they're often crushed along with everything else on them. This often includes sticks, insects, rodents, and even larger mammals. Wine-makers label this "ingredient" MOG, or "Material Other than Grapes." Mmm...good old rat wine.

And it gets even worse, hence the title of this article. Marni, in an essay titled "Beaver Butt Juice" continues:

> So, imagine my shock at myself when I read about castoreum and actually said to myself, I don't want to know about this! This has got to be one of the fowlest, most urp-evoking ingredient known to man. Worse than gelatin. Worse than German porn, even. Two Girls, One Beaver...coming to YouTube soon!
>
> Castoreum is the extract from beaver anal glands and is used extensively in perfumes and...brace yourself...sometimes in food. But wait, it gets even better. Because it is derived from a natural source (uh...that would be the ass of a beaver in case you weren't paying attention...you know...where the beaver sh*t comes out), under the Code of Federal Regulations it can be listed

as "natural" flavor. Grab something out of your cabinet right now and read the ingredients. Do you see "natural flavorings" listed? I thought I smelled beaver ass on your breath.

But why? Well, according to the Nov/Dec 2007 issue of *VegNews Magazine*, castoreum "gives a smooth, round finish to raspberry flavors in a handful of baked goods, condiments, and candies." Ugh! It's in candy? Not exactly what the kids had in mind when they said, "Trick or treat!"

And if these nasty ingredients weren't enough to turn you off, you should also keep in mind that you get what you pay for. When you buy those cheapo candies from the Dollar Store, you might have more to worry about that bug and beaver booty. In the past few years, news stories have surfaced about titanium dioxide (a known carcinogen) in candy canes, and melamine (another carcinogen, known to cause reproductive damage and/or kidney stones) in candy and dairy products (including infant formula) from China. Yet another reason to think twice about (A) eating bullsh*t candy, snacks, and sweets; and (B) buying food products from the dollar store.

> **Did You Know?**
> Children who spend more than two hours a day in front of the television in early childhood are twice as likely to develop asthma as those out playing, a major study has found. Another study has found that children who start watching TV before age 2 are more likely to develop the symptoms associated with ADHD. Other studies have found that programs like *Baby Einstein* don't boost the intelligence of babies, and that young children are unlikely to learn real language skills from television alone. *Your Baby Can Read* might teach them some words, but most of that is due to the heavy parent interaction and multiple learning methods (flashcards, etc.). What does all that mean? In a nutshell, it means television is bad for your babies.

Feed that sweet tooth differently. Dry fruits can be gummy, sweet, and healthy.

D.O.A. (DEATH OF ADD/ADHD)
BY C'BS ALIFE ALLAH

"Let the Boys Be Boys"

When my son entered into pre-K, the teachers constantly stated that he wasn't paying attention and that he had learning difficulties. This would carry over into his kindergarten years. His mother at the time was devastated because she thought that it immediately pointed to her as a horrible mother. **My own mother was a teacher so what she heard as "something is wrong with your child" I automatically translated as "we don't know how to educate your child at this point."** I knew at that moment that they were on the road to classifying him as a child with ADHD (Attention Deficit Hyperactivity Disorder). The only thing preventing it was my active involvement in my child's educational future.

The Legal Dope Boys

A general definition of ADD (Attention Deficit Disorder) or ADHD is that a child's behavior is in conflict with the expectations or demands of parents/teachers. The FDA says they have the answer to that 'problem' in the form of legal drugs. The one that most people are familiar with is Ritalin.

Medicating children started in the United States in the 1950s. In 1999 they did a study on medicating children and found that Ritalin use increased six fold from 1990-1995. **90% of the world's Ritalin use comes from the United States.** It has been estimated that 10-14% of all children in the United States are being prescribed Ritalin or some other behavior modifying stimulant. **This is most distributed amongst boys and then most highly concentrated amongst boys of color.** In some areas 20% of the students are on Ritalin. Amongst the 53 million children in school in the United States approx. 5 million are being medicated with these drugs. Also there has been a 3 fold increase in medicating children between the ages of 2-4 yrs. old.

ADD/ADHD: That Imaginary Disease
Now yes, there are a range of biological reasons which may interfere with the way children process information. There are legitimate learning disorders that are cataloged. All of those disorders share one common factor. They have identifiable biological foundations that can be located in the brain that serve as the reasons for their disabilities. **Guess what the NH consensus development conference of 1998 and the American Academy of Pediatrics in 2000 both ruled? They ruled that there is no biological basis for ADD and ADHD in the brain.** In fact in the 'diagnosing' of ADD/ADHD such 'scientific' terms are used to detect it like "fidgeting", "squirms in seat", "unwanted behavior", "answers question before teacher finishes it", etc. Man that describes EVERY boy who I ever went to school with, including myself.

Also nowadays, with the success of the "push Ritalin on children" campaign, children are being diagnosed with a whole host of 'disorders'. There is OCD (Obsessive Compulsive Disorder), ODD (Oppositional Defiant Disorder) and PDD (Pervasive Development Disorder). All of the descriptions of the disorder read just like someone who can't figure out how to interact with a child. Terminology is used in their descriptions like "often deliberately annoys people", "often loses temper", etc.

Ritalin is a helluva drug!
By many people, Ritalin has been compared to cocaine. Ironically this is not too far off point. It is a stimulant just like cocaine. In fact it's classified in the same class as methamphetamines (Meth), cocaine, and the most potent opiates/barbiturates.

And the list of side effects is sickening.

❏ Chest pains, Cardiac Arrest (yes in children!)

- ☐ Mania, Psychosis, Hallucinations, Anxiety, Emotional Sensitivity, Withdrawal, Drowsiness, Dopiness, Zombie/Robot behavior, OC behavior
- ☐ Nausea, Vomiting, Stomach issues
- ☐ Weight Loss, Pituitary Dysfunction, Messing with their Growth Hormones
- ☐ Blurred Vision, Rashes, Hives

Notice that most of the side effects interfere with what the goal of taking Ritalin is supposed to do. Can you imagine a child who is supposed to be helped by taking Ritalin being hit with those side effects? Yeah, I'm sure he'll be able to pay attention now.

What Can You Do?

First off make sure that the biological foundation is checked. I mean in terms of real issues. Make sure that your child has no food allergies. Make sure that they haven't been afflicted by environmental toxins like lead paint or heavy metals. Next make sure that your child's diet is stepped up to the next level.

Become friends with the teacher. Set up meetings with the teacher before they set up meetings with you. Show that you are interested in the welfare of your child. I have seen that when a teacher doesn't like a child they aren't looking out for the child. Make sure the teacher doesn't give up on your child.

> **Did You Know?**
> Prescription drugs are on record for being notorious gateway drugs. Those who utilize prescribed stimulants are very likely to become cocaine users when they become adults.

See if you can have it set up where your child can have a smaller teacher to student ratio. You explain that your child is exploring the world in their own way and that everyone isn't supposed to learn the same way.

Discover how your child best learns. Is it by sight? Is it by sound? Is it by touch? Whatever the best method is, reinforce whatever they learn in school at home by immersing you in that method. I remember when I was teaching my son his numbers and letters. I wrote all of them on different stickies and placed them all around the house. We ran around the house finding them and had him recite them. Sitting down and looking at them on a static paper didn't do anything for him yet that running around had it in his brain right away.

It is not about you. It is about your child. They are not having difficulty in school to piss you off. Although your child may manifest certain type of behavior in order to try to communicate their emotions. My son would be dealing with anger, sadness, and anxiety. One of the best things that I ever taught him was to breathe and to clearly identify what was bothering him at a particular moment in time.

Let your child know that you are invested in their success. It is possible that by 'not conforming,' your child actually has the makings of a leader, so nurture that. Yet a leader is accountable, so for everything that they do, ask them for explanations. Have them examine their motives and behavior. Come up with ways for them to take control of their environment so that it serves them, without them destroying it.

For more on ADHD, see the article in the Psychological Health chapter of this book.

Have a plan for your child. Make parenting adjustments, don't feed them to the wolves (uncaring teachers and doctors).

STUPID PRESERVATIVES

BY SUPREME UNDERSTANDING

Did you know that those wonderful chemicals in your kids' snacks are literally making them stupid? It's true. Artificial food colorings, preservatives and other additives can cause behavioral and psychological changes in children aged 3 to 9, British researchers reported in September of 2007. **Tests on more than 300 children showed significant differences in their behavior when they drank fruit drinks spiked with a mixture of food colorings and preservatives, according to Jim Stevenson and colleagues at the University of Southampton.** "These findings show that adverse effects are not just seen in children with extreme hyperactivity (such as ADHD) but can also be seen in the general population and across the range of severities of hyperactivity," the researchers wrote. The additives included popular ingredients in children's drinks like sunset yellow coloring, tartrazine, the preservative sodium benzoate, and other colors. Naturally, the 3-year-olds reacted more severely. The following year, Stevenson found that chemical food additives were doing as much damage to children's brains as lead in gasoline, accounting for over 5 points difference in IQ, among other effects.

> **Did You Know?**
> Studies show that just one sausage a day can significantly raise your risk of bowel cancer, one of the deadliest forms of the disease. Eating 1.8 ounces of processed meat daily – about one sausage, 2 slices of bologna, or 3 pieces of bacon – raises the likelihood of the cancer by 20%. Processed meats may also trigger cancer in the prostate, lung, stomach and esophagus. The World Cancer Research Fund recommends people avoid eating all processed meats.

If you think that's bad, a study of one million students in New York showed that students who ate lunches that included artificial flavors, preservatives, and dyes did 14% worse on IQ tests than students who ate lunches without these additives. As a result of the British study, the UK started banning such chemicals from their foods, and a list of more than 900 products containing the additives was published on the British Food Commission's site (www.actiononadditives.com). Because they're more informed (and thus empowered), people in the UK routinely shut down the crap we accept without question in the US. This is why the UK bans dangerous chemicals that the US still uses, and why many foods (even McDonald's Chicken McNuggets) have different ingredients in these two places, with the US always having the unhealthier end of the stick.

Find ways to gradually remove artificial additives and preservatives from your children's diet. Find or make healthy alternatives to there favorite junk food.

VACCINATIONS 101
BY QUEEN ZAFIRAH AQUEOUS

What is a Vaccine?

"A vaccine is a medical preparation providing immunity from a vaccine specific disease....vaccines change the immune system by promoting the development of antibodies that can quickly and effectively attack a disease causing microorganism when it enters the body, preventing disease development." – The Gale Encyclopedia of Science

"Valence" is a term used to describe how many different viruses or strains of viruses the vaccine is designed to immunize against. For example, a trivalent influenza vaccine is designed to immunize against two strains of Influenza type A and one strain of Influenza type B.

Live, attenuated vaccines, like the MMR, are very commonly used. They are vaccines that are alive and infectious but have been treated with a chemical (often formaldehyde) that is supposed to weaken them to the point that they do not actually because the disease against which they are immunizing. They can multiply and are more effective unlike killed/inactivated vaccines. Some vaccines, such as the DTaP vaccine, contain portions of the microorganism attached to a chemical that allows it to stimulate the immune system.

> **Did You Know?**
> The idea of vaccination was introduced to the West in an earlier form, known as inoculation, by an enslaved African named Onesimus. In 1721, Onesimus taught his master, Rev. Coton Mather, how his people traditionally immunized themselves against smallpox with a prick of a thorn that had been poked into a smallpox pustule. This method was likely first practiced in Africa (where smallpox originated), then India and China (where it spread) long before 1714, when it was introduced to Europe by traders from the Turkish Ottoman empire. It was Onesimus' method that helped George Washington's army win the Revolutionary War without falling victim to a smallpox outbreak.

What's in a Vaccine?

Formaldehyde, other animal viruses, cow blood, traces of human DNA, MSG, heavy metals like mercury and aluminum, disinfectants, antibiotics, sugar, gelatin, egg. The common disinfectant used in vaccines is both cancer causing and toxic. Shockingly, the chickenpox vaccine involved the use of a cell line that was started using tissue from human embryos obtained through illegal abortions in the 1960's. Some research has been done implicating the SV 40 virus, a monkey virus, which was not removed from some vaccines during cleaning, in cancer cases.

What are some diseases that we currently vaccinate against?

- ❏ Measles, mumps, rubella (MMR)
- ❏ Diphtheria, pertussis, tetanus (DPT)
- ❏ Human papilloma virus (HPV)
- ❏ Influenza
- ❏ Chickenpox/Varicella
- ❏ Polio
- ❏ Hepatitis
- ❏ Hib (Haemophilus influenza, type b)

Why Vaccinate?

- ❏ Some of these diseases can be fatal. It gives parents peace of mind by helping to shelter their children from preventable illness and potential death. Conditions in schools make it easier for children to transmit pathogens as do some crowded living situations.
- ❏ Babies have immature immune systems and it's seen that giving them some immunity protects them.
- ❏ In some countries, it's easier to contract illnesses with less access to effective medical care.
- ❏ Some diseases are worse when contracted as an adult. Rubella, for instance, isn't a very serious illness on its own, but can lead to a disorder called congenital rubella syndrome (CRS) when contracted by a pregnant woman. CRS can lead to serious birth defects and sometimes death of the child. Chickenpox is also more serious in adults. Thus, it's better to intentionally expose children to vaccine preventable diseases.
- ❏ Some public assistance programs require recipients to vaccinate their children for full benefits.

The Illness and the Vaccine

With certain vaccines, the risks associated with being infected are similar to being injected with the vaccine. It seems that, as well as presenting the risks of a natural infection, vaccines also introduce other potential complications.

Both the measles illness and measles vaccine are associated with brain inflammation, seizures, hearing loss, and the development of irritable bowel disorder. Specific only to measles vaccination is the risk of experiencing atypical measles infection. An atypical infection is a more severe case of measles striking only those that have been previously vaccinated. The risk of death is higher in atypical measles infections than in natural infections.

Mumps and its vaccine share the potential of aseptic meningitis. The mumps vaccine alone is associated with the development of insulin dependent diabetes.

Both rubella and its vaccine can lead to arthralgia or arthritis.

There is a possibility that children who were vaccinated for chickenpox will develop shingles as an adult.

Aviva Romm, in *Vaccinations: A Thoughtful Parent's Guide: How to Make Safe, Sensible Decisions about the Risks, Benefits, and Alternatives*, suggests that the diphtheria, pertussis and tetanus (DPT) vaccine is associated with a significant number of frequently occurring adverse reactions. These reactions seem to outweigh the discomforts common to a natural infection. Pertussis and its vaccine may both cause encephalitis.

Why not Vaccinate?

It's hard for anyone to tell how safe vaccines are, despite the soundness of the fundamental idea of how vaccines work. In the 1930s, a vaccine for the poliovirus was administered to patients and it caused the paralysis it was designed to prevent. More recently, the CDC changed their recommendation from the oral poliovirus vaccine to the inactivated polio vaccine after studies showed that all polio cases since 1980 were caused by the vaccine. Additionally, Curtis Cost, in his book *Vaccines are Dangerous*, has collected evidence that some of the illnesses that vaccines have been created for were declining prior to administration of the vaccines.

A 1991 study published in the *Lancet* showed correlations between hepatitis B vaccines and central nervous system problems. Another study in the *Lancet* found that children who received a new measles vaccine died in significantly greater numbers from common childhood diseases than children who did not receive the vaccine. **Another *Lancet* study found that people who were vaccinated were 3 times more likely to develop Crohn's disease and more than twice as likely to develop ulcerative colitis.**

> **Did You Know?**
> The Swine Flu Epidemic of 1976 inspired the vaccination of over 40 million people. A little known fact was that those vaccinations caused devastating side effects to over 4000 victims. Swine flu itself only killed one person.

Current research is focusing on the H1N1 Vaccine and the seasonal influenza vaccine (also known as the "flu shot"), with most of the current concern focusing on the mercury content (and possible links to Alzheimer's) and their role in weakening the immune system (rather than strengthening it).

Harris Coulter, in his book *Vaccines, Social Violence and Criminality: The Medical Assault on the American Brain* says that much developmental impairment trace back to cases of encephalitis which, Coulter says, are primarily caused by the childhood vaccination programs in industrialized countries. Death and encephalitis have been reported as adverse effects of the MMR, DTP, polio and flu vaccines.

Just how necessary are some vaccinations?

In her 2010 article, "Using Fear and Prejudice to Attack Vaccine Exemptions," Barbara Loe Fisher mentions how polio-vaccinated children expose unvaccinated children to the poliovirus because they become infectious after receiving the vaccine.

Sometimes reactions can also be fatal. The National Childhood Vaccine Injury Act, using your tax dollars, has given money to families of infants who have passed because of the pertussis vaccine. These deaths were originally classified as SIDS deaths. It has been a long time question of my own if vaccines are as necessary as the profits reaped by pharmaceutical companies as well as the Centers for Disease Control (CDC) which is responsible for purchasing and distributing a large number of childhood vaccines. According to Money magazine, a safer form of the pertussis vaccine, a cellular pertussis vaccine, was withheld from the public for years after it was licensed, for reasons of production costs.[18]

There are risks associated with taking the vaccines such as allergic reactions and certain syndromes like Guillain-Barre Syndrome (GBS). GBS has symptoms of muscle weakness and paralysis that can cause respiratory dysfunction that may be fatal. Seemingly the symptoms are caused by nerves outside of the central nervous system losing their covering (myelin). A known risk for many vaccines is destruction of the covering of nerves. Myelin is necessary for normal brain and neurological function. The development of allergies and bowel problems are known to be increased when vaccines are given.

> Did You Know?
> Combination vaccines overwhelm the immune system – it's highly unlikely that a person would get measles, mumps, and rubella all at the same time.

Since breastfeeding gives newborns immunity passing it from mother to child in the breast milk it may not be necessary to immunize newborns. Breast milk also contains chemicals that protect babies from infections like Hib, pneumonia and other respiratory and intestinal infections along with promoting the maturation of the immune system. Some practitioners see that vaccinating prevents diseases that help the immune system mature thus vaccinations cripple the immune system later on in life. Some practitioners even see that aside from physiological maturity, mental maturity also occurs during an illness.

What do I do if I want to abstain from vaccination?

There are 3 types of exemptions: Philosophical, Medical, and Religious. Look at the National Vaccine Information Center (NVIC) website (www.909shot.com) to investigate the type of vaccination exemptions your state allows and file one. There may still be issues with your child entering or remaining within the public school system. Go to the NVIC site for more information and resources and on how to obtain assistance.

---

[18] Romm seems to think that the acellular version of the pertussis vaccine appears to be safer than whole cell pertussis in some populations because those populations vaccinate children later in life.

What if I want to vaccinate?

Some pharmaceutical companies list age ranges for which the vaccine is intended. DPT shouldn't be given to children over 7 years old. Find out the specifics of the vaccine product (drug name and manufacturer) your doctor will use and research it at the pharmaceutical company's website or a site like rxlist.com or drugs.com

Risk of anaphylaxis is a reality for all shots, so be sure that a chemical used to treat such a reaction, epinephrine, is present at the time of injection. **If your child does suffer a bad reaction to a shot, be sure that it's reported to VAERS, after doing all you can to ensure your child's safe recovery.** It is also important to keep detailed records of any adverse events.

Whether or not to vaccinate is a very serious issue for many families and, in my research, journalists, holistic practitioners and even medical doctors concur that being informed is crucial in making decisions about whether or not to vaccinate. Fear should not be your primary motivating factor. However, fear is instilled in the readers of much of the literature provided by the CDC, National Institutes of Health (NIH), the public school system and various initiatives whose objective is to increase vaccination. On the other end, fear is propagated by those who oppose vaccines leaving parents in a difficult position. Ultimately, the decisions are made for indecisive caregivers by mandates of the public school system, pressure by doctors, and persecution by vaccinating parents.

Research is crucial to making a decision. Please start by reading some of the literature I've cited here. The most strategic starting point is a book I've consulted throughout this article, *Vaccinations: A Thoughtful Parent's Guide: How to Make Safe, Sensible Decisions about the Risks, Benefits, and Alternatives* by Aviva Romm. She offers a wide scope of bare-bones information about vaccines and multiple considerations while not invoking the fear many writers do. Other books on the subject include *A Shot in the Dark* by Harris L. Coulter, *The Parents' Concise Guide to Childhood Vaccinations: From Newborns to Teens, Practical Medical and Natural Ways to Protect Your Child* by Lauren Feder, and *What Your Doctor May Not Tell You About Children's Vaccinations* by Stephanie Cave.

As a parent, you have a right to decide whether your children are vaccinated and when. Check out the following sites for more: njvaccinationchoice.org, www.cfic.us, and www.vaccinechoice.org

Don't be discouraged. Don't feel alone. There are many parents all over the world that share this struggle. I'm one of them.

Visit the National Vaccine Information Center website to find information on vaccines your child has taken or is "required" to take.

WHAT DOES DYSLEXIA LOOK LIKE?

BY SUPREME UNDERSTANDING

"Coulda ended up in Spofford, juvenile delinquent/ But Pops gave me the right type'a tools to think with Books to read, like X and stuff/ 'Cause the school said the kids had dyslexia" – Nas, "Bridging the Gap"

Dyslexia is a recognized disability affecting 10% of the population. **Dyslexia doesn't mean you're stupid or that you won't be able to succeed in a world that values reading ability**...but it will be more challenging. Some famous dyslexics include Whoopi Goldberg, Danny Glover, Edward James Olmos, Muhammad Ali, and a bunch of rappers who would never admit it. Nas might have been telling us something in the verse above, but who knows? On "We Don't Care," Kanye West raps:

> You know the kids gonna act a fool/ When you stop the programs for after school/ And they DCFS them; some of them dyslexic/ They favorite 50 Cent song's "12 Questions"/...We ain't retards the way teachers thought/ Hold up, hold fast; we make mo' cash/ Now tell my momma I belong in the slow class/ It's bad enough we on welfare/ You tryina put me on the school bus with the space for the wheelchair

Dyslexics have a hard time telling left from right. If you told someone with dyslexia, "Use your left finger to point to your right foot," it would be ridiculously hard for them. Dyslexics also have a hard time spelling "easy" words like: friend, enough, they, because, island, any, said and many. Dyslexic people are extremely disorganized. Dyslexics are often unable to write down what they feel on paper. Dyslexics find it hard to retain what is said to them. Dyslexics find it hard to follow specific instructions, especially those with multiple steps. With all that being said, can you imagine how hard school would be for a child with undiagnosed dyslexia? The following checklist can help you tell if a child (or adult) you know has dyslexia.

Characteristics of Dyslexia

According to the scale developed by Ronald D. Davis, "Most dyslexics will exhibit about 10 of the following traits and behaviors. These characteristics can vary from day-to-day or minute-to-minute. The most consistent thing about dyslexics is their inconsistency."

General
- ❒ Appears bright, highly intelligent, and articulate but unable to read, write, or spell at grade level.
- ❒ Labeled lazy, dumb, careless, immature, "not trying hard enough," or "behavior problem."
- ❒ Isn't "behind enough" or "bad enough" to be helped in the school setting.
- ❒ High in IQ, yet may not test well academically; tests well orally, but not written.
- ❒ Feels dumb; has poor self-esteem; hides or covers up weaknesses with ingenious compensatory strategies; easily frustrated and emotional about school reading or testing.

- [ ] Talented in art, drama, music, sports, mechanics, story-telling, sales, business, designing, building, or engineering.
- [ ] Seems to "zone out" or daydream often; gets lost easily or loses track of time.
- [ ] Difficulty sustaining attention; seems "hyper" or "daydreamer."
- [ ] Learns best through hands-on experience, demonstrations, experimentation, observation, and visual aids.

Vision, Reading, and Spelling
- [ ] Complains of dizziness, headaches or stomach aches while reading.
- [ ] Confused by letters, numbers, words, sequences, or verbal explanations.
- [ ] Reading or writing shows repetitions, additions, transpositions, omissions, substitutions, and reversals in letters, numbers and/or words.
- [ ] Complains of feeling or seeing non-existent movement while reading, writing, or copying.
- [ ] Seems to have difficulty with vision, yet eye exams don't reveal a problem.
- [ ] Extremely keen sighted and observant, or lacks depth perception and peripheral vision.
- [ ] Reads and rereads with little comprehension.
- [ ] Spells phonetically and inconsistently.

Hearing and Speech
- [ ] Has extended hearing; hears things not said or apparent to others; easily distracted by sounds.
- [ ] Difficulty putting thoughts into words; speaks in halting phrases; leaves sentences incomplete; stutters under stress; mispronounces long words, or transposes phrases, words, and syllables when speaking.

Writing and Motor Skills
- [ ] Trouble with writing or copying; pencil grip is unusual; handwriting varies or is illegible.
- [ ] Clumsy, uncoordinated, poor at ball or team sports; difficulties with fine and/or gross motor skills and tasks; prone to motion-sickness.
- [ ] Can be ambidextrous, and often confuses left/right, over/under.

Math and Time Management
- [ ] Has difficulty telling time, managing time, learning sequenced information or tasks, or being on time.
- [ ] Computing math shows dependence on finger counting and other tricks; knows answers, but can't do it on paper.
- [ ] Can count, but has difficulty counting objects and dealing with money.
- [ ] Can do arithmetic, but fails word problems; cannot grasp algebra or higher math.

Memory and Cognition
- [ ] Excellent long-term memory for experiences, locations, and faces.
- [ ] Poor memory for sequences, facts and information that has not been experienced.
- [ ] Thinks primarily with images and feeling, not sounds or words (little internal dialogue).

Behavior, Health, Development and Personality

- ❏ Extremely disorderly or compulsively orderly.
- ❏ Can be class clown, trouble-maker, or too quiet.
- ❏ Had unusually early or late developmental stages (talking, crawling, walking, tying shoes).
- ❏ Prone to ear infections; sensitive to foods, additives, and chemical products.
- ❏ Can be an extra deep or light sleeper; bedwetting beyond appropriate age.
- ❏ Unusually high or low tolerance for pain.
- ❏ Strong sense of justice; emotionally sensitive; strives for perfection.
- ❏ Mistakes and symptoms increase dramatically with confusion, time pressure, emotional stress, or poor health.

You can also do a free online dyslexia test at www.dyslexia.com

Use the above checklist to assist you in identifying whether you or someone you know has dyslexia.

RESPONDING TO CHILD SEXUAL ABUSE

BY SUPREME UNDERSTANDING

"They shoulda thrown the book at you/ Because I hate you so much that it burn when I look at you"
– Nicki Minaj, "Autobiography"

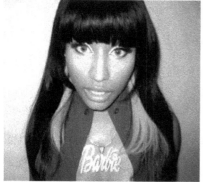

I used to wonder why Nicki Minaj came off like she was rapping for an audience of perverts and pedophiles. If you listened to her delivery, and the way she used to dress, she was impersonating a child. She even had a giant lollipop and schoolgirl dress on in some pictures. Yet she was selling sex. It seemed kind of sick to me. But as I paid attention to how many grown men found that exciting, I understood what her industry handlers had put her up to. She wasn't in control of her own image. And when she realized how many teenage girls were trying to become slutty "Barbie's" and "Harajuku girls" (a trend that comes from pedophilic elements in Japanese culture), she realized there was a problem. In the July 2010 issue of *Vibe Magazine*, she explained that before 'finding her groove' at drama school (where she could 'create characters' for herself), she was psychologically wrecked by an abusive father:

> I thought we would just be happy, but with a drug-addicted parent there is no such thing as being happy. When you have a father who is stealing your furniture and selling it so that he can buy crack, you suffer. You come home from school and your couch is gone. You're like, 'what happened?'

Most people who have been abused won't share all the details of their abuse, partly because they don't even want to think about it. Minaj continued:

All my dolls, all my stuffed animals, all my pictures are burnt. I was one of those kids that kept all that stuff. I cared a lot. I swear you'd have to hypnotize me to get me to remember some things that happened. I think psychologically I blocked them away.

I can only imagine what else happened, because the chances are good that it was even worse than she'd admit to. But among people of color, we rarely talk about physical abuse. And even LESS about sexual abuse. It's just something we brush under the table. Because we don't talk about it, most of us continue to suffer long into adulthood. At some point, we might tell what happened, as The Game did on his tragic song "Lost":

> My pops is a pedophile/ How you stick your 28-year-old dick in your child/ And now how it feel to be 52/ and have a son that's a millionaire and he don't f*ck with you?/ Daddy, she was only in the sixth grade/ The day I heard her scream, I shoulda hit you with the switchblade

But by then it's too late. We're scarred. We're hardly survivors. We're more like victims. Countless studies have shown that people who suffered sexual abuse as children were more like to feel isolated, abandoned, hopeless, and disconnected (from society and/or reality). **70% of victims develop alcohol and drug problems (80% among males).** Victims are also more likely to have depression, PTSD, eating disorders, physical health issues (somatization), other psychological issues (like self-hatred or aggression towards others), and serious difficulty maintaining healthy relationships (including being unable to tell sex from love).

Does this Sound Like a Lot of People you Know?

It should. In this country, 1 out of 4 girls and 1 out of 6 boys are sexually abused before they turn 18. In fact, most sexual assaults in this country are not perpetrated on adults, but on children. And those estimates are probably too low, considering that 88% of sexual abuse goes unreported. Bottom line is that **for every 5 people you know, one of them was most likely sexually abused at some point.** And for most people, it's not a one-time occurrence, because people are rarely molested or abused by "creepy old strangers." While that also can happen, we should know that **90% of sexual abuse comes from people who are known by the family of the victim.** Often, these are people who are trusted by the family. These can be clergy who volunteer to work "hands-on" with youth (like Bishop Eddie Long), teachers who spend extra one-on-one time – unsupervised – with students (like several who've made the news in recent years), and even record label owners and managers who take a "special interest" in developing a young artists career (I won't name any names here, because I'm sure you've heard the rumors about what happens to young artists in today's entertainment industry). Or these can be a step-parent (as Ludacris raps about in the first verse of "Runaway Love"), babysitter, or uncle (more Blacks are abused by their uncles than their fathers).

Why Don't They Just Tell?

Because of the abuser's status, victims can be scared to "snitch." They fear that no one will believe them, or that they will hurt someone else through their confession (such as what happened when Raz-B of B2K charged manager Chris Stokes with molesting him, his brother Ricky, and Marquez Houston...and then soon retracted).

30-40% of victims are sexually abused by family members themselves. Many times, victims are so "changed" by the abuse that their understanding of people and the world shifts entirely. Often, they are unable to tell sex from love, to know what is "right" or "wrong" or to protect themselves against future abuses. That was the case with Tyler Perry, who was molested by a neighbor for years, then seduced by a friend's mother at age 10, and physically abused by his own father, who he

later learned was molesting his female friend. **Many don't know that Tyler Perry's first play, *I Know I've Been Changed*, was about adult survivors of childhood abuse.** But audiences weren't ready for it, so he changed his formula. The Madea plays and films that followed paved the way for Perry to again address the topic of abuse by releasing the film *Precious*.

What Happens to the Victims?

Not only is child sexual abuse more common than we'd like to think, it's also more devastating than we'd like to admit. Do you think all those teen pregnancies in the hood are some "glitch" in our children? **The statistical truth is that more than 60% of teen first pregnancies are preceded by experiences of molestation, rape, or attempted rape.** The average age of the offenders is 27 years old. Another study found that 66% of pregnant teens report a history of abuse (but of course, most were never treated). Not only are victims of sexual abuse more likely to be promiscuous (especially engaging in unprotected sex and other risky behaviors), but they're also more likely to engage in prostitution. **Two-thirds of all prostitutes were abused as children.** What's most concerning is the cycle of abuse in which all this occurs. **30% of male victims later violently victimized others. And 70-80% of serial rapists were sexually abused as children.**

To make matters worse, this abuse tends to be more brutal in the hood. Incestuous abuse among Blacks was more than three times more likely to be "very severe" and violent, compared with the abuse experienced by whites. While it goes without saying that some of these victims will grow up to do worse than their own abusers, sexual abuse has other, more subtle, side-effects in the community. For starters, much of the dysfunction we see in the hood can be traced back to instances of abuse. **Sylvia Coleman identifies dozens of coping mechanisms used by victims/survivors of child sexual abuse at www.BlackSurvivors.org**, including promiscuity, attracting chaos, using religion to avoid intimacy, trouble saying no to others or trouble setting healthy boundaries, engaging in risky sexual behavior (unprotected sex, sex with strangers), falling for unavailable men, always feeling like a victim in life, and persistent low self-esteem, among other traits we have probably seen exhibited by many of our close friends and colleagues. Coleman adds:

> Men who have been abused are more commonly seen in the criminal justice system than in clinical mental health settings. Some men even feel societal pressure to be proud of early sexual activity (no matter how unwanted it may have been at the time).

When Did all This Start?

Most researchers trace the occurrence of child sexual abuse in the Black community back to European intervention. While some authors credit early contact (citing the ancient Greek emphasis on pedophilia being normative for much of European history, and then later emerging in European contact with indigenous populations), **others – like Sylvia Coleman – argue that "African-Americans have a history of victimization and sexual abuse dating back to their initial arrival in this country as slaves."** Coleman cites, as factors, the forced and often incestuous nature of sex on the slave plantation, the molestation that occurred regularly (beginning with the physical "inspections" at slave auctions), and the repression of dialogue about abuse:

> To survive, our ancestors learned to act complacent and submissive, to put on a mask to navigate through life. To talk about sexual attacks could result in lashings, sale or even death. So not talking showed a bravado that was passed down from generation to generation. Today this is called splitting or disassociation.

So How Can you Tell if a Child is Being Abused?

Physical signs are not common, but can include redness, rashes, or swelling in the genital area, urinary tract infections, and similar symptoms. Physical symptoms can also include constant headaches and stomach aches.

More common are the psychological symptoms. Some of these can range from "too perfect" behavior to withdrawal and depression to unexplained anger and rebellion. If you see a mood shift or a pattern of emotional behavior you can't explain, you may be seeing the signs of child sexual abuse.

Other signs include nightmares and bedwetting in children who have outgrown it, runaway behavior, cruelty to animals and fire-setting, self-mutilation and negative self-talk ("I'm ugly," "I'm worthless"), early alcohol/drug use, and inappropriate sexual behavior and language at an early age.

Above all, however, intuition is the first step in seeing clearly.

Recommendations

❒ Monitor (or avoid) any one adult-one child settings, which is where 80% of sexual abuse occurs. If there are to be any, drop in unexpectedly (even with family members) and ask questions (of the adult beforehand and of the child afterwards).

❒ Be mindful of allowing older children around your young child, because 40% of child sexual abuse is perpetrated by older or larger children. Comedian/talk show host Mo'nique, confessed that she'd been molested by her older brother from age 7 to 11. She said her parents didn't believe her, and her brother eventually went to prison for 15 years for sexually abusing another girl. Queen Latifah also admitted that she'd been sexually abused by a teenage babysitter.

❒ Part of the problem is the abuser, but a much larger part of the problem is the much larger number of people who do nothing about the problem. Some of us "look the other way."

❒ Others do even worse, sticking up for the accused, without even bothering to investigate. That's the case with South Park Mexican, a Houston rapper who sexually assaulted several children (impregnating one of them), before he was finally convicted and sentenced to 45 years in prison. Yet he continues to record music while incarcerated, and there are persistent messages from online posters calling for his release. This kind of behavior has to stop.

❒ While it's good to be aware of who's a registered sex offender in your area (using a site like www.FamilyWatchdog.us), it's more important to be aware of who actually has access to your children. Set some serious limits on who can watch your child, because it's not something everybody and anybody should have access to.

❒ Prepare your children for this sick world. Don't wait until it's too late to have those "talks" you've been putting off. You don't have to freak them out to be real with them.

❒ You can also help protect your children by not sending them out into the world looking like they're older than they are. While many child predators prey on children who look like children, there are also plenty of older people who are attracted to children who look, dress, or act "grown," which they feel makes their advances acceptable ("She looks like she's already doing it," "I thought he was 18," etc.)

❒ Encourage your children to tell you everything and anything as soon as it happens. Children who disclose abuse soon after its occurrence may be less traumatized than those children who live with the secret for years.

❒ Ask open-ended questions like "Then what happened?" Make sure the child knows you are there to trust, support, and protect them no matter what. Thank them for telling you, let them know it's not their fault, and then seek help.

- There are two agencies that handle most reports of child abuse: Child Protective Services (known by a different name in some states) and the Police. To find out where to make a report in your area, visit www.reportchildabusenow.com for the specific reporting numbers for your state.

- If the legal system doesn't handle the issue, visit the National Center for Victims of Crime (www.ncvc.org or 1-800-FYI-CALL) or Stop It Now (www.stopitnow.com or 1-888-PREVENT). You can also call 1-866-FOR-LIGHT or 1-800-4-A-CHILD.

- You can also visit a Children's Advocacy Center. To find a center near you, contact The National Children's Alliance at www.nca-online.org or 1-800-239-9950.

- Children and adults who were sexually abused as children have indicated that family support, extra-familial support, high self-esteem, and spirituality were helpful in their recovery from the abuse.

- Victims also report that attending workshops and conferences on child sexual abuse, reading about child sexual abuse, and undergoing psychotherapy have helped them feel better and return to a more normal life.

Finally, if you were a victim of child sexual abuse yourself, you can't allow yourself to be a victim anymore. In life, we choose either to be victims or survivors. Survivors find the strength to emerge from the shadows of shame to tell their stories and empower others to heal with them. Survivors of child sexual abuse include Oprah Winfrey, Laveranues Coles, Dorothy Dandridge, Antwone Fisher, Mary J. Blige, Iyanla Vanzant, Donnie McClurkin, Maya Angelou, Gabrielle Union, Jill Scott, Fantasia Barrino, Missy Elliot, Queen Latifah, Kenny Lattimore, Mo'nique, Tyler Perry, and thousands of others. You're not alone.

Recommended Reading
- African Americans and Child Sexual Abuse by Veronica Abney
- *Boys into Men: Raising Our African American Teenage Sons* by Nancy Boyd-Franklin, Pamela Toussaint, and A. J. Franklin
- Broken Boys, Mending Men: Recovery from Childhood Sexual Abuse by Stephen D. Gruban-Black
- I Will Survive: The African-American Guide to Healing from Sexual Assault and Abuse by Laura Robinson and Julia Boyd
- No Secrets, No Lies: How Black Families Can Heal from Sexual Abuse by Robin Stone
- Stolen Women: Reclaiming Our Sexuality, Taking Back Our Lives by Gail Wyatt
- Know who is around your child. If you aren't sure about someone's character, this includes relatives, don't leave them alone with your child.

Know who is around your child. If you aren't sure about someone's character, this includes relatives, don't leave them alone with your child.

6. WASTED: DRUGS AND ALCOHOL

On "Building Minds Faster," Lupe Fiasco raps, "Who use most the drugs? Americans! What's in Afghanistan? Heroin!" He's right, and he's not exaggerating. **The U.S. has only 4% of the world's population, but consumes 65% of its hard drugs.** And drug use (and addiction) is not something you only find in the hood. It's just something you only go to jail for in the hood. The truth is that – across the board – whites do more drugs than Blacks or Latinos. Both numerically and percentage-wise. Even marijuana. Just ask Bill Clinton…and while you're at it, ask George W. Bush about cocaine. But "Black" drugs like crack-cocaine receive the hardest sentencing and the least opportunities for rehab. **It's a telling fact that cities that are mostly white are the easiest on drug use** (in some areas, you can have an ounce on weed on you and not go to jail)**, while cities that have high minority populations respond, ahem, very differently.** These disparities are obvious even in the celebrity world, when you look at how they treat Lindsay Lohan, for example, versus someone like Lil Boosie. That's probably what was on Boosie's mind when he said, "If I made a mistake with marijuana, why am I not eligible for rehab? I've been on marijuana since a teenager. I need some rehab. Jail is not rehab."

He's got a point, but Boosie's story should tell you something. This system is not design for you to thrive. So if you're trying to kick an addiction, your chances of being assigned to a rehab program are slim. You might do better finding one on your own and checking yourself in. But even that may not go well. When all else fails, all you've got is you (and hopefully your family, unless your addiction has run them away). So you've got to take your life into your own hands. This starts with understanding how chemical addiction works.

"It was my decision to get clean, I did it for me/ Admittedly I probably did it, subliminally, for you/ So I could come back a brand new me, you helped see me through/ And don't even realize what you did, believe me you" – Eminem, "Not Afraid"

What is Addiction?

Addiction is no joke. I'm sure everyone reading this has lost somebody to addiction…especially if you consider that some of us are "gone" but not physically dead. They're just part of the "walking dead." Public Enemy rapped about em on "Night of the Living Baseheads" and Nas called them "Black Zombies." Addiction has taken the lives of thousands of notable figures, from legendary singer Marvin Gaye (whose own father shot him because he'd become violent during a cocaine binge) to rapper Ol' Dirty Bastard, who had a lethal mixture of cocaine and the prescription painkiller Tramadol in his system at the time of his 2004 death. Pimp C's 2007 death was caused by the effects of a large dose of promethazine and codeine (prescription cough syrup) coupled with a preexisting sleep apnea condition. Fellow Texas pioneers DJ Screw and Fat Pat also fell victim to deadly doses of cough syrup. Even Cam'ron claimed that he could no longer do business with Juelz Santana because of his addiction to syrup.

The latest news regarding drug addiction in HipHop wasn't Whitney and Bobby on crack or D'Angelo on coke. It was Lil Wayne and – once again – syrup. After Wayne admitted to his addiction in April of 2009, *Rhapsody* caught up with Bun B to get his take on Wayne, syrup, and quitting drugs:

Rhapsody: Lil Wayne recently made a lot of headlines by admitting to being addicted to syrup. What were your thoughts?

Bun B: I wish they would just leave the kid alone. When you have 100 people telling you to not do something, that sh*t doesn't work like that. Now me, I hadn't sipped syrup for a while before Pimp died. Does that mean I let all my vices go? F*ck no. I'm still drinking and smoking weed. Ike Turner died of cocaine use. People haven't stopped snorting cocaine. Thousands of people die drunk driving every year and somebody is going to drive home drunk tonight. People stop doing things whenever they sort of feel their way up to it. **The kid said he would love to stop, but the withdrawal symptoms are too intense for him. Anybody going through something like that knows that's what it is. I say this to all media, you can't force Lil Wayne to stop sipping drank. That's gonna be a personal choice. For all these people that love to put his sh*t on blast, I would love for them to put their vices on front street. Walk around with your proverbial white cup with you all day and see if you could handle the pressure.**

And this was Lil Wayne's take on his situation:

No, [Bun] hasn't talked to me. But I'm going through that same sh*t with my friends, with my mom. **Everybody wants me to stop all this and all that. It ain't that easy. Do your history, do your research. It ain't that easy – feels like death in your stomach when you stop doing that sh*t. You got to learn how to stop, you got to go through detox. You got to do all kinds of stuff.** Like I said, I'm a selfish-ass nigga. I feel like everything I do is successful and productive. It's gonna be hard to tell me I'm slipping. It's hard to sit and tell a nigga 'Stop.' 'F*CK, how can we tell this nigga to stop when every f*cking thing he do is successful? This nigga is making progress. He just went and talked to kids and that sh*t was amazing.' Feel me? So what am I doing wrong? Let me do me. Everybody's got their thing. Why focus on me? Don't compare me to no one. Don't compare me to no one who has passed, and why they passed. I can walk out this bitch right now and get hit by a bus. Don't judge me. You want to judge me, put on a black gown and get a gavel. Get in line with the rest of them that's about to judge me. I got court dates every other month. It's me against the world, that's how I feel...I don't escape. I don't. I'm too shelled-in by it. It's in my own circle. Everybody around here be looking down. I deal with it...I never been one to run. I stand there and take it and throw it right back at them bitches. That's always been my game...It's inspiring me, but I'mma tell them now they better stop. Cause they [are trying to] push me off the edge. If I jump, I'm taking the world with me. That's my word.

Sounds like a true addict talking. That is, it sounds like someone who knows they have a problem, but just can't find a solution...yet.

Addiction involves 3 main elements:

1. chemical need (at the physiological cellular level)
2. learned habit (chronic use/behavior and associations)
3. denial of both need and habit

Some addictions, like alcoholism, develop over a period of years. Others are much quicker, like addictions to cocaine and meth (which is said to only require "one hit"). In any case, the addiction becomes "Priority One," something separate from everything else...something that eventually negates everything else as a priority in your life.

There are 3 stages to the addiction process:

1. Preoccupation/anticipation
2. Binge/intoxication
3. Withdrawal/negative effect

These stages occur in cycles, up to several times a day, depending on how strong the addiction is. With each use, a person's body and brain chemistry begin to alter in such a way that the drug effects become a normal part of the addict's internal chemistry. This leads to a physical dependency where the body relies on the drug for normal functioning.

The most significant changes occur in your central nervous system, starting with your brain. Drugs cause the brain to release dopamine and serotonin, the "feel good" neurotransmitters. Meanwhile, the drugs make it harder for your brain to process dopamine and serotonin. So not only do you need the drugs to feel good, you continuously need more and more just to feel the same level of good. After certain point, the reward/punishment pathways within your brain become permanently altered, making you susceptible to addictive behavior long after you stop using.

If you were to stop "cold turkey," your central nervous system would basically punish you for not giving it what it thinks it needs. This is known as withdrawal, producing symptoms such as sweating, tremors, irritability, insomnia, nausea, depression, extreme cravings (and worse), all caused by your brain's inability to function normally without the drug.

"I'm not afraid to take a stand/ Everybody come take my hand/ We'll walk this road together, through the storm/ Whatever weather, cold or warm/ Just let you know that, you're not alone/ Holla if you feel that you've been down the same road" – Eminem, "Not Afraid"

But these symptoms are all temporary. They may feel like hell (so bad with some drugs that people often rely on doctor-prescribed "transition" drugs to quit), but most withdrawal symptoms do nowhere near the damage you're doing to your body with long-term drug abuse. **Any drug that is addictive is also toxic to your health.** From missing teeth to heart disease, drugs are bad for you. They wreck your brain but they also affect the rest of you. For example, Ecstasy interferes with the body's ability to regulate temperature, and can cause liver, kidney, and cardiovascular failure. But addictive drugs (including prescription painkillers, so don't get it twisted) are more likely to wreck your life before they wreck your health. By the time you start getting real sick, you'll be so f*cked up and out of it that no one will even notice. Probably not even

you. You'll probably die sick, while still trying to get your next fix.

Why Do We Do It?

*"If it feels so good, why do we call it getting f*cked up?" – Bro Akil, From Niggas to Gods*

Most alcoholics and addicts have someone in their family who has already fallen victim. In fact, being prone to chemical dependence can be inherited…or even a genetic trait. And while those are factors in why some of us develop addictions, put simply, chemical dependency is a mask for depression. People who are miserable about their lives "self-medicate" with alcohol and other stimulants/depressants to feel better (or just feel "out of it") temporarily. I didn't learn that in a book. I lived that. And it wasn't until I felt better about myself, my life, and my future, that I could easily give up drinking and smoking.

With that said, there are some of us who can drink or smoke weed on occasion, and it's not a symptom of depression. But there's a lot more of us who THINK we don't have a problem and we really do. Earlier, you read an example of this from Lil Wayne. He said those words in April of 2009. But fortunately, things seem to have changed. And it's likely that the change was brought on by all that pressure he was complaining about. In February of 2010, he told *Rolling Stone*, "I haven't f*cked with that in a long time," insisting he quit drinking cough syrup and juice May in 2009, doing it "cold turkey." Wayne might have been screaming "Leave me alone," but it looks like the harassment helped. And it appears that Wayne was looking forward to his prison sentence, because it offered him a chance to 'get clean.' "I just say I'm looking forward to it," he told *Rolling Stone*, "I know it's an experience that I need to have if God's putting me through it." Going to prison is a hell of a way to detox, but it works. The only problem is that if you go back to the same circles once you're back in the free world, you'll be back to your old problems in no time.

Know what "drives" an addiction, how addicts usually behave and "rationalize."

FROM ILLIN TO HEALIN
AN ADDICT'S PLIGHT TO FREEDOM FROM ACTIVE ADDICTION
BY ANONYMOUS

I am the epitome of a dope addict. As a little boy, I literally believed every family in the world got high off something, because every adult in my family got high off something, even my great grandmother who smoked trees. Coming up in my hood, every family in my reach was in a similar position.

I started out smoking cigarettes at 13. The buzz I got made me want to smoke even more, but by my fifth cig, the buzz was gone. I needed something else. Over time, I realized this would be for every drug I used. Next, I drank 40 Oz's and cheap wine. Then I started a love affair that would take me to some of the darkest places in the universe, a gate way to a path of destruction that I thought I'd never travel. Her name was known in many languages, but in the hood she was called Weed, Trees, Sess, Dro, Purp, Chronic, and most recently Kush. I had a love affair with Mother Mary or Marijuana. I sold it to support my habit. I made decent money but I smoked so much of my supply that I didn't make as much money as I could have.

So I got the bright idea to sell cocaine. I thought that I could make more money and not use up my supply. Well I was sadly mistaken. When weed's high wasn't enough, I eventually laced my blunts with base or freebase, which is crack cocaine. I got to a point where I smoked at least five cocaine-laced blunts, a day. And when the weed ran out I smoked the crack with cigarette tobacco in joints. I got so high daily that I couldn't sleep without snorting heroin. I was miserable and depressed and so was everyone around me.

Although I was slowly committing suicide by getting high, I couldn't figure out why I felt so sad and depressed. The drugs had me so lost that I didn't realize I was out of my mind. My life was a constant path of destruction. I was living in a fantasy world, though I had jolts of reality. During one of my moments of clarity, I noticed enough was enough. I went to my mom's house and told her I'd had enough. She suggested I get help. Based upon her suggestion, I signed myself into a drug detoxifying unit. I discovered a 12 step program there and I learned that my addiction was a clinical illness which meant, just like any other illness, that I needed treatment. I learned that drugs had driven me to a point of insanity and I needed recovery. I needed to recover my sanity, myself respect, and most importantly my inner peace. I went to a rehabilitation unit after I left the detox unit. I stayed in rehab for 30 days. (Ironically both the detox and rehab were housed in mental health wards.) It was suggested of me to continue attending the 12 step support groups, so when I left rehab, I immediately went to one. I knew where to go because, in treatment, they gave me a list of where they were.

Once there, I raised my hand and told the people there that I was an addict and I needed help. They gave me many suggestions, many of which I still use today, such as staying away from people, places, and things I used with, going to support group meetings, getting phone numbers and calling other recovering addicts, learning and working the 12 steps, and many more.

It has been over 7 years since I used drugs. I still attend 12 step meetings. I lost the desire to use drugs and found a new way to live. My worst days clean are better than my best days using drugs. I have the love and support of my family again. I've become a productive member of society and I've been blessed to help others find their way to recovery.

I have received many gifts during my years of being clean but the greatest gift has been the connection with my Higher Power that exists within me. See, I learned that I was powerless over my addiction and my life had become unmanageable, but my Higher Power, the God within, is more powerful than the disease of addiction.

In the past I felt all alone in the mean streets of the hood. Now my support network is so vast, I'll never feel alone again. If you're reading this and you want help from drug abuse, or if you know anyone who wants help, Google "12 step programs" in your area and see which one best suits your needs. And don't be afraid to tell someone who you know and trust that you need help. Remember, alone we can do some things, together we can do anything.

Drug Abuse Screening Test (DAST)

This 20-question self-test may help you become aware of your use or abuse of drugs. To take the questionnaire, please mark the choice which best reflects how each statement applies to you. The questions refer to the past 12 months. For the purposes of this screening test, "drug abuse" refers to the use of prescribed or "over the counter" drugs in excess of the directions, and any non-medical use of drugs. Remember, for the purposes of this screening test, the questions do not refer to alcoholic beverages. Carefully read each statement and decide whether your answer is "yes" or "no." Please give the best answer or the answer that is right most of the time.

1. Have you used drugs other than those required for medical reasons?
❒ Yes ❒ No

2. Have you abused prescription drugs?
❒ Yes ❒ No

3. Do you abuse more than one drug at a time?
❒ Yes ❒ No

4. Can you get through the week without using drugs?
❒ Yes ❒ No

6. Are you always able to stop using drugs when you want to?
❒ Yes ❒ No

7. Have you had "blackouts" or "flashbacks" as a result of drug use?
❒ Yes ❒ No

8. Do you ever feel bad or guilty about your drug use?
❒ Yes ❒ No

9. Does your spouse (or parents) ever complain about your involvement with drugs?
❒ Yes ❒ No

10. Has drug abuse created problems between you and your spouse or your parents?
❒ Yes ❒ No

11. Have you lost friends because of your use of drugs?
❒ Yes ❒ No

12. Have you neglected your family because of your use of drugs?
❒ Yes ❒ No

13. Have you been in trouble at work because of your use of drugs?
❒ Yes ❒ No

14. Have you lost a job because of drug abuse?
❒ Yes ❒ No

15. Have you gotten into fights when under the influence of drugs?
❒ Yes ❒ No

16. Have you engaged in illegal activities in order to obtain drugs?
❒ Yes ❒ No

17. Have you been arrested for possession of illegal drugs?
❒ Yes ❒ No

18. Have you ever experienced withdrawal symptoms (felt sick) when you stopped taking drugs?
❒ Yes ❒ No

19. Have you had medical problems as a result of your drug use (e.g., memory loss, hepatitis, convulsions, bleeding, etc.)?
❒ Yes ❒ No

20. Have you gone to anyone for help for a drug problem?
❒ Yes ❒ No

21. Have you been involved in a treatment program especially related to drug use?
❒ Yes ❒ No

Scoring

This quiz is scored by allocating 1 point to each 'yes' answer –	Score:

	except for questions 4 and 5, where 1 point is allocated for each 'no' answer – and totaling the responses.	
Scoring Ranges and Explanation		
0	None Reported	
1-5	Low Level	
6-10	Moderate Level	
11-15	Substantial Level	
16-20	Severe Level	

The Proactive 12 Steps

Many of us have heard of "12 Step" programs for addiction recovery and sobriety. The "Proactive 12 Steps" are an alternative inspired by the Twelve Steps of Alcoholics Anonymous and other addiction programs. **They employ a non-religious approach that provokes positive results for people from all walks of life, without being constricted to religious ideology.** They can be used for alcohol addiction as well as drug addiction. They are as follows:

Step 1: I realize I'm stuck. It makes no sense to keep trying to solve my problems with "solutions" that aren't working.

Step 2: I'm willing to let go of my usual ways, in the hope that this will help me see things from a broader perspective.

Step 3: I shift my focus, from being fixated on my problems, to seeking a sense of wholeness and contentment in my life.

Step 4: I honestly look at the effects of my actions on others and myself.

Step 5: I take responsibility for my actions.

Step 6: I see that my knee-jerk reactions have to do with being in the grip of more or less conscious fears.

Step 7: I strive to find my motivation in a deeper sense of who I really am, rather than fear and defensiveness.

Step 8: I stop blaming and feeling blamed, with a willingness to heal the wounds.

Step 9: I swallow my pride, and sincerely apologize to people I've hurt, except when it would be counterproductive.

Step 10: I live mindfully, paying attention to the motives and effects of my actions.

Step 11: I stay tuned inside, in touch with a broader sense of who I really am, and a deeper sense of what I really want.

Step 12: As I feel better about myself, I reach out to others who feel stuck.

Memorize "The Proactive 12 Steps." Apply them to your every day life and live them out. Focus on being effective and getting results.

---

101 STRATEGIES TO STAY CLEAN AND SOBER

The following comes from recovering addict and alcoholic Patrick Meninga, who maintains a recovery blog at www.spiritualriver.com:

- ❏ Don't underestimate your disease. Every single person does at first.
- ❏ Take care of yourself spiritually. Be mindful of your connection to your higher power today.
- ❏ Ignore the dismal relapse rates. You are creating your own success.
- ❏ Make a zero tolerance policy with yourself concerning relapse. Don't even allow your mind to go there.
- ❏ Avoid fundamentalism, even in recovery. Rigid thinking and dogma can undermine your sobriety.
- ❏ You are creating a life of recovery and you are responsible for ALL OF IT. Yes, others can help you. Their "help" is mere advice. It is up to you to recover.
- ❏ Don't confuse enthusiasm for action. Figure out what you need to do to stay sober and then do it.
- ❏ Listen to what the relapsing addicts keep preaching. Then do the opposite.
- ❏ Take care of your social network. Reach out to others in a meaningful way.
- ❏ Figure out a way to help other addicts or alcoholics.
- ❏ If you attend 12 step meetings, find one to start chairing. Consider H&I meetings (taking meetings into jails and treatment centers).
- ❏ Use mindfulness and a heightened awareness to overcome ego. Use meditation to overcome self.
- ❏ Practice forgiveness. Forgive all your past transgressors. Forgive yourself. You must do this to get long term relief from resentment.
- ❏ Be aware of diminishing returns, and spread out your recovery efforts (i.e., don't focus on just "spiritual" growth).
- ❏ Rearrange all the furniture in your house. Anything to get through the night sometimes.
- ❏ Clean your house from top to bottom. Same as above.
- ❏ Go for a long walk.
- ❏ Adopt a pet and care for it.
- ❏ Eat a gourmet meal.
- ❏ Cook a gourmet meal.
- ❏ Practice the arts. Paint, draw, sculpt, sing, and dance. Etc.
- ❏ See a therapist.
- ❏ Work on a puzzle.
- ❏ Connect with someone else who is hurting.
- ❏ Start a project that is bigger than you.
- ❏ Revisit an old hobby.
- ❏ Teach someone something. (Anything!)
- ❏ Learn something new each day. (Anything!)
- ❏ Write in a daily journal.
- ❏ Stretch yourself spiritually by suspending disbelief for a day.
- ❏ Write a letter to your addiction where you say farewell to it.
- ❏ Join a recovery forum online.
- ❏ Start a free blog over at blogger.com and tell the world about your progress in recovery. Figure out your own tips on staying sober.
- ❏ Go back to school.
- ❏ Learn a new skill or trade.
- ❏ Sponsor a newcomer.
- ❏ Make a commitment to chair a meeting each week.
- ❏ Celebrate the recovery of a friend.
- ❏ Spend time with your family.
- ❏ Email the spiritual river guy and tell him your problems.
- ❏ Celebrate your clean time with a cake.
- ❏ Write out a gratitude list.

- [ ] Read through your old journal entries and see how much you've changed.
- [ ] Try a new form of meditation (or make up your own...there is no "wrong" here). Some of the best tips to stay sober come from within.
- [ ] Write out a to-do list and cross each thing off as you accomplish it.
- [ ] Always have a big goal in the back of your mind that is challenging for you, but would make your day if you met it.
- [ ] Practice balance. Challenge your daily habits.
- [ ] Forgive yourself and move on with your life.
- [ ] Sit down and write 2 goals out for yourself: one big one and one little one. Keep the paper in your pocket.
- [ ] Inspire someone else to grow. Challenge them to be a better person in some way. Encourage them through your own success.
- [ ] Learn to relax. Find your quiet place of rejuvenation and return to it often.
- [ ] Elevate your consciousness. Watch your own mind and see how it responds to events. Repeat often. Learn.
- [ ] Find the beauty in life. Appreciate all of it. Be grateful for beauty itself.
- [ ] Ask yourself with each decision: "Is this the healthiest choice for me right now?"
- [ ] Quit smoking cigarettes already.
- [ ] Be grateful for existence.
- [ ] If you go to the same AA meetings all the time, switch it up and go to a completely new meeting.
- [ ] Write a poem about how you are overcoming addiction.
- [ ] Turn off your television and read a book. Better: read recovery literature. Best: write your own recovery literature.
- [ ] Use overwhelming force to conquer a goal.
- [ ] Learn how to stay sober through creation of a new reality. Don't settle.
- [ ] Create the life you really want in recovery.
- [ ] Write your bucket list. Then, act.
- [ ] Figure out your life purpose.
- [ ] Write out a fourth step and share it with your sponsor.
- [ ] Take care of yourself physically. Exercise. Take a walk. No excuses.
- [ ] Keep your priorities straight. Physical abstinence is number one. Simple and effective.
- [ ] Keep a high price on your serenity. Don't sacrifice it for just anyone and their whims.
- [ ] Use a sponsor for stage 2 recovery. Let them guide you through holistic living.
- [ ] Take care of yourself mentally. Go back to school. Get that degree.
- [ ] Find your own path. It is your responsibility to do so.
- [ ] Practice humility and stay teachable. Always be learning.
- [ ] Go to long term treatment and be done with it. Best decision I ever made.
- [ ] Don't pin your hopes on a short stay in rehab. It takes more than that.
- [ ] Call your sponsor.
- [ ] Get a sponsor.
- [ ] Use a zero tolerance policy when it comes to self-pity. Never allow it for yourself ever again. Ever. It is poison.
- [ ] Join a recovery forum.
- [ ] Use outpatient treatment if that works for you. Take it as seriously as possible and connect with the others in your group.
- [ ] Meditate.
- [ ] Pray.
- [ ] Go out for coffee with a friend in recovery.
- [ ] Find your passion.
- [ ] Work out.
- [ ] Join a church.
- [ ] Volunteer.

- ☐ Take care of yourself emotionally. Don't get knocked too far off your square.
- ☐ Stay vigilant against potential relapse. The disease can find many routes (gambling, prescription drugs, sex, etc.).
- ☐ Go to a meeting.
- ☐ Don't pin your hopes on long term treatment. It takes a lifetime of learning for alcoholics and recovering drug addicts to recover.
- ☐ Use long term strategic thinking. Care for yourself, network with others, and pursue conscious growth.
- ☐ Don't ask "why me?" Instead, ask "how can I create the life I really want now?"
- ☐ Call a friend in recovery.
- ☐ Sit down and write out a gratitude list.
- ☐ Don't live in fear of relapse. I wasted 5 years on this. Embrace the creative life and know you are strong in recovery.
- ☐ Get extreme. Figure out what you need to do to stay sober...then double it and add ten. That's how hard you have to push yourself.
- ☐ Raise the bar. Stop settling. Use your talents as a gift to the world and make a difference in some way.
- ☐ Live consciously. Set deliberate goals and go after them with overwhelming force.
- ☐ Embrace the creative life in recovery and live holistically.

Get a healthy routine going. Make these suggestions work for you.

I CAN'T PUT THE CIGARETTES DOWN!
BY SUPREME UNDERSTANDING

Tobacco use kills at least 5 million of us every year. It's the leading preventable cause of death. The World Health Organization (WHO) estimates that tobacco could kill about 8 million people every year by 2030, mostly in developing (Black and brown) countries. And it's not just affecting the people with the cigarettes in their hands. **Secondhand smoke – nearly as toxic – kills about 600,000 people every year, including children who grow up with serious asthma and respiratory conditions, only to die later in life.**

But the WHO isn't doing much to change that. According to Patrick Basham, director of the Democracy Institute, WHO recommendations like increasing tobacco taxes and banning advertising don't address the root causes of why people smoke. Smoking declines when people become less stuck in the hells of poverty and limited opportunity. I guess that's why we smoke 90% of the stuff we smoke, from cigarettes to crack. Same with drinking alcohol. Anytime you look at a displaced, disenfranchised, disadvantaged and/or discriminated against group of people anywhere in the world...they're probably smoking and drinking. The people in the slums of Mumbai, India smoke bidis and opium (that's what the fathers of those Slumdog Millionaire kids blew all their movie money on), the Bushmen people of South Africa take snuff, smoke Makaranga tobacco and get drunk on plum wine…and you already know how it goes in our hoods. People who feel great about their futures are a lot less likely to smoke than people who think their life is hell.

But if we can't (immediately) make the world a better place to live, what will it take to get people to stop smoking their stress away? After all, we all know smoking causes cancer. Hell, it's on all the boxes now, and those "Truth" commercials on TV have made the message even clearer. Of course, there are some statistics they don't share. Such as how – like almost anything else – **if it's bad for everybody, it's even worse for Black people:**

- ❒ Black men are at least 50% more likely to develop lung cancer than white men.
- ❒ Black men also die more often from cancer of the lung and bronchus than do white men.
- ❒ Tobacco related cancers account for almost half of new cancer cases in Black men and about 1/3 of cancer deaths.

In fact, the cancer death rate among Black men has a higher rate of increase than any other ethnic group in this country. By eliminating tobacco use, most of these deaths could be prevented. Even if we don't know the specifics, we at least know that smoking is killing us. But even though we call them "cancer sticks," we can't leave them alone. Why? The chemicals in cigarettes are addictive! The main one, Nicotine, is one of the most addictive substances known to man. And guess what? **According to a study published in 2009 in the journal *Pharmacology, Biochemistry and Behavior*, nicotine is more addictive for people of color than white people.** In fact, the darker your skin, the longer nicotine and tobacco's cancer-causing agents tend to linger and accumulate in other melanin-containing tissues like the heart, lungs, liver and brain, potentially putting those organs at increased risk for tobacco-related diseases. Scientists have already found that Black and brown people have a harder time quitting cigarettes due to higher levels of stress and awareness of racial discrimination, but

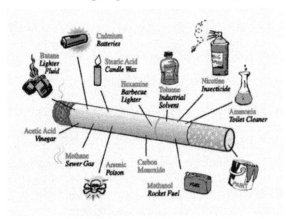

this study explains another factor for why Black people have a more difficult time quitting and suffer from more tobacco-related diseases. And what about Menthol? Approximately three out of four Black smokers prefer menthol cigarettes (versus one in four whites). And guess what? Menthol may increase the body's absorption of the harmful ingredients in cigarette smoke.

And it's not just nicotine in there. Cigarette smoke contains over 4,000 chemicals (literally), including over 60 known carcinogenic (cancer-causing) compounds and 400 other toxins. These include...

❑ Tar – about 70% of the tar in the smoke is deposited in the smoker's lungs

❑ Benzene (gasoline additive) – A colorless cyclic hydrocarbon obtained from coal and petroleum, used as a solvent in fuel and in chemical manufacture – and contained in cigarette smoke. It is a known carcinogen and is associated with leukemia.

❑ Formaldehyde (embalming fluid) – A colorless, highly poisonous lipid, used to preserve dead bodies. Known to cause cancer, as well as respiratory, skin and gastrointestinal problems.

❑ Ammonia (toiler cleaner) – Used as a flavoring, frees nicotine from tobacco turning it into a gas, found in dry cleaning fluids.

❑ Acetone (nail polish remover) – Fragrant volatile liquid ketone, used as a solvent – found in cigarette smoke.

❑ Carbon monoxide (car exhaust fumes) An odorless, tasteless and poisonous gas, rapidly fatal in large amounts – it's the same gas that comes out of car exhaust and is the main gas in cigarette smoke, formed when the cigarette is lit.

❑ Others you may recognize are: Arsenic (rat poison), Hydrogen Cyanide (gas chamber poison), and DDT (banned cancer-causing pesticide)

> Did You Know?
> For many smokers, it may be hard to quit because they also have depression. 43% of adult smokers age 20 and older have depression. Depressed smokers are also heavier smokers. Depressed people were more likely to smoke within five minutes of awakening and to smoke more than one pack of cigarettes a day. 28% of adult smokers with depression smoked more than a pack a day, which is almost twice the rate for adult smokers without depression. Smokers with depression were also much less likely to have tried quitting. However, smokers with depression can succeed with intensive treatment, including therapies focused on depression and quitting smoking. Information on quitting smoking for people with depression can be found at www.smokefree.gov/topic-depression.aspx

For those of you who avoid pork, Glycerin (a pork by-product) is sprayed on tobacco leaves, and researchers have recently found that cigarette filters contain pig blood. There are plenty of reasons to quit. If you're Black or Latino, for example, there's the reason one of my friends offered: He doesn't smoke cigs simply for the fact that most owners of tobacco companies and fields are inheritance/descendants of the slave owners who kept a whip on his ancestors' backs, forcing them to tend the tobacco fields without pay or dignity. They benefited from our labor back then and benefit from our pockets now.

The Benefits of Quitting

☐ Within 20 minutes of quitting - your blood pressure and pulse rate drop to normal and the temperature of your hands and feet increase to normal.

☐ Within 8 hours of quitting - your carbon monoxide levels drop and your oxygen levels increase, both to normal levels.

☐ Within 24 hours of quitting - your risk of sudden heart attack decreases.

☐ Within 48 hours of quitting - nerve endings begin to regenerate and your senses of smell and taste begin to return to normal.

☐ Within 2 weeks to 3 months of quitting - your circulation improves and walking becomes easier; even your lung function increases up to 30%.

☐ Within 1 to 9 months of quitting - your overall energy typically increases and symptoms like coughing, nasal congestion, fatigue, and shortness of breath diminish; also, the small hair-like projections lining your lower airways begin to function normally. This increases your lungs' ability to handle mucus, clean the airways, and reduce infections.

☐ Within 1 year of quitting - your risk of coronary heart disease is half that of someone still using tobacco.

☐ Within 5 years of quitting - the lung cancer death rate decreases by nearly 50% compared to one pack/day smokers. The risk of cancer of the mouth is half that of a tobacco user.

☐ Within 10 years of quitting - your lung cancer death rate becomes similar to that of someone who never smoked; precancerous cells are replaced with normal cells; your risk of stroke is lowered possible to that of a nonuser; your risk of cancer of the mouth, throat, esophagus, bladder, kidney, and pancreas all go down.

No matter how long you've been smoking, it's never too late to quit.

QUITTING METHODS THAT WORK

Studies show that having an incentive to quit smoking can help more than having information alone. So find a friend or family member you can trust with money, and have them hold about half your month's pay until you've quit for a month. Better yet, have your friends and family take up a collection for a "Help _____ Quit Bribe/Incentive"

I quit my habit through sheer willpower, but that's not realistic for many of us, especially those of us with pack-a-day habits. So we ran a contest for ex-smokers to provide step-by-step strategies that worked for them. We then asked our Facebook friends who smoked to vote on which method sounded most promising.

Jah's Creation:

The winner, Jah's Creation of Dallas, Texas, explained her reason for quitting:

> I grew up watching my grandparents smoke cigarettes and cigars. Imagine putting on clean clothes every day and goin to school smellnig like a chimney.. That was ME! I would see my mom wake up with hacking coughs JUST TO PUT A CIGARETTE BACK IN HER MOUTH! But, when I grew up I would smoke too, until I realized – WHY AM I DOING THIS?

When I had children they would come home crying and telling to stop because the elementary school had shown them pictures of what lungs, stomachs and the like looked like when full of cancer. It was not easy. Yet, I had to break down the essentials to stop the want to pick up anything and light it. So, I sat down and wrote the approach you see here. What matters the most is that you pick things in your life you can CHANGE. Get away from environments that are smoking-friendly and most importantly, remember you are killing your future.

☐ Make a budget of your household needs – Tally how much you spend on cigarettes.

☐ Throw away any and all cigs, lighters and ashtrays in your house.

☐ Let ALL friends, family and co-workers know you have quit. (Not "are" quitting – make it final)

☐ DON'T dine at old hang-outs where you smoked. Do not use the smoking entrance to your job or any familiar buildings.

☐ Invest in Wrigley's Spearmint gum. The money you will spend will rival your cig bill for at least 6 months. Chew at least two pieces at a time. The taste is as strong as the inhaled smoke your body is used to (Psyche your senses out).

Dierdra Baptiste:

☐ Nicotine is a drug. Acknowledge that you are an addict by repeating out loud to yourself each time you light up. (Do this in a mirror, carry a compact if you must – yes men too! – as you must face yourself doing this.)

☐ Do NOT go cold turkey if you are a half pack or more per day smoker, the withdrawals/mood swings etc., will put you right back where you started and sometimes actually smoking more.

☐ Take a few of your clothing items without washing them and store them in a tightly sealed container or box in the back of closet or basement

☐ Find a flight of stairs, preferably two or more and run up and down them once. Test how winded you are...

☐ Write down what you are doing each time you light up as habit is a huge component with smoking

☐ Pick habit action number 1, i.e. with morning coffee or while driving car and do not have a cigarette with that one particular action each day for at least two weeks.

☐ Go to next habit and progress from there until you get down to one

☐ Reward yourself for each day you go without one cigarette during each action, i.e. praise yourself on your accomplishment, enlist family/friends to assist you by acknowledging that you didn't smoke today while on your lunch break, etc. (achieving a goal and being rewarded for it will take the place of the high felt from smoking or the relief felt from stress).

☐ Once a week, after each day of one less cigarette, run those flights of stairs and test your increased lung capacity.

☐ Go back to the closet where your clothes in the box are kept and smell your clothes. Your ability to smell better will increase over time. Eventually, you'll smell how rancid you smell to others.

☐ The first full week without a cigarette reward yourself with something special, i.e. dinner out, a date, whatever suits you.

- Realize that if you slip, you are only human and this is after all an addiction. Tell yourself this in the mirror. And resign yourself to one per day at that point until the need subsides.

Letitia Patterson:

A "Drug Bomb" (Show this to a health food store. They'll know what to do):

- 1000 mil niacinamide
- 5000 IU Vitamin A
- 400 IU Vitamin D
- 800 IU Vitamin E
- 2000 mil Vitamin C
- 500 mil magnesium carbonate
- 25 mil B6
- 200 mil B complex
- 300 mil B1
- 100 mil pantothenic acid
- Drink with milk and powdered amino acids
- Eat meal before drinking
- Eat yogurt or drink raw milk to coat stomach while taking
- 4x daily every 6 hours
- Exercise
- Use sauna to sweat (nicotine has to get out of fat tissue)
- Take normal vitamins
- Eat real food when possible: fruits, vegetables, anything that grows

Telisa Bee:

The one thing that needs to happen is for people to find their triggers. When you make a conscious effort to recognize your pattern, only then can you begin to break some of the sub-conscious habits and deal with the physiological addiction. Do you smoke when you: drive, drink, smoke weed, work hard, over eat, feel sad, etc. That's a critical step many of us miss.

Prentice Sams:

- Everybody doesn't have the luxury of being able to buy exotic herbs and foods with cleansing/healing properties, so find alternatives to cleanse yourself naturally with what you have available.
- Give your smokes away whenever asked, leaving less for you to smoke.
- Spend money on other things so you have little left to buy cigs
- Use breathing exercises to restore/increase lung capacity/strength, over time the tar will break up, the body will flush the tar and build up from the lungs.
- Flush toxins from the body. Keep water on hand to drink constantly, go on a fast (juice-only or water-only) for detox if needed. Do something to make yourself sweat – Exercise (walk, run, dance, stairs, sex, etc.) (drink water); put on multiple layers and sit in the car w/ the windows up on a hot day, if it's cold outside run the heater (drink plenty of water during).
- Eat/drink fruits and vegetables [juices] to restore nutrients from all the water and sweating.
- If you're really ready to quit, you will do what you need to do to quit.

Josh Lawler:

- Find a hobby or passion. Mine is/was Muay Thai. I dropped the smokes and picked up a pair of 16 oz. gloves. Same went for drinking.

- Do it 'til you drop. Choose a winter month when the humidity is high and the temperature low. Buy a new pack and chain smoke it until your stomach hurts and your neck burns. The next day when you have to call in sick from work because you can't breathe and your head feels like a hand-grenade went off, you'll realize that smoking has NOTHING to offer you.

Take the initial step to a smoke free life.

BIDIS ARE HAZARDOUS TO YOUR HEALTH
BY SCIHONOR DEVOTION

Some of us have seen the commercials growing up that said that smoking was actually good for us and was encouraged, even amongst pregnant women. But now, we have all seen the commercials, advertisements and billboards telling us that smoking cigarettes is not good for us. Many states like New York have even banned smoking in public places. Because of this, those who are looking for alternatives, have explored the options of Electronic Cigarettes, Herbal Cigarettes and Clove Cigarettes also known as Kreteks. Unfortunately, some of us are either so addicted or just so caught up in the term "Herbal" or "Natural" that we think these alternatives can actually be better than tobacco cigarettes.

Aren't Bidis Safer than Cigarettes?
Bidis (pronounced Bee-Dees), which look similar to marijuana "joints," have become more popular these days. Their aromas, candy like flavors, and frequently lower prices have contributed to their popularity. Although these bidis are legal, they have proven to have arresting powers over those who smoke them. Many of them are unfiltered and are more dangerous than regular cigarettes.

Studies show that the smoke from a bidi has 3 times as much nicotine and carbon monoxide, and 5 times as much tar, as smoke from regular filtered cigarettes.

Studies in India have shown that they pose a greater risk for throat, mouth, and lung cancer.

Smoking Bidis Have Been Proven to Cause...
- Cancer of the tongue
- Cancer of the gums
- Cancer of the floor of the mouth
- Other squamous cell oral cancers
- Cancer of the larynx
- Lung cancer
- High blood pressure
- Coronary heart disease

In 1996 a report done by the Human Rights Watch exposed that children were working at least 10 hours a day, six days a week to make them.

What about Clove Cigarettes?
Cloves (or "Kretek") cigarettes are produced mainly in Indonesia and contain 60%-80% tobacco and 20%-40% ground cloves and other additives. They also contain nicotine, so addiction is possible. When

burned, they release many of the same toxins as cigarettes and herbal cigarettes and come with the same health risks.

What about Herbal Cigarettes?

Let me start by saying everything that's called "herbal" isn't good for you. Herbal cigarettes are basically cigarettes made from herbs such as ginseng, rose petals, licorice root, passion flower, red clover flower, mint, etc. They come in different flavors, which attract young. They don't contain tobacco or nicotine which makes them legal to sell to young people in most states throughout the U.S. Although they don't contain nicotine or tobacco, when burned, they produce many of the same toxins that are found in tobacco products like carbon dioxide, tar and other toxins, so there are still risks to smoking them such as heart problems, lung problems and even cancer.

What about Electronic Cigarettes?

Electronic cigarettes are little "machines" which look similar to a cigarette, but change the nicotine and other ingredients to a vapor that the user inhales. The FDA has tested these devices and has found some E-Cigs contain diethylene glycol, nitrosamines, and nicotine (in difficult to measure amounts). E-Cigs are often marketed to young people who believe they are safer than cigarettes. They have not been approved by the FDA and Canada fully banned them in 2009. **There are no regulations for E-cigs since they aren't tobacco products, so even though they contain nicotine, children can actually buy them.**

There are no healthy alternatives to cigarettes. It's best to take the initiative and quit.

BEER IS GOOD FOR YOUR BONES
BY SUPREME UNDERSTANDING

As we'll explore in the upcoming book, *The Science of Self*, our cultural traditions aren't new. Instead, the unique and diverse elements associated with modern Black culture (even "ghetto" culture) are actually part of an unbroken continuum that spans thousands of years. Dreadlocks, braids, rappers, gold teeth (with jewels in them!), baggy pants, weed smoking, hard beats, graffiti (cave paintings and uncommissioned hieroglyphics), and even dice games all go back thousands of years, finding their origins in ancient Black civilizations. It turns out you can add drinking beer to that list. **An analysis of ancient Nubian bones from North Africa has found that not only were prehistoric Black societies drinking beer, but many of us were using it as a health tonic!**

Anthropologist George Armelagos and his team say the Nubian bones they dug up contained tetracycline, an antibiotic. How? It appears the brew was made from a recipe that produces tetracycline as a byproduct.

Today tetracycline is used to treat ailments ranging from acne flare-ups to urinary-tract infections. But the antibiotic only came into commercial use about 50 years ago. Yet the Nubians were using it consistently over 2,000 years ago, as all the bones examined were infection-free – thanks to the beer.

Charlie Bamforth, a professor of biochemistry and brewing science at the University of California, says that beer has been a staple of the human diet for thousands of years and that the health benefits of beer were well known in ancient times. "There is a whole series of Egyptian pharmacopoeias (medicine books) that talk about things beer can help with," Armelagos says, adding that the Egyptians used beer as a gum-disease treatment and a dressing for wounds.[19] Ain't it amazing how all of our proudest developments have been turned against us? From hip-hop (once the way our griots preserved thousands of years of history by rapping stories over drums) to the dice game (an ancient method for studying mathematical probability and predicting the future), all of our best has been made into our worst. Nowadays, drinking tons of beer is the LEAST likely thing to make you healthy.

But if you just can't live without your beer, you should at least choose the best rather than the worst. What's that mean? First, malt liquor is out. There's a reason why that stuff is marketed directly to the Black community and no one else. It's cheap to buy because it's super-cheap to make, meaning they use the worst of everything. They even use pig intestines in the process, as many of us remember seeing on the *Faces of Death* DVD series back in the day. After that, you've got the popular brands like Budweiser. Mostly garbage. **Since beer and wine ingredients do not have to be labeled, manufacturers dump in a variety of unhealthy chemicals such as preservatives, flavor enhancers, etc.** Natural food stores often sell alcoholic beverages without lots of chemicals... And Certain American beers like Coors and Anchor Steam have no additives. Many German and Austrian beers are also toxin-free. Most microbrews (independent brands) are decent as well.

Once you eliminate the 'el cheapo' beers that are full of garbage, beer actually turns out to be one of the healthiest alcoholic drinks (in moderation of course). Why? Beyond the B Vitamins and other nutrients (magnesium, selenium, potassium, phosphorus, and biotin), it seems it would be the same health benefits as in the beer from ancient Nubia. Modern beer contains between 6 and 57 mg (per liter) of silicon, a nutrient needed for healthy bones. **The most silicon was found in beers with the most hops and malted barley (more common in**

---

[19] It also appears that Egyptians were the first (in recorded history) to discover penicillin, evidenced by the fact that they placed molded bread inside wounds to treat infections.

microbrews than the main brands). Most people get between 20 and 50 mg of silicon per day from their diets. Although beer has a more bioavailable form, it's also found in certain foods, like bananas and brown rice.

But don't get it twisted. Once you get past two servings of alcohol a day (and we're talking wine or beer, not the hard stuff), you fall right into potential health problems. And since you can get all these benefits from food anyway, there's no need to drink if you're not drinking (so don't say we told you to have a drink). **In fact, if you're eating enough fruits and berries, you don't need to drink wine to get that "good for your heart" effect they talk about in France.** And if you do drink wine, make sure you're not drinking more than 2 glasses a day, because that's the point when it goes from being okay to being a straight-up health risk. As always, moderation is key.

Try brewing beer yourself. Look up how it's done and potential risks. Look for healthy brews or foods that contain the same nutrients.

ARE YOU AN ALCOHOLIC?
BY SUPREME UNDERSTANDING

What if you're a drinker, and "moderation" ain't nowhere in your vocabulary? I can relate. In *How to Hustle and Win, Part One,* I describe my battle with alcoholism, which began at age 13.

> I simply couldn't see through the clouds of smoke and the blur in the bottle. I couldn't see that my way of escaping the pain was actually making the pain worse day by day. I looked at weed and liquor like they were my medicine, when they were just making me sicker. But I couldn't see that, because I was never sober long enough to think seriously about my life and what I was doing. Many days, I hated what my addictions were doing to me. I hated how I felt, but I felt that I needed them still. I couldn't get away, even though I told other people I could. In a way, the liquor and the weed were taking control of me.

Fortunately, I was able to reclaim myself...though it certainly didn't happen overnight. I continue:

> It took a few years for me to get rid of all my vices. But I began by quitting hard liquor and weed. It was hard for the first few weeks, but I found other things to do with my free time. I knew I was doing the right thing when I began seeing life so much clearer than I ever had. I was focused. I still got stressed, but I found other ways to handle it. I went from dependent to independent. And once I did that, I began to see that the misery I was trying to escape wasn't just my problem. I started seeing that we're all suffering. And I became determined not to run from that pain, but to fight it head on like a man. So, in a way, I didn't become a man, until I stopped letting other things have power over me, and I took control of myself.

Alcoholism is not easy to shake. But it's not impossible either. Just as you can quit your "addiction" to fast food (the chemicals in fast food ARE literally addictive), you can discipline your mind and body enough to quit any fixation. And if you plan on being worth anything in a screwed-up society that needs us to be strong, productive builders, you can't be "stuck" on anything, especially not a substance that makes you totally unproductive. Hell, even Frederick Douglass saw what alcohol did to his people over a hundred years ago.

> We were induced to drink, I among the rest, and when the holidays were over we all staggered up from our filth and wallowing, took a long breath, and went away to our various fields of work, feeling…glad to go from that which [we thought was] freedom, back again to the arms of slavery… It was about as well to be slave to master, as to be a slave to whisky and rum. When the slave was drunk, the slaveholder had no fear that he would plan an insurrection, or that he would escape to the North. It was the sober, thoughtful slave who was dangerous and needed the vigilance of his master to keep him a slave.

Don't forget that they pacified the Indians the same way. Drinking isn't recreation for many of us. It's escapism. Ironically, that escape eventually becomes a prison.

Are you Trapped?

Take the following informal quiz and see how you fare.

Am I drinking too much? YES, if you are:

> Did You Know?
> A survey by the University of Toronto revealed that more than 70% of recovered problem drinkers said they overcame their alcohol troubles without formal treatment. A similar study in the U.S. by psychiatrist George Vaillant, at Cambridge Hospital reported that of those who either quit or cut back drinking, 75% did so without benefit of treatment or AA. These findings are consistent with published studies on the Smoking Cessation Site (quitsmoking.about.com), which indicate that 80 to 90% of successful quitters give up cigarettes without professional help.

❒ A woman who has more than 7 drinks[20] per week or more than 3 drinks per occasion

❒ A man who has more than 14 drinks per week or more than 4 drinks per occasion

❒ Older than 65 years and having more than 7 drinks* per week or more than 3 drinks per occasion

Am I drinking heavily? YES, if you are:

❒ A woman who has more than 3 drinks every day or 21 drinks per week

❒ A man who has more than 5 drinks every day or 35 drinks per week

Am I taking risks with alcohol? YES, if you:

❒ Drink and drive, operate machinery or mix alcohol with over-the-counter or prescription medicine

❒ Don't tell your doctor or pharmacist that you are a regular drinker

---

[20] One drink = one 12-oz bottle of beer (4.5 percent alcohol) or one 5-oz glass of wine (12.9 percent alcohol) or 1.5 oz of 80-proof distilled spirits.

- Are pregnant or are trying to become pregnant and drink at all (even small amounts of alcohol may hurt an unborn child)
- Drink alcohol while you are looking after children
- Drink alcohol even though you have a medical condition that can be made worse by drinking

Has my drinking become a habit? YES, if you drink regularly to:

- Relax, relieve anxiety or go to sleep
- Be more comfortable in social situations
- Avoid thinking about sad or unpleasant things
- Socialize with other regular drinkers

Is alcohol taking over my life? YES, if you:

- Ever worry about having enough alcohol for an evening or weekend
- Hide alcohol or buy it at different stores so people will not know how much you are drinking
- Switch from one kind of drink to another hoping that this will keep you from drinking too much or getting drunk
- Try to get "extra" drinks at a social event or sneak drinks when others aren't looking

Has drinking alcohol become a problem for me? YES, if you:

- Can't stop drinking once you start
- Have tried to stop drinking for a week or so but only quit for a few days
- Fail to do what you should at work or at home because of drinking
- Feel guilty after drinking
- Find other people make comments to you about your drinking
- Have a drink in the morning to get yourself going after drinking heavily the night before
- Can't remember what happened while you were drinking
- Have hurt someone else as a result of your drinking

Want a more official result? Take the following screening test, which is used to make clinical assessments of alcoholism.

Michigan Alcohol Screening Test (MAST)

This 22-question self-test may help you become aware of your use or abuse of alcohol. The questions refer to the past 12 months. Carefully read each statement and decide whether your answer is yes or no. Please give the best answer or the answer that is right most of the time. This test specifically focuses on alcohol use, and not on the use of other drugs. A separate test called 'DAST' focuses on non-alcohol drugs. Please note: This test will only be scored correctly if you answer each one of the questions. Please check one response for each item.

1. Do you feel you are a normal drinker? ("normal" = drink as much or less than most other people)?
□ Yes □ No

2. Have you ever awakened the morning after some drinking the night before and found that you could not remember a part of the evening?

☐ Yes ☐ No

3. Does any near relative or close friend ever worry or complain about your drinking?

☐ Yes ☐ No

4. Can you stop drinking without difficulty after one or two drinks?

☐ Yes ☐ No

5. Do you ever feel guilty about your drinking?

☐ Yes ☐ No

6. Have you ever attended a meeting of Alcoholics Anonymous?

☐ Yes ☐ No

7. Have you ever gotten into physical fights when drinking?

☐ Yes ☐ No

8. Has drinking ever created problems between you and a near relative or close friend?

☐ Yes ☐ No

9. Has any family member or close friend gone to anyone for help about your drinking?

☐ Yes ☐ No

10. Have you ever lost friends because of your drinking?

☐ Yes ☐ No

11. Have you ever gotten into trouble at work because of drinking?

☐ Yes ☐ No

12. Have you ever lost a job because of drinking?

☐ Yes ☐ No

13. Have you ever neglected your obligations, your family, or your work for two or more days in a row because you were drinking?

☐ Yes ☐ No

14. Do you drink before noon fairly often?

☐ Yes ☐ No

15. Have you ever been told you have liver trouble such as cirrhosis?

☐ Yes ☐ No

16. After heavy drinking have you ever had delirium tremens (D.T.'s), severe shaking, visual or auditory (hearing) hallucinations?

☐ Yes ☐ No

17. Have you ever gone to anyone for help about your drinking?

☐ Yes ☐ No

18. Have you ever been hospitalized because of drinking?

☐ Yes ☐ No

19. Has your drinking ever resulted in your being hospitalized in a psychiatric ward?

☐ Yes ☐ No

20. Have you ever gone to any doctor, social worker, clergyman or mental health clinic for help with any emotional problem in which drinking was part of the problem?

☐ Yes ☐ No

21. Have you been arrested more than once for driving under the influence of alcohol?

☐ Yes ☐ No

22. Have you ever been arrested, even for a few hours, because of other behavior while drinking?

☐ Yes ☐ No

Scoring

This quiz is scored by giving 1 point to each 'yes' answer – except for questions 1 and 4, where 1 point is given to each 'no' answer – and totaling the responses.	Your Score:
Scoring Ranges and Explanation	
0-2	No Apparent Problem: Your answers to this alcohol screening test

	suggest that you are in the normal range and at low risk of problem drinking.
3-5	Early to Middle Problem Drinker: Your answers to this alcohol screening test suggest that you are at risk of problem drinking. The authors of this test would recommend that you contact your doctor about your drinking.
6 or More	Problem Drinker: Your answers to this alcohol screening test suggest that you are at risk of alcoholism. The authors of this test would recommend that you contact your doctor about your drinking.

Families of People with Alcohol Problems

And for the families of those who have a drinking problem, support is available, regardless of whether the drinker is an alcoholic or just a problem drinker. **If someone else's drinking is a problem for you, there are resources available to help you find your own peace. You can check out www.alcoholism.about.com/cs/info2/a/blfam.htm for where to start.**

And we can't wrap this up without talking about our children and drinking. Some parents assume that teenagers will drink alcohol and there is little they can do to prevent it. Now, research does indicate that parenting has little effect on whether kids decide to *try* alcohol. But your attitudes and actions can make a big difference in *how much and how often* your teenager drinks.

Researchers at Brigham Young University surveyed 5,000 adolescents about their drinking habits and their relationship with their parents. They found the kids least like to be heavy drinkers had parents who scored high on accountability (knowing where their kids were and with whom) and warmth. It was no surprise that having so-called "indulgent" parents (low on accountability but high on warmth) nearly tripled the risk of the teen participating in heavy drinking. But what may be surprising to some is that "strict" parents (high on accountability and low on warmth) didn't do much better. In fact, this parenting approach more than doubled their teen's risk of heavy drinking. These results were apparent even when researchers controlled for other influences, such as peer pressure, religious and economic background.

"Authoritative parents tend to be highly demanding and highly responsive," the authors wrote. "They monitor their children closely and provide high levels of support and warmth. Our data suggest that peer encouragement to drink might have less impact when parents are both highly supportive and highly attentive." Lesson!

Powerless

For those who are in fact alcoholics, who actually have the disease, all the willpower and self-resolve in the world, will not help. These drinkers find themselves powerless to stop or control their drinking without help.

Those who have tried repeatedly to curtail or quit drinking and found that they simply cannot, will surely require outside help to do so – either from the treatment center industry or from a self-help program of recovery, such as Alcoholics Anonymous. While Alcoholics Anonymous focuses on religious belief as a strategy towards sobriety, there are other organizations that employ a non-religious approach, such as Secular Organizations for Sobriety, also known as "Save Our Selves," (www.cfiwest.org/sos), LifeRing (www.lifering.org), Smart Recovery (www.smartrecovery.org), or Rational Recovery (www.rational.org).

Get the necessary help. Get in contact with an organization that makes the most sense to you.

IS WEED BAD FOR YOU?

BY TESNIM HASSAN

A Little History

Cannabis is believed to have originated in the mountainous Himalayan region, with it being found originally throughout Central and Southern Asia. The Hindu Vedas may provide the first and earliest reference to the use of the plant as a religious sacrament. It was written about in the Vedas as early as 2000 BCE and eventually began to be called in India, the "food of the gods." Cannabis was used during the Hindu festival, Holi. Among Chinese Shaman cannabis was used as early as 1000 BCE and Buddhists have used cannabis for meditation since 500 BCE. The Chinese also used hemp to make clothing. Ancient German cultures used the herb and associated it with the Norse goddess of love, Freya. Jesus was almost certainly a cannabis user and an early proponent of the medicinal properties of the drug, according to a study of scriptural texts published in 2006. The study suggests that Jesus and his disciples, in a well-established Judaic tradition, used the herb to carry out "miraculous" healings. Sufis have used cannabis for spiritual purposes since the 13th century CE. Arab traders introduced the plant to the African continent, and in Central and Southern Africa, it's referred to as "dagga." Cannabis began to be imported to European countries during the 19th century CE from India and Arabia in the form of hashish.

Presently, many people associate cannabis use with Rastafarians. Interestingly, the smoking of cannabis may have been introduced to the Caribbean by Indian sadhus. These "mystics" arrived, along with many thousands of Indian migrants, to the Caribbean during the 20th century CE. Sadhu "holy men" have smoked cannabis for centuries. Along with their use of cannabis for meditation, sadhus also allow for their hair to grow in long and matted "locs." The term, "ganjah" (or "ganga") is actually taken from its ancient Sanskrit name, Ganjika.

Aside from alcohol, caffeine and tobacco, cannabis is the most commonly used drug worldwide, including the United States. Still, many of us haven't done the knowledge on cannabis's benefits or negative effects.

Cannabinoids or Tetrahydrocannabinol, (THC, for short)

Cannabis has two main strains: *Cannabis sativa* and *Cannabis indica*. *Cannabis sativa* is valued primarily for the strength of its' hemp fibers, which can be used to make clothing, and rope. This strain grows in milder climates. *Cannabis indica* is valued for its' intoxicating effects, growing in hot, dry climates like India, Arabia and Persia. *Cannabis sativa* is found in three forms: as the dried flowers of the plant, as a resin (hashish), or as an extract (hashish oil).

Everyone has cannabinoid receptors in their brain. These are mostly located in the part of the brain which controls the central nervous system. Because we've all got these receptors, researchers figured out that we naturally produce cannabinoids on our own. THC attaches to the cannabinoid receptors in the brain. This causes cannabis users to experience feelings of well-being and relaxation. THC also changes the way that they experience time, and changes the way that they hear, smell and see. The "high" that one experiences can last up to three hours.

On the flip side, THC may also cause users to feel sleepy, anxious, disoriented and hungry. Since cannabis can make users sleepy, it logically follows that their productivity can be reduced. The more time that you spend smoking and sleeping, the less time you have to do other things.

"Strong/Loud/Bomb" weed is weed that has a lot of THC. THC is found in the crystals that you may see covering a cannabis bud, which is the female, flowering part of the cannabis plant. There are a lot of different types of weed, ranging from "high grade" to "reggie" (or regular). A lot of the "high grade" weed is grown indoors in soil, or in water based (hydroponic) set-ups. "High grade" usually has fewer seeds and leaves than lower grades. Less potent strains of weed are grown outdoors, sometimes in Mexico, sometimes in State Parks, sometimes in back yards, (as in "back yard boogie"). Of course, price increases with quality and availability.

Unless you grow your own, you can't be sure about where or how your weed is grown. As with other outdoor crops, weed bushes are often sprayed with pesticides. You inhale these pesticides along with your weed as you smoke. Mold is another concern. Molds attack various plants and typically, a grower won't destroy a profitable crop. Research is limited regarding the effects of smoking molds, but it's well known that inhaling mold in its' original form can cause many forms of lung disease. Also, once your dealer gets his supply, there's no telling what he may do to "hype" it up. I've heard of dealers pissing on the weed and microwaving it. This gives it a stronger odor so that buyers think they're paying for a higher grade. I've also heard people claim that dealers add cocaine or PCP ("wet") to weed before selling it so that they can increase the potency.

So...You Smoke Weed...

Cannabis can be smoked in papers, blunt wraps, fanta leaf, pipes or water pipes, (or bongs). Folks also roll herb in banana leaf or bible papers (no joke). There's even a huge selection of flavored wraps at almost every liquor store. Because cannabis is an organic material, when it's burned, it releases particles that irritate the airway. These particles, along with the particles that are released by whatever the weed's been wrapped in, may cause the smoker to cough violently. The smoke is inhaled, travels through the airway and into the lungs. You've seen people hold their breath until they're damned near blue after inhaling, right? This gives the THC more time to enter the blood stream through the lungs. All the blood in the human body passes through the right side of the heart, then through the lungs, then through the left side of the heart, where it's pumped back through the body. As blood goes through the lungs, it releases carbon dioxide and picks up oxygen. When you're smoking weed, the blood picks up THC, too, and when the blood reaches the brain, this makes the smoker "high."

Because cannabis and tobacco share many of the same smoke particles when they're burned, researchers thought that cannabis could be responsible for causing lung cancer or other lung diseases, like COPD (Chronic Obstructive Pulmonary Disease). Tobacco smokers suffer from lung diseases 20 times more than non-smokers. What about weed smokers? Donald Tashkin, M.D. is an Emeritus Professor of Medicine and the Medical Director of the Pulmonary Function Laboratory at the David Geffen School of Medicine at UCLA. He conducted the largest study, ever, to find out whether cannabis causes lung disease. His 2007 study was funded by the National Institute for Health. **More than 2,200 "heavy [cannabis] smokers" were found to have "no elevated cancer risk." This study also found that THC has an "anti-tumoral effect", meaning that THC causes cells to die before they can become cancerous.** After this study was conducted, Dr. Tashkin was quoted as saying:

> At this point, I'd be in favor of legalization. I wouldn't encourage anybody to smoke any substances, because of the potential for harm. But I don't think it [cannabis] should be stigmatized as an illegal substance.

He has also said, "Tobacco smoking causes far more harm. And in terms of an intoxicant, alcohol causes far more harm." Although no link was found between cannabis smoking and lung disease, it was found that cannabis smoking can cause disease in the airways. Because cannabis smoke contains so many smoke particles, it irritates the airway, causing it to swell. This disease is called Chronic Bronchitis.

Hungry? Thirsty?

When weed is swallowed, it takes the THC longer to reach the brain because the weed has to be digested, and has to move through the intestine's walls, into the blood stream. The "high" experienced from ingesting weed can last up to 24 hours, depending on how slowly a person metabolizes the drug. Some people say that using these methods causes a different kind of high than one feels when smoking cannabis. Of course, when cannabis is swallowed, you don't have to be concerned with injuring the airways or the lungs.

The Legalities

California passed one of the earliest state laws against cannabis use. At the time, many Mexicans laborers were crossing the border with weed. Cannabis was so strongly associated with Mexicans, that the more 'Spanish-sounding' name, "marijuana" came to replace the use of the word, "cannabis" in legislation and common use. There were already tensions about the use of Mexican labor, and the Mexicans' use of weed made for an easy scapegoat. Marijuana was used as an excuse to jail Mexicans. After California criminalized weed, a lot of other border, western and mid-western states did too, including Texas, Nevada, Iowa and Nebraska. By the time of the Great Depression during the 1930s, many other states had outlawed weed with the Federal government not far behind. Harry Aslinger, the first Commissioner of the Federal Bureau of Narcotics, when testifying to Congress in 1937 said:

> There are 100,000 cannabis smokers in the US, and most are Negroes, Hispanics, Filipinos and entertainers. Their Satanic music, jazz and swing, result from cannabis usage. This cannabis causes white women to seek sexual relations with Negroes, entertainers and any others.

He's also been quoted as saying, "Reefer makes darkies think they're as good as white men," and "...the primary reason to outlaw cannabis is its' effect on the degenerate races." It's pretty clear that from early on, cannabis's criminalization was closely tied into racism.

The subject of cannabis's legalization hasn't really been revisited with much honesty or clarity. The U.S. Drug Enforcement Agency classifies cannabis as a Schedule 1 drug, meaning that it's considered by the government to have "a high potential for abuse", "no currently accepted medical use in the United States", "and a lack of accepted safety for use of the drug." Other Schedule 1 drugs include PCP and Meth! If you've had any experience with cannabis use, you probably disagree.

Addiction

The National Institute on Drug Abuse's website says that, "Long-term cannabis abusers trying to quit report irritability, sleeplessness, decreased appetite, anxiety, and drug craving, all of which make it difficult to quit." The paragraph then goes on to say, "These withdrawal symptoms begin within about 1 day following abstinence, peak at 2–3 days, and subside within 1 or 2 weeks following drug cessation." Although cannabis users tend to have a psychological dependency, meaning that they REALLY like smoking weed, there are very limited physical withdrawal symptoms, and these symptoms go away after two weeks.

Medical Cannabis

Recently, many states have passed laws legalizing the use of medicinal cannabis. This contradicts the DEA's classification as a Class 1 drug, or a drug that has "no currently accepted medical use in the United States." THC has many pharmacological benefits, and has fewer "side-effects" than many other commonly prescribed drugs. THC is an analgesic. Analgesics are "pain killers" that don't cause you to lose consciousness. Examples of other analgesics are aspirin, Tylenol, Advil, morphine and oxycodone.

THC has been shown to benefit cancer and AIDs patients. Cancer and AIDs patients often receive medications that cause nausea and vomiting. Currently there are two oral, (or pill), forms of cannabis that are available by prescription in the United States for the treatment of nausea and vomiting associated with chemotherapy treatment. These are dronabinol (Marinol) and nabilone (Cesamet). Some glaucoma patients benefit from medicinal cannabis because it decreases the pressure inside the eye.

Multiple Sclerosis is a disease that affects the central nervous system, (the brain and the spinal cord). Currently, the National Multiple Sclerosis Society is sponsoring studies to find out if THC can reduce the amount of muscle spasms. Sativex, a spray which is used beneath the tongue, has been approved for use in Canada for individuals suffering from MS.

Because THC causes a sense of relaxation and well-being, it's being studied by researchers who are trying to combat Post-Traumatic Stress Disorder in Jerusalem.

The FDA does sometimes facilitate cannabis research, but because of its' illegal status in many other countries, research is really limited. However, as you can see from the examples provided above, THC has the potential to cure MANY diseases and ailments.

The Negatives

It's important to know that there has NEVER been a documented human death from "overdosing" on cannabis. One study has estimated that it would be necessary to smoke 1,500 pounds of cannabis in a fourteen minute period to cause a human death.

Keep in mind, though, that any inhaled irritant can possibly cause airway inflammation. This is especially concerning for people that have Asthma. Asthma is triggered by many different air particles, including smoke. People that have Asthma and who also smoke put themselves at risk of having an "Asthma attack".

Cannabis smoking is often a "communal activity", meaning it's something that people tend to do in groups. Imagine that you receive a blunt from someone that has a cold, or a flu, or worse yet, oral herpes? You've just put yourself at risk for contracting a communicable disease. Not to mention, sharing blunts with strange people also puts you at risk for smoking more than weed. Some people mix their weed with cocaine, mushrooms, PCP, etc.

There has been speculation about links between mental illness and cannabis use. Although it has not been proven that cannabis causes schizophrenia, it's possible that it can quickly trigger their disease. And according to a recent study, smoking marijuana barely affects driving performance. The researchers found there were no differences between the performance of marijuana smokers and those who were given a placebo in a simulator's driving segment or its collision-avoidance scenarios. In fact, the only difference between the two groups was that weed smokers were actually more likely to slow down during certain parts of the simulation.

Recent studies have shown that cannabis use affects male fertility. Apparently cannabis "confuses the movement" of the sperm, making them less likely to reach the female's egg and achieve fertilization. Although this may be true, I personally know MANY Rasta's with large tribes that would argue otherwise. And if it's true that male infertility is caused by cannabis use, many would argue that it should be researched as a contraceptive!

Pregnant Puffers

Make no mistake! If you're pregnant and test positive for THC, you can face very stiff penalties. In many places a positive drug test can result in you losing your baby to the state because you will be deemed an unfit parent. This is based on the claims that cannabis use during pregnancy leads to prematurity, low birth weights, and a decrease in the infant's ability to think because of poor brain development.

In 1994, the American Academy of Pediatrics published an article titled, "Prenatal Cannabis Exposure and Neonatal Outcomes in Jamaica: An Ethnographic Study." This study looked closely at the brain development and behavior of babies whose mothers smoked while they were pregnant. Twenty-four infants whose mothers smoked while pregnant were compared with twenty infants whose mothers didn't smoke while pregnant. The researchers visited with the babies when they were three days old and again when they were three months old. On day three, all of the babies' brain development and behaviors were pretty much the same. Surprisingly, at three months the babies that had been exposed to cannabis in the belly, "had better scores on autonomic stability, quality of alertness, irritability, and self-regulation and were judged to be more rewarding for caregivers."

Keep a detox handy, car freshener if you smoke in the car, a plan if you get arrested, know where to smoke and where not to.

ADDICTED TO CAFFEINE
BY SUPREME UNDERSTANDING

Caffeine is the world's most popular drug. The white, bitter-tasting, crystalline substance was first isolated from coffee in 1820. Both words, caffeine and coffee, are derived from the Arabic word qahweh (pronounced "kahveh" in Turkish). The origins of the words reflect the spread of the beverage into Europe via Arabia and Turkey from northeast Africa, where coffee trees were cultivated in the 6th century. Coffee began to be popular in Europe in the 17th century. By the 18th century, plantations had been established in Indonesia and the West Indies.

Is Caffeine Bad for Me?

A lethal dose of caffeine is about 5000 mg. There haven't been any proven cases of people dying from caffeinated drinks, but people have overdosed (and died) from caffeine pills (like No-Doze). Even an energy drink like Cocaine contains about 280 mg, so it would take an unrealistic amount of drinking to straight up kill you with no other factors involved. But medical studies show that just two cans a day of a popular energy drink increase blood pressure and heart rate in healthy adults. In the book, *Poison With a Capital C*, by Agatha Thrash M.D. and Calvin Thrash M.D., the authors state, "Many people take about 1/10 the lethal dose every day, and even in one cup of coffee lurk substances that seriously alter the body. Women who drink only one cup of coffee per day have almost three times greater risk of getting bladder cancer than abstainers!"

Addicted?

Can you be addicted to caffeine? Absolutely. How else could you explain Brooke Robertson, a 23-year-old New Zealand mother who lost 88 pounds after drinking nothing but Red Bull (from 10 to 14 cans a day) for 8 months? Of course, she also developed severe pain and cramping in her stomach and bowels, anxiety attacks, a heart murmur, and then finally had a small heart attack. It was during her two-week stay in the hospital that she finally managed to wean herself off the energy drink. She said, "I had severe withdrawals – sweating, nausea, shaking. It was an addiction. The doctors stated that."

Of course, Red Bull's PR department claims caffeine is not addictive, but studies suggest otherwise. Regular use of just 350 mg of caffeine a day (about 3-4 cups of coffee or 2 energy drinks) causes "physical dependence" on the drug, another way of saying "addiction." At this point, missing caffeine can cause withdrawal symptoms like constant headaches or feeling irritable and tired. At 650 mg a day (about 8 cups of coffee or 4 energy drinks), you're not just addicted, but now the caffeine is starting to have a toxic effect on your body, leading to symptoms like chronic insomnia, persistent anxiety, depression, and stomach ulcers. Heavy caffeine use also affects your heart, causing irregular heartbeat and possibly raising cholesterol levels.

Recommendations

Lower your caffeine intake to 300 mg or LESS a day. What does that mean in terms of what you're drinking? It depends. A regular cup of coffee has about 108 mg (but a Starbucks cup might have double or triple that). A small can of Red Bull has (surprisingly) 80 mg, but a can of Monster has much more. For the specific caffeine quantities in nearly any beverage you can think of, check out the caffeine database at www.energyfiend.com/the-caffeine-database

Either way, anything more than 300 mg daily and you're dealing with problems. For natural methods to have more energy and stay awake, see "Magic Potions" and "How to Stay Awake Naturally."

Look into things that are more enjoyable, effective, and less costly. Change is great, especially when changing for a better. Embrace it.

ADDICTIVE PERSONALITY DISORDER

We all know about Eminem's battle with drug addiction. He's been on damn near everything, from weed to Ecstasy to mushrooms to Xanax. And on his last album, he claimed he'd gotten himself sober...finally. But he recently admitted that he was worried he was now addicted to – of all things – exercise. He got concerned after he tried to cut down on his fitness regime but instead started making it tougher and tougher for himself every day:

> I'm actually at the point where I think I've got a little obsessive/compulsive about it. Like running on a treadmill – I started doing two miles a day. Then I did four. Then I got up to six, then 10, 15 until at 17, I had to take a break. I couldn't stop.

Nah, Eminem, that's not obsessive compulsive disorder. That's addictive personality disorder.

People with addictive personalities are more likely to "fall victim" and becoming dependent on things like drugs, gambling, overeating, sex, stealing, and even surfing the Internet. For example, while marijuana is not chemically addictive on its own (See "Is Weed Bad For You?"), people who are more prone to addiction will become "hooked" on smoking weed and have a harder time quitting than others. When they do quit, they often find a new addiction to take its place. The following are some of the traits associated with addiction. If you notice 5 or more of them in yourself or someone you care for, it's time to get help.

- ❑ Low Self-Esteem: People with addictive personalities often have low self-esteem and negative self-concepts. They feel better about themselves when they achieve the highs of indulging in their addictions.
- ❑ Stress: Addictions can create stress. People can feel pressured to relieve stress through their addictions, creating a cycle that never ends.
- ❑ Depression and Antisocial Behavior: People with depression or antisocial behavior often turn to addictions to make themselves feel better instead of finding treatment.
- ❑ Self-Destructive Behavior: Addictive people sometimes engage in self-destructive behaviors. This can be in order to further their addiction (like a gambler selling his house), or to end their addiction once and for all (like a drug addict ODing on purpose).
- ❑ Satisfaction: Most people with addictive personality disorder gain pleasure from their addictions. The high feeling they get can come in the form of endorphins being released in the brain. Endorphins are the brain's natural opiate, and the addict will continue his behavior to achieve the good feelings that come with it.
- ❑ Mood Swings: A person will become irritable or defensive when a family member or friend wants to discuss a perceived addictive behavior. In the book, Addiction Recovery Tools, author Robert H. Coombs argues that consequences of addiction affect everything in a user's life. They become suspicious of people's motives and believe they are being persecuted.
- ❑ Guilt: Feelings of guilt are common characteristics in an addict. They feel guilty about lying to friends and family, ashamed of their problem and lack of control, guilty knowing that their money and time was wasted on their addiction and that they didn't spend that time with kids or people who are no longer around. This guilt leads to stress, and the stress leads them back to their addiction.
- ❑ Secrecy: When people are ashamed of being unable to give up their addition, or fearful of losing access to their addiction (by a parent, jail or rehab, for instance) they hide their addiction from friends and family and become more secretive.
- ❑ Loss of Control: Once an individual has lost all ability to stop whatever they're stuck on, people around them may start noticing erratic behaviors like random arguments, missing work or disappearing for days at a time.
- ❑ Isolation: Fearful of being "exposed," many addicts find it easier to avoid those who know them. Isolating themselves is a way for those with an addiction to keep others from knowing about, or challenging, their habits.

Too much of anything is bad. Add new changes to your daily routine.

ARE YOU ADDICTED TO THE INTERNET?
BY SUPREME UNDERSTANDING

If you're prone to addiction, you can be addicted to just about anything. In this digital age, there's a lot of us addicted to technology. We act like we can't live without it. But some of us have got it so bad, that we'll actually die from it. It's even worse though, when someone else dies due to your addiction. Check out this recent piece of news:

> An internet-addicted South Korean couple have been found guilty of letting their baby starve to death as they played online. They spent most of their days at an internet cafe raising a virtual daughter in an online game instead of caring for their baby. The three-month-old died last September. The husband, 41, and the wife, 25, were given two years in prison. The wife's term was suspended because she is pregnant with a second child. Earlier this year, the South Korean government said there were two million "internet addicts" in the nation, which is considered one of the worlds's most technologically wired.

Nicholas Carr's book, *The Shallows: What the Internet is Doing to Our Brains* argues that technology is literally ruining our brains. His book examines how society shifted from an oral tradition to the printed word and then to the Internet, rewiring our brains along the way. Being bombarded with little "bites" of information across dozens of open tabs has us thinking short-term, unable to do the deep thinking of people who normally read books, long essays and articles. The Internet generation finds it harder to focus, concentrate and be introspective and contemplative, Carr writes. "We never engage the deeper, interpretive functions of our brains," he said. Carr suggests that we slow down, turn off the computer and practice the skills of contemplation, introspection and reflection. "It is pretty clear from the brain science that if you don't exercise particular cognitive skills, you are going to lose them," he said. "If you are constantly distracted, you are not going to think in the same way that you would think if you paid attention." Not only are we losing the ability to think critically and meaningfully, we're also getting way too much of our "information" from unreliable sources. Any self-proclaimed "expert" can string together a bunch of false claims on YouTube, add some flashy pictures and a beat…and the next thing you know, half of Facebook will swear it's true. That's a problem. Dumb AND dumber.

And this kind of addiction isn't limited to the Internet.[21] A new study from the International Center for Media & the

> **Did You Know?**
> In 2007, a Nevada couple was charged with child neglect after their kids became malnourished while they played online video games as well.

---

[21] The TV viewing habits for millions of Americans also fits the criteria for substance abuse, with numerous dependency symptoms, including the inability to control viewing, using TV as a sedative, feeling a lack of control while watching, angry feelings about watching too much, and being upset when unable to watch.

Public Agenda found that most college students are functionally unable to manage without digital media (like iPods, laptops, video games, BlackBerrys, etc.). Stripped of technology for only 24 hours, the students described their feelings in literally the same terms associated with drug and alcohol addictions: *In withdrawal, Frantically craving, Very anxious, Extremely antsy, Miserable, Jittery, Crazy.* They also reported that they felt disconnected from the world without social media, meaning they were growing more and more unable to relate to people in real life! So many of us are unable to live when not "plugged in," but what are we plugged into? Try a 24 hour fast for yourself and see how you do. Better yet, take the following test and see if you fit the description for an addict.

Internet Addiction Test

Most psychologists don't consider excessive internet use to qualify as a bona "real addiction," but this 20-question self-test may help you to identify areas of your life which are being impacted by excessive internet use. To take the questionnaire, please circle the selection which best reflects how each statement applies to you. Be sure to base your answers only on the time you spend online for non-academic and non-job related purposes. Please note: This test will only be scored correctly if you answer each one of the questions.

Limit how many sites you can visit in a day, how long you can be online, and time spent thinking about something internet related.

> **Did You Know?**
> A recent study found that young men who were video game addicts had the most self-reported aggressive behavior, as well as different patterns of brain activity than young males who weren't obsessive gamers. "Changes in aggressive behavior do not mean someone will become violent and...shoot other people. The point is that our mental skills will be reduced. The effect of video games is the same as if we're watching too much television," says psychiatrist Donald Hilty, MD.

1. How often do you find that you stay online longer than you intended?

    A. Rarely   D. Often
    B. Occasionally E. Always
    C. Frequently   F. Does Not Apply

2. How often do you neglect household chores to spend more time online?

    A. Rarely   D. Often
    B. Occasionally E. Always
    C. Frequently   F. Does Not Apply

3. How often do you prefer the excitement of the internet to intimacy with your partner?

    A. Rarely   D. Often

4. How often do you form new relationships with fellow online users?

    A. Rarely   D. Often
    B. Occasionally E. Always
    C. Frequently   F. Does Not Apply

5. How often do others in your life complain to you about the amount of time you spend online?

    A. Rarely   D. Often
    B. Occasionally E. Always
    C. Frequently   F. Does Not Apply

B. Occasionally E. Always
C. Frequency   F. Does Not Apply

6. How often do your grades or school work suffer because of the amount of time you spend online?

A. Rarely   D. Often
B. Occasionally   E. Always
C. Frequently   F. Does Not Apply

7. How often do you check your email before something else that you need to do?

A. Rarely   D. Often
B. Occasionally   E. Always
C. Frequently   F. Does Not Apply

8. How often does your job performance or productivity suffer because of the internet?

A. Rarely   D. Often
B. Occasionally   E. Always
C. Frequently   F. Does Not Apply

9. How often do you become defensive or secretive when anyone asks you what you do online?

A. Rarely   D. Often
B. Occasionally   E. Always
C. Frequently   F. Does Not Apply

10. How often do you block out disturbing thoughts about your life with soothing thoughts of the internet?

A. Rarely   D. Often
B. Occasionally   E. Always
C. Frequently   F. Does Not Apply

11. How often do you find yourself anticipating when you will go online again?

A. Rarely   D. Often
B. Occasionally   E. Always
C. Frequently   F. Does Not Apply

12. How often do you fear that life without the internet would be boring, empty, and joyless?

A. Rarely   D. Often
B. Occasionally   E. Always
C. Frequently   F. Does Not Apply

13. How often do you snap, yell, or act annoyed if someone bothers you while you are online?

A. Rarely   D. Often
B. Occasionally   E. Always
C. Frequently   F. Does Not Apply

14. How often do you lose sleep due to late-night log-ins?

A. Rarely   D. Often
B. Occasionally   E. Always
C. Frequently   F. Does Not Apply

15. How often do you feel preoccupied with the Internet when offline, or fantasize about being online?

A. Rarely   D. Often
B. Occasionally   E. Always
C. Frequently   F. Does Not Apply

16. How often do you find yourself saying "just a few more minutes" when online?

A. Rarely   D. Often
B. Occasionally   E. Always
C. Frequently   F. Does Not Apply

17. How often do you try to cut down the amount of time you spend online and fail?

A. Rarely   D. Often
B. Occasionally   E. Always
C. Frequently   F. Does Not Apply

18. How often do you try to hide how long you've been online?

A. Rarely   D. Often
B. Occasionally   E. Always
C. Frequently   F. Does Not Apply

19. How often do you choose to spend more time online over going out with others?

A. Rarely   D. Often
B. Occasionally   E. Always
C. Frequently   F. Does Not Apply

20. How often do you feel depressed, moody, or nervous when you are offline, which goes away once you are back online?

A. Rarely   D. Often | C. Frequently   F. Does Not Apply
B. Occasionally E. Always |

Scoring

Scoring Key	Items Marked		Points
A. Rarely: 1 point	A: ___	x 1 =	
B. Occasionally: 2 points	B: ___	x 2 =	
C. Frequently: 3 points	C: ___	x 3 =	
D. Often: 4 points	D: ___	x 4 =	
E. Always: 5 points	E: ___	x 5 =	
F. Does Not Apply: 0 points	F: ___	x 0 =	
TOTAL SCORE =			
Generally speaking, the higher your score, the more impact internet usage may be having on your life. Very high scores (above 80) indicate that internet usage is causing significant problems in your life, and you may benefit from evaluating the impact of the internet on your life and addressing the problems directly caused by your internet usage.			
Scoring Ranges and Explanation			
0 to 19	Below Average Range		
20 to 49	Average Range		
50 to 79	Above Average		
80 to 100	Significantly Above Average		
The Internet Addiction Test is adapted from Dr. Kimberley S. Young's book, *Caught in the Net*.			

7. GET YOUR MIND RIGHT

MENTAL HEALTH

MENTAL WELLNESS IN THE HOOD
BY ROBERT L. WILLIAMS, CPS

*"One out of 4 people in this country is mentally imbalanced.
Think of your 3 closest friends – if they seem okay, then you're the one." – Ann Landers*

There's been a silent situation in the inner city that has crushed many families over the years. This phenomenon exists within the lives of many men, women and children in hoods all over the world. It causes some people to believe they can fly and jump off buildings. It has caused frightened mothers to murder their babies. It made others depressed to the point that they've completely given up on life. And still others were left to believe they were the toughest gangster alive; only to approach the wrong person with such aggression and become the toughest gangster no longer alive. These are all reflections of the same phenomenon. This phenomenon is commonly called Mental Illness. There are many variations: Bi-polar Disorder, Manic Depression, Post Traumatic Stress Disorder, Postpartum Depression, Schizophrenia, ADHD – the list goes on. These titles are considered to be psychiatric diagnoses which can be clinically and/or holistically treated. Let's take a closer look at some of these issues and some relative solutions.

Silent No More

Many people have symptoms of mental illnesses but are never diagnosed. In some cases that's good because quite often people are misdiagnosed and left to believe the diagnosis is accurate. Not knowing what to do they resort to psychiatric medicine and become a lab rat of sorts as they are prescribed numerous types of medication until they find what they think works best for them. On the other hand there are those who strongly exhibit mental health symptoms that go unaddressed. When this occurs it's not rare for a person to be laughed at and ridiculed in the street, you know like the lady in every hood that dresses ghetto couture and talks to herself or cusses people out for no good reason, which is a symptom of schizophrenia. Another common symptom is outbursts of laughter without an apparent reason.

Another commonly unaddressed mental health situation is the person in everyone's family doesn't seem to catch on to the flow of life for some reason. He or she sits at home every day watching television or playing video games. They don't have the motivation to get a job or attend school. This person doesn't say anything when you speak to them and seems to have a difficult time maintaining a complete thought. This person can be suffering from Clinical Depression.

There are many unaddressed mental health situations in the hood, like the girl grew up in a single parent home; mom abuses drugs and is verbally and physically abusive towards her. The men her mom dates are also abusive and in many cases sexually abusive. The state found out about the abuse of the young girl thus she is placed in foster care only to experience further abuse. The young girl runs away from her foster parents to the streets in search of love and is discovered by a pimp who convinces her to prostitute and further abuses her. After being beaten and forced to sleep in closets, she escapes from the pimp and attempts to live a "normal life" but she can't seem to have peace of mind, she has regular nightmares of her past and she seems to feel as if being abused is the norm. She is angry or agitated most of the time and she finally becomes abusive towards herself and others including violent outbursts to some people in her circle. It sounds like she may have Post Traumatic Stress Syndrome, and if left untreated, this vicious cycle will wreck havoc in her life.

> Did You Know?
> Blacks are over-represented in all the "high-need" populations that are particularly "at risk" for mental illnesses:
> A. People who are homeless. While representing only 12% of the U.S. population, Blacks make up about 40% of the homeless population.
> B. People who are incarcerated (See "Prison is Bad for Your Health").
> C. Children in foster care and the child welfare system. Black children and youth constitute about 45% of children in public foster care and more than half of all children waiting to be adopted.
> D. People exposed to violence. Blacks of all ages are more likely to be victims of serious violent crime than are whites. One study reported that over 25% of Black youth exposed to violence met diagnostic criteria for post-traumatic stress disorder (PTSD). Among Vietnam War veterans, 21% of Black veterans, compared to 14% of white veterans, suffer from PTSD, apparently because of the greater exposure of Blacks to war-zone trauma.

Holistic Thoughts

All health-related diagnoses are essentially holistic situations and should be resolved in a holistic manner. Holistic means the whole person; mentally, physically, emotionally, and spiritually. All health related issues/dis-eases are a result of chemical imbalances in the body. As far as mental health is concerned it's all too common for someone with a mental health diagnosis and people who advocate for them to focus only on their mental and emotional stability. Although most mental health diagnosis surface as a result of some sort of trauma in one's life, one of the main culprits is improper physical consumption.

High Priest Kwatamani writes in his book *Raw and Living Foods: The First Divine Act and Requirement of a Holistic Living Way of Life*, "A diet of dead and devitalized foods not only perpetuates mental, physical, and spiritual illnesses for the consumer, but has an even more devastating impact on that individual's children."

Many studies suggest that men diagnosed with ADHD often have children with the same diagnoses. Is it merely genetic or is it passed down as a result of consumption and mannerism?

In *124 Ways Sugar Ruins Your Health*, Nancy Appleton, PhD states that sugar can cause depression and can worsen the symptoms of children with ADHD. Meanwhile, Amanda Gardner of *Health Day* magazine reports:

> Exposure to high levels of organophosphate pesticides, commonly found on berries, celery and other produce, could raise the odds for attention-deficit/hyperactivity disorder (ADHD) in children.

The vast amount of chemicals used to mass produce meats and poultry also has an effect on our chemical response in the body. The improper digestion of meats alone causes a chemical imbalance in the body that may result in mental health diagnosis. Our bodies were not constructed to digest animal flesh therefore most meat eaters store undigested meat in the colon and the spoilage of this animal flesh creates chemical imbalances that leads to mental and physical disease.

> **Did You Know?**
> The psychiatric drug Prozac has a similar effect as cocaine does to the body. As a result of drug abuse there have been cases of people who were improperly diagnosed as being Bi-polar. False Bi-polar diagnoses have caused many people to believe they needed treatment when what they really needed was to stop their abuse of drugs - including marijuana and alcohol.

Jay Basemeyer, Stress Management Certified Trainer comments that for people with Bi-polar Disorder, "the effects of regular caffeine consumption in coffee, teas, soft drinks or chocolate can linger in the body for days or weeks and then add fuel to the fire of the manic high! If not full blown mania, then even a nervous restless night's sleep can be relieved by reducing or eliminating caffeine from the diet."

Most mental and physical imbalances also embody emotional imbalances. Feelings of sadness, hopelessness, anxiety, stress, paranoia, and general fear are reduced when we have proper nutrients in our bodies. We can also alter our emotions by avoiding watching too much TV or movies that trigger negative emotions such as horror movies, gangster movies, or any other depressing films. We can also avoid music with a depressing message as well such as rap that degrades woman or glorifies crime. We can also avoid gossip and counterproductive conversations.

Be Open-Minded for Your Healing
As mental health pertains to spiritual wellness I suggest you do what works for you as sincerely as you can but be careful to "avoid dogma". In other words, if you practice a religion or culture and not doing your best can result in feelings of guilt, stress, and many other unhealthy feelings.

Avoiding dogma and realizing that true spirituality is the connection one has with a higher being within (higher self/higher power) we can be open-minded to all sorts of suggestions from the divinity that breathes through us. Regular meditation, yoga, and affirmations such as "I am healing," "I am not mentally ill; I'm mentally able," and "I can do it" can make a great mental and spiritual difference in the life of someone with a mental health diagnosis.

It is important that if you feel as though you may be severely depressed or in any other mental health crisis, don't take it for granted. Talk to someone you trust and take action for your own healing. I was once diagnosed as Bi-polar. Through Holistic Living the symptoms were reversed and the doctor who I was seeing at the time said there was no way I was Bi-polar. I haven't taken any medication in four years to the date of this writing. Get a doctor who you feel comfortable with, one who doesn't give you a prescription and send you on your way after three minutes of each visit. Keep the Doctor around in case you stumble but don't wait for the doctor to tell you that you can overcome, KNOW IT IN YOUR HEART! Then take all the necessary actions to prove it to yourself and let the doctor know what YOU are doing for yourself.

Know when to get help and when to be the help. Read the following articles and come up with a way to help yourself and/or community.

MENTAL HEALTH IN THE HISPANIC COMMUNITY
BY DENIZ LOPEZ

Among Latinos with a mental disorder, less than 1 in 11 ever gets diagnosed. Depression and anxiety go unaddressed and sometimes only expressed by the sufferer as nervousness, fatigue, restlessness, or having some trouble remembering and concentrating on things. **Latino youth, since before 1999, have shown to experience more anxiety-related and delinquency behaviors than do White youth.** The statistics all read that Latinos are the least likely to go to the doctor when suffering mental illness. How can this be happening? Don't we pay attention and want to help when people don't seem right? The truth is, we may be involved and paying attention, yet the factors that create and magnify mental illness have been accepted as natural states of being for Latinos. To expand, here is a breakdown of things that affect the mental health of Latinos:

Discrimination/Criminalization – Unless you've really been keeping yourself busy and not paying attention to the world around you, you've seen what the media describes as a drug cartel takeover along the border. You've watched Gangland on the History Channel, and seen how Arizona has become so fearful of the 'browning of America' that it's passed a law that allows police to racially profile, harass, and act as immigration officers in that state (SB 1070). If you look at all these things in connection, you see how the Latino is the new face to fear in America, characterized as delinquents, illegals, gangsters, drug addicts, and a main reason for the failing U.S. economy.

Poverty/Unemployment – While Latinos (documented and not) are often looked upon as the scapegoat for bad economic times, many Latinos are under constant pressure to stay above poverty – often living paycheck to paycheck and having to take on several jobs in order to keep food on the table...or keep up with the Joneses – Sound familiar? Additionally, poverty rates among Latinos have averaged about 22% since 2000, with rates increasing most rapidly for undocumented Latinos.

Access to Mental Healthcare – Lack of knowledge of where to seek treatment, lack of proximity to treatment centers, lack of insurance, transportation problems, and a lack of mental health workers who are culturally and linguistically trained to work with Latinos, are all barriers to seeking out and receiving treatment for mental illness. Studies have shown that only 24% of Latinos with depression and anxiety received appropriate care and both Latinos and Blacks have a high rate of being misdiagnosed with schizophrenia when seeking help.

A Disconnection from our Roots – Like the average Black person, who has little knowledge of what their origins are prior to the enslavement of their ancestors, as generations pass, Latinos have become more and more disconnected with their ancestry. Through slavery, assimilation, and acculturation, what it means to be Latino/Hispanic (so-called) has come to be represented by remnants, mockery, and novelty. You can hate a Mexican, but love to eat tacos. You can be all for 287G and down with the Minutemen, but throw parties yearly for Cinco de Mayo. The tradition that has survived through our abuelas y abuelos comes in constant conflict with what we are expected to believe in as Latinos in America.

Learn to explain your understanding of mental disorders in Spanish and English. Look into the research published by predominant "Spanish-speaking" countries on mental disorders, and compare it to what is known in the West.

SCHIZOPHRENIA AND MULTIPLE PERSONALITY DISORDER
GETTING PAST "THEY'RE JUST CRAZY"
BY SUPREME UNDERSTANDING AND LANDRIA CARR

I was watching this film, *Besouro*, which is based on the life of legendary Capoeira "hero" Besouro. The film features some excellent themes of Black resistance to European rule in Brazil, but it also highlights African spiritual traditions as they emerged in the West. What I like about the film is that it shows the African gods as being timeless principles found in both our psyche and genetic memory. This was a welcome break from the European version that made god, even indigenous gods, appear to be something totally outside of self, independent entities that do their own thing like the Greek gods on Mount Olympus.

Returning to the film, there's a scene where the god Exu – who demands respect and reverence for the balance of positive and negative in life – is confronting one of the brothers, who has just had his leg broken by the Europeans. The brother is so angry and hurt that he gets into an angry clash with Exu – who almost no one else can see. So it appears the brother has gone crazy, talking and arguing with himself, swinging a knife at the air. This made me think about African and indigenous conceptions of mental illness, versus the European constructs. **A Western psychologist would diagnose this brother as schizophrenic, and would begin him on a heavy dose of medication meant to keep him in check** (since there's no cure for schizophrenia). **A traditional African healer would say that he is talking to the spirits or the orishas or having some spiritual conflict in his head.**

What's interesting is that both experts would simply be using their culture's language and terminology to make the same diagnosis (psychological imbalance), except only an indigenous healer would attempt to get to the root of the problem and fix whatever went wrong. While we can talk trash on "witch doctors" and "medicine men," in "primitive societies," the truth is that these same societies have much less mental illness, and they deal with the issues fairly effectively, when compared to the real "witch doctors"[22] and "medicine men" here in the West, who simply dose out drugs that NEVER fix the problem, and only create drug dependency and semi-zombies.

So what IS Schizophrenia? First, let's talk about what Schizophrenia is NOT. It's NOT the same as *Dissociative Identity Disorder (DID)* – also known as Multiple Personality Disorder (MPD) – They are two completely *different* disorders. Dissociative Identity Disorder is a rare disorder in which a person exhibits two or more distinct and alternating personalities. This disorder is usually brought on by a really, REALLY horrible and traumatic event that has happened to someone. This is common with people who've been abused.

One famous example is Shirley Ardell Mason, best known as "Sybil," a young woman who had a documented *sixteen* personalities raging inside of

---

[22] In fact, most translations of Revelation 18:23 now read "For your merchants were the important people of the world, and all the nations were deceived by your witchcraft." But the original Greek used the word "Pharmacia," which doesn't mean witchcraft or sorcery, but actually means mind-altering drugs. However, while we're on the subject of Revelation, it's also important to note that several scholars have described the role of European Christianity (especially its devil concept) in promoting mental illness among indigenous people.

her. This disorder was brought on by the sexual, emotional, and physical abuse brought on by her schizophrenic mother, Martha Alice "Mattie" Hageman. There was a novel and two films created—each titled *Sybil*—telling the story of Shirley. Now, imagine the brain as a pie. Sybil's "pie" was whole up until her mother started doing these horrible things to her. As Sybil grew up, still subjected to this abuse, her "pie" was cut into *slices*, each slice representing a personality. The pie was cut to protect Sybil from dealing with all that pain alone and all at once. She could basically retreat into her other "minds."

While plenty of rappers use "alter egos" in their rap careers, sometimes taking on completely different personas in their songs, it's not just entertainment. In fact, some individuals in the hood can be so traumatized by the stress of their everyday lives (See "PTSD) that they unknowingly begin creating new personalities, who they hold responsible for their failures and wrongdoing. This can begin  inauspiciously enough, but can grow into a real problem. In one extreme example, a 43-year-old Jersey City man named Dwayne Wilson recently pleaded guilty to killing his sister, niece and nephew in a horrific attack that he said he watched his other personality, Kiko, carry out.

Now, let's get back to Schizophrenia. Schizophrenia is defined as a group of severe disorders characterized by disorganized and delusional thinking, disturbed perceptions, and inappropriate emotions and actions. The three classifications of Schizophrenia are Classical, Catatonic, and *paranoid*. Classical (or disorganized schizophrenia) is mild, but still sucks to have; it's characterized by lack of emotion and disorganized speech. Catatonic is physical as it reduces or increases movement of an individual. The movie *A Beautiful Mind* is based on the life of a Nobel Economist, John Forbes Nash, Jr. who suffers from Paranoid Schizophrenia…which so happens to be the worst of the three classifications of schizophrenia.

> "I'm hearin voices in my head, think I'm schizophrenic/ Swear they sayin 'let's get it' from another planet."
> — Young Jeezy, "Lose My Mind"

So, let's take it back to the "pie" for a second. Remember when I said that the "pie" of someone suffering from DID is split into slices? Well, the pie of a schizophrenic isn't separated into slices; the pie's still whole, but it's a *bad* pie. DID pie is sliced, but still good and edible; a Schizophrenic pie is whole, but *bad,* baked with a whole bunch of evil, hallucinogenic ingredients. At any rate, the Schizophrenic pie is so bad—despite it being whole–that the sufferer feels as though the pie is subject to crumbling. Get it?

Now, the worst–and ironically, most common–type is paranoid schizophrenia. Paranoid schizophrenia is when you hear voices telling you to do harmful things to yourself and/or other people; you'll also suffer sensory delusions, in which you either see things in a way they aren't meant to be perceived, or just see stuff that just ISN'T there at all.

Both DID and Schizophrenia are serious mental inflictions, but Schizophrenia is different, and much worse. It's usually diagnosed between the ages of 18 and 24. DID is curable; Schizophrenia is *treatable*. There's a DIFFERENCE.

And even though some people believe a "crazy" person can't get any "worse" by smoking weed, doing a line, popping pills, etc…they couldn't be more wrong. Just think: If these drugs screw with your mind by themselves, can you IMAGINE what they'll do to you if you already see ten-foot tall killer clowns with machetes and hear random voices telling you to fling yourself off of the nearest bridge?

Studies show that Black Americans tend to feel more *denounced* when diagnosed with one of these disorders…or with any other form of mental illness for that matter. We already have one strike against us (our skin color) when it comes to what it takes to succeed in society, such as getting a job, and African-American *women* have two. A mental disorder just adds to the difficulty. As a result, you probably haven't heard of many "famous" examples of people of color with serious mental illnesses like these…unless you count Jamie Foxx's portrayal in *The Soloist* or Samuel Jackson in *The Caveman's Valentine*.

Then again, there is **Thelonious Monk**, the American jazz legend. He died at age 65 in 1982, leaving a legacy of brilliant music in his wake. He did it all while wrapped tightly in the clutches of Paranoid schizophrenia AND manic depression, both of which were "missed" by his psychiatrist at the time. So there's one "famous" example for you. But unfortunately, most other people of color who develop these disorders (and go untreated) end up homeless (as in the two films named above), in prison, or in a public mental health facility.

This is why early diagnosis is critical. That man or woman you see living on the street talking crazy" is someone's family member. But we rarely figure these things out early enough to secure adequate treatment…and before long, "Uncle Jimmy" is getting kicked out of the house because his "crazy behavior" has gotten out of control. Now let's be clear: Most people suffering from DID or Schizophrenia are HARMLESS. At least in terms of violence. But these disorders can certainly wreck lives in other ways…so, again, early diagnosis is critical.

A Screening Test for Dissociative Identity Disorder

Want to know if you fit the description? The following 28-question self-test was developed as a screening test for Dissociative Identity Disorder, formerly known as Multiple Personality Disorder. To answer the questions, please determine how much the experience described in the question applies to you. Circle the percentage of the time you have the experience. The left of the scale, labeled 'NEVER', corresponds to 0% of the time, while the right of the scale, labeled 'ALWAYS', corresponds to 100% of the time; the range covers 0% to 100% in 10% increments. It is important, however, that your answers show how often these experiences happen to you when you are not under the influence of alcohol or drugs.

Please note: This test will only be scored correctly if you answer each one of the questions.

	NEVER	10%	20%	30%	40%	50%	60%	70%	80%	90%	ALWAYS
1. Some people have the experience of driving or riding in a car, bus or subway and suddenly realizing they don't remember what happened during all or part of the trip.	0%	10%	20%	30%	40%	50%	60%	70%	80%	90%	100%
2. Some people find that sometimes they're listening to someone talk and suddenly realize they didn't hear part or all of what was said.	0%	10%	20%	30%	40%	50%	60%	70%	80%	90%	100%
3. Some people have experiences of finding themselves in a place and having no idea how they got there.	0%	10%	20%	30%	40%	50%	60%	70%	80%	90%	100%
4. Some people have the experience of finding themselves dressed in clothes they don't remember putting on.	0%	10%	20%	30%	40%	50%	60%	70%	80%	90%	100%
5. Some people have the experience of finding new things among their belongings they don't remember buying.	0%	10%	20%	30%	40%	50%	60%	70%	80%	90%	100%
6. Some people sometimes find that they're approached by people that they don't know who call them by another name or insist that they have met them before.	0%	10%	20%	30%	40%	50%	60%	70%	80%	90%	100%
7. Some people have experiences of feeling as though they're standing next to themselves or watching themselves do something as if they're looking at another person.	0%	10%	20%	30%	40%	50%	60%	70%	80%	90%	100%
8. Some people are told that they sometimes do not recognize friends or family members.	0%	10%	20%	30%	40%	50%	60%	70%	80%	90%	100
9. Some people find they have no memory for some important events in their lives (for example, a wedding or graduation).	0%	10%	20%	30%	40%	50%	60%	70%	80%	90%	100%

	0%	10%	20%	30%	40%	50%	60%	70%	80%	90%	100%
10. Some people have experiences of being accused of lying when they do not think that they have lied.	0%	10%	20%	30%	40%	50%	60%	70%	80%	90%	100%
11. Some people have experiences of looking in a mirror and not recognizing themselves.	0%	10%	20%	30%	40%	50%	60%	70%	80%	90%	100
12. Some people have experiences of feeling that other people, objects, and the world around them are not real.	0%	10%	20%	30%	40%	50%	60%	70%	80%	90%	100%
13. Some people have experiences of feeling their body does not seem to belong to them.	0%	10%	20%	30%	40%	50%	60%	70%	80%	90%	100
14. Some people have the experience of sometimes remembering a past event so vividly they feel as if they're reliving that event.	0%	10%	20%	30%	40%	50%	60%	70%	80%	90%	100%
15. Some people have experiences of not being sure whether what they remember really happened or if they just dreamed them.	0%	10%	20%	30%	40%	50%	60%	70%	80%	90%	100%
16. Some people have experiences of being in a familiar place but finding it strange and unfamiliar.	0%	10%	20%	30%	40%	50%	60%	70%	80%	90%	100%
17. Some people find that when they're watching tv or a movie they become so absorbed in the story that they're unaware of other events happening around them.	0%	10%	20%	30%	40%	50%	60%	70%	80%	90%	100%
18. Some people find that they become so involved in a fantasy or daydream that it feels as though it were really happening to them.	0%	10%	20%	30%	40%	50%	60%	70%	80%	90%	100%
19. Some people find that they sometimes are able to ignore pain.	0%	10%	20%	30%	40%	50%	60%	70%	80%	90%	100
20. Some people find that they sometimes sit staring off into space, thinking of nothing, and are not aware of the passage of time.	0%	10%	20%	30%	40%	50%	60%	70%	80%	90%	100%
21. Some people sometimes find that when they are alone they talk out loud to themselves.	0%	10%	20%	30%	40%	50%	60%	70%	80%	90%	100%
22. Some people find that in one situation they may act so differently compared with another situation that they feel almost as if they were two different people.	0%	10%	20%	30%	40%	50%	60%	70%	80%	90%	100%
23. Some people sometimes find that in certain situations they're able to do things with amazing ease and spontaneity that would usually be difficult for them (for example, sports, work, social situations, etc.).	0%	10%	20%	30%	40%	50%	60%	70%	80%	90%	100%
24. Some people sometimes find they cannot remember whether they've done something or just thought about doing it (for example, not knowing whether they've just mailed a letter or just thought about mailing it).	0%	10%	20%	30%	40%	50%	60%	70%	80%	90%	100%

	0%	10%	20%	30%	40%	50%	60%	70%	80%	90%	100
25. Some people find evidence that they have done things that they do not remember doing.											
26. Some people sometimes find writings, drawings, or notes among their belongings that they must have done but can't recall doing.											
27. Some people sometimes find that they hear voices inside their head that tell them to do things or comment on things they're doing.											
28. Some people sometimes feel as if they are looking at the world through a fog so that people and objects appear far away or unclear.											
TOTAL NUMBER CIRCLED (for each %)											

Scoring

This screening test for Dissociative Identity Disorder is scored by totaling the percentage answered for each question (from 0% to 100%) and then dividing by 28: this should yield a score in the range of 0 to 100. If not, you did the math wrong.

Number Circled for 0%:		x 0 =	
Number Circled for 10%:		x 10 =	
Number Circled for 20%:		x 20 =	
Number Circled for 30%:		x 30 =	
Number Circled for 40%:		x 40 =	
Number Circled for 50%:		x 50 =	
Number Circled for 60%:		x 60 =	
Number Circled for 70%:		x 70 =	
Number Circled for 80%:		x 80 =	
Number Circled for 90%:		x 90 =	
Number Circled for 100%:		x 10 =	
	TOTAL		
DES SCORE	Total divided by 28		

Generally speaking, the higher the DES score, the more likely it is that the person has DID.

The figure shown below plots the distribution of DES scores (horizontal scale) in the general population. Finding your score in this chart lets you know where you fall in comparison with most people. Being closer to the extreme end can be a sign you have a problem. But the DES is not a diagnostic instrument. It is a screening instrument. High scores on the DES do not prove that a person has a dissociative disorder; they only suggest that clinical assessment for DID is a good idea. Studies have found that only 17% of people scoring above 30 on the DES actually had DID. And people

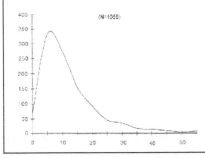
(N=1065)

experiencing DID can also have low scores, so a low score does not rule out DID. The average DES score for a person who actually has DID is in the 40s, but roughly 15% of clinically diagnosed DID patients scored 20 or below on the DES. Note: This test is meant to be used as a starting point, not as a diagnosis tool. This score is not intended as a mental disorder diagnosis, or as any type of healthcare recommendation.

"Our Survey Says...!"

So, you've screened yourself for Dissociative Identity Disorder and you just may have it! What to do, what to do?!

First off: DON'T PANIC! Trust me, it could be a LOT worse. Second, buckle down some funds and hire a good therapist. Psychiatry is rooted in mental illness and disorders. Contrary to popular belief, psychiatry and psychology are two *different* practices; what you want for a DID treatment plan is a *psychiatrist*.

Don't have the funds? Find someone trustworthy and willing to administer some tough love for free. The first step is tracing back your deepest darkest memories to what traumatic event caused your pie to split in the first place.

Once you've confronted that fear and accepted it as a stitch in your past, you can face your other selves and perhaps even embrace them in such a way that they become parts of you again rather than different versions of yourself. Just like Sybil, with the help of her therapist.

Make sure you don't go without help. Look up the type of treatments professionals would use and try to get them. You if can afford it, come up with alternatives to every single part of their treatment plans.

PERSONALITY DISORDERS
BY SUPREME UNDERSTANDING AND EM'MAYA JEWEL

A personality disorder is defined as "a severe disturbance in the character or psychological constitution and behavioral tendencies of an individual." Basically, this means you're thinking ain't right. Now, of course you could argue that this oppressive, often barbaric, society is not a fair judge of who is thinking right or wrong, and you're right...to some extent. But personality disorders – whether they are caused by living in foul conditions or some other factor – are a very real part of our urban landscape. Just think about yourself and the people you know...chances are good that there's some undiagnosed problems going on. I'm not saying they (or you) need psychiatric treatment, but if someone has a psychological problem that's keeping them from functioning at the optimum level, then that person needs to treat that problem. And there's plenty of ways to treat and resolve those issues. But it all begins with awareness and acceptance. Sure, we know that most of these disorders are byproducts of being besieged, put in bondage, beaten, brainwashed, and bullied into believing this corrupt way of life is the best thing ever...but that doesn't change the fact that some of us are just "out there" or "out of order" nowadays. Black and Latino communities are home to the most psychological OVERdiagnoses and UNDERdiagnoses...meaning we get tons of labels like ADHD, ODD, and other "disorders" to explain away our natural disconnect with this European society. For more on that, see my essay in *How to Hustle and Win, Pt. One*, "Mental Illnesses in the Black Community" where I explain how the first "mental diseases" ascribed to African slaves were Drapetomania, which caused Blacks to have an uncontrollable urge to run away from their "masters" (The "treatment" for this illness was "whipping the devil out of them"), and Dysaesthesia aethiopis, which caused disobedience, answering disrespectfully, and refusing to work (The "cure" for this was to force the person into hard labor, which would send "vitalized blood to the brain to give liberty to the mind"). I write:

> In the modern era, these bogus disorders have been replaced by new disorders. These new disorders are just as popular among doctors diagnosing Black children as the old ones were for slaves. They are ADHD and ODD, and instead of whippings and forced labor, the new treatments are medications that dope our children up into complacent zombies.

I go on to discuss a number of real psychological syndromes affecting Blacks in America, including Post Traumatic Slave Syndrome (made famous by Dr. Joy Leary), Baby Boy Syndrome (Dr. Frances Cress Welsing), Mentacide (Bobby Wright and Mwalimu Baruti), Psychological Slavery (Dr. Naim Akbar), Stockholm Syndrome, and True Believer Syndrome.

But beyond that, we are also notoriously UNDERdiagnosed for conditions like schizophrenia, mania, depression, and all that other "crazy sh*t" you see when you walk down any street in the hood. What's the solution to all this madness? It starts with finding out what's wrong, then investigating WHY, and then proceeding with the appropriate treatment. But NOTHING happens until you start LOOKING. So I don't want you to become a hypochondriac and think everything's wrong with you and your loved ones, but just take an honest look and you might find something worth following up on. If you're wondering if you or someone you know fits the criteria for any of the conditions above, you can visit www.CounsellingResource.com where there's more information on the criteria for each, and even some online diagnostics to make things crystal clear.

For now, here are some basics. A personality disorder usually involves several areas of your personality, and typically causes considerable personal and social disruption. Basically, because of your disorder your life is out of order. A personality disorder tends to appear in late childhood or adolescence and continues to be manifest into adulthood. Child abuse, especially sexual abuse, is often a major factor in the development of these disorders.

Personality disorders generally fall under the following main headings:

❏ Paranoid personality disorder: characterized by irrational suspicions and mistrust of others. It is characterized by at least 3 of the following:

❏ Excessive sensitivity to setbacks and challenges.

❏ Tendency to bear grudges persistently, i.e. refusal to forgive insults and injuries or slights.

❏ Suspiciousness and a tendency to distort experience by misconstruing the neutral or friendly actions of others as hostile or contemptuous.

❏ A combative and tenacious sense of personal rights not related to the actual situation.

❏ Recurrent suspicions, without justification, regarding faithfulness of spouse or sexual partner.

❏ Tendency to experience excessive self-importance (making everything "about them")

❏ Preoccupation with conspiracy explanations – without need for evidence – for events in both their personal life and the world beyond.

Schizoid personality disorder: lack of interest in social relationships, seeing no point in sharing time with others, and endless introspection. Schizoid is characterized by having at least four of the following criteria:

❏ Emotional coldness, detachment or reduced affection.

❏ Limited capacity to express either positive or negative emotions towards others.

❏ Consistent preference for solitary activities.

❏ Very few, if any, close friends or relationships, and a lack of desire for such.

❏ Indifference to either praise or criticism.

❏ Taking pleasure in few, if any, activities.

❏ Indifference to social norms and conventions.

❏ Preoccupation with fantasy and introspection.

❏ Lack of desire for sexual experiences with another person.

Schizoid is rare, compared with other personality disorders, affecting less than 1% of the general population. But a study by Valliant & Drake (1985) found that over 40% of a particular sample group of inner city males were Schizoid. Detached or neglectful parenting is hypothesized to play a role in the disorder.

Schizotypal personality disorder: characterized by a need for isolation and odd behavior or thinking. Schizotypal often evolves into full schizophrenia if left untreated. It can be identified by the following traits:

❏ Inappropriate or constricted affect (the individual appears cold and aloof).

❏ Behavior or appearance that is odd, eccentric, or peculiar.

❏ Poor rapport with others and a tendency to social withdrawal.

- Odd beliefs or magical thinking, influencing behavior and inconsistent with the cultural norms of one's peer group.
- Suspiciousness or paranoid ideas.
- Obsessive ruminations (focusing on distress and anxiety).
- Unusual "experiences," including out-of-body experiences or other perceptions of depersonalization or derealization.
- Vague, circumstantial, metaphorical, overelaborate, or stereotyped thinking, manifested by odd speech or in other ways, without sounding totally incoherent (totally incoherent = schizophrenia = gone).
- Occasional quasi-psychotic episodes with intense illusions, auditory or visual hallucinations, and delusion-like ideas, usually occurring without external provocation (again, when it's no longer "quasi" = gone).

Antisocial personality disorder: a pervasive disregard for the law and the rights of others. People with antisocial personality disorder are sometimes referred to as "sociopaths" and "psychopaths." So this isn't the average crook that breaks the law to make a living. This is the guy who set cats on fire when he was a kid. However, nearly 80-95% of felons would meet the criteria for ASPD, which means it's bogus. A better measure of psychopathic or sociopathic tendencies is the Hare Psychopathy Checklist, which looks at more important factors, like lack of remorse, lack of empathy, superficial charm, and pathological lying.

Borderline personality disorder: Extremely polarized (everything is "black or white") thinking, chaotic relationships, unstable self-image and identity, and unpredictable behavior.

Histrionic personality disorder: Pervasive attention-seeking behavior, including inappropriate sexual seductiveness and shallow or exaggerated emotions.

Narcissistic personality disorder: A pervasive pattern of grandiosity, need for admiration, and a lack of empathy.

Avoidant personality disorder: Social inhibition, feelings of inadequacy, extreme sensitivity to negative evaluation and avoidance of social interaction.

Dependent personality disorder: Pervasive psychological dependence on other people.

Obsessive-compulsive personality disorder (not the same as obsessive-compulsive disorder): Characterized by rigid conformity to rules, moral codes and excessive orderliness.

Depressive personality disorder: Pervasive pattern of depressive cognitions and behaviors beginning by early adulthood.

Passive-aggressive personality disorder (or "negativististic personality disorder"): Pattern of negative attitudes and passive resistance in interpersonal situations. This one is an issue I need to spend a few extra minutes on, because it's one I've seen growing at a ridiculous rate among us. This is where a person will have a problem with you, and tell everyone else BUT you…and then when you confront them, it's all love. This is where a LOT of drama starts in the hood. Because these people set others against you. Or they will sabotage you some other way. Worst part about it is, no matter how wrong they are, these people always play the victim People with this issue may not be aggressive, but they will passively create some serious problems for you. Either address their issues or leave em alone. Houston rapper Paul Wall hinted at this disorder (without knowing its name) when he talked about Mike Jones:

> When he left Swishahouse, he was dropping salt on everybody from Swishahouse and not giving us any credit at all. He was talking down on a lot of us and he would never directly say our names, but he was still hating. There were times when I felt disrespected and I would call him out on it, and he'd be like, "Nah, I wasn't talking about you. I would never do that." I'm sure there's a psychological term for this problem that Mike Jones has. He has a problem. His perception of reality ain't the real perception of reality. In his mind he feels like he hasn't done anything wrong to me, Trae, or Chamillionaire. He feels like everyone else is trippin' and he's the victim. But that ain't how it happened. We always say there's three sides to every story. There's your side, the other person's side, and then there's the truth. But in his mind, he's the victim and he never did anything wrong to anybody. When somebody thinks that way, there's no point in arguing with them.

Common Factors of Personality Disorders

The set of common diagnostic guidelines which apply to all personality disorders are that the condition is not caused by brain damage, disease, or another psychiatric disorder, and meets the following criteria:

- ☐ Imbalanced attitudes and behavior, involving one or more areas of functioning, e.g. affectivity, arousal, impulse control, ways of perceiving and thinking, and style of relating to others;
- ☐ the abnormal behavior pattern is long-term, and not limited to episodes of mental illness;
- ☐ the abnormal behavior pattern is persistent and clearly unable to adapt well to a broad range of personal and social situations;
- ☐ the above symptoms always appear during childhood or adolescence and continue into adulthood;
- ☐ the disorder leads to extensive personal distress but this may only become apparent late in its course;
- ☐ the disorder is usually, but not always, associated with significant problems in business and social performance.

It is an accepted notion that for different cultures it may be necessary to develop specific sets of criteria with regard to social norms, rules and obligations. However, while the Chinese have done some of this, there aren't really any sets of criteria specific to Black or Latino people. As a result, things can get a little cloudy for us when it comes to diagnosis.

As noted by my brother Jeffrey C. Johnson:

Too often, the stigmas surrounding mental illness prevent us from dealing with our folks appropriately. Misunderstanding mental illness and writing mentally ill people off as societal pariahs forces too many of us with very real needs to go into hiding about our issues. A mental illness is a disease – like diabetes is – but mental illness is treated as an entirely different animal due in large part to a vacuum in our collective understanding of mental health issues, particularly as they relate to people of color. When you need help, get help. When someone you know needs help, encourage them to get help. Some mental health issues are temporary, others (as far as we know) are permanent. All of them need to be addressed appropriately, and not tucked under the rug out of convenience.

I also need to say that a person does not have to have hallucinations and severe mood swings to be in less-than-optimal mental health. Anxiety, depression, eating disorders, etc., are all examples of mental health issues that are not seen in the same light as more obvious mental health problems. **Sometimes, something as simple as a daily meditation routine can ease stress, anxiety, and depression, while other times drastic changes in diet, counseling, or psychiatric interventions are necessary to deal with these issues.** Mental health problems are not one-size-fits-all, and neither are treatment options. The beauty of all this is that there ARE options, there is help, and that OWNING these issues and the events/circumstances that created them can help people make incredible strides towards wholeness, health, and happiness.

Check your city, local colleges and universities, for free resources, professional diagnosis, and treatment centers.

OCD

BY MECCA WISE

I diagnosed myself with Obsessive Compulsive Disorder (ODC) when I was about 19 years old.

OCD is an anxiety disorder where anxious thoughts constantly invade your mind and you do whatever is necessary repeatedly to ease your anxiety. I define it as an irrational fear of what might happen if I don't do something.   Obsession is the thought. Compulsion is the behavior. Although it may be very real to us, our rituals do not make sense to people who are not inflicted with this disorder. At times, we even realize that some of your behaviors are irrational, but many times still can't help ourselves.

I was always checking…the stove to make sure I turned it off, the door to make sure that I locked it, the post office drop box , to make sure the mail went down…you name it, I checked it. Then there was the mysophobia aspect and the washing of the hands. I must have washed my hands more than 20 times a day, after shaking some ones hands, after touching door knobs, the bus seat, the shopping cart… You name it, I saw it as contagious.

I can recall how much time I wasted, how much hand lotion I used and how my 'normal' friends sometimes found it difficult to deal with my weird behavior. I've worried profusely, been a hoarder, a perfectionist, a control freak...I've done some irrational things as it relates to this disorder and not wanting to admit it, have found many ways to rationalize my behaviors. But I will say, I have come a long way since then.

Wait, Black people have OCD?

Yes. Blacks experience OCD at similar rates as everyone else, but are over 30% less likely to receive treatment. Blacks are absent in OCD specialty clinics and in research studies. **There are almost no published studies focused on the diagnosis, assessment, or treatment of African Americans who have OCD.** The little research that exists makes it clear that Blacks experience OCD differently from whites:

Black Americans are more likely to have a later age of onset (32 years), as opposed to late adolescence (19 years).

Standard tests for OCD don't properly assess Blacks.

Blacks are often misdiagnosed for OCD (like other disorders) based on cultural norms or personal quirks (like frequent hand-washing).

Once they are finally diagnosed, Blacks are more likely be "stuck" with OCD and not get better.

What causes OCD?

Scientists don't really know! Some think it's just another anxiety-type psychological disorder. Others are unsure if it's genetic, environmental or something else altogether. I've heard someone speculate that it was another byproduct of "Western culture" which has taught us that our environment must be "controlled" and we have to regulate/rule everything in our reach. All those "my space"/ "my stuff"/ "my time" issues can translate into a lot of craziness, so it makes some sense, especially when you consider that you don't find OCD in our more "relaxed" homelands.

What fixes OCD?

Again, scientists haven't found the answers. Can a serotonin boost help? That looks like a major part of it, but there's a lot that's still unknown. What I CAN tell you is that OCD is a real issue to someone who suffers from it. If you are close to someone who suffers from this, have patience and search for ways to help them before you criticize. If you are a sufferer, try getting facts about the issues that cause your anxious thoughts, you may find that you have misinformation about your fears. Although the thoughts behind the anxiety are not rational, this may help. Also, if you are a 'checker' try repeating out loud once you have completed a task or try carrying a piece of paper with a check list. I think the key is working hard to create balance in your life. In general, think about the time you will lose and the freedom that you can enjoy.

Either way, there's no "cure" for OCD, so don't expect a magic medication to set you straight. There are some herbal approaches that have shown promise, but nothing has been "proven" to work all the way, every time. Here's what's been found so far:

May help	May make it worse
St. John's Wort. This herb has proven to be effective in the treatment of depression and anxiety. Several small studies have been done regarding its effectiveness for OCD, and some of them have shown success equal to medications, with some studies going so far as to compare it to the clinically effective equivalent of Prozac. Other studies though have shown no effect greater than a placebo effect. St. John's Wort is the only clinically demonstrated herbal aid for OCD, and is a good option for those unwilling or unable to try a prescription medication.	Marijuana. Weed may provide some short term relief, but it ultimately causes symptoms to later worsen. For some people, OCD symptoms were actually trigged by using marijuana. Marijuana can also interfere with other approaches, prevent new learning in therapy, and make depression more severe.
Valerian Root	Ephedra
Ginseng	Cocaine
Gotu Kola	Methamphetamines

Create a "rational phrase" or mantra to manage your anxiety. This will help disprove an irrational impulse, limiting your need to pay it immediate attention. Limit your OCD impulses to a certain number a day. And begin to decrease that number weekly.

ARE YOU AN ADULT WITH ADHD?
BY SUPREME UNDERSTANDING

I make my "disorder" work for me. ADHD is how I can manage a dozen projects at one time and constantly find new opportunities where others wouldn't think to look. And apparently I'm not alone in my thinking. Multi-millionaire Wilson Harrell (former publisher of Inc. Magazine), in his book *For Entrepreneurs Only*, devotes two chapters to his own ADHD and his belief that ADHD is "essential" for the success of an entrepreneur.

But I also know a lot of people who have these same symptoms and it DOESN'T work for them. Whether it's a lack of focus at work or the inability to maintain a committed relationship, adult ADHD can make your life pretty shaky. Sure, the chemicals in our food and environment are making our brain chemistry a little funny, but it's not like there weren't people with these same symptoms back in the day. As I explain in "If Einstein Were Black" in *How to Hustle and Win, Part Two*, there have ALWAYS been historical examples of people who managed these exact issues. Many were considered geniuses, like Thomas Edison, Leonardo Da Vinci, Nikola Tesla, etc. Certainly some Black historical figures also qualified, but people haven't researched/written much about that. (Why don't you?) But even in indigenous society, we've had people with those traits. We gave them names that meant "Follows the Birds" or "Running Deer" but we didn't punish them and try to make them go about life the same way as everyone else ("conforming to the norms").[23] **So if you're an adult with ADHD, it's not a death sentence or a poverty sentence, but it will be rough for you, if you try to succeed in a field that values conforming.** If you qualify based on the quiz below, I'm not saying quit your day job…but entrepreneurship is definitely something you should look into.

The Adult ADHD Self-Report Scale

Research suggests that the symptoms of ADHD can persist into adulthood, having a significant impact on the relationships, careers, and even the personal safety of patients who may suffer from it. Because this disorder is often misunderstood, many people who have it do not receive appropriate treatment and, as a result, may never reach their full potential. Part of the problem is that it can be difficult to diagnose, particularly in adults.

The following quick ADHD screening quiz includes just 6 questions which have been found to be the most predictive of symptoms consistent with adult ADD/ADHD. Please choose the one response to each item that best describes how you have felt and conducted yourself over the past 6 months.

Please note: This test will only be scored correctly if you answer each one of the questions.

1. How often do you have trouble wrapping up the final details of a project, once the challenging parts have been done?

    A. Never   B. Rarely   C. Sometimes   D. Often   E. Very Often

2. How often do you have difficulty getting things in order when you have to do a task that requires organization?

    A. Never   B. Rarely   C. Sometimes   D. Often   E. Very Often

3. How often do you have problems remembering appointments or obligations?

    A. Never   B. Rarely   C. Sometimes   D. Often   E. Very Often

4. When you have a task that requires a lot of thought, how often do you avoid or delay getting started?

---

[23] In fact, some scholars say that indigenous "hunter-gather" societies embodied the traits of ADHD when compared to more settled agricultural societies. But now scientists are trying to say that ADHD is genetically inherited, which is simply a way to say (again) that Black people are "naturally" screwed up…and thus another argument for eugenics, or the elimination of undesirable populations and their genetic traits.

A. Never   B. Rarely   C. Sometimes   D. Often   E. Very Often

5. How often do you fidget or squirm with your hands or feet when you have to sit down for a long time?

    A. Never   B. Rarely   C. Sometimes   D. Often   E. Very Often

6. How often do you feel overly active and compelled to do things, like you were driven by a motor?

    A. Never   B. Rarely   C. Sometimes   D. Often   E. Very Often

Scoring

Questions 1 to 3: 1 point for "Sometimes", "Often", or "Very Often"	Score:
Questions 4 to 6: 1 point for "Often" or "Very Often"	Score:
Total Score:	A total score of 4 or above suggests symptoms highly consistent with ADHD in adults, and further investigation is warranted.

This score is not intended as a mental disorder diagnosis, or as any type of healthcare recommendation. The actual diagnosis of ADHD can only be made on the basis of a detailed history and mental status examination. High scores on this screening quiz may also be related to anxiety, depression or mania. These conditions must be ruled out before a diagnosis of ADHD can be made. This book also includes a screening test for a related disorder, mania.

Find a way to make your ADHD work for you. Adjust your work ethic, goals, abilities, and ADHD to complement each other.

THE GREAT DEPRESSION

On Biggie Smalls's classic *Ready to Die* album, he raps:

All my life I been considered as the worst/ Lyin' to my mother, even stealin' out her purse/ Crime after crime, from drugs to extortion/ I know my mother wished she got a f*ckin' abortion/...I swear to God I just want to slit my wrists and end this bullsh*t/ Throw the Magnum to my head, threaten to pull sh*t/ And squeeze until the bed's completely red/ I'm glad I'm dead, a worthless f*ckin' buddah head

Biggie wasn't the only one feelin like that. In fact, I could write an entire book on suicide and depression in Hip Hop. From Bushwick Bill to Eminem to The Game to T-Pain (yes, even T-Pain), nearly half of the rap game has – at some point – mentioned wanting to end it all somehow. Hell, even Grandmaster Flash rapped about suicide on "The Message"! But that's because Hip Hop, for the most part, is a reflection of what's happening in OUR consciousness at the time. And you'd be surprised how many of us are depressed or even suicidal. But talking about depression just isn't cool among people of color. We think that's a "white people problem," so we don't talk about it. But think about the following:

- ❏ At least 10.4% of Blacks in America (and 12.9% of Blacks from the Caribbean) reported having MDD (Major Depressive Disorder)
- ❏ More than 1 in 10 Blacks in America has had suicidal thoughts
- ❏ 4.1% of Blacks in America have attempted suicide
- ❏ Suicide is the 3rd leading cause of death among Black youth ages 15-19
- ❏ Black youth are the fastest growing percentage of suicide victims
- ❏ From 1980-1995, suicide among Blacks ages 10-14 increased 233%
- ❏ In general, Blacks have higher depression rates than whites (8.0% vs. 4.8%). Among the poor, the Black-white gap is even bigger, and poor Blacks are more depressed than Blacks with higher incomes.
- ❏ Serious depression can also lead to "suicide by proxy" or "indirect suicide" meaning you *create* the circumstances that get you killed

And don't think fame, status, or money will make things easier, if your mind ain't right. Never forget that for every rich person who kills themselves, somebody homeless is happy with how things are going. It's about how you process things.

Remember that cover of *XXL* with The Game on the cover with the pistol to his head? Shock value aside, he was really contemplating suicide.

In the magazine, The Game revealed he was in such a dark place emotionally and physically, he almost chose to end his life. He told *XXL*:

> My life is f*cked up right now. I'm in a f*cked up place. My fans love me, and I know what they want but in a minute, I'm not gonna be physically capable of pleasing the world with music. Because my mind isn't right. People are driving me under God's good earth...Sometimes I wanna be at peace so bad that I wish myself off of the earth.

My Story

Growing up, I remember a lot of us were either depressed or full-blown suicidal by the time we were teenagers. When we played chicken by pretending to tie our shoes in oncoming traffic, we weren't just being badasses. When we jumped across rooftops and scaled buildings (the origins of *parkour* – look it up on YouTube), we weren't just being reckless. We were making it clear that we didn't want our lives. We were all ready to die. After all, the world made us feel disposable like trash, while the elders who should've helped us didn't do much more than yell at us. To make a long story short, I grew up in a dysfunctional family, and my neighborhood was pretty sh*tty. I spent a lot of time feeling miserable and alienated. I made my first suicide attempt at 14. If nothing else, it was a cry for help. I just had no idea how I'd get it.

Over the next few years, I began reading up on depression: its symptoms, its causes, and its treatment. After the suicide attempt, they'd put me on anti-depressant medication but it made me feel more like a dopehead than a regular kid, so I stopped taking it. Instead, I started reading up on the subject of depression and began treating myself. I learned that my depression resulted from having an idealized view of where I should be, and what my life should be like…and comparing that perfect picture with how f*cked up I thought I really was.

"You cannot see the future with tears in your eyes." – Navajo proverb

I began with trashing that ideal image I had for myself. I wasn't rich, I wasn't handsome, and I wasn't the captain of the football team. I didn't have a good family, and I didn't live in a good neighborhood. I had bad days, and sometimes I had bad weeks. But I learned that was all a part of regular life. I stopped hating life, and started learning to live with it. After all, tons of people had it ten times worse than me.

The crazy thing is, once I learned to live with it, it was ten times easier to change everything. Instead of beating up on myself for having problems, I could focus on beating my problems.

I learned about why life was so hard for people like me. I learned about what people of color have been put through (slavery, exploitation, abuse, rejection, dehumanization, etc.), and I understood why I couldn't let myself fall victim to that pit of despair.

"Waste not fresh tears over old griefs." – Euripedes (485-406 B.C.)

I changed my perspective. I refused to be a victim, and I chose to be victorious. Every time I felt the thoughts of depression coming back, I reminded myself that clinical depression usually is the result of a chemical imbalance in the brain.

That means it's not real. All those feelings that life wasn't worth living, that everything was terrible, that I was a failure, they weren't based on reality. So, like the hallucinations I had when I was trippin on acid that one time (another story), I ignored them when they came up. Eventually, I outgrew them. Choosing to see myself as the problem-solver instead of the problem allowed me to take control of my life, and my mind.

That was over ten years ago. I haven't had a weak thought since.

Alonzo Heyward: A True Story of Suicide-by-Proxy

In *How to Hustle and Win*, I used a fictionalized account, but this time around I'm sharing one pulled fresh from the local news:

CHATTANOOGA, Tennessee (AP) – August 19, 2009 – Alonzo Heyward carried a rifle around his low-rent Chattanooga, Tennessee, neighborhood one day last month, ranting about suicide and ignoring the pleas of friends for hours before six city police officers surrounded him on his front porch and decided it had to end.

His father says Heyward told the officers, "I'm not out here to hurt anybody." But the police, who tried unsuccessfully to disarm Heyward, fired

59 rounds to kill him on July 18. The medical examiner found 43 bullet wounds in his chest, face, arms, hands, legs, buttocks and groin. Police contend Heyward was a danger to others and threatened the six officers.

Chattanooga police spokeswoman Jerri Weary described the case as "suicide by cop." As questions continue to surround the shooting, Heyward's family and civil rights leaders take issue with the police response. Heyward, a 32-year-old moving company employee, was black. The six officers are white. They were temporarily placed on administrative leave but have since returned to work.

Reactionary vs. Revolutionary Suicide

The above story is not rare. There's even a word for it nowadays, and they mention it in the movie *Phonebooth*. It's called "cop-assisted suicide." In general, it's also known as "suicide-by-proxy" or "indirect suicide." It's what happens when a person who doesn't know he's depressed and suicidal goes out on a mission that will almost definitely end up killing him. And dozens of us do it every day. It's what Tupac was trying to tell us in so many of his songs. For example, on "So Many Tears," he raps:

> Now I'm lost and I'm weary, so many tears/ I'm suicidal, so don't stand near me/ My every move is a calculated step, to bring me closer/ to embrace an early death, now there's nothin left/ There was no mercy on the streets, I couldn't rest/ I'm barely standin, bout to go to pieces, screamin "peace"/ And though my soul was deleted, I couldn't see it/ I had my mind full of demons, tryin to break free/ They planted seeds and they hatched, sparkin the flame/ inside my brain like a match, such a dirty game/ No memories, just a misery/ Paintin a picture of my enemies killin me, in my sleep

> Did You Know?
> Signs and symptoms more likely to occur with male depression include:
> Violent or abusive behavior
> Inappropriate rage
> Escapist behavior, such as over-involvement in work or sports
> Risky behavior, such as reckless driving
> Sexual liaisons
> Alcohol or substance abuse
> More frequently thoughts of suicide
> Having these kinds of symptoms can make it more difficult to link them to depression, making diagnosis and treatment harder.

"All around I felt suicidal," Tupac once confirmed. "But I couldn't kill myself. I just wanted somebody to kill me for me." I think this is part of why we love Tupac so much. He was a whole person, flaws and disorders and all…conflicted but genuine…and so much like us, whether good, bad or ugly.

We're killing ourselves like never before, and nobody understands why. Well, a few of us do. I know Huey P. did. He said we kill ourselves in reaction to the misery we experience, when we should instead be giving our lives trying to destroy the bullsh*t that made us so miserable.

"The greatest tragedy in the ghetto is watching people become accustomed to the prospect of a bleak future" - Ice T

He coined the term "revolutionary suicide" to describe the actions of Black people – oppressed by racism and poverty – who risk their lives for the people, for positive change, by standing up to the system. He argued that this was very different from the "reactionary suicide" commited by so many others through drug addiction, criminal activity, and other self-destructive behaviors that result from hopelessness. He argued that "the slow suicide of life in the ghetto" should be replaced by a revolutionary struggle that would end only in victory (change of the system) or revolutionary suicide (death).

Almost poetically, he said in "I am We, or Revolutionary Suicide":

> So many of my comrades are gone now. Some tight partners, crime partners, and brothers off the block, are begging on the street. Others are in the asylum, penitentiary, or grave. They are all suicides of one kind of another...The difference lies in hope and desire. **By hoping and desiring, the revolutionary suicide chooses life; he is, in the words of Nietzsche, "an arrow of longing for another shore."** Both suicides despise tyranny, but the revolutionary is both a great despiser and a great adorer who longs for another shore. The reactionary suicide must learn, as his brother the revolutionary has learned, that the desert [the American nightmare] is not a circle. It is a spiral. When we have passed through the desert, nothing will be the same.

Did You Know?
In the book, "*Disappearing Acts* by Terry McMillian," the author doesn't directly focus on the main male character, Franklin, as being "depressed." However, in his attempts to improve himself financially, emotionally, and personally, he faced many obstacles that catapulted him into a cycle of self-loathing, depression, and giving up.

Mwalimu Baruti has written that "Black men kill themselves with their futures ahead of them, and white men when their futures are behind them." It's true. The way we give our lives is very different from everyone else. White people typically commit suicide once their company crashes or they go bankrupt. Sh*t, most of us *start out* bankrupt! Many of us feel like we were "born dead," so we don't need to lose anything in particular for us to feel like everything is lost. Having so little, and being treated like we're less than nothing...it's enough to send someone over the edge. It's not so amazing that so many of us are "damaged goods," but that so many of us somehow can still make it. As James Baldwin observed several decades ago:

> All over Harlem, Negro boys and girls are growing into stunted maturity, trying desperately to find a place to stand; and the wonder is not that so many of them are ruined but that so many survive.

But now our survival rate is dropping. We're killing ourselves in dozens of ways, some of them too subtle to notice. Some of us are so unhealthy psychologically and emotionally that we've used the endless pursuit of money as a "mask" to cover up our own illness. Even you may fit the profile. But instead of dying for nothing, dying over nothing, dying with nothing...try living FOR something...and even if you die, it won't be for nothing.

And it's not just men. Black and Hispanic women are highly depressed (perhaps even more), except they exhibit their symptoms differently. "I find that there's a shadow, a cloud of sadness amongst women of color, from all walks of life," says Stacey Muhammad, director of *Out of Our Right Minds: Trauma, Depression and the Black Woman*. She continues, "It's time to have this discussion. My commitment is to not only explore our behavior but to also examine the environment in which we've been embedded for more than 400 years and to encourage us to begin to examine what this environment has done and continues to do to people of color."

According to author and social activist Terri Williams:

> **Today, nearly 70% of Black children are born to single mothers, a third of which live below the poverty line.** This means that these mentally distressed women are raising our children, more often than not by themselves, and under very harsh circumstances…It should come as no surprise that depressed mothers often lead to depressed children. Unfortunately, even those mothers who recognize that they themselves are depressed don't recognize the signs in their own children. Many depressed and busy parents may also not be as attentive of their own children and not realize that their dysfunction is deeply affecting the rest of the family.
>
> **Children whose mothers suffer from depression may be more likely to exhibit the same symptoms.** Moreover, the harmful consequences of poverty coupled with the mediating effects of maternal depression jeopardize the development of our young boys and girls. These children are slow to develop and their problems often only come to our attention when their pain becomes public manifested as violence and self-destruction at the hands of drug and alcohol abuse or additional behavioral disorders.

And guess who is being prescribed the most anti-depressants nowadays? Not Black men, not Black women, but Black children. So yes, depression is a serious problem that affects the whole population. It's not just "the blues."

What causes clinical depression? It could be cognitive issues (e.g., negative thinking patterns), biological and genetic factors, the effects of medications, other illnesses, and situational factors, like stress and discrimination. To make matters worse, some people try to "self-medicate" through the abuse of alcohol or illegal drugs, which only leads to more problems.

The good news is that over 80% of people with depression can be treated successfully. Be careful where you go for treatment though! Blacks tend to be diagnosed more frequently with schizophrenia and less frequently with affective disorders. In addition, one study found that 27% of Blacks compared to 44% of whites received antidepressant medication. Moreover, new medications with fewer side effects are prescribed less often to Blacks than to whites. Finally, even though data suggest that Blacks may metabolize psychiatric medications more slowly than whites, Blacks often receive higher dosages than do whites, leading to more severe side effects. As a result, they Blacks are more like likely to stop taking their medications than whites with similar diagnoses.

Besides regular exercise, the herb St. John's Wort is possibly the best natural remedy for depression and anxiety, even though all the studies done haven't agreed on its effectiveness. Dr. Andrew Weil recommends taking 300 mg of a St. John's Wort extract three times a day, along with cutting fat and protein (meat) from your diet.

Of course, there are people who want immediate help of the clinical variety. For help finding treatment, support groups, medication information, and other mental health-related services in your community, you can visit Mental Health America at www.nmha.org (but keep in mind that Western medicine's "last resort" treatment for severe depression is electro-shock therapy).

Finally, suicide does not need to cross your mind. Beat that thought away every time it comes. **If you or someone you know is in crisis right now, seek help immediately.** Call 1-800-273-TALK to reach a 24 hour crisis center or dial 911 for immediate assistance.

The Different Types of Depression

Major Depression: This type of clinical Depression is characterized by a severe lack of interest in the things that were once enjoyed, or nonstop feelings of sadness.

Bipolar disorder or manic depressive illness: Also called Manic Depression, bipolar disorder is a type of depression that has either subtle or extreme "high" periods alternating with "low" periods of Depression.

Dysthymic disorder: This type of Depression is characterized by ongoing yet mild symptoms of Depression.

Cyclothymic disorder: is a relatively mild form of bipolar II disorder characterized by mood swings that may appear to be almost within the normal range of emotions. These mood swings range from mild depression, or dysthymia, to mania of low intensity, or hypomania.

Postnatal depression (PND) or Postpartum depression: is a complex mix of physical, emotional, and behavioral changes that occur in a mother after giving birth. It is a serious condition, affecting 10% of new mothers. Symptoms range from mild to severe Depression and may appear within days of delivery or gradually, perhaps up to a year later. Symptoms may last from a few weeks to a year. Recent studies have found that dads can suffer from a form of postpartum depression as well.

Seasonal affective disorder (SAD): See "Why are you so S.A.D.?"

Wakefield Depression Screening Questionnaire

1. I feel miserable and down.	2. I find it easy to do the things I used to do.
A. No, not at all C. Yes, sometimes	
B. No, not much D. Yes, definitely	A. Yes, definitely C. No, not much

B. Yes, sometimes D. No, not at all

3. I get very panicky or paranoid for apparently no reason at all.

 A. No, not at all   C. Yes, sometimes

 B. No, not much D. Yes, definitely

4. I have crying spells, or feel like breaking down crying (even though I don't).

 A. No, not at all   C. Yes, sometimes

 B. No, not much D. Yes, definitely

5. I still enjoy the things I used to.

 A. Yes, definitely   C. No, not much

 B. Yes, sometimes D. No, not at all

6. I am restless and can't keep still.

 A. No, not at all   C. Yes, sometimes

 B. No, not much D. Yes, definitely

7. I can go to sleep easily without sleeping pills, drugs, or alcohol.

 A. Yes, definitely   C. No, not much

B. Yes, sometimes D. No, not at all

8. I feel anxious when I go out on my own.

 A. No, not at all   C. Yes, sometimes

 B. No, not much D. Yes, definitely

9. I've lost interest in things that I used to enjoy.

 A. No, not at all   C. Yes, sometimes

 B. No, not much D. Yes, definitely

10. I get tired for no reason.

 A. No, not at all   C. Yes, sometimes

 B. No, not much D. Yes, definitely

11. I am more irritable than usual.

 A. No, not at all   C. Yes, sometimes

 B. No, not much D. Yes, definitely

12. I wake early and then sleep badly for the rest of the night.

 A. No, not at all   C. Yes, sometimes

 B. No, not much D. Yes, definitely

Scoring

Scoring Key	Items Marked		Points
A: 0 points	A: ____	x 0 =	
B: 1 point	B: ____	x 1 =	
C: 2 points	C: ____	x 2 =	
D: 3 points	D: ____	x 3 =	
TOTAL SCORE =			
Scoring Ranges and Explanation			
Less than 15	No High Levels of Depressive Symptoms		
15 or Over	High Levels of Depressive Symptoms		

Most depressed people score 15 or above on the Wakefield, whereas most non-depressed people score between 0 and 14. It is important to realize that a rating scale such as the Wakefield does not diagnose clinical depression. The Wakefield measures the frequency and intensity of symptoms often associated with depression. Some high scores may be attained by individuals with other emotional problems or physical illnesses. Therefore, use the test as a guide, and consider consulting a professional for an evaluation if your score is 15 or more. Scores lower than 15 may still warrant consultation with a doctor if your distress or dysfunction is substantial. Repeating the Wakefield approximately two weeks after its first use may be helpful, and if your score is still below 15 but rising, you should strongly consider consulting a doctor.

ARE YOU BIPOLAR?

BY LANDRIA CARR

"Funny how it break down, but never mind me/ Forever grimy, I guess it's just Philly shinin/ Rock roller, bipolar like Phyllis Hyman"
– Black Thought, The Roots "Doin It"

Philadelphia songstress/actress Phylis Hyman, known best for her top ten hit "Can't we Fall in Love Again" was diagnosed with bipolar disorder in the late 80s. She battled alcoholism before committing suicide via overdose in 1995 at age 45, leaving a note that read (in part): "I'm tired. I'm tired. Those of you that I love know who you are." From Phyllis Hyman to DMX, Bipolar disorder is more common than you'd think.

We often think someone having a mood swing is the same as being "bipolar," or we think someone being clinically bipolar simply means they are prone to crazy mood swings. It's time we get some clarity. Bipolar disorder is a mental illness that consists of alternating periods of elevated moods, called manic episodes, and depression. These mood swings run on a spectrum from mild to more severe ("crazy") highs. Periods of mania can last for hours, days, weeks or even months before the person plunges back into depression. See? NOT the same as a run-of-the-mill mood swing. For more on those, see the chapter on Emotional Health.

Bipolar disorder is often misdiagnosed as depression because the manic symptoms (increased energy, heightened mood and increased sex drive) are considered positive – so it's not perceived as a problem. It's the depression that makes people look for help. But Mania has problems too. If you know anyone who goes from being down in the dumps to reckless and impulsive (symptoms of the "mania" part), then you already know bipolar disorder can wreak havoc in a person's life. Properly treated, however, a person with bipolar disorder can lead a peaceful and productive life without the extremes of mood.

You may think you only have depression alone, when you may actually have bipolar disorder. The following two screening tests can help you tell. The first, the Goldberg Mania Questionnaire can help you become familiar with the symptoms of mania, determine if you may have experienced a manic episode in the past. If you've already been diagnosed with depression (or think you may meet the criteria), the second test, the Goldberg Bipolar Spectrum Screening Questionnaire, can help you tell if you have bipolar disorders. While these quizzes cannot take the place of a professional psychiatric evaluation, they will give you an idea where to start a dialogue with your healthcare provider.

Goldberg Mania Questionnaire

To take the questionnaire, circle the selection which best reflects how each statement applies to you. Be sure to choose the statement that applies to how you have felt and behaved during the past week. Please note: This test will only be scored correctly if you answer each one of the questions.

1. My mind has never been sharper.
   A. Not at all   D. Moderately
   B. Just a little   E. Quite a lot
   C. Somewhat   F. Very much

2. I need less sleep than usual.
   A. Not at all   D. Moderately
   B. Just a little   E. Quite a lot
   C. Somewhat   F. Very much

3. I have so many plans and new ideas that it's hard for me to work.
   A. Not at all   D. Moderately
   B. Just a little   E. Quite a lot
   C. Somewhat   F. Very much

4. I feel a pressure to talk and talk.
   A. Not at all   D. Moderately
   B. Just a little   E. Quite a lot
   C. Somewhat   F. Very much

5. I have been particularly happy.
   A. Not at all   D. Moderately
   B. Just a little   E. Quite a lot
   C. Somewhat   F. Very much

6. I have been more active than usual.
   A. Not at all   D. Moderately
   B. Just a little   E. Quite a lot
   C. Somewhat   F. Very much

7. I talk so fast that people have a hard time keeping up with me.
   A. Not at all   D. Moderately
   B. Just a little   E. Quite a lot
   C. Somewhat   F. Very much

8. I have more new ideas than I can handle.
   A. Not at all   D. Moderately
   B. Just a little   E. Quite a lot
   C. Somewhat   F. Very much

9. I have been irritable.
   A. Not at all   D. Moderately
   B. Just a little   E. Quite a lot
   C. Somewhat   F. Very much

10. It's easy for me to think of jokes and funny stories.
   A. Not at all   D. Moderately
   B. Just a little   E. Quite a lot
   C. Somewhat   F. Very much

11. I've been feeling like "the life of the party".
   A. Not at all   D. Moderately
   B. Just a little   E. Quite a lot
   C. Somewhat   F. Very much

12. I have been full of energy.
   A. Not at all   D. Moderately
   B. Just a little   E. Quite a lot
   C. Somewhat   F. Very much

13. I have been thinking about sex.
   A. Not at all   D. Moderately
   B. Just a little   E. Quite a lot
   C. Somewhat   F. Very much

14. I have been feeling particularly playful.
   A. Not at all   D. Moderately
   B. Just a little   E. Quite a lot
   C. Somewhat   F. Very much

15. I have special plans for the world.
   A. Not at all   D. Moderately
   B. Just a little   E. Quite a lot
   C. Somewhat   F. Very much

16. I have been spending too much money.
A. Not at all   D. Moderately
B. Just a little   E. Quite a lot
C. Somewhat   F. Very much

17. My attention keeps jumping from one idea to another.
A. Not at all   D. Moderately
B. Just a little   E. Quite a lot
C. Somewhat   F. Very much

18. I find it hard to slow down and stay in one place.
A. Not at all   D. Moderately
B. Just a little   E. Quite a lot
C. Somewhat   F. Very much

Scoring

Scoring Key	Items Marked		Points
A. Not at all: 0 points	A: ____	X 0 =	
B. Just a little: 1 point	B: ____	X 1 =	
C. Somewhat: 2 points	C: ____	X 2 =	
D. Moderately: 3 points	D: ____	X 3 =	
E. Quite a lot: 4 points	E: ____	X 4 =	
F. Very much: 5 points	F: ____	X 5 =	
TOTAL SCORE =			

The higher the number, the more severe the mania. If you take the quiz again weekly or monthly, changes of 5 or more points between tests may be significant.

Scoring Ranges and Explanation	
0-9	No Mania Likely
10-17	Possibly Mildly Manic, or Hypomanic
18-21	Borderline Mania
22-35	Mild-Moderate Mania
36-53	Moderate-Severe Mania
54 and up	Severely Manic

The Goldberg Mania Questionnaire was developed by Dr. Ivan Goldberg, MD.

Goldberg Bipolar Spectrum Screening Questionnaire

This test is designed to screen for the possibility of a disorder in the bipolar spectrum in individuals, 18 or older, who have had at least one depression episode severe enough to have caused them distress and/or interfered with their functioning at home, work, school or in their interpersonal relationships. **In other words, this quiz assumes that you have already experienced a depressive episode.**

To take the questionnaire, choose the answer that best reflects how each statement applies, how you have felt and behaved over much of your life. If you have usually felt one way, and have recently changed, your responses should reflect how you have USUALLY felt. Please note: This test will only be scored correctly if you answer each one of the questions.

1. At times I am much more talkative or speak much faster than usual.

  A. Not at all   D. Moderately
  B. Just a little E. Quite a lot
  C. Somewhat F. Very much

2. There have been times when I was much more active or did many more things than usual.

  A. Not at all   D. Moderately
  B. Just a little E. Quite a lot
  C. Somewhat F. Very much

3. I get into moods where I feel very speeded up or irritable.

  A. Not at all   D. Moderately
  B. Just a little E. Quite a lot
  C. Somewhat F. Very much

4. There have been times when I have felt both high (elated) and low (depressed) at the same time.

  A. Not at all   D. Moderately
  B. Just a little E. Quite a lot
  C. Somewhat F. Very much

5. At times I have been much more interested in sex than usual.

  A. Not at all   D. Moderately
  B. Just a little E. Quite a lot
  C. Somewhat F. Very much

6. My self-confidence ranges from great self-doubt to equally great overconfidence.

  A. Not at all   D. Moderately
  B. Just a little E. Quite a lot
  C. Somewhat F. Very much

7. There have been GREAT variations in the quantity or quality of my work.

  A. Not at all   D. Moderately
  B. Just a little E. Quite a lot
  C. Somewhat F. Very much

8. For no apparent reason I sometimes have been VERY angry or hostile.

  A. Not at all   D. Moderately
  B. Just a little E. Quite a lot
  C. Somewhat F. Very much

9. I have periods of mental dullness and other periods of very creative thinking.

  A. Not at all   D. Moderately
  B. Just a little E. Quite a lot
  C. Somewhat F. Very much

10. At times I am greatly interested in being with people and at other times I just want to be left alone with my thoughts.

  A. Not at all   D. Moderately
  B. Just a little E. Quite a lot
  C. Somewhat F. Very much

11. I have had periods of great optimism and other periods of equally great pessimism.

  A. Not at all   D. Moderately
  B. Just a little E. Quite a lot
  C. Somewhat F. Very much

12. I have had periods of tearfulness and crying and other times when I laugh and joke excessively.

  A. Not at all   D. Moderately
  B. Just a little E. Quite a lot
  C. Somewhat F. Very much

Scoring

Scoring Key	Items Marked		Points
A. Not at all: 0 points	A: _____	x 0 =	
B. Just a little: 1 point	B: _____	x 1 =	
C. Somewhat: 2 points	C: _____	x 2 =	
D. Moderately: 3 points	D: _____	x 3 =	

E. Quite a lot: 4 points	E: ____	x 4 =	
F. Very much: 5 points	F: ____	x 5 =	
TOTAL SCORE =			
Scoring Ranges and Explanation			

Roughly speaking, the higher the score, the higher probability of a bipolar spectrum disorder, as opposed to major (unipolar) depression. (Remember, this quiz assumes that you are 18 or over and have had at least one depressive episode or depression severe enough to have caused you distress and/or interfered with you functioning at home, work, school or in your interpersonal relationships.)

0-15	Major/unipolar depression
16-24	Major Depression or a Disorder in the Bipolar Spectrum
25 or Above	Bipolar Spectrum

The Goldberg Bipolar Spectrum Screening Questionnaire was developed by Dr. Ivan Goldberg, MD.

Take the above questionnaire. When going thru mood swings, keep in mind they are only emotions and they will change. Find activities, songs, books, and places to help manage your emotions.

ALZHEIMER'S DISEASE
BY RODNEY JONES

My mom's favorite Aunt, Katie, used to ask me that same question seven times within 20 minutes. I would politely answer all seven times. My mom's explained to me that Aunt Katie was developing a serious case of Alzheimer's. At this point, my Aunt's memory was just about gone. She didn't remember much past 5 minutes.

Alzheimer's is a debilitating brain disease which affects more than 5 million Americans at any time. Alzheimer's Disease has more than doubled since 1980. *Science News* predicts that Alzheimer's Disease will quadruple by 2050.

While old age is still the biggest risk factor, Blacks and Latinos are in greater danger than any other group. Blacks are twice more likely to develop Alzheimer's than our white counterparts, while our Latin amigos are 1.5 times more likely than whites to be affected. Yet studies also show that these groups still tend to be the least likely to be diagnosed with Alzheimer's (meaning they won't get the help they need). According to the Aging, Demographics and Memory Study more than 1/5th (21.3%) of Black people past age 70 are into any given stage of Alzheimer's.

Alzheimer's is the most common form of dementia. Dementia does not mean crazy as is the general belief. Dementia by definition describes memory loss and a decrease of intellectual functions. An early sign of Alzheimer's is short term memory loss. Things like forgetting information that was told to you 10 minutes prior, being suspicious or fearful of people you've been around or trusted with your life (without good cause) and forgetting the directions to a friend's house that you've been to 500 times, are all signs of Alzheimer's. When these things occur often, they are signs that you are either developing early signs of Alzheimer's or are already knee-deep into it.

The brain is made up of more than 100 billion nerve cells called neurons. These neurons communicate via neurotransmitters (electrical signals) to other neuron groups through paths called synapses or branches. Think of each branch as a telephone cable. These neuron branches also keep you from getting confused, by regulating thoughts and problem solving ability. Other neuron groups control bodily functions as simple as finger movement or as intricate as scent memory. In Alzheimer's patients, these neurons or brain cells deteriorate and die. Missing neurons means screwy brain communication. The more neurons you lose, the worse off you are and, you'll become more susceptible to Alzheimer's disease. So what technically occurs in a brain developing Alzheimer's? When you lose so many neurons, your brain size shrinks and shrivels, damaging areas involved in thinking, personality, planning and remembering. Protein clumps build up around and in between neurons, inhibiting neurotransmitters and neuron branches.

What Should I Avoid?

Nutrient Deficiency: Vitamin C & E have been known to delay the development of Alzheimer's while Vitamin B and Essential Fatty Acids are widely known to improve brain memory. Zinc is also associated with healthy brain functionality.

Sleep deprivation: According to *Smart Nutrients*, written by Abram Hoffer and Morton Walker, "People who are sleep deprived for a day have the brain functionality of a person who is legally drunk." Over time, this adds up.

Heavy Metals: Mercury, which is in High Fructose Corn syrups and even some immunizations, which can cause headaches and memory loss.

Lack of Good Cholesterol: People with lower levels of HDL are at a heightened risk (more than 50%) of developing Alzheimer's.

Prescription Drug Use: Drugs also play a role, particularly among older African-Americans. According to a study appearing in the July 13, 2010 issue of the medical journal *Neurology*, the medications people take for a variety of common medical conditions (such as insomnia, allergies, or incontinence) negatively affect the brain over time, causing long-term "cognitive impairment" in older African-Americans (thus possibly contributing to Alzheimer's).

Another risk factor is smoking. Come to think of it, Aunt Katie smoked cigarettes for years. I can't say that's what did it, but I know that it didn't help. There's also alcohol consumption and brain injuries such as concussions. Desertion is another factor in the development of dementia. When elders get up in age, they are too set in their ways for some younger people to deal with, so elderly people tend to spend much of their time alone.

High blood pressure and diabetes are also indicators for Alzheimer's and dementia susceptibility. Also, according to a 2010 report from the Alzheimer's Association:

> Lower levels of education and other socioeconomic characteristics that are associated with increased risk for Alzheimer's disease and other dementias are more common in older African-Americans and Hispanics than in older whites and probably also account for some of the differences in prevalence among the groups.

Preventative Measures

When people learn new things, their brains make new connections (branches) improving their cerebral health. At the same time you are losing neuron branches from daily life (toxin inhalation, diet, and natural body deterioration) so it's imperative to keep our elders minds exposed to new experiences. Be open-minded. It is really easier than you think, It can be as easy as teaching your Grandma how to do the stanky leg (please refrain though…lol). **Playing memory games as old as concentration is an easy way to improve memory health among older people. Or challenging their memory via a crossword puzzle book (which old timers love anyway) is a great way.** Teaching them critical thinking through a game like Chess works wonders.

Take trips to the doctor with them to learn about their current health condition; then use that information to better their lives. Learn what they should and shouldn't be eating and take the time to iron chef it up for them once or twice a week. Foods such as whole grains, leafy green veggies, beans, nuts and seeds promote healthy brain function. Hit up a yoga class with them; join them on their morning walk. Take them to the hoop court. Don't be dunking on em' and thinking you raw though, because you're not. Overall, exercise encourages the forming of new brain matter. There's a lot more ideas in a book titled *100 Simple Things You Can Do to Prevent Alzheimer's: And Age Related Memory Loss* by Jean Carper.

One last way to help out our elders, is to build with them about *themselves*. If you know about Black history, then pick their brains to see what they can teach you, and then sprinkle THEM with a little of the game you've acquired, as a beneficiary of being born into the information age. You might become a student, a teacher, or (ideally) both. Take them to cultural museums and events. Buy them books on ancient Black and Brown civilizations (pre-1492). You would be surprised to see how receptive they are to the information if you present it in the right fashion. Besides, what else does their old ass have to do after retirement? But don't say things like that. At least not to their face.

Come up with memory games and other thinking activities, you can play with your elders. Play chess instead of watching TV together.

ONE MINUTE MENTAL HEALTH CHECK

Look quickly!

What catches your eye in this drawing?

If you saw the frown face instantly, you've got good attention skills, which is a sign of intelligent memory, the thought process that allows you to be creative and make fast decisions, says Barry Gordon, MD, PhD, director of the Memory Clinic at the Johns Hopkins School of Medicine.

But if it took you a few seconds, you need to boost your ability to focus. Try to avoid multitasking (chatting on the phone while replying to an e-mail while surfing the Web while grabbing for your ringing cell). "It may seem efficient, but it's much more tiring than just focusing on one thing at a time, so it takes you that much longer to get anything done and do it well," says Dr. Gordon.

And that clear-mindedness may actually prolong your life. Researchers recently discovered that intelligence, indicated by the ability to respond quickly to circumstances, is a far better gauge of longevity than blood pressure, exercise levels or weight. Men and women who recorded slow response times were over two and half times more likely to die prematurely.

"It has been hypothesized that reaction time, as a measure of speed of the brain's information-processing capacity, may be a marker for bodily system integrity," wrote the researchers. "This way, slower reaction times, or poorer information-processing ability, might be an indication of suboptimal physiological functioning, which may in turn be related to early death."

For more activities to develop your brain, visit www.sharpbrains.com/teasers

---
Take the exam then test your friends.

---

8. EMOTIONAL HEALTH

GETTING PAST TRAUMA AND TOXICITY

WHAT IS EMOTIONAL HEALTH?
THE IMPORTANCE OF EMOTIONAL HEALTH AND MENTAL STABILITY
BY QUEEN CHUNIQ EARTH

Emotional health is an aspect of mental health that encompasses stress management, depression and other mental/emotional factors that can slow you down or damage your overall health. Dealing with difficult people lead to dealing with situations that can be stressful or emotionally draining. I was once told, "If you can't change your situation, change your attitude." This means that instead of complacency or complaining, having a positive outlook and hopeful attitude will enable you to make the best of your situation. When life gives you lemons, you should make lemonade right? Absolutely.

Poor emotional health can lead to poor physical health. Have you ever seen a person and thought to yourself, "She MUST be going through something!" This person can be well-dressed, smelling good and even seem to have everything, yet we can always tell if deep inside a person isn't truly happy. Our body carries energy that speaks louder than designer brands and luxurious threads. A person carrying negative energy can be felt once they walk into the room! You don't want to be that person. If you can visually see and feel stress on another person, you must be able to identify it within yourself.

What are some signs of emotional distress?

- ❏ Acting out or lashing out
- ❏ Depression/extreme sadness
- ❏ Social withdrawal
- ❏ Stress
- ❏ Anxiety
- ❏ Anger
- ❏ Mood swings
- ❏ Unhealthy attachments
- ❏ Compulsive behavior
- ❏ Bodily dysfunction (constipation, headaches, hair loss, infections/ sudden illness, spontaneous weight loss or gain, lack of energy, sexual dysfunction)
- ❏ Physical violence to yourself or others

One of the first symptoms of emotional distress is detachment and depression. If you have watched yourself slowly fade away from friends, work, school and family, you may need to start addressing your issues. Relationship troubles? Family stress? Work overload? Whatever it may be, identify what's bothering you and then you can begin to turn your life around. Being in control of our emotions is key to managing life and the ups and downs that will inevitably occur.

Emotions are "energy in **motion.**" Either that energy is going downhill or uphill and it's your choice what direction that energy is going to travel. Don't let it drag you down! Successful people understand the power of the mind and can manipulate that to their advantage. Not every path is paved smoothly; resilience is a characteristic of happy people.

If you still find yourself having trouble getting your mind on track, seeking the guidance of a trusted friend or family member, self-help books or professional help is available. If you have exhausted all of your resources and are considering seeing a therapist or support group, DO SO. Don't worry about what anyone else thinks of that decision. It may save your life.

As a man (or woman) thinketh, so is he (she). The true power of you lies within your mind!

Think of people you know who may be showing signs of emotional distress. When watching television, notice the body language, facial expressions, language, and tones actors use to portray emotions.

> Did You Know?
> Mood swings can be brought on by pancreatic functions as well as sudden changes in your blood-sugar levels? Similar to remedies for anxiety, therapies for mood swings include nutritional supplements, aroma therapy, herbal remedies and even physical therapy.

PTSD

BY RODNEY JONES

What does an Iraq War veteran have in common with a Rollin' 60's Crip…or any young boy of color from any hood across America? For one, that War vet probably is "of color" too, but more importantly, they are probably experiencing some form of Post-Traumatic Stress Syndrome. According to the National Institute of Mental Health "Post-Traumatic Stress Disorder, PTSD, is an anxiety disorder that can develop after exposure to a terrifying event or ordeal in which grave physical harm occurred or was threatened." Events that can induce PTSD include violent assaults (such as gang violence), prison stints, natural or human-caused disasters (such as Hurricane Katrina), accidents, sexual assaults or military combat. PTSD is silently running rampant in urban communities, mainly because we tend to pass it off as anger. Well, here's two reasons why we ain't just angry as hell:

First, Blacks and Latinos make up a large segment of the military, particularly in those fields designated for combat. In fact, www.heritage.org reports that 35% of newly enlisted male recruits were from "ethnic" backgrounds. The typical soldier is also likely to come from a financially challenged background. So that basically spells A LOT OF

US. With the United States' most recent wars in Iraq and Afghanistan, and new "conflicts" certainly on the way, you are almost guaranteed to be shipped overseas to serve at least a year of active duty. When we are put out on the frontline, possibly "stop-lossed" and made to serve ANOTHER round on the frontline, and then finally returned home, without proper evaluation or time to psychologically heal, this is when PTSD takes effect. A report from *ABC News* states that "After nine years of war, the U.S. Army is showing signs of stress because of repeated deployments and inadequate support for soldiers when they return." These factors affect our community when these stressed-out, possibly traumatized, adults come home.

Second, there's high rates of exposure to violence and abuse experienced by children in our communities, creating wounds that won't heal anytime soon, if ever. Dr. Caren Goguen states that "While one-third of children ages 10-16 have reported being a victim to violence, an even higher number of urban children reported being exposed to indirect violence," which means they witnessed it or somebody close to them was harmed. It doesn't matter which hood. And these kids become what kind of adults? Traumatized. Nobody traumatized is fully functional or healthy until they start the healing/therapy process. But where is the access? Even our country's soldiers have a hard time getting help for PTSD, so imagine what a gang member or abuse victim would have to go through to "get better." And you wonder why we self-medicate! It's no different from the Vietnam vets hooked on heroin or the Iraq vets now hooked on painkillers or crystal meth. There's a reason our young men in the hood consider themselves "soldiers." Like our soldiers, they face constant threat of physical harm, whether it's a molliwoppin, a stabbing or a shooting. Like Pac said, Death is always right around the corner when you're living that lifestyle. There's only destruction in a life like that. Destruction of the body and of the mind, so the last thing we need to be doing is losing our heads. After all, it's not like we need any more stress than we already have on us. We ain't exactly healed from the trauma of slavery yet…which is older and deeper rooted than any of these gang wars (it's ALL gang wars if you think about it).

"The Africans become insane, we are told, in some instances, soon after they enter upon the toils of perpetual slavery in the West Indies" – Benjamin Rush, MD (1746-1813), the "Father of American Psychiatry"

So you don't need to be a Crip or a Marine to be traumatized. It's in your heritage if you're Black or Latino. For Blacks in America, it's known as Post Traumatic Slave Syndrome. That isn't a "blame the white man" term (for those of you who like to yell that when Black people start stating facts). It is REAL. As a matter of fact, Dr. Joy Leary has a book titled just that, "Post Traumatic Slave Syndrome." On her website, Dr. Leary states:

P.T.S.S is a condition that exists as a consequence of multigenerational oppression of Africans and their descendants resulting from centuries of chattel slavery; A form of slavery which was predicated on the belief that African Americans were inherently/ genetically inferior to whites. This was then followed by institutionalized racism which continues to perpetuate injury.

So if you know a Black person that isn't affected by P.T.S.S, get at me because I want to meet them. With that said, we are basically surrounded by traumatized people, and should tread lightly and with compassion as we walk on our own roads to self-discovery.

Know the signs of PTSD, how to deal with someone with PTSD, and know the location of centers in your community that treat PTSD.

Do You Have an Anger Problem?

BY SUPREME UNDERSTANDING

ORIGINALLY PUBLISHED IN HOW TO HUSTLE AND WIN, PT. ONE

There's one weakness that will destroy you faster than any other, its anger.

Think about it…we kill each other over anger. We lose our jobs due to anger. We end up doing life in prison after one fit of anger. We are f*ckin angry.

Why? Look around, and it's obvious. We're all pretty cool as little kids (unless we were abused from an early age). But by the time we hit 3rd or 4th grade, we're hip to the game. We know the teachers are lying about how useful and helpful the bullsh*t they're teaching is…We know adults are lying when they say school and hard work will equal success (and all we see around us is broke-ass adults)…We know the world is lying to us with its promises of freedom, justice, and equality. The Black man in America knows he's f*cked from an early age.

That does some things to you, whether you know it or not. For one, it creates an "I Don't Give a F*ck" attitude (See "Who Gives a F*ck?" in *How to Hustle and Win*). For another, it makes us angry with ourselves, angry with each other, and angry with the world. We never really figure out how to take our anger out on the people who put us in such a f*cked up predicament in the first place, so we lash out at the closest ones to us. First, we torture our mothers for bringing us into such a f*cked-up life and giving us so little with which to defend ourselves. Nine times out of ten, our mothers are completely unprepared to raise Black boys in a world set out to destroy them. Many of them have no idea what it will take to keep us from becoming yet another victim. It's not their fault…they simply don't have a magic formula.

After we've burned our bridges with our families, we end up going to war with anyone who we feel wrongs us in any way. Step on my shoes or pass me without saying "Excuse me," and it's on. We aren't dying over

Jordan's, we're dying because we are angry with our lives and the world steadily sh*ttin on us, and the dude who stepped on our Jordan's was just that last straw of disrespect that broke the camel's back.

There's nothing wrong with being angry about a f*cked-up situation. That's natural. What's wrong is to take that anger out on people who had nothing to do with it. What's wrong is to ignore what you are doing to make your situation f*cked up, while blaming everyone else. What's wrong is to throw your life away because you're angry. Instead of wasting your life over something the news reporters will call "trivial" and the church folks will call "ignorant," here's the number one thing you need to do, followed by several other suggestions to help you deal with anger.

- ☐ Know why you're angry, and who you're angry with. Leave other people out of it.
- ☐ When you're angry, tell people before they start bothering you and making things worse.
- ☐ Before you do something stupid, breathe and count for at least 20 seconds.
- ☐ If you're going to destroy something, make sure it doesn't belong to someone else. Your anger has nothing to do with them.
- ☐ If you feel like violence is the only option, weigh out the consequences. Will you get away with murdering someone in the street? Doubt it.
- ☐ Listen to some music, write something, or work out. Turn your negative energy into something else. If nothing else works, jog until you're tired.
- ☐ Find someone you can talk to when you're stressed or pissed. Look at what they do that calms you down.
- ☐ When you finally figure out what you've been so mad about all your life, deal with it like an adult.

Finally, if you don't think that anger and other emotions have any effect on your health, you're really missing a big part of the picture. That's why there's a whole chapter in this book dedicated to Emotional Health. The relationship between your emotional state and your physical well-being is well-document. Study after study has proven that not only can your moods and mind states be affected by what you eat or do, but your emotions themselves can have a big impact on your wellness. As Dr. Craig Sommers writes in the *Raw Foods Bible*:

> Emotions have been scientifically proven to have a powerful effect on the immune system...Immune cells such as T-cells, B-cells and macrophages (the white blood cells) have receptors for neuropeptides. Neuropeptides are created in our body every time we have a thought, and our immune cells listen for and react to the emotional dialog. Positive thoughts such as love, joy, happiness, forgiveness, and so forth, create health-promoting neuropeptides that boost the immune system, while negative thoughts such as fear, hate, jealousy, possessiveness, and so forth, create neuropeptides that can depress the immune system and lead to disease...
>
> If you could only remember one thing from this book, I suggest you remember this. If there is someone in your life towards whom you feel

animosity and refuse to forgive, you are not hurting them, you are hurting yourself. Forgive them and your health will benefit. I once heard someone say that holding a grudge against someone is like drinking poison and expecting the other person to die. Many researchers are now convinced that our emotional state is just as important as our nutritional state in the quest for optimum health.

Write a set of rules you can't break when angry. (I won't hurt myself or someone else, damage property, pursue that which is angering me, etc.) And find a safe way to let it all out. (sprints, pushups till failure, music.)

WHAT'S STRESS?
BY SUPREME UNDERSTANDING

"Keep a rugged dress code, always in this stress mode/ (That sh*t will send you to your grave!) So?/ You think I don't know that? (BLOW!) Nigga hold that!" – M.O.P., "Ante Up"

Stress is defined as "failure of a human or animal body to respond appropriately to emotional or physical threats to the organism, whether actual or imagined," of "the disruption of homeostasis (balance) brought about by physical or psychological stimuli." That means stress is an internal thing, completely based on how you react to something you perceive (or imagine), not the reality of that thing. That's why some people could be terribly stressed about losing their job, while someone who's used to changing jobs won't feel the same. So, since it's all on you, it's also on you to do something about it…if it's become a problem for you.

Is Stress a Bad Thing?

Contrary to what most people believe, "stress" ain't all bad. We all need a certain amount of stress to be able to respond to challenges effectively. Without stress, we don't get the necessary push to overcome adversity, and become complacent. This is just like how our people were "lulled to sleep," becoming politically passive after the Civil Rights era passed. Without any idea of what we should be fighting (since the system never really changed), we actually lost the will to fight. This would happen to us on a physical level also…if it weren't for our natural tendency to have stress. According to success coach Susan Castle:

> My coaching philosophy is that stress is a signal – we often treat stress as something to be avoided, as something negative and harmful but in reality we need stress to motivate us. The same way as if we went to the gym and never got out of breath or lifted a weight that was even slightly challenging – we would never achieve anything.

According to the Canadian Mental Health Association's publication, *Coping with Stress*:

> How we perceive a stress-provoking event and how we react to it determines its impact on our health. We may be motivated and invigorated by the events in our lives, or we may see some as 'stressful' and respond in a manner that may have a negative effect on our physical, mental and social well-being.

But excessive, unmanaged stress can lead to major health problems. Cortisol, also known as "the stress hormone" because it's released only when the body is under stress, is believed to affect the metabolic system causing faster heartbeat, quicker breathing and higher blood pressure and metabolism. Norepinephrine, another stress hormone, is believed to play a role in depression and hypertension. Excess stress also wears down our immune system and can play a role in obesity. Chronic stress has been shown to cause both short-term and permanent hair loss. Too much stress can even induce a heart attack which could lead to death.

Job-Related Stress

❑ Work-related stress can also make you sick, and 25% of all employees view their jobs as the number one stressor in their lives. The other 75% must be too scared of losing their jobs to tell the truth. According to the *Encyclopedia of Occupational Safety and Health*:

❑ Psychologically demanding jobs that allow employees little control over the work process increase the risk of cardiovascular disease.

❑ It is widely believed that job stress increases the risk for development of back and upper-extremity musculoskeletal disorders.

❑ Studies suggest that increased rates of mental health problems (such as depression and burnout) for various jobs may be due in part to differences in job stress levels.

❑ There is a growing concern that stressful working conditions interfere with safe work practices and set the stage for injuries at work.

❑ Some studies suggest a relationship between stressful working conditions and suicide, cancer, ulcers, and impaired immune function.

❑ A 2002 study found that workers who perform meaningless work with minimal chance for input were at higher risk for dying young.

❑ A 2003 study shows that working for an unfair or unreasonable boss can result in dangerously high blood pressure.

❑ Another study found that long term-strain on the job is more harmful for the heart than aging 30 years or gaining 40 pounds.

❑ According to the *Journal of Occupational and Environmental Medicine*, health care expenditures are nearly 50% greater for workers who report high levels of stress.

Are You Stressed Out?

If you feel exhausted most of the time, feel close to tears or "breaking down", shout at the people around you at work or at home, find yourself unable to concentrate, your normal eating pattern is disturbed, and/or you have trouble sleeping, you're stressed out for sure. But let's be all the way sure. The following list, based on a test design by Clinical Psychologist, Dr. Thomas Yarnell, contains symptoms generally related to stress. Make copies of this page and keep track of your score as you rate each symptom according to the following rating scale:

How Serious/ How Often	Not A Problem	Mild and Occasional	Mild and Often	Severe but Occasional	Severe and Often

Points	0 pts.	1 pt.		2 pts.	4 pts.	5 pts.
Stress Symptoms		Pts.	Stress Symptoms (Contd.)			Pts.
Unusual breathing (fast, shallow)			Unusual heart beat (fast, pounding, irregular, etc.)			
Feels warm/hot when it isn't			Sweat more than normal			
Obsessive worrying			Too serious			
Muscles feel tight or tense			Dry mouth			
Uncomfortable around other people			Nervous stomach (gas, diarrhea, constipation)			
Unhappy when there is no apparent reason			Urinate more than normal for you			
Panic attacks			Headaches			
Perfectionist			Often have colds			
Heartburn			Often get the flu			
Increase in appetite			Loss of appetite			
Frequent aches and pains			Workaholic			
Lack of concentration			Nausea			
Memory loss			Insomnia			
Depressed			Feel self-conscious			
Sexual problems (any kind)			Crying spells			
Lonely			Irritable			
Anxiety			Fearful			
Fatigue			Anger			
Restless feeling (feels like you have to move)			Shy, withdrawn, or uninterested in socializing			
Difficulty giving emotional support to others			Dissatisfied with where you are in your life			
SUBTOTAL			SUBTOTAL			
TOTAL (BOTH SIDES)						

Scoring

Total Score:	A total score of 20 points or more indicates that you need to do something to reduce the amount of stress in your life.

According to Susan Castle, you can put stress to good use as "a signal that you are reaching the boundaries of your comfort zone." But this zone, which Castle calls the "Learning Zone...where all breakthroughs occur" has a boundary. Past that boundary is burnout, breakdown, and health problems. When stress levels pass your comfort zone, and cross over into being seriously uncomfortable, the first thing you should do is immediately take a break, whether it's five minutes or five hours, and put the situation into proper perspective.

"I'm delving into the emotionality of what it means to be human... If I didn't address these emotions, I'd probably get cancer." – Alanis Morisette on her songwriting therapy

There are tons of other ways to alleviate stress, both short-term and long-term. Different personalities have different stress thresholds and the coping mechanism that works for one person doesn't always work for another. According to Dr. Hamden. "Choosing one that fits your lifestyle and personality is what will have the greatest benefit."

Take the survey, figure out what you're stressed about, and then read this next article for tips on how to manage it.

---

37 WAYS TO REDUCE YOUR STRESS

☐ Do something different from what's stressing you out. It doesn't mean you have to quit. But either you take a break, or break down. It's your choice.

☐ Smile (even if it's just to yourself), and tell yourself you feel good, and you can handle it, whatever it is. Consider that any crisis can be an opportunity. You'd be surprised how powerful self-affirmation (positive thinking) can be in bringing about real results.

☐ Get comfortable in a chair, close your eyes and take 3 deep breaths. As you exhale, let your whole body relax. Enjoy it for a minute and then go back to what you were doing.

☐ Find your tense muscles (See "The Benefits of Massage") and relax them.

☐ Go for a walk. It can be around the block, or through a nice area where the sights are pleasant. It's therapeutic.

☐ Seek the help and advice of the people you trust. It's kind of like a support group, without making you feel like something's seriously wrong with you (though there might be!).

☐ Listen to some relaxing music. Music therapy can help people reduce daily stress. Music heals indirectly by stimulating the body to heal itself. We're talking Sade here, not Waka Flocka. Not that music like that doesn't serve a purpose. In fact, music that makes you want to jump up and elbow somebody in the head can actually be good for your health. It can offer you a therapeutic release by releasing some pent-up tension and getting your blood flowing, which helps with stress. However, it can also raise adrenalin levels, which does the opposite. You have to see what works best for you.

☐ Get organized and kill the clutter in your life. One of the most common causes of stress is being disorganized at work or at home. By reorganizing yourself, you can use your time and energy more effectively. Decide what is important for you and do it. Prioritizing tasks helps you to minimize stressful situations

☐ When a situation is not worth the fight, time, or energy let it go. It is not giving in but an acknowledgment to yourself to move on for your own emotional freedom. Think about something you need to let go of. Accept that there are events that you cannot control.

☐ Plan, but don't become anxious. Avoid worrying about problems ahead of time. (The "what if..." question). It's easy to make something a bigger deal than it needs to be, creating stress about something that hasn't even happened (and might not happen at all!).

☐ Pay attention to the signs you are getting stressed (and what's triggering it). Take regular mini relaxation breaks. A twenty-minute nap can do wonders.

- Making unrealistic demands on yourself is a big cause of stress. Sometimes, you just need to be easier on yourself (if you're doing a lot, not if you're a lazy ass). A healthy attitude will reduce wear and tear on your physical and emotional energy and lower tension. According to Dr. Raymond Hamden, a psychologist with the Human Relations Institute in Dubai: "People who have a higher anxiety level are more prone to stress

- than others. But for everyone it's important to set realistic goals. **A common cause of stress is the frustration that comes from setting goals too high.** The inability to reach goals is frustration. Frustration leads to aggression and aggression can lead to violence or depression."

- Take frequent, short vacations. Even if you can't afford Aruba, you can afford a trip to the nearest lake.

- Measure your strength and capabilities. To help realize yours, on a piece of paper, try listing five strengths that you possess, which can get you through a crisis. Below them, list five weaknesses that can prevent you from reaching your goal. Commit yourself to change one each day. List five attributes that you would like to have and explain why you want them. Finally, record your activities in the previous week and list things you most enjoy doing. You may be surprised at the result of this self-examination.

- Exercise vigorously at least 3 times a week. Exercise is great at combating stress, and strengthening the body's defense against future stress-related problems. Warren G recently told an interviewer: "People [in Hip-Hop deal with] stress a lot and have anxiety. I used to stress when I had pressure to meet a deadline or something. So, when I work out, that's kind of what makes me calm. It makes me feel good. I don't get all riled up and all crazy."

- Get more sleep than you are currently getting. Your brain can sort a lot of things out while you're resting. (See "Get Some Damn Rest")

- Even people living in war-torn countries can remember when things were better. And they still play soccer in the middle of those dirt fields with the land mines in 'em. Why? To keep the good times fresh in their mind.

- Leave early enough so you don't have to rush. And allow time in your schedule, whether daily or monthly, for the unexpected. Factor unexpected

- Learn to say "no." People can drain you. You're helping them to be more stress-free, while killing yourself in the process.

- Avoid chemical "stimulants" (which are sometimes actually "depressants"). Stop smoking and cut down on alcohol. Reduce your intake of caffeine. It might pick you up, but it also puts you down hard. And it raises stress levels throughout your body.

- Decide on a risk you have been considering (changing jobs, or moving). List all that could go wrong, what you have to lose, and then, if it seems worthwhile, do it.

- Think good thoughts about the people you encounter every day. Find the good even in the worst of us. It's there.

- Add some variety to your life. Do something completely out of the ordinary, like riding the back of a shopping cart through Wal-Mart until they kick you out.

- Keep in touch with friends and relatives, especially the ones who have the least drama. Unless hearing about their crazy life makes you feel better about your own.

☐ Learn to give and accept compliments. It's all part of that positive state of being. You'll need to bounce stress off you like a hater's criticisms.

☐ Be yourself and accept your own. Look in the mirror and accept who you are and your situation in life. Develop a sense of humor and keep a positive attitude about it, all of it, even the crappy parts. This can help you not take life so seriously. As long as you are working at it, everything will eventually work out the way you want it too. Treat yourself with that kind of respect, and treat others with the same respect (or better!).

☐ Take responsibility for your feelings. When you get angry, take a break and cool down before you act. (See "Do you Have an Anger Problem?")

☐ Know your values and priorities and be true to them.

☐ Laugh more. A University of Maryland School of Medicine study found that when people laughed during a comedy, their blood vessels expanded, increasing blood flow to their arteries and reducing their heart disease risk. Comedian Mark Curry, from the sitcom Hangin' with Mr. Cooper, was moments away from committing suicide in the Spring of 2006, after an accident that burned 18% of his body. "I wanted to kill myself and, by the fourth day, I said, 'I can't do this.' I felt less than a man," Curry explained. "I couldn't even look at my own body. I saw my hand with the peeling skin and threw up, and I didn't look at myself again." What stopped him from overdosing on his pain medication, as he'd planned? According to him, it took a few calls to old friends like Sinbad and Bill Cosby. "They made me laugh, and that helped a lot," he said.

☐ Realize that life is continually subjected to growing pains. And that, with each growing pain, you will learn tolerance and become a happier, better person. Whatever doesn't kill you, only makes you stronger.

☐ Eat a more balanced diet. Stay away from foods that create stress on the body's systems, such as processed foods.

Learn to identify the major stresses in your life. Remember, there's no escape from stress but you *can* learn to gain control, handle it, and benefit from it.

Take your favorite ideas from the list and try them. Something like "laughing more often" won't take up much time or effort.

DEALING WITH ANXIETY
BY LANDRIA CARR

Anxiety is defined as "distress or uneasiness of mind caused by fear of danger or misfortune."

It doesn't mean you'll be viciously scrubbing your hands every ten minutes or feeling the urge to faint whenever you're put in front of a crowd; it just means that you're stressing about something. It could be as simple as getting ready to fly or waiting in line for a roller coaster.

Anxiety can also lead to phobias, which are anxiety disorders marked by a persistent, irrational fear and avoidance of a specific object or situation. Phobias…are 100% curable as is anxiety. As aforementioned, it's just a matter of choosing who you want to help you overcome it. Now in the case of phobias, **the most common and successful cure for any phobia—via both methods [self-help and professional]—is called aversion therapy, which is basically curing the fear with the fear itself.** For example, if someone was suffering from arachnophobia, aversion therapy would be placing him or her in a room full of spiders. Depending on the case, this therapy could be gradual (shadow of a spider → toy spider → dead spider → living spider) or sporadic and or all at once (being placed in a room full of living spiders). Sounds cruel, but it works! 100% Success rate!

But for the simpler forms of anxiety, there are ways to help yourself relax and face whatever challenge awaits you head-on!

Herbs! (No…not THAT kind)

So, there is a list of plants that are considered very relaxing and calming. These plants can be mixed into drinks and are ideal for anxiety relief. And guess what? ALL LEGAL! Balm, Catnip, Hops, Lime flowers, Oat straw, Orange blossom, Passiflora, Skullcap, Valerian, Vervian, and Wood Betony just to name a few. Should you need pictures of these plants or information on where and how to grow them, Google is your friend.

> **Did You Know?**
> Although most clinical studies have failed to demonstrate that aromatherapy alone can produce significant health benefits, even in terms of reducing anxiety, aromatherapy massage – perhaps because of the massage component – has been more successful. But recently, an international team of scientists found that burning frankincense (resin from the Boswellia plant) activates ion channels in the brain to alleviate anxiety or depression. This is a small step towards scientific evidence that aromatherapy does more than make your room smell good.

Aromatherapy (No…it is not a "girl thing"; this works for everyone)

Scents and water have been the considered therapeutic remedies since the dawn of time. Albeit, the media tends to overdo the idea a bit, it doesn't make it any less true. Men and women are able to draw a bath, but the activity is primarily female. Why? Who knows? It's just one of those things; right up there with women making sandwiches? (Who comes up with these gender schemes?)

Anyway, the top five therapeutic scents include, Basil, Geranium, Lavender, Melissa, and Rose. Two or three drops of this stuff in a bath…or extracted for a massage oil…and you're in business.

Create a "feel good regiment" made up of aromatherapy, some herbs, mediation, good music, and you're set.

HOW DO YOU FEEL?

BY SUPREME UNDERSTANDING

You'd be surprised, but you can actually make yourself feel better just by FEELING something…literally. As in touching. While whatever you're thinking about is also a way to relieve stress (See "Sex is Good for You"), that's not what I'm talking about here. At least not entirely. A recent study published in the journal *Science* found that tactile contact – touching something light or heavy, smooth or rough, soft or hard – can have a profound effect on your perceptions and judgments, even when the object has nothing to do with the task at hand. For example:

❑ A resume on a heavy clipboard made readers think an applicant was more serious about the job than the same resume on a lightweight clipboard.

❑ People who did a puzzle made of sandpaper-covered pieces later judged a social situation as "harsher" than people who did a smooth puzzle.

❑ People sitting in wooden chairs drove a harder bargain in a mock car sale than people sitting in cushioned chairs.

The study confirms what we've been saying all along when we use metaphors and slang: heavy = serious, rough = uneasy or harsh, hard = strict or difficult. What does that mean for you? Well, other **studies have shown that children who have emotional/behavioral problems can be calmed by squeezing a soft stress ball** (the kind you can squish and it returns to its normal shape). Other **research has shown that people can improve their mood by looking at pleasant images** (like landscapes), **reading motivational literature, touching "feel-good" surfaces and even looking at certain colors.** The subconscious mind is that deep. **German researchers have even found that being exposed to an unpleasant smell while you sleep can cause you to have bad dreams.**

In *How to Hustle and Win, Part Two,* I write about the colors worn by politicians (dark blue suit, red tie) to make people feel they have integrity, and the colors painted on prison walls (pastels) to decrease feelings of aggression among inmates. And **a new study published in April of 2010 in the journal *Psychological Science* suggests that the very sight of sickness prompts the immune system to mount defenses against illness.** So our brain is steadily processing many layers of information, including colors and textures. Why not help it move in the right direction by giving it something it will like?

For example, if you're stressed, try sitting in a comfortable chair, or sliding your hands across something smooth (but not cold). If you need a boost, trying rubbing your fingers across something bumpy or looking at bright colors. Sounds weird, but science says it works.

Wouldn't hurt to try, would it?

MUSIC MAKES ME LOSE CONTROL

BY BEAUTIFUL SEEASIA

"Do what I gotta, to eat a decent meal, brothers is starvin'/ Don't try to find a job son, it's all about robbin'/ So don't be alarmed, when we come through, cause we supposed to/ If you opposed to, get your face blown dude, off the map." – Mobb Deep, "Give Up the Goods"

It's up blasting, the seatbelt is off, I'm doing about 15 over the speed limit and suddenly I'm in a Tri-state state of mind. It's a sound that makes me feel that I would be willing to lose it all if provoked.

"Murder Music," as Mobb Deep calls that sound, puts me in straight guerrilla mode, although I personally have a knowledgeable foundation to stand on. I'm swerving between extreme feelings of cautiousness to recklessness just because of the tone of music that I'm listening to, which are really the feelings of the artist being transferred to its listeners. So what could that mean for the moods of unstable people who DON'T care about cautiousness or sensibility, or those who have no foundation of knowledge to ground them? For all the young impressionable minds out there, whether they're of biological age or just young in the mind, music can influence you to be in an extreme state of emotions that cannot be produced without its aid.

Many of our parents have acknowledged how Luther Vandross or The Whispers helped bring a lot of babies in the world with their ballads because of the "This is what I do to get you in the mood" lyrics these brothers kicked. And because of the composition and live instruments played by creative souls, jazz music was vital in calming the moods and focusing the goals of many of our grandparents' journeys in life. Similarly, Hip Hop's positive messages were once largely responsible for the wave of young men standing on the corners in the 80's & early 90's feeling empowered like the ancestors they were debating about.

With today's music lacking the subtle themes of baby-making love that it once had, or the live instruments that brought forth perspective, or the

> Did You Know?
> It's well known among psychologists and neurologists that music affects your brain patterns and moods. But can you imagine that listening to dancehall artist Sean Paul could cause someone to have seizures? That's exactly what doctors learned about Stacey Gayle, a young Canadian woman, who has a rare condition called musicogenic epilepsy. It causes her to experience epileptic seizures (the big kind, known as "grand mal" seizures) whenever a Sean Paul song plays within earshot. She visited the hospital and played Paul's hit "Temperature" on her iPod for doctors. She soon suffered three seizures. So doctors implanted more than 100 electrodes in the right side of her brain to pinpoint the abnormal area of her brain and then surgically removed the electrodes, along with parts of her brain suspected of causing the seizures, effectively curing Gayle of her epilepsy.

empowering message, what remains in the mainstream is pretty toxic by comparison. It is clear that the current state of volatile emotions spilling over is related to the music we listen to. People are unconsciously aware that music is used to put them in a desired state of emotions. If you're feeling depressed about a breakup, it wouldn't be wise to put on music that focuses on the matters of the heart unless you're truly ready to heal. If you're pissed about poverty, incarceration rates, and murder, then it may not be a good idea to put on Tupac's music, unless you plan to utilize his words to empower yourself and promote social change.

Music is a manipulator of the emotions that can either take you to heaven or hell instantly. The key is to use music to make you feel better, because destiny stands on the premise of will accompanied by feelings. If you want to live in a Nino Brown fantasy and feel like a hood superstar, then put on a Rick Ross track and envision your destiny. Of course, you might find your destiny in prison or 6 feet in the earth's soil. But if you plan to author your reality in a world of happiness and in a circumference of abundance, then put on that Teddy Pendergrass song that goes, "So good, good lovin' somebody and that somebody loves you back. It's so good needin' somebody and that somebody needs you back."

Use music as a tool to meet your needs. When you want to do something you're not in the mood for, play the type of music that'll encourage you to do it.

MEDITATION: A PATH TO INNER FREEDOM
BY JAMIL SULEMAN

Simply defined, meditation is being aware of your thoughts and emotions (your inner environment) and observing it without judging it or using your mind to label it. It's being present as "the watcher" of this inner environment. Really the ultimate aim of meditation is to still your mind completely, so that you can tap into the greater powers of the Universe.

I know what you're thinking, "Don't I need my mind? Isn't it what empowers me, and isn't it what oppressive and manipulative people try to control? Isn't regaining this ability to use my mind a good thing?" The answer is yes, but the fact is most people don't use their mind...their mind uses them.

Steven Bantu Biko, a South African freedom fighter who was assassinated in the 1970's, famously said, **"The greatest tool of the oppressor is the mind of the oppressed."** This means that, when you let your mind dictate your life unchecked, it controls you and not vice versa. It's like the dog walking the owner. And when your mind is left open to influence, without your awareness of what the input is, it's susceptible to influences from anywhere. **This is where subliminal advertising comes in. Cats watch so much TV or are on the internet so much, leaving their minds usually unchecked and opened to ideas that may not benefit them.** Basically, when you don't observe your mind and become the watcher of your thoughts and emotions, you can get brainwashed and live a reactionary life repeating tapes that you didn't even want to listen to. It's like leaving your iTunes open for anyone to drop in tracks, and then you loop em. If you're not happy with Vanilla Ice on repeat, it's time to take control of your playlist.

Besides the calming, relaxing effects on the mind, meditation can also boost your immune-system and increase your amount of vital energy. This is because you are releasing internal resistance that you were not even conscious of before. Once you make something unconscious, conscious (like self-limiting beliefs), you have the option of choosing to keep that pattern or not. This is why you may hear people say, True Power comes from Within.

You might be thinking, "This sounds great, but who has the time to just sit and do nothing, while I got a hundred things to do?" I assure you, if you just take 15 minutes of your time in the morning before you start your day to tap into a quiet state of internal presence, it will increase your productivity and you will be less stressed out while you do those hundred things. It's not that hard to dedicate a few minutes a day to meditation, and you'll probably see such an improvement in your life that you'll start increasing how much time you meditate (and even invite your friends and family to join you).

If you are new to meditation, here is a simple method to try out. There are hundreds of forms of meditation, but don't get caught up in a particular school. Try out stuff, and go towards what you intuitively feel. Trust me, the more you become centered, the more you will clearly sense what your mind and body naturally prefer.

❏ Find a quiet and peaceful place, free from distractions. Be sure to turn off your phone, and let anyone around you know you wish to be left undisturbed for a moment. If they are stressing you, let them know it will only take a few minutes (you can start with just 10 or 15 minutes).

❏ Sit in a position that is comfortable to you, either on the floor, in a stool, or in a chair. Some people use meditation cushions which you can purchase. Try not to lie down if possible.

❏ Make sure that your back and neck are straight. This will help you stay alert, and allows for energy to freely move through your body.

❏ Close your eyes and begin to focus on your breathing. Don't try to control it, count it, or visualize it. The point is to still your mind, so just observe your breathing, and focus on the sensation of the air moving through your nostrils.

❑ Allow all your thoughts and emotions to rise up and pass away. This is really the "work" in meditation, as our main motivation tends to be attachment. Now is the time to release those attachments, and tap into your basic essence.

❑ If you can, start to scan the sensations of your body from the top of your head to the tips of your toes. "Check in" with your whole body, and try to focus on what you feel, as opposed to visualizing it in your mind.

❑ As you become more sensitive, try and feel the whole body, and the subtle energy running through your inner-body. Your ability to do so will increase as you quiet your mind and focus on the sensations in your body without judging them.

❑ To close the meditation, return to your breathing, and tell your mind and body to relax. Open your eyes and rest for a moment. Return back to what you were doing, refreshed and re-energized.

Meditation and Depression

Meditation has been around for eons, and has been passed down by indigenous and original peoples for just as long. Meditation was one of the original prescriptions for depression, anxiety, and other mental agitations, and studies are now proving that not only does it work – it may work more effectively in the long-term than prescription medication.

The Autonomic Nervous System, which regulates the internal activity of the body and its organs, consists of two parts: the sympathetic system and the parasympathetic system. The sympathetic system activates when one is preparing for a stressful situation ("fight or flight"). The parasympathetic system is usually active the rest of the time ("rest and digest"). When one is in a depressed, anxious, or negative state, they tend to be operating from the sympathetic nervous system, which causes a host of internal problems if a stress factor is habituated (like a prolonged depressed state) causing chronic health issues.

When one goes into a meditative state, they begin to activate the parasympathetic part of their nervous system, slowing down their heart rate and decreasing internal stresses to organs. This results in more mental clarity, which relieves many symptoms of chronic depression. In a way, meditation may be the direct opposite of a depressed, fearful, or negative state of mind and body.

Find a way to add mediation to your everyday life. Learn to notice when you're in Sympathetic or parasympathetic mode.

Panic Attacks
BY JUSTICE RAJEE

A "panic attack" is one of those conditions, like depression, that we just don't like to talk about in the hip-hop community. We associate "panicking" with "punking out" or being so nervous you lose it, a very un-hip-hop thing to do. But panic attacks are real, and are actually more common than you'd think...and they can be pretty serious. In 1998, Violent J, a member of the notoriously white "horror-core" rap group Insane Clown Posse, was hospitalized for two days following a series of panic attacks that forced them to cancel their U.S. tour. In 2008, Eve had a panic attack on her flight to perform in Australia for the first time. So the causes might be different (you might be reasonably freaking out about something real, or you might just "naturally" have some issues). The point is, if rappers can have em, so can you. In fact, you may have had one, and just didn't know.

What is a Panic Attack?

According to the DSM-IV, the official diagnostic manual of the American Psychological Association, victims of panic attacks experience the following symptoms: pounding heart or rapid heart rate, sweating, tremors, sensations of smothering or shortness of breath, feeling of choking, chest pain or discomfort, nausea or abdominal distress, dizziness, lightheadedness or faint derealization, depersonalization, fear of losing control or going crazy, fear of dying, paraesthesia or hot flashes. Additionally, a single attack could be followed by a month or more of more anxiety, such as worrying about future attacks, worrying about whether the attacks will cause physical illness, and/or significant behavioral changes.

The damage done by the attack is less severe than the long-term feeling of losing self-control. In our community the discussion of even a minor mental health issues is unheard of. Most people suffer through an attack and its aftermath alone. They will deal with accusations of faking ill to get attention or hiding some other substance addiction, without support. Since we do not usually seek mental health services even informal ones like confiding your frustrations with a close friend or an elder, we suffer the insecurity and fear alone. Panic/anxiety disorders are often hereditary, so the family up the street that always seems to have these events is not just crazy, they need some care.

How Can you Prevent a Panic Attack?

Here are some steps you can take to lower your risk:

❏ Avoid caffeine, alcohol and other stimulants
❏ Stay away from food with artificial colorings, additives, and sugar
❏ Learn a meditation or controlled breathing technique and make it apart of your regular routine
❏ Pick up Yoga or Tai Chi, or another martial art
❏ Exercise daily and eat a balanced diet
❏ Read labels on over-the-counter medicines and herbal remedies. Some chemicals and herbs can increase panic/anxiety symptoms.

- Seek wise council and support following a traumatic or disturbing experience. Do not suffer alone; ask for help.

Panic attacks are preventable and treatable if you take the proper steps. All the prevention measures above depend on your ability to honestly assess how you are doing, what you are doing, and when you may need a little help. Meditation and the practice of martial arts are age old means of managing stress and building your capacity to deal with whatever you encounter. Learning how to get in tune with what your body is saying will provide a lifetime of benefits.

Start by removing stimulants from your diet, then get support from family and friends, and start a yoga, meditation, or exercise routine.

LET IT GO

BY MECCA WISE

Buildup of any kind in our physical bodies can cause disease/toxicity. Feeling angry, sad, jealous... holding grudges or being stagnant for long periods of time is NOT good for our emotional health. When something is not useful to us physically, our bodies eliminate it. So why can't we do the same when it comes to the things that create emotional distress? Sometimes we hold on to people, possession, and behaviors that are not useful anymore and we therefore inhibit our growth.

Possessions
- Have your broke appliances become decoration?
- Have you kept shoes and clothes for years although you can't fit them/or haven't worn them?
- Do you have more than 1 non-working car in your driveway but you are not a mechanic?
- Do you have magazines from the 90's saying one day you will make time to read them?
- Do you have Valentines memorabilia from middle school?

If you haven't already done so in 3 years, you are not going to use it, read it or wear it anytime in the future. It won't come back in style, you won't get it fixed, and it's not a good idea to save it for your unborn child. If you paid too much for it to give it away, then sell it. Eliminate the clutter from your life.

People
- Have you stayed in a relationship and you don't know why?
- Do you see your mate as a place holder until you find better?
- Are you getting nothing from a relationship but still stick around?
- Do you stay in relationships for fear of how to get out or fear that you won't find better?
- Do certain relationships make you miserable but you still engage in them?

☐ Have you outgrown old behaviors and have absolutely nothing in common with some friends?

Abusive or Parasitic relationships don't change until you change them. Don't stay in relationships to use others or be used. Don't let fear of any kind keep you in a relationship where you have no business being. Although you love your friends, sometimes it's time to move on. If they are not willing to change, then eliminate negative or stagnant people from your life, because they will actually keep you from growing.

Behaviors

☐ Are you still mad at something that was done to you five years ago?

☐ Do you not speak to someone and you can't even remember why?

☐ Do you not like him/her because at some point one of your friends did not either?

☐ Do you jump at the opportunity to talk bad about someone?

☐ Do you sit around waiting for someone to offend you?

☐ Do you continue behaviors that you don't enjoy just because you have done them for so long?

☐ Do you have self-limiting beliefs that you are unworthy?

☐ Do you fear change?

Eliminate those negative behaviors, perspectives, and habits from your life.

Although some of the above questions may seem humorous, the reality is that people hold on to far too much, for far too long. When something stops working, or working for you, it becomes time to let it go. We must leave some people, possessions, and behaviors behind in order to grow and develop – in order to find new opportunities. Elimination is a natural and necessary process. So stop holding on to things that will make you sick, leave you miserable, or keep you stagnant. Let it go.

Plan a garage sale, it'll be easier if you get friends to help you. Open an ebay account, and get money for your unused items.

WHAT'S UNDER ALL THAT CULTURE?

BY BEAUTIFUL SEEASIA

No matter how one articulates Supreme Mathematics, gets thorough with Black's Law Dictionary, recites the Al-Fatihah in Arabic, or divinely sings a Kirk Franklin gospel tune, there's serious, RESIDUAL mental health issues with our asses (trauma)! Negroes are depressed, angry, crazy, compulsive liars, have extreme mood swings, etc. You cannot hide behind a hijab, kufi, headwrap, suit, fez, locks, afro, beret...Healing is a responsibility!

I'm not impressed by any of the costumes anymore. Underneath all of these labels, good jobs, titles, memberships, loc jewelry in hair, bandanas, Muslim oil, dashiki, tattoos, mud cloth, Yoruba white...underneath allll that, is a freak show of pain, fear, and trauma. And until I hear more confessions about the steps taken to fix the voids that come with blackness, universal oppression, molestation, violence, death, prison, drug addiction, abandonment, ass whoopins, baby daddy/babymama drama, bad relationships, whatever…I'm not impressed. When I hear people who have dealt with all the Negro trauma that come with being us in this world yesterday and today, then I'll trust your character with what you represent. For now *yawn*

What's your confession? Cause all our Black asses have one. What? Schizo, bipolar, depressed, paranoid, bitter, ADD, ADHD, what do they label you with? Whatever it is, we got to get through *that*, and THEN you can come to fully accept and represent your Islam, your Christ, your lessons, your oath, your Torah, your sovereignty, your worldview. Healing is key. Let's go.

It's the same thing with running to a new relationship without truly getting over the one before. Like I said earlier, RESIDUAL. Root word? Residue! I've been the shot out girlfriend, tyrant daughter, impatient mother, emotionally unavailable sibling, negative influence for a friend, temperamental chick, whatever. And in this period of time (really the last year) that I chose to actually deal and heal with what I was, and some of its ugliness (which is my responsibility when co-existing in a world with billions of other people), I had to admit that I can go as natural-haired as I like, be thoroughly known as an activist or hustler, appear to be civilized/cultured, even relocate, whatever…But all of it didn't matter if I kept running from healing.

Supreme living is without damaged emotion. That's what trauma is and that's what I find among so many of us, now that I am beginning to see much clearer since I am healing. The fog is removing itself, and many of you all are some ugly mofos. Because for one, I see my old self in many of you, the person that hides. And for two, because I know I am not really looking at you, but an agent of our own continued oppression. Take off the suit. Be yourself. Heal yourself.

Create a "Self-Reflection Routine." Set aside a couple hours a week to reflect and be honest to yourself. Better yet, do it whenever you're uncomfortable, confused, or hurt by something, personally

---

42 WAYS TO IMPROVE YOURSELF

❑ Read a book (or a few pages of a book) every day.

❑ Learn a new language.

❑ Pick up a new hobby.

❑ Take up a new course.

❑ Create an inspirational room.

❑ Overcome your fears.

❑ Level up your skills.

❑ Wake up early.

❑ Have a weekly exercise routine.

❑ Start your life handbook.

- ☐ Write a letter to your future self.
- ☐ Get out of your comfort zone.
- ☐ Put someone up to a challenge.
- ☐ Identify your blind spots.
- ☐ Ask for feedback.
- ☐ Stay focused with to-do lists.
- ☐ Set big, ambitious goals.
- ☐ Acknowledge your flaws.
- ☐ Get into action.
- ☐ Learn from people who inspire you.
- ☐ Quit a bad habit.
- ☐ Cultivate a new habit.
- ☐ Avoid negative people.
- ☐ Learn to deal with difficult people.
- ☐ Learn from your friends.
- ☐ Start a journal.
- ☐ Start a blog about personal development.
- ☐ Get a mentor or coach.
- ☐ Reduce the time you spend on chat programs.
- ☐ Learn chess (or any strategy game).
- ☐ Stop watching TV.
- ☐ Start a 30-day challenge.
- ☐ Meditate.
- ☐ Join Toastmasters (Learn public speaking).
- ☐ Befriend top people in their fields.
- ☐ Let go of the past.
- ☐ Start a business venture.
- ☐ Show kindness to people around you.
- ☐ Reach out to the people who hate you.
- ☐ Take a break.
- ☐ Read at least 1 personal development article a day.
- ☐ Commit to your personal growth.

Add as many suggestions to your daily routine as possible. Think about what you need and what you'll benefit from the most. Don't do it to be "busy," do it to get results!

YOUR TIME IS NOW!
BY COACH BRANDI

With numerous adversities coming our way, many people have a tendency to put their own hopes and dreams on the backburner. As a life coach, I find prioritizing to be the biggest challenge that I face with clients. We sit down, set goals, and they aren't accomplished. And why? Because people have been conditioned to put others first, and to not be "selfish" enough to work on themselves. Or they rather spend their money on instant gratification vs. something that brings lasting peace and satisfaction.

Today, I would like to remind you…If you do not build yourself up and accomplish the goals you set for yourself, then how can you edify others? An empty vessel has nothing to give…

So, I want you to make the decision that you are going to focus on creating the best you. YOUR time is NOW!!!!!!! Here's a couple of tips to get started…

Accept responsibility. Often times we blame our past, present, and future situations on other people/events. Remember that we are a people of free will, and that we create situations in our lives, even if we don't want to accept it. (For example: Bad budgeting can be prevented; signs are given in bad relationships; parents do not dictate our adult lives.)

Get on your mission. Every organized business has a mission statement which provides guidance and focus. It is my belief that individuals need mission statements as well. There are several websites that provide online mission statement wizards to assist you in creating your very own personal mission statement. One you have your statement, print it, memorize it, and reflect on it **every day.**

The next thing to do is **build your resilience.** Once you make a decision to live a life of freedom, prepare for adversities. There will be haters, bills, challenges, etc. that will come your way. I tell people all the time that being a life coach does not make me immune to the troubles of the world. It is the way that I handle those adversities is how I show resilience. Prepare to do a spiritual detox of the people, places, and things that hinder your growth.

Prepare yourself for a **life-long learning** experience. The reason that all great leaders and entrepreneurs constantly read is because they embrace continuing education. Take the initiative to read daily, attend workshops, enroll in audit classes (where you can "sit in" on a college class without being enrolled), etc. The more you learn, the more you grow, and the more you can teach to others. (I have included a beginner's self-improvement book list on my website to get you started).

Network your way to success. The old saying is true: "Your network is your net-worth." Surrounding yourself with success-minded people is one of the ultimate keys to success. Anything else is draining, and will eventually take you down a notch. Attend events to address your goals, join associations/ organizations, and communicate with members beyond the meetings. Build a website, create contact cards, and travel! And most importantly, find a mentor that can provide a gateway to your goals.

Take care of **your body.** A person who is unhealthy, stressed and tired definitely cannot be an asset to others (or themselves). When was the last time you exercised? It is on a regular basis? When was your last annual physical? Do you sleep 6-8 hours daily? How are your eating habits? These are all things to think about. We are at a critical point of our lives. We are too old to treat our bodies any type of way, yet young enough to make corrections and prevent chronic and genetic diseases.

Get your mind on your **money.** Again, we are at the age to correct past mistakes, and prepare for the future. Yet, some of our peers do not have savings accounts, create piles of credit mistakes, and don't even know what an IRA is, so how can they have one?!? Today, get a free copy of your credit report, set aside 10% of your income to pay down debts, and reprioritize your money. Create a budget, do not acknowledge raises (save the new found extra money), and live within your means!

Your last lesson for today: address the **spirit** that is within. Take the time every day for meditation, journaling your progress, and blessing others. Give your time, gifts/talents, and tithes when you are able. All great leaders know to delegate responsibility and power.

These are just a couple of tips from one of my workshops, "The Seven Secrets That all Leaders Know." And yes, YOU are a leader! If you need any assistance in implementing these strategies, or want to bring this workshop to your city, do not hesitate to Contact the Coach!

Find ways to nurture your gifts and strengths. Create a "Success Incubator" for you and your friends.

---

3 STEPS TO A LIBERATING SENSE OF SELF-WORTH
BY BRYAN OGILVIE

Your value as a person is not to be measured by your achievements: while your desire for success is healthy, the false notion that you *need* success to be important or desirable is not…

If you have this false notion, the following cycle might sound familiar: (1) you get inspired to do something, (2) you make a *minor* attempt at it, (3) you experience a natural setback, (4) you lose motivation and give up, and (5) you *beat yourself up about it continuously after the fact.*

Your internal dialogue might go something like: "Look at me, here I go messing things up AGAIN." "What the hell is wrong with me? **Why can't I get this right?**" "I'm just stupid… stupid, stupid, stupid." "See, I knew this would happen. *Why do I even bother?* Just forget it…"

This is low self-worth, and in time, the negative self-talk associated with it becomes **ingrained**. It finds a reason to come up even in insignificant mistakes (oversleeping, missing a deadline, less-than perfect cooking, etc.), so when you have low self-worth, almost EVERY experience is an opportunity for a mental beat-down, and eventually, *negative self-talk turns into an internal monster*: a hidden gremlin that keeps you defeated and depressed. (If you're perceptive, you'll notice this gremlin both in yourself and in almost everyone comfortable enough share their deeper thoughts with you.)

So an opposite, more positive self-talk which encourages success (an internal champion) might seem unimaginable for you. You might have adopted negative thinking habits through years of repetition, and so now, **you accept them as true without question**, and even subconsciously *look* for reasons to give the gremlin validation.

The first step to liberate yourself from this is to **SEPERATE YOUR EXPERIENCES FROM YOUR IDENTITY**; to learn to see yourself as separate from your results...

If you can't seem to stay motivated, that just means you don't know how to motivate yourself (which is a skill you can learn). If you can't seem to build anything with the people you meet romantically, that just means you don't know how to build intimate relationships, and if you can't seem to manage your finances, that just means you don't think strategically about your income and expenses, but these are all skills you can learn! None of this means that something is wrong with *YOU* – only that you don't know how to do a particular thing.

Remember that **failure is a stepping stone to success**. You have to fail multiple times in everything you do before you learn to do it, so stop interpreting your failures as indications of your personal value.

Goals are meant to unfold your potential and improve your life experience, NOT to prove your worthiness to exist. Nothing you could ever do will prove your worthiness to exist, because that's proven by your existence in and of itself (there are no mistakes in the Higher Plan).

The second step to liberation is to **LEARN TO FORGIVE YOURSELF**...

Self-forgiveness is hard because *we harbor extreme guilt and shame towards ourselves for what we've done in the past.* In the past, our selfishness or lack of self-control might have caused someone else – maybe even someone we loved – to experience pain, and through anger, we may have even done this intentionally.

If this is you, **accept the fact that it happened** and that there's nothing you can do about it now.

Shame and guilt about the past prevents you from making the most of your life in the present, and therefore, it denies the world of the brilliance only you have to share. We ALL have things in our past that we're ashamed of, so your mistakes (even the most terrible ones), don't make you a bad person, they make you *human*.

"How can I forgive myself if I knew exactly what I was doing at the time, but I still went ahead and did it anyway?" The answer is to realize that *everyone you know, including you, is, at all times,* **only doing the best they can**.

Everyone's doing the best they can; everyone's operating to the highest level their consciousness allows them to. While we may know something intellectually, that doesn't mean we really KNOW it – it doesn't mean we've integrated it into our core of our being, and that's the difference between knowledge and wisdom: While it's relatively easy to understand a concept, it takes life experience to internalize it, and this life experience usually comes in some form of pain, **such as the guilt you feel from your mistake now**.

Wisdom is a bio-feedback mechanism. The prefix *bio* means life, and wisdom is the mechanism that obtains lessons from life by reflecting on it. You have to make mistakes in order to learn, because if you REALLY knew, you wouldn't have made the mistake in the first place. Forgive yourself for not having enough wisdom at the time, and move forward with the lessons you can extract from it now...

Debbie Ford talks about this in her audiobook *The Secret of the Shadow: The Power of Owning Your Whole Story*, where your "shadow" is the past that you've been avoiding or feeling guilty about and your "secret" is **the hidden jewels of insight contained within that same past**.

While you THINK your past is negative, it actually holds keys central to self-knowledge and your life purpose... if your shadow has something to do with a significant other, the secret might lead you to devote yourself to creating love in all of your relationships. If your shadow has something to do with your family, your secret might lead you to dedicate yourself to becoming a wonderful parent and helping others to do the same, so on and so forth.

You can't play cut and paste with your life history, and you can't relegate the parts that you're ashamed of to some place in the back of your mind (or they'll haunt and limit you from the subconscious realm). You have to "own your whole story" and accept **everything** that's happened – the good, the bad and the ugly – in order to get the wisdom you need to be your Complete Self.

The third and last step is to **REALIZE THAT THINKING IS A HABIT**. You have the same thoughts over and over again not because they're valid or accurate, but simply because you're in the habit of thinking them... .

If you're in the habit of thinking limiting and discouraging thoughts, then you have to get into the habit of thinking supportive and encouraging thoughts, and you can gain this habit in the same way you gain any other: **repetition**.

At the start of a new year, when you write down the date, you accidentally write down last year's number because of **repetition**. When you check your e-mail online, you type out your username and password without even thinking about it because of **repetition**, and when you stop using an alarm clock, you get up at the same time everyday anyway because of **repetition**.

To be positive, motivated and proactive in your life, you have to condition yourself, through repetition, to automatically think thoughts conducive to positivity, motivation and effectiveness. To free yourself of anxiety, depression and low self-esteem, you have to condition yourself, through repetition, to automatically think thoughts conducive to faith, joy, and high self-esteem. By consistently forcing yourself to think thoughts of your own design, you gain control over your mentality and your emotions, as well as their consequent behavior. It's called *The Science of Auto-Suggestion.*

So take affirmations seriously, and find creative ways to make them part of your automatic, habitual mind state.

Remember, in your life, you're the sole-controller, so free yourself from *what* happened and take charge of *what is* happening. **Today is the first day of the rest of your life,** so clean the slate mentally and start building something right and exact in the here and now.

After all, *the "you" that you dislike is not even the real you anyway* – it's simply a garment which holds your essential spirit, and just as the wardrobe in your closet can change, so too can the character which adorns your soul…

Incorporate peaceful thoughts to every day routines turning them into peaceful practices. Example, associate cleansing the body with cleansing the mind, when showering. Now that's multitasking!

TOXIC RELATIONSHIPS
BY SHERIESE NICOLE TANAHESI

All relationships are soooo tricky, even amongst good people. They take time, energy, understanding, consideration, compromise, and effective communication. Honest, caring and genuine communication is key to healthy, thriving relationships.

Baby Mamas and Baby Daddies

This is a phenomenon that we must master. Children should have both parents in the home together. But in our world that is not the case a lot of times. **All relations between the split parents directly or indirectly affect the child.** Never speak negative to a small child about their parent. It is disrespecting and hurting them. If a child is older and able to understand certain concepts – honesty about the other parent can still be loving and empathetic. Talk to them as you would want someone to talk about them when they got older. Don't let selfish emotional attachments and unnecessary resentments lead to scaring the child's emotion/mental development. Extreme situations may exist that are traumatizing and more challenging to speak of with love and empathy. With wisdom and willingness one can learn to balance this for the healthy development of the child.

The thing about split parent confusion that always boggled my brain is how a person can lay down with someone, have a baby, then…they ain't

S***. Everything you refer to a person you share so much with is a direct reflection of self! Even if you were really the one done wrong, look at what in and about you attracted and chose it. Don't waste your time resenting a parent of your child. Look at yourself, heal, forgive, and place any current toxic behavior from another in its rightful place in your life.

Training the Mental

Some years ago I was mad and complaining about something I was going through to an elder and he said "Sheriese, focus on what you want and you will attract it." In other words, instead of complaining about hate and envy, focus on what I want, to give and receive Love. Instead of being consumed by the ills of the world, focus on what you want the world to be and what you can do to make it better. Give no energy to negative energy and don't assume anything. Simple stuff that even great intellectuals can sometimes find to be a task but a gratifying healing process when practiced. We Master the Mind/Emotions. We apply universal righteous principles to all negative thinking.

We learn to respond with logical truth and to not react with emotions. This is the toxicity you address with a clear head, don't sweep it under the rug and act like foul stuff ain't happen. **Part of effective communication is allowing another person to know that issues need to be addressed in order to move forward within a healthy relationship.** Have an unbiased, level headed elder mediate the dialogue if needed. That conversation has to involve all parties being honest and if that can't happen, get away quick! With time the truth will come to light itself.

"Watch what you think, it will manifest into your words and actions; watch what you say and do, it will manifest into your habits; watch your habits, they manifest into your character; and your character will manifest destiny."

True Self Love

Ultimate love for self and true self-acceptance is the key to more harmonious relationships. Due to lack of English words to define, describe and conceptualize feelings, emotions, and spiritual phenomenon, we throw around the word LOVE with various meanings.

While teaching parenting at a shelter, a recovering crack addict mother said, "I love my kids." I explained that love manifests within our actions and she could only treat and love her children as well as she treated and loved herself.

As long as we live, the ability to love self will always be in development. Acceptance of personal liabilities as well as assets is essential to a better relationship with self, and others, in turn. No extremes like "I'm perfect" arrogance or "I'm stupid" negative self-talk. Just stay in the middle, "I'm perfect with all my imperfections" and take responsibility for what needs to change. Never accept a growth stunted self and keep an open mind about things you might not know that can assist in your growing process.

When you know everything, you can't learn anymore. Always accept and be in your own lifelong process of development. When we are able to love ourselves through emotional scars and distorted cognition due to past experience, then we can truly love others and attract healthy, meaningful relationships.

Make the best of things when possible. Get out, if it's not worth it. Think of ways to come to an understanding and be happy.

WHAT IS A HEALTHY RELATIONSHIP?

BY AFYA AND KHNUM "STIC.MAN" IBOMU

FROM OUR UPCOMING BOOK, REVOLUTIONARY LOVE

A healthy relationship between a young Black man and woman is characterized by the following:

- ❏ Both are grounded in their respect for and love for their community.
- ❏ Each is individually motivated to be providers and self-sufficient in their own talents and interests.
- ❏ The integrity of their words and actions does not contradict and when it does it's acknowledged and corrected with love, understanding, and self-discipline.
- ❏ The man is 100% sure and clear on his commitments to his woman and chooses to because of his own values and thoughts and his assessment that she is worthy to him of such commitment and not because of any outside influence, tradition, physical urge or circumstance.
- ❏ The woman is sure of her own character and self-respect, and has evaluated her man prior to their relationship going past the "friend" stage, so she knows deeply that he is worth her loyalty, love and camaraderie without a doubt.
- ❏ The views of the two are in sync naturally and not due to manipulation of any kind.
- ❏ There are good vibes and humor, passionate sex, healthy activities, intellectual activities, community activism, and shared interests to keep one another engaged and interactive.
- ❏ Each allows the other the space needed for growth without nagging, judgment or betrayal, but without lessening personal standards or accepting bullsh*t.
- ❏ They are spiritually connected. Meaning they are both striving to be in harmony with the greater good and not just out for material things.
- ❏ They support each other's endeavors and always speak to each other, and about each other, with great respect. Their arguments are not full of personal attacks, name calling, and immature emotional rants and tantrums. They communicate by listening and respecting each other's viewpoints striving not to win over the other, but to win in the battle over self and needed to be right. They each seek to master their emotions for the benefit of themselves and for the success of their relationship.

Signs you have a Healthy Relationship

We came up with our lists separately. Based on what we each put down is a testament to our chemistry, unity and cohesiveness as a family.

Afya:

☐ You show affection regularly.
☐ There's plenty of laughter.
☐ Arguments are light/short term.
☐ There's honest communication.
☐ You have a satisfied sex life.
☐ You enjoy spending time together.
☐ There's complimentary growth.
☐ You're supportive of each other in both words and deeds.
☐ You're loyal to each other, especially through hard times.
☐ There's emotional control.
☐ You put up with each other's bullsh*t.

Khnum:

☐ You're actually friends, not just co-parents or sex partners.
☐ You look forward to time together.
☐ You both feel motivated by the other.
☐ You respect each other's strengths and have compassion for the things that challenge each other.
☐ You don't seek to manipulate one another for own pleasure over your partner's misery.
☐ You are each living fully productive lives, doing things in your own right that are important to you and fulfilling, both individually and collectively.
☐ When you argue, you are able to disagree without violence, verbal abuse or immature emotional tantrums. You're able to resolve issues with positive communication and principled understanding
☐ When you seek win-win conflict resolution, not a winner/loser paradigm.
☐ When you see your relationship as a top priority for what you want in your life
☐ When you realize that you are gonna have to put in work at any relationship and if you gotta put up with some bullsh*t, you're happy to put up with your spouse's bullsh*t, because you realize they feel the same way about you and your bullsh*t.
☐ You both accept the responsibility of being happy as a couple.
☐ You are patient with each other.
☐ You are respectful of each other's privacy.

Discuss what you value the most in a relationship with your partner or write it down like in the above article. It'll be easy to compare when written down.

---

9. DYING TO BE BEAUTIFUL

Image is everything. Or is it? And in whose image are we making ourselves? Just think about it. Think about all the things we do to "improve" or "enhance" our appearance. From hair dye to nose jobs, there's a lot to consider. Most of it started with us. In ancient times, we invented makeup, tattooing, piercing, exotic hairstyles, and other forms of "body modification" like embedding jewels in our teeth. But while some of it was cosmetic (just to show off or attract the opposite sex), and some of it was practical (like eyeliner, which was used to protect our eyes from direct sunlight and smoke), how much of it was done in attempt to look like another group of people? And how much of it was done even at the expense of

our health? Today, we've got women bleaching their skin, frying their hair, dying it blonde, and even getting nose jobs and lip reduction surgeries...often DYING in the process...and who do we end up looking like? The people who told us we were ugly in our natural state. And I'm not just talking about women here, because not only are more and more men doing the same things nowadays, but men are encouraging this madness.

Skin-lightening causes cancer, mercury poisoning, and all kinds of other problems. We ain't never done that in ancient times. In fact, Marco Polo reported that we used to rub sesame oil on our babies to make them darker!

Hair dyes are linked to bone cancer and bladder cancer, and haven't been monitored by the FDA since 1938! We colored our hair, but we used henna (which is made from plants) or red clay from the earth.

And the list goes on. We get liposuction (which is often fatal, especially for Black women) instead of using diet and exercise...just to acquire a body type that probably wasn't meant for us in the first place!

There's even a new surgery where Black women are having their eyes permanently turned blue (just Google it!) and the results are disastrous, leaving women blind.

We're not saying there's anything wrong with wanting to look better. The question is what is your idea of what "better" looks like (and why), and what risks are you willing to take to get there?

LIGHT SKIN IS ALWAYS IN
BY SUPREME UNDERSTANDING

We all know Lil Kim did it. We all know Sammy Sosa did it. And while

some of us have noticed folks like Beyoncé and Mary J. Blige gradually getting lighter over time, we're not sure whether it's the makeup, the airbrushing, or something bigger. But cases like Lil Kim and Sammy Sosa are clear. They bleached their skin chemically because they believed light skin to be preferable over dark skin. In Sosa's case, he also changed his hair texture. In Lil Kim's case, she changed everything, down to the shape of her nose and cheekbones. The worst was when she challenged the choice of a dark-skinned actress portraying her in the *Notorious* film, claiming light-skinned singer Ciara looked more like her! The light skin obsession is that deep. It's definitely more psychology than style. And it's not rare. In fact, it's more global than Coca Cola.

When Dr. S. Allen Counter found reports of high levels of mercury poisoning among patients in Latin America, Saudi Arabia, West Africa, East Africa, and even among newly arrived Bosnian and Albanian refugees in Germany, he struggled to find the common thread. At first glance, most of the patients with mercury poisoning had two things in common. They were (a) people of color and (b) women.

It wasn't long before Dr. Counter discovered the rest. In his 2003 article for the *Boston Globe*, he writes:

> In every case, clinical questioning revealed that the women had used skin-whitening creams – many for years. In other words, these women had tried so desperately to whiten their skin color that they had poisoned their bodies by applying mercury-based "beauty creams."
>
> **Ninety percent of the women entering border clinics in Arizona with mercury poisoning were Mexican-American, and they like their Mexican counterparts had been using skin-whitening creams.** These skin-whitening creams contain mercurous chloride, which is readily absorbed through the skin. Saudi, African, and Asian women were also using these skin-

bleaching chemicals in a tragic attempt to change their appearance to that of white women.

Mercury poisoning is known to cause neurological and kidney damage and may also lead to psychiatric disorders. Upon finding high levels of mercury in the urine of women and men in Tanzania, scientists initially thought that the indigenous people had been accidentally exposed to elemental mercury vapors from gold mining operations or methylmercury from the consumption of fish from Lake Victoria that had been contaminated by the liquid mercury discharge from gold mines [Sound familiar? See "Fish...With Extra Oil"].

It was later discovered that the high levels of mercury in the urine of Tanzanians living around Lake Victoria were the result of the use of mercury-based skin-whiteners. In other parts of Africa, including Nigeria and Kenya, one finds widespread mercury poisoning from the use of skin-lightening creams and soaps.

When asked why she thought women in Saudi Arabia used skin-whitening creams, and in some cases even applied these creams to their children, one woman from an Arab-American family replied directly, "Oh, that's simple. It is well known that in many Arab families the whiter looking children are the most preferred. People will often respond positively to the lighter-colored child and simply ignore the darker one."

So, the prevalent medical evidence of high levels of mercury poisoning among women of Saudi, African, Asian and Mexican backgrounds reflects a common and prevailing belief that whiter skin has greater currency and appeal.

Apparently, the patients...believe that removing the healthy melanin from their skin with toxic creams and soaps makes them more valuable in their own cultures and in European and Euro-American societies in general.

In an interview with one Latin American woman about identification and self-image, I was told that "whiter-looking Spanish women are generally perceived as more attractive to many Latino men and vice versa." The woman, a journalist, went on to say that during her childhood, her parents and her friends' parents had always carefully screened the children invited to their parties "to be certain that they were light enough in color" and thus "of sufficient socioeconomic value to be included."

Of course, there will be health complications that accompany ANY chemical that shuts down the melanin in your body. First, your skin never becomes consistently lighter throughout. According to Sharon Parry, a Jamaican salon owner in London:

> You can always tell (they're using it) because the knuckles on their hands and feet never change. Also, they look ghostlike. Their appearance looks gray and dull, especially if they're dark-skinned people. In Jamaica, if we see someone like that, we call them 'duppy' (which means ghost).

It gets worse from there. According to Thomas Fuller, in his *New York Times* article on skin whitening in East Asia:

> Some patients also develop leukoderma, where the skin loses the ability to produce pigment, resulting in patches of pink like those on Ms. Panya's face and neck. When she first began using the cream, which was packaged under the name 3 Days and cost the equivalent of $1, she said she was very happy

with the results. Her skin started itching, but she tolerated it because her complexion lightened considerably. She got bigger tips at the restaurant, where she sang folk songs, she said. But when her face became blotchy two months later, her boss told her she could no longer sing at the restaurant because she was unsightly. In April, she told her story on a Thai television program, breaking down as she described how she ruined her face and lost her job. But first, the announcer ran through a list of the show's sponsors, including a cream called White Beauty. "Use this cream," the announcer said. "It gives you expert treatment."

How does this stuff work? Skin-lightening treatments work by breaking down melanin through a chemical process or blocking melanin production. The strongest (and cheapest) skin whiteners contain toxic mercury such as mercury (II) chloride or ammoniated mercury as the active ingredient. Still cheap, but considered a "safe" chemical, Hydroquinone is found in most other whiteners, and has been shown to cause leukemia and cancer in mice and other animals. The European Union banned it from cosmetics in 2001, but it still shows up in creams in the developing world (many of which are made in Europe!). Oh and it's still sold over-the-counter in the United States.

In Malangu Ntambwe's article on skin lightening among South Africans (noting similar practices among Black Americans, Cubans, Jamaicans, Japanese and South Asians), he describes the following effects of various skin lightening agents:

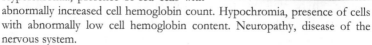

Mercury derivatives: Neurotoxic problems such as ataxia, speech and hearing impairment; mental problems such as irritability, fearfulness, and depression; kidney problems such as mercury-induced nephropathy; and immunotoxicity

Hydroquinone preparations: Ochronosis, a blue-black discoloration caused by deposits of ochre-colored pigment. Hyperchromia, presence of red cells with abnormally increased cell hemoglobin count. Hypochromia, presence of cells with abnormally low cell hemoglobin content. Neuropathy, disease of the nervous system.

Topical steroid products: Contact eczema, bacterial and fungal infections, Cushing's syndrome, acne, skin atrophy and pigmentation disorders.

According to Ntambwe, some of these effects take a while to appear, and others mimic known disease patterns. As a result, they are sometimes misdiagnosed even by doctors, especially since most patients deny using skin lighteners. **Research says up to 69% of those who practice skin lightening may suffer from at least one complication. And these problems are not limited to the users themselves. In one medical report, a 3-month-old patient was found to have kidney, eye and blood disease because the mother had used mercury-containing cosmetics during pregnancy and later during breast-feeding.**

The whitening cream industry is estimated to be worth around $432 million in India and $7 billion in China. In 2005, 62 new skin-whitening products were introduced in supermarkets or pharmacies across the Asia-Pacific region, a jump from the average of 56 per year over the past four years. In fact, in 2009 worldwide sales increased at a rate of 14% throughout non-European markets. And throughout Asia, all your favorite cosmetic companies are involved. Olay has a product called White Radiance. L'Oréal markets products called White Perfect. Nivea even has a skin whitening lotion for men. The more toxic combinations are created by smaller companies, like "Crema de Belleza-Manning," which is manufactured in Mexico (and includes mercury). Even stronger (and more dangerous) chemicals are created by local bootleggers and are available – where else – throughout Africa and the Caribbean.

In "India's Hue and Cry over Paler Skin," Amrit Dhillon writes that not everyone has been pleased with the spread of these products:

> "We are against the product," said Brinda Karat, the president of the All-India Democratic Women's Association. "It is downright racist to denigrate dark skin."...Protests by Miss Karat's group recently forced another company – Hindustan Lever, the Indian arm of Unilever – to withdraw television advertisements for its women's fairness cream, Fair and Lovely. The advertisements depicted dejected, dark-skinned women, who had been snubbed by employers and men, suddenly acquiring new boyfriends and glamorous careers after the cream had lightened their skin.

> Yet most of India's 800 million population are puzzled to hear such creams described as symptomatic of an unhealthy self-image. In the matrimonials, the classified newspaper advertisements through which brides and bridegrooms are sought, a potential bride's porcelain skin is ranked as a more desirable attribute than a university degree. Film stars who are not naturally light-skinned are touched up to look paler on screen.

> In everyday conversation, the ultimate compliment on someone's looks is to say someone is gora (fair). "I have no problem with people wanting to be lighter," said a Delhi beauty parlor owner, Saroj Nath. "It doesn't make you racist, any more than trying to make yourself look younger makes you ageist."

Keep reading...because I want you to see how much we have in common with Original People (People of Color) throughout the world. It should show you two things (once you get past the main point that lighter skin is not "better." That is, (1) we've all been done the same way, almost the EXACT same way, and (2) we were done that way by the same people, so why are looking down at each other? Thomas Fuller continues:

> **Sociologists have long debated why Asians, who are divided by everything from language to religion to ethnicity, share a deeply held cultural preference for lighter skin. One...theory is that the waves of lighter-skinned conquerors, the Moguls from Central Asia and the colonizers from Europe, reset the standard for attractiveness.** [Duh]

> Films and advertising also clearly have a role. The success of South Korean soap operas across the region has made their lighter-skinned stars emblems of Asian beauty. [Sound familiar yet?]

Nithiwadi Phuchareuyot, a doctor at a skin clinic in Bangkok who dispenses products and treatments to lighten skin, said: "Every Thai girl thinks that if she has white skin the money will come and the men will come. The movie stars are all white-skinned, and everyone wants to look like a superstar."

In Thailand, as in other countries in the region, the stigma of darker skin is reflected in language. One common insult is tua dam, or black body. Less common but more evocative is dam tap pet, or black like a duck's liver. [Sounds like how the kids in my hood tease each other]

Oscar Bamwebaze Bamuhigire, author of *The Healing Power of Self Love*, writes:

According to BBC, more than half of the women in Mali are bleaching their skins, and the same could be said about any other region with black people, including the rest of Africa, Jamaica, USA, UK, etc.

Asians are facing a similar trend – 4 out of 10 women in Hong Kong, Malaysia, Philippines, South Korea and Taiwan use a skin-whitening cream…

 **A recent study revealed that 61 percent of Asians in Hong Kong, Malaysia, the Philippines, South Korea and Taiwan said they felt they looked younger with a fair complexion.** It also revealed that half of Filipino women, 45 percent of Hong Kong women and 41 percent of Malaysian women were currently using a skin-whitening product. "Everybody else basically wants white skin," said Leeyong Soo, the international fashion coordinator at Vogue Nippon (Japan). The Ancient Chinese used to say that, "one white covers up three ugliness."

Another survey by a research company, Asia Market Intelligence, revealed that three quarters of Malaysian men thought their partners would be more attractive with lighter complexions. In Hong Kong two thirds of men had a preference for fairer skin, while half the local women wanted their men paler. Almost half of Asians aged 25 to 34 years have bleached their skins…

Non-white people could not defend themselves against their white abusers, and so they identified with them instead! They learned to adore the white skin, and everything associated with it, and to hate the nonwhite skin, and everything associated with it. The great psychiatrist Frantz Fanon explained: "In the man of colour there is a constant effort to run away from his own individuality, to annihilate his own presence."

According to Karl Bostic's article on skin lightening among people of color in Europe at www.theGrio.com:

The magazines we saw in the predominantly Asian neighborhood of London called Southall featured only ads showing near-white models. When I called the editor of the biggest Asian magazine in London to ask why only fair or near-white models were used, she admitted that this was already a well-documented complaint…

Unfortunately an obsession with changing skin color can go much further. A recent documentary airing on Britain's Channel 4, "Bleach, Nip, Tuck: The White Beauty Within," suggested that there is now a movement of "global de-racialization," where surgeons can change your identity. "Longer legs, less body hair, a Caucasian nose, wider eyes," were some of the examples they feature. A crying Asian woman says, "I dream about how to look white, how to become white, how to look white and beautiful."

And then there's Jet, a black valley-girl sounding model who doesn't like her nose. Michael Jackson is her role model. She says, "I can understand why Michael Jackson wants to get rid of the typical black nose, because in order to fit into European society, you've got to get rid of the black nose and that's what he did." She then tells her radio listeners, "I want a straighter more European nose, because if I smile, my nose goes wide." [And THAT'S another piece of the same puzzle. See "What's Wrong with Your Nose?"]

And as you already know, Black Americans are in the same boat. Skin bleaching has been present in the Black community since the slavery era, and hasn't gone anywhere. The products might have prettier names and more pleasant promises ("fading cream" "will give you a radiant glow") but they're the same stuff. Even the Tyra Show recently did an episode on skin bleaching in the Black community. And if Sammy Sosa is any indication, it's even worse for Black people outside the U.S.

> **Did You Know?**
> In addition to the traditional products (and the bootlegs), some Jamaicans use a mix of toothpaste, curry powder, milk powder, household bleach and cornmeal.

In a 1999 *Washington Post* article on Jamaican skin bleaching, Serge F. Kovaleski writes:

"With Jamaica so close to North America, we are bombarded with images of a white culture. People have come to feel that lighter skin is a passport to better relationships and making it in this world," said Kingston dermatologist Clive Anderson. "The use of skin bleaching is spreading rapidly, and unfortunately men are starting to use it as well."…"I know they can do bad to your skin, but I have nothing to lose in wanting to be a brownin'. I am poor and bored, and being whiter would make me happier," said Sheri Roth, 22, who had just bought a tube of cream that promised "a brighter, cleaner, smoother complexion." She added, "I want people to think I am more than a ghetto girl…I want to walk into dance halls and feel like a movie star, a white one."

"There is no safe way to bleach your skin beyond your natural color," says Sujata Jolly, a research scientist. "Initially, [the bleaching cream] will appear to lighten the skin," she says. "The reaction between the sun and chemicals triggers an oxidation reaction, which then starts turning the skin darker… and as the skin gets darker, one uses more cream more vigorously. By doing that you start to break the skin, and then the chemicals will then penetrate into the bloodstream and reach your liver and kidneys. And that's where it could cause more damage," she says. As usual, we're dying for nothing.

> Eliminate as many things, as possible, that make you insecure about your skin. This includes magazines, relationships, TV shows, and thoughts.

WHAT'S WRONG WITH YOUR NOSE?

NOSE JOBS AND BLACK WOMEN

BY SUPREME UNDERSTANDING

What do Keisha Cole, Lil Kim, Toni Braxton, Janet Jackson, Patti Labelle, Halle Berry, Naomi Campbell, Amerie, and possibly Beyoncé, have in common? Compare their noses ten years ago and now. I'll wait.

In 2008, 907,141 Black Americans had cosmetic or plastic surgery procedures, nearly TRIPLE the number from 2002. Latinos were in the same boat, getting 1.2 million procedures in 2008.

The increase among Black women doesn't surprise Dr. Emily Pollard, who has been a plastic surgeon for 18 years. Pollard typically does body contouring, breast lifts and eyelid surgeries on Black women. But she doesn't perform nose jobs. Why? "What they see is not what I see," she explained. "They see something different." So what is it that they see? Hmm...let's think about it. What's the most distinct African feature of your face? Your nose. Yes, that big, wide nose. That nose that we once couldn't afford to change, That Nina Simone/Pam Grier/Keisha Cole nose that screams authentic Blackness. Oh wait...Keisha Cole swapped hers out. But most of the women

> Did You Know?
> For face work, the average cost for Botox injections is $417, and a facelift is roughly $6,532, according to the American Society for Aesthetic Plastic Surgery. Rhinoplasty (nose job) averages $4,277. Insurance rarely covers the costs of such procedures. Translation: People are paying out of pocket to "fix" their face. For that much money, you can afford to hire a personal trainer, dietician, or style coach, and get some real improvement in your life!

getting nose jobs don't even have noses that prominent. They're just not narrow "enough." And what do we replace our noses with? Noses that are pencil thin with pointy tips and small nostrils. But that's not self-hatred, huh? Nah, it's just cuter right?

Well, what makes a European-style nose better? Who said it was better? How did we come up with what's cute and what's not? This is no different from how Asian women are currently spending millions of dollars on eyelid surgery (which makes their "chinky" eyes nice and round like a European's). It's no different from the millions of dollars we spend on "fixing" our hair and skin complexion (often giving ourselves cancer in the process). And for those who say it's just a "different look" (not us trying to look like them) how many of us are making our features look more African? Seems like the only people trying to frizz their hair, fatten their lips and darken their skin are white people! Well, maybe when white models start widening their noses, we'll start being happy with ours again!

BOOTY SHOTS

BY SUPREME UNDERSTANDING

Kim Kardashian has em, Amber Rose has em, Angel Lola Luv has em, Nicki Minaj has em, and just about every stripper making a decent living nowadays has em. Seems like booty shots are a substitute for talent! Because I can't tell you why Kim Kardashian and Amber Rose are famous, besides their backsides!

MediaTakeOut.com has highlighted the recent increase in women getting silicone booty injections. But the silicone booty craze has a serious downside to it. Here is the story of one MTO reader (Warning: It's pretty gross):

I had silicone injected into my butt in 2006. I almost died from it. It took me over a 1 year to heal after having a surgery to drain the silicone out of my buttocks. I regret it sooo much. The person was unlicensed. My bigger [butt] got lots of compliments and men chasing me, but it almost cost me my life. I had to get a blood transfusion. I lost lots of blood from doing this to myself. My hospital bill was 100,000 from being in the hospital for about 3months. My friend and I went through this pain at the same time. I couldn't drive. They had to insert a pic line into my arm. I lost lots of weight. My butt is terrible. Men was running from me. I couldn't get a man – they were scared of my butt. I had a leaky booty. Silicone had to leak out of my butt so I could get better. I really couldn't wear clothes. If I did it would leak through, leaving a big wet spot. Embarrassing. I had to drive sitting on pillows in my convertible. The wounds wasn't healing after being treated at wound care. So I used aloe and it healed up after a month. Wow. Now I want to have fat transferred into my buttocks and later have a skin graft to cover up my scars, but I'm scared, thinking I might die.

> **Did You Know?**
> In March 2010 alone, six women from the Newark, New Jersey area ended up in hospitals after receiving buttocks-enhancement injections containing the same material contractors use to caulk bathtubs. The women checked into hospitals after their procedures, apparently done by unlicensed providers, went horribly wrong. Different from medical-grade silicone, the substance used in the botched procedures was believed to be a diluted version of nonmedical-grade silicone. "The same stuff you use to put caulk around the bathtub," said Steven M. Marcus, executive and medical director of the New Jersey Poison Information and Education System. Mr. Marcus said there have been other incidents of people providing implants of nonmedical-grade silicone, then getting put out of business – only for other shady providers to surface. "Caveat emptor: Buyer beware," Marcus said. "If it looks too cheap, there's probably a reason it's too cheap."

Buttock injections are a surgery that changes the shape of your body by injecting a substance (Hydrogel or PMMA) into your body that will stay with you forever. This substance can leak, because infections, and end up out of place, so that your booty looks totally ridiculous. Why would any sane woman, who's not a prostitute desperate for more clientele, get a booty shot? Is it because it's quick? So quick that you can go to a "booty shot" party where one "doctor" (probably one without a license) is giving a dozen girls injections (probably with the same needle). In fact, there were over a dozen arrests for these types of parties and unlicensed procedures in 2009 alone. Or is it because they're cheap? The most expensive procedure for "fixing" your booty is the Brazilian butt lift, which actually uses fat from your own body, but it runs about $14,000. Then there's butt implants, which average about $4,000. Finally, there's buttocks injections, or booty shots, which can cost anywhere from $1,000 to $2,000.

Now, guess which one is most likely to go wrong? Guess which one is most likely to cause health complications? Guess which one is hardest to get reliable information on? Guess which one is most likely to be done by someone unlicensed and unprofessional? And guess which one you can't sue for when they screw up? Since most women who choose booty shots are simply considering "quick, easy, and cheap" maybe I should ask if that's what you want to be associated with…quick, easy, and cheap? If not, try a much better, safer, and free alternative to getting surgery. It's called exercise. Your ass, tummy, thighs, and waist don't need any surgical sculpting if you simply start jogging and doing squats.

Look up fitness routines specifically for the legs, thighs, butt, and waist. YouTube and the rest of the internet is full of them.

DYING TO BE THIN
WHAT ARE YOU WILLING TO LOSE?
BY MECCA WISE

Most women have been on a diet at least once in their lives. The problem is that many women don't diet to be healthy, but only to lose weight, to fulfill some body image that is said to be standard or sexy. **Did you know that models weigh 25% less than the average American woman? Not only that, but most Black and Brown women throughout the rest of the world are considered "sickly" if they are whatever is considered "normal" here.** Yes, most of the world celebrates a little meat on their women. But here we are told that something is wrong with us if we aren't a size 6 or smaller. We think we're "fat" when we have curves, even though that's the way we're naturally made! (See "Am I Fat?") It seems that its only when white girls started wanting a "Black girl butt" that "Black girl butts" became acceptable for us! So yes, the media is selling us a false image. And although not ALL of us want to look like those models that we see on television or in magazines, most of us want to see quick results when we're not happy with our size and shape. But wanting to lose 5-10 pounds by the next week to fit into an outfit just may not be realistic.

If we really care about our health, then we should create a healthy way of living and not constantly jump to the next fad diet (See, "HipHop And Weight Loss.") Don't get me wrong – there ARE some healthy plans out there, but it's so important to carefully examine whatever diet plan or diet pills you are using. Some diet pills sound natural or are even endorsed by celebrities, but many diet pills contain drugs that can not only affect your heart and lungs but can have other unfavorable side effects, including nausea, back pain, heart palpitations, and even death

But we're so serious about achieving a certain body image that we'll risk death for it! That is, we're "serious" as long as it happens quickly. This is why you have so many Black women dying from liposuction procedures nowadays (See "Get the Fat Out"), not to mention the rising rates of bulimia among Black and Brown women. Did you think bulimia (forcing yourself to throw up after eating) and anorexia (not wanting to eat, for fear of gaining weight) were "white people" problems? Not anymore. Now they're considered "American" problems, meaning they affect just about kind of woman living here, regardless of color. And the more people in other countries look to the West for their standards, the more you see anorexia and bulimia rates rising there (See "Fat and Drunk in East Asia").

> **Did You Know?**
> Studies have found that women with cosmetic breast implants – in addition to having other issues, like risky leaks – are three times more likely to take their own lives, and three times more likely to die from drug and alcohol abuse. Why? The research suggests these women had pre-existing body image and self-esteem issues before getting the implants. Apparently, Captain Obvious commissioned these studies.

Many times we want more out of something than we are willing to put in. We want quick fixes without making real changes. And we pay for it, one way or the other. It's time to think about everything that we are putting into our bodies (foods, drugs, ideas, etc.).

To see the best weight results, choose being healthy overlooking cute/sexy. Don't risk losing essential nutrients that can cause future health issues.

To see the best weight results, choose being healthy overlooking cute/sexy.

GET THE FAT OUT: THE DANGERS OF LIPOSUCTION

BY SUPREME UNDERSTANDING

37-year-old Rohie Kah-Orukotan went into the Weston Med Spa in Weston, Florida a healthy mother of three just looking to "shed a few pounds." She left on a stretcher and is now braindead as her family struggles with whether to pull the plug. She'd gone in for a non-invasive liposuction procedure that uses a laser to melt away fat underneath the skin.

"It's a procedure so safe, that the government allows us to do it in an office setting under local anesthetic, without the regulatory equipment that an anesthesiologist would require," said Dr. Jason Shapiro, who specializes in aesthetics. Safe? Right. Turns out the spa didn't have a license from the state Health Department to do full liposuctions, and only asked for a basic blood test to move forward. Lawyers think Ms. Kah-Orukotan was given too much lidocaine, a local anesthetic, which can cause seizures like the one she experienced. Out of respect for the family, I won't repost her picture from the CBS news article, but Ms. Kah-Orukotan was a beautiful African woman without the surgery.

This kind of story is not uncommon. Every year, at least a dozen women die from procedures related to liposuction. And it's happening to more and more women of color. Sometimes, it's the way the anesthesia is administered, often without an anaesthesiologist present. Other times, it's the doctor's incompetence, because you don't have to be an actual plastic surgeon to do these procedures. You just have to be doctor, of any kind. You can even be a dentist (like Dr. Kurt Dangl, who charged a woman $25,000 for a botched procedure that nearly killed her).

And this isn't just happening to Black and brown women who can't afford good surgeons. I'm sure you know the tragic story of what happened to Dr. Donda West, Kanye's mother, who continued to pursue liposuction even after doctors (and her son) told her she shouldn't. Similarly, Tameka Foster, Usher's ex-wife, secretly flew down to Brazil in February of 2009, telling everyone, including her husband at the time, that she was attending her nanny's child's birthday party. She was really there to get Lipo. And it went wrong. She was rushed to ICU after suffering cardiac and respiratory arrest while being anesthetized for the procedure. She was put into an induced coma and eventually recovered. But damn, when will we learn? **There's a safer way to go about all this, known as exercise. If you can afford surgery, you can even afford a personal trainer, chef, or dietician (probably all three).** But some of us really need to begin by accepting ourselves, and loving ourselves, the way we are. From there, you can do what you want, and it probably won't be life-threatening, image altering or impulsive.

If you are going to go through with a surgery, and won't reconsider…Pollard's advice is that you at least educate yourself, learn the statistics, ensure that your surgeon is board certified, check if they are on staff at a local hospital, make sure they keep an anesthesiologist on hand, and to check out the surgeon's reputation and the facilities where the procedure will take place.

MY advice is eat better and exercise. It'll actually save your life instead of ending it. It's much cheaper to hire a personal trainer.

TATTOOS AND THE HOOD
BY I ATOMIC ALLAH

History of Tattooing

The word tattoo comes from the word *Tatau* which means "to tap." This comes from tribes who would "tap" ink into skin to produce designs. Arguably, according to recent recorded history; tattoos originated with the Polynesian, Tahitian, and New Zealand tribes. However every indigenous people on the planet indulges in some form of body art, typically as a part of some sort of ceremony or celebration. Whether it's the tattooing of the Polynesians, the scarification and piercings of the many Afrikan tribes, or the application of henna, red ochre, or face paint in various other cultures, body adornment has been a part of indigenous cultures for as long as people have been on the earth. There's nothing new under the sun, right? Archeologists have even discovered tattoos on mummies!

Tattoos and the Hood

Until the early '90s, as far as the United States are concerned; tattoos were a white boy rocker/biker thing. Even though you might have had an occasional uncle or cousin who'd come home from prison with a name or two, it was nowhere near as big as it is now. What happened, you ask? There are three key figures to whom I attribute the rise in popularity and acceptance of body art in the hood: Tupac Shakur, Dennis Rodman, and

Rasheed Wallace. Although it was their celebrity status that put them in positions for the world to see, the more important factor is the different social paradigms of the hood each these cats represent. Pac, from the hip hop perspective, represented the cousin or uncle that had come home from prison inked up. Dennis Rodman represented that cat that was always doing his own thing. As a matter of fact, I would go so far as to say that Dennis Rodman is the father of this skinny jeans-wearing, "rock star" look that we see on the streets these days. Rasheed Wallace came along a little later in '96. What he represented was the working class cat that had an urge for ink every now and then. From this era, tattoos exploded in the hood. Then throw in a couple video vixens with tats and you have a cultural phenomenon. After the above names came on the scene, others followed, pushing the envelope even farther. Mike Tyson, for instance, later introduced the hood to facial tattoos. Danger, from the Ray J show, introduced the idea of facial tattoos on women. Now Lil Wayne and Baby are taking it to levels that would make some Punk Rockers blush.

Art Imitates Life

And life also imitates art. For people in the hood, entertainers such as rappers and ball players represent an escape from poverty and the other problems in our communities. So the emulation and imitation of their favorite entertainers serve as an attempt to move in the same in hopes that they will achieve the same results. As of late, there has been a dramatic increase in the amount of facial tattoos in the hood. From an artist's perspective, I have no problem with that. However, as a responsible adult, I must advise that you think it through before you decide to get a tattoo on your face. Keep in mind that your favorite entertainer is in the career of his/her choice.

More likely than not, they're in positions where are financially independent and will not have to go asking anyone for a job. They may never have to go to an interview again. In fact, the facial tattoo may help them get more publicity, which will make them more money. If you're in a similar position, then get tatted up!! However, if you're not in a position of absolute independence, then you may want to hold off on the facial tats until you reach your goal!! How about this? I challenge you to use this as a motivating factor in attaining absolute independence. Let that facial tattoo be your crowning. Ya dig?!?

Risks

Although the art of tattooing is a beautiful medium of expression, it does come with a certain degree of risks. Some can be fatal. **Hepatitis C, Syphilis, MRSA (staph), and possibly even HIV can be transmitted** through the application process if a tattoo artist doesn't adhere to the necessary sanitation processes that go with applying a tattoo. The absolute safest way is to **ask your artist if he/she uses disposable tubes and needles.** Step two would be to sit back and watch that same person during their set up process. This will show you a lot about how committed to sanitation he/she is or isn't. **Some things to look for: if a person has just got out of the chair, you want to see the artist** disassemble the tattoo machine throwing both the tube and needle into a red biomedical waste container. That's shows you that this artist disposes of every needle and tube that he/she uses. Now, you may see some disassemble the machine and put the metal tubes in an ultrasonic solution and throw the needle into a biomedical waste container. There's nothing wrong with this, you just need to make sure that this studio has an autoclave sterilizer.

If it's a reputable establishment they won't mind showing you. Also during the sanitation process, at some point you should see him/her spray down his station, chair, and patron's chair with disinfectant and thoroughly wiped down. You should see him/her pull out an individually packaged needle and tube upon preparing to do a tattoo. He/she should put on a new pair of gloves. He should have laid all instruments out on a dental bib or whatever he/she uses as a barrier between the instruments and the table that is being used. All bottles should be clean.

If ink bottles look like they've never been wiped down, with all different colors smeared all over the bottle, this should be your red flag. This is an indication of cross contamination. Cross contamination occurs when an artist isn't careful about what he/she touches with contaminated gloves. Combined with not wiping the bottles and machines down with saniwipes or whatever sanitizer he/she chooses. There's no telling how many people this artist may have tatted using these same unsanitized bottles. This is a no go!!

Professional Artists vs. Street Artists

With the proliferation of tattoos in the hood, so came tattoo artists as well. Even though the tattoo hit the scene hard first, it took a little longer for the Black tattoo artists to emerge and make an impact on the culture. Shameless plug: When I started in '95, in Atlanta there were few shops that catered to Black clientele. When I hit New York in '98, it was easier to find bin Laden than it was to find a Black tattoo artist. Now days however, it seems that there are as many Black artist and shops in the hood as there are liquor stores and churches. Salute to all my colleagues and comrades getting it in all across the country!!

Day and time; things have changed…dramatically. Now, we're everywhere. With this sudden proliferation of professional Black tattoo artists, came the phenomenon that is known as the "street artist." What's the difference? A professional tattoo artist has had some form of formal training, via apprenticeship under another professional. The professional will have vast experience in working in tattoo parlors and understanding of the safety issues and precautions that come with the application of tattoos. For the most part, most street artists haven't gone through the apprenticeship process. A lot of artist will tell you such as a badge of honor. What happens when this occurs is that the street artists, for the most part, loses out on some of the most important aspects of the art.

Most of the street artists that I've met throughout my career don't take the sanitation aspect of the art as serious as the professional does. That's not to say that all street artists slack in this area. There are some professional artists that have "taken it to the street." That is, there are some tattoo artists that were properly trained and have worked in many studios and parlors who at some point decided to either work from home or go on some mobile freelance type sh*t. That's "taking it to the streets."

There's nothing wrong with this. The only problem with this is if you as a customer don't know what to look for, you're not going to know the difference. Any artist that is serious about what they do will take the necessary precautions to protect you and him/her. However, a person can only do what they know. The sad truth is that by going to a street artist, you run a bigger risk of running into an artist that actually doesn't know. This not only puts you at risk, but the rest of your family and community as well.

Don't Rush In...

It's definitely easier to take a wedding band off than it is to remove a tattoo. Please keep this in mind when you're trying to prove your point or convince yourself that your relationship is not dying. From my experience, this is one of the most irrational and impulsive decisions that people make. This is not to say that this is not for you and your significant other. If you're in a relationship with someone whom you've been with for years, then by all means – knock yourself out. Now if this is some puppy love teenage sh*t, then I strongly advise against you getting anyone's name other than your family members. I have seen cases where people have come back to get a name covered before it even had time to heal.

Why is it Addictive?

One of the most frequently asked questions that I've come across is: Why do tattoos seem to be so addictive? Tattoos are another form of expression as is all mediums of art. So for a lot of people tattoos become their medium for expression. So for the shy and timid chick and the corporate executive, tattoos become their outlet. Then there are more personal, therapeutic reasons. For the ex-heroin junkie, tattoos serve as a survival tool, a pacification of sorts. For the memorial tattoo recipient, tattoos have become a way to not only honor his loved ones but, himself also. So for these people the art form serves a deeper purpose than merely cosmetic.

Does it Hurt?

The answer is subjective: what's painful to some, bring others pleasure. I have absolutely no idea what hurts you or make you feel good. Are you going to feel it? Yes. Is it an excruciating pain? No, however this depends on your pain threshold. I can only tell you like I tell everyone else, the only way to know how it feels is to sit down and get one. It's that simple, because there aren't too many things that the feeling can be compared to.

Aftercare

Finally, as it applies to tattoos; when your artist's job ends your job begins. What that means is you bare the full responsibility of nurturing the healing process. Your artist should give you a copy of specific instructions on how to take care of your tattoo. **What you have to remember is that your tattoo is a controlled scar. So you have to take care of it accordingly.** Everyone's body is different. Since such is the case, the healing time and process is going to vary according to your physical makeup. Whatever the case here are some general instructions:

❏ Remove the bandage after an hour to an hour and a half.
❏ Wash with antibacterial soap and water.
❏ When washing, wash with hands, no cloth.
❏ Towel blot dry.
❏ Now apply a thin film of lubricant.
❏ For best results, I recommend; Aquafor or AandD ointment.
❏ Repeat this process two to three times a day for the next forty eight hours.
❏ After the forty eight hour process you can just apply lotion when it starts to itch or if it's too dry. It usually itches when it's too dry.
❏ Recommended lotions: Lubriderm, Keri, Eucerin, Vaseline Intensive Care.
❏ Continue until your tattoo no longer looks ashy or has opaque shine to it.

Removal?

Speaking of decisions, what happens when you've already gotten a tattoo and later decide you made a mistake? It's estimated that over 45 million **Americans have tattoos and around 17% of those people end up regretting it.** That's almost 8 million regrets! What do you do if you're one of them? Some people cover up their tattoos (make sure you find an artist, like myself, who specializes in "cover-ups," or else you'll end up like The Game did, with pieces of your old tattoo still showing underneath your new tattoo (the letters "LA").

Often, people want to get rid of the tattoo altogether. Unfortunately, most of the store bought products that promise tattoo removal don't live up to their promises. At best, tattoo removal creams only succeed in fading a tattoo, leaving you with the same tired image you no longer want, only a little out-of-focus and less vibrant. And as for less advanced methods – burning or excision (rubbing or cutting it off your skin) – just think serious PAIN and some serious health risks you don't want.

The safest and most effective way of getting rid of a tattoo is though laser tattoo removal. This is what 50 Cent did recently. To help with his growing acting career, he had all of his tattoos lasered off his skin.

Laser tattoo removal works by breaking down the tattoo ink with a targeted beam of light (a laser). Over a series of treatments, the ink is progressively degraded and absorbed by the body, as would naturally happen over time or due to sun exposure. The procedure must be tailored to the individual, making it difficult to estimate cost, but – unless your tattoo is teardrop-tiny – expect it to be in the four-digit range. The bigger (and deeper) your ink, the more sessions it will take. Laser removal usually requires 3-12 sessions, lasting about 15-90 minutes each…and it still hurts. Oh, and you'll look like you have a bad case of eczema (like 50 Cent) until those laser burns heal. So what does all this mean to the person considering a tattoo? Simple: Decide wisely!

Find a qualified tattoo artist or tattoo parlor, and know their quality of work. Be on the look out for possible Cross-Contamination!

TO PIERCE OR NOT TO PIERCE

BY SCIAMOOR ETERNAL EARTH

ORIGINALLY PUBLISHED IN THE 14TH DEGREE AND BEYOND

Body piercing is ancient. According to author Ted Polhemus it's "arguably the most widespread of all the permanent (semi-permanent) body arts." Piercing has been practiced throughout the world, and presumably has its origins in Africa, where the oldest examples can still be found.

Lip Piercing. The piercing of the lips for the insertion of objects into them is very widely practiced throughout the world; however, only two tribes pierce the lips with a ring; the Dogon tribe of Mali, and the Nuba of Ethiopia. Among the Dogon the piercing of the lip has religious significance. They believe that the world was created by their ancestor spirits *"Noomi"* weaving thread through their teeth, but instead of thread, words came out, creating the origins of speech.

All the other lip piercing that is practiced in the world is done with labrets, which can either be a pin of wood, ivory, metal, or even quartz crystals. Among the tribes of Central Africa, and South America the Labret piercing is stretched to extremely large proportions and large wooden or clay plates are inserted.

The Makololo tribe of Malawi wears lip plates in the upper lip called *Pelele*. The European explorer Dr. Livingstone asked a chief the reason for this, in surprise, the chief answered:

> For Beauty! They are the only beautiful things that women have. Men have beads, women have none. What kind of person would she be without Pelele? She would not be a woman at all.

Dr. Muraz referring to the Saras-Djinhas tribe near Lake Chad, who insert plates to 24 cm in diameter in both lips, observed:

The plug of wood in the lips, which became little by little a disk, and then a real plaque, was in some manner a sign of possession of the husband of the Djinja woman. It is the man who is to marry her, and very often him alone who operates, transfixing the lips of the young girl with a blade of straw forms the first sign of the deformation to which she will be subject as an adult. It is in sum, a betrothal rite.

Among the ancient Aztecs and Mayans, piercing was reserved for the male members of the higher castes, they wore beautiful *tentetl* (labrets) fashioned from pure gold in the shape of serpents, golden labrets with stones inset and ones of jade or obsidian. The Native Americans of the Pacific Northwest and the Inuit peoples of northern Canada and Alaska wore labrets fashioned from walrus ivory, abalone shell, bone, obsidian, and wood. The Carafa Indians of South America wear a thin cane in the lower lip; this denotes one being in their prime of life.

Tongue Piercing. The ancient Aztec, Mayas of Central America and the Haida, Kwakiutul, and Tlinglit tribes of the American Northwest practiced tongue piercing in a ritual form. The tongue was pierced to draw blood to propitiate the gods, and to create an altered state of consciousness so that the priest or Shaman could communicate with the gods. Today, tongue piercing is one of the most popular piercings; mostly because it's provocative and often used for oral sex.

Nose Piercing. The nose is the face's most prominent feature. Nose piercing was first recorded in the Middle East approximately 4,000 years ago and is mentioned in the Bible in Genesis 24:22. Abraham requested his oldest servant to find a wife for his son Isaac, the servant found Rebekah, and one of the gifts he gave her was a "golden earring." The original Hebrew word used was *Shanf*, which also translates as "nose-ring."

This practice is still followed among the nomadic Berber and Beja tribes of Africa, and the Bedouins of the Middle East. The size of the ring denotes wealth of the family. It is given by the husband to his wife at the marriage, and is her security if she divorced. Nose piercing was brought to India in the 16th century from the Middle East by the Moghul emperors. In India, a stud (*Phul*) or a ring (*Nath*) is usually worn in the left nostril. It is sometimes joined to the ear by a chain, and in some places both nostrils are pierced. The left side is the most common to be pierced in India, because that is the spot associated in *Ayurveda* (Indian medicine) with the female reproductive organs. The piercing is supposed to make childbirth easier and lessen period pain.

In the west, nose piercing first appeared among the hippies who traveled to India in the late 1960's. It was later adopted by the Punk movement of the late 1970's as a symbol of rebellion against conservative values, and conservative people like parents and employers still don't react well to it, so consider their reaction carefully before getting it done. Nowadays, nose piercing is gradually becoming more socially acceptable.

Ear Piercing. The ear lobe was probably man's first attempt at body piercing due to the ease with which it can be pierced. The oldest mummified body in the world was found frozen in an Austrian Glacier in 1991; tests showed the body to be over 5,000 years old. The body had pierced ears and the holes had been enlarged to 7-11mm diameter. Ears were probably first pierced for magical purposes. Many primitive tribes believe that demons can enter the body through the ear, because demons and spirits are supposed to be repelled by metal, ear piercing prevents them from entering the body.

Sailors used to have an ear pierced to improve their eyesight. Also the earring was a form of insurance, because if their body washed up somewhere, the earring would pay for a Christian burial. In many societies, ear piercing is done as a puberty ritual. In Borneo the mother and father each pierce one ear as a symbol of the child's dependence on their parents. Ear piercing is an almost universal practice for men and women; it's only in western society that it's deemed effeminate.

Genital Piercing. The ancient Indian Kama Sutra refers to the *apadevya*, a genital piercing, while a similar piercing, the *ampallang*, is said to have originated in Borneo.

Nipple Piercing. Nipple piercing was once practiced by the Karankawa Indians of Texas and is still practiced in the mountains of Algeria by women of the nomadic Kabyle tribe. However, nipple piercing has been mostly a European style. Roman Centurions wore leather armor breast plates, and rings were placed where the nipples would be, and used to hang their capes. This has led to the belief that the actual nipples were pierced to hang a cape from, but anybody who has had their nipples pierced would tell you that this would be a very uncomfortable practice.

In the middle of the 14th century, many women suddenly wore such low necklines that you could see nearly half of their breasts, Queen Isabella of Bavaria introduced the "Garments of the grand neckline" where the dress was open to the navel. This fashion eventually led to the application of rouge to freely displayed nipples, and to placing diamond studded rings or small caps on them, even to piercing them and passing gold chains through them decorated with diamonds.

In the late 1890's, the "Bosom Ring" came into fashion briefly, and was sold in inexpensive Parisian jewelry shops. These "Annex De Sien" were inserted through the nipple, and some women wore on either side linked with a delicate chain. The rings enlarged the nipples and kept them in a state of constant excitation. The medical community was outraged by these cosmetic procedures, for they represented a rejection of traditional conceptions of the purpose of a woman's body.

Modern Body Piercing

There seems to be two main schools of thought as to how modern body piercing arose, one based in America and the other in the United Kingdom. These theories are covered in books like *Eye of the Needle* and *Modern Primitives* which document piercing's development and expansion from the gay and S&M (sadomasochistic) communities. The major factor behind body piercing going from being exclusive to such groups, to becoming common and even mainstream, was the opening of the first shop to produce jewelry specifically for body piercing.

This shop, called Wildcat, is based in Brighton and is one, if not the, largest supplier of medical grade stainless steel body jewelry in the UK. It was the availability of affordable hypo-allergenic jewelry that contributed to the piercing rise in popularity. The sudden change in the nature of body piercing occurred like another baby boom. This change was brought about by a number of factors.

Most notably the rise of navel and eyebrow piercing by the fashion world as well as the increased amount of exposure given to the fetish scene on British television. This made piercing fashionable, and "safely accessible" to the general public. Not to mention that, psychologically speaking, to specifically draw attention to oneself is the goal of an ever-increasing number of people who are dissatisfied with "traditional" Western culture, which many regard as oppressive.

To Pierce or Not to Pierce?

Piercing is a profoundly personal experience. It changes not only the way in which others perceive a person but also the way that person perceives himself or herself. Self-identification is built up through numerous life experiences. In some cases, piercing is used by many as a way of celebrating particular "life crises" or a trophy of a rite of passage. It is the highly personal thing that you'd rather not verbalize.

In order to understand the motivations behind people's decisions, James Myers, in his work on non-mainstream body modifications, divided the motivations behind "severe" body art and manipulation into a number of distinct categories. The categories, listed as motivations and rationale, include sexual enhancement, pain, affiliation, aesthetics, trust or loyalty, religion or mysticism and shock value.

Myers' research goes into great depth as to how each category influences people to get involved in such forms of body art. An explanation for piercing was given by a homosexual man who was abused when he was young. He stated that piercing allowed such people to come to terms with their emotional pain by re-experiencing physical pain in an environment which they controlled and in such a way reclaim their bodies.

Raelyn Gallina stated a similar observation, "Piercing is really a rite of passage. Maybe a woman is an incest victim and wants to reclaim her body."

The writings of psychologist Freud explore the dichotomy between biological human drives and rules imposed by social life. However, pain and danger are to be avoided at all costs and human life is to be preserved above all else. This has given rise to new ways to escape the pressures of social life; adrenaline sports and thrill seekers, recreational drugs, and the rise in the practice of sadomasochistic practices and amongst these the wish to test oneself against society fears of pain.

While I am aware that there are those who find piercing utterly painless, and indeed those who find it so painful that they have, at the most extreme, lost consciousness, the experience of piercing of the flesh has been said to cause an intense sensation which, while most easily associated with pain, is not painful. Such a feeling cannot be described using available vocabulary sufficient to say it is a sensation, which, in part, drives many to acquire more piercings in order to experience and understand it.

Think about why you want to get a piercing; excitement, pleasure, tradition, to stand out? If you think of better alternatives to these things, but still want to get pierced, go right ahead.

AVOIDING PROBLEMS WITH PIERCINGS
BY I ATOMIC ALLAH

Much of the sanitation procedures, risks, and precautions that are associated with tattoos are synonymous with those in piercing. However, there are some risks such as keloids that are more commonly associated with piercing than tattoos. Keloids occur in people as a reaction to jewelry or sanitation procedures. **Some people's skin is very sensitive. So much so that if they are not pierced with high grade metals then they will have a reaction that more often than not will result in keloiding.** This can be avoided by making sure that your piercer is using surgical steel, niobium, gold, platinum, or titanium. **Sterling silver, stainless steel, and gold-plated are no no's when it comes to piercing your body.**

Another risk involved in the piercing process is loss of feeling in different sensitive areas. For example, clitoris piercing. This is probably the most sensitive of all piercings. In terms of sensation, that is. Women who get this piercing are looking to have an around the clock arousal going on. For the most part, it works. However there are times where the clitoris can become desensitized as well. One way is if the piercer pierces the actual clit (instead of the hood). Yikes!!! By the time the actual healing is done, you may lose sensation. Also, over time, the constant stimulation of the jewelry's movement can become such a routine/normal feeling that it may require much more to stimulate you. As a result, the orgasms that you were in search of are now fewer and farther in between.

Another area where loss of sensation may occur is the nipples. The nipples are full of nerve endings. Where there is a congregation of nerve endings there will be heightened sensitivities. Piercing such areas usually intensifies these sensitivities. However, like with the clitoris piercing; desensitizing can occur. With the nipples though, this usually happens over a period of time. The longer you have the piercing the more stimulation they require. Gradually they may lose sensation altogether. Again, this is not the norm, yet as a professional tattoo and piercing artist I have heard plenty of such cases.

NON-Professional Piercing Places

The Piercing Pagoda kiosk and Claire's Boutique are not the places to get your child pierced. First of all, the instruments that places like these use cannot be sterilized nor are they disposable. So, your baby is about to be pierced with the same instruments that possibly everyone else in the mall has been pierced with. Of course that was an exaggeration.

However, the point is you don't know how many people have been pierced with that "gun." **Now for piercing infants, the "gun" is the best method because it quick enough to do before the infant moves. However, these guns aren't usually sterilized. So either think twice about getting your baby pierced, or make SURE the gun's been sterilized.**

Another thing you have to worry about is the quality of the jewelry. For the most part this jewelry is of the lowest quality. Gold is usually plated

Another thing you don't see in these establishments is the "piercer" wearing gloves. Not even when they put the jewelry in the gun. This is cross contamination in its simplest form. (See, "Tattoos And The Hood.")

Professional Piercing Places

When you go to a place where there is a professional piercer, or a tattoo parlor or piercing parlor; you will notice an obvious difference in sanitation practices immediately. Or, you should be able to see an obvious difference. If not, then you shouldn't be there either. If you're not sure what to look for, don't worry, I got you.

When you walk into the spot, the first thing you should notice is the floor. If the floor is dirty, then you may want to reconsider.

However, if that's not a big issue for you then you should look for a display case. Actually, you shouldn't have to LOOK for the display case. It (or they) should be in plain sight. The jewelry in the case should be neatly organized and individually packaged in either plastic transparent jewelry containers or sterilization pouches. If they are in sterilization pouches, ask to check out a piece of jewelry.

When the piercer hands you the jewelry, the pouch will more than likely be folded in thirds so that potential customers will be able to see the jewelry. What you should do here is **unfold the pouch, then flip it over to the side with the company name on it. You're looking for either a brown arrow or brownish black dot.**

When you see either one of these, it's an indication that this jewelry has gone through the sterilization process. The arrow or dot will only change to this color under the heat of sterilization. By the way, **if the pouch isn't sealed then don't bother even patronizing this spot.** They've already tried to deceive you off top, so there's no telling to what other extents they will go to make a buck.

Next you should notice the piercing station where the process will take place. As a matter of fact, you should watch the piercer's set up process from start to finish. He/she should first spray the station down with some form of germicide. Then they should lay down a dental bib to serve as a barrier between the surface and the piercing utensils. If they haven't already, at this point he/she should have on some gloves.

You should now see them lay out the individually packaged jewelry, individually packaged forceps (if needed), and an individually packaged needle. All of these instruments should bear the same sterilization markings that I mentioned earlier. Don't be shy. Ask to see them. There should be no problem with that request. If there seems to be a problem with that, then that should be a red flag. Now once you see all the things that I've described, just sit back and enjoy the pain.

Know what sanitation and cross contamination issues to look for before getting pierced. Professionalism beats a good price any day.

HEALTHY SKINCARE PRODUCTS

BY WALASIA NOOR EL SHABAZZ

Since my Granny was my age, the women in my family have had a skin-care "secret" – 100% pure extra-virgin olive oil. We use two brands of soap/cleanser – Kiss My Face, a bar soap made from olive oil, and Dr. Bronner's Magic Soap, which contains olive oil. I prefer the Peppermint for a face wash, Almond for a body wash, and both of those kinds of Dr. Bronner's also make an excellent tooth cleanser, substituting for toothpaste.

As far as moisturizing after cleansing, my mother uses straight olive oil on a cotton pad every night to clean and moisturize, all in one, and she easily looks 20-30 years younger than her actual age. I'm not the purist my Granny was (though I'm still wrinkle-free at 36), so I use the olive oil trick only in the coldest/driest winter months, or as a pre-cleanser before I wash my face.

For a facial moisturizer, I go with whatever is fragrance-free and has the fewest hard-to-pronounce ingredients from the local co-op, health food store, or even the corporate giant whole foods. For those of us with a RushCard or pre-paid credit card, and a library card for internet access, some really great skin-care products are just a click away. My favorite lines are Inky Loves Nature, a vegan/organic/fair-trade/hand-made line of skin and hair care.

I also love Carol's Daughter's products, which can be pricey but worth saving up for. Both Inky and Carol are Melanin-rich women who started their companies because they were sick and tired of skin- and hair-care products full of additives, pork and/or whale-oil derived ingredients, bleach, glycerin, and other unsavory things.

Always look for discounts before making purchases.

Makeup or Made Up?

BY DR. KANIKA JAMILA

In many African cultures, men and women wore makeup for spiritual purposes. Different colors symbolized deities or evoked different energies for ceremonies and other rituals. The black worn around the eyes protects the eyes from the sun (and from smoke), or represented the eye of Heru (the resurrection of the divine self) in Khemetic teachings. **The notion that all makeup is unnatural to us is beyond me. Makeup, gold teeth, hairstyles of various colors, and spiritual dances are beautification rituals that have survived the middle passage and beyond.** Even though we no longer have a direct connection to why we do the things we do, we know mother Afrika is breathing through our lungs and guiding our spirits.

Just as with any spiritual health and healing, beauty plays its part in the healing of our minds, bodies, and souls. We must be conscious of what we put in our bodies and what we beautify our body temples with. The ancestors said, "If you look good, you feel good." The mental state of being comfortable in your own skin is a struggle that many of us fight with daily. We come in all sizes, shapes, and colors. The constant struggle to be in acceptance of who we are and be happy with our own beauty is internal.

The beauty industry has not taught us that black is beautiful, but that for some reason we have to change what we look like to feel good about ourselves. History books, magazines, television, and all forms of media feed us messages through images of beauty that most of us do not identify with. (See, "Light Skin Is Always In.")

There is something about human nature that makes us unsatisfied with the way we are. If our hair is wavy, we want it to be straight. If it's nappy, we want it straight. If we are dark, we would like to be lighter, etc. Changing our appearance to look like the opposite of who we are is not a reflection of true beauty. Enhancing our bodies with natural oils, makeup, and beautiful garments is an expression of true beauty. We must hold our beauty sacred with daily rituals of using essential oils of flowers and plants that have therapeutic properties to heal the skin.

Holistic skin and hair care is a healing art. It has the power to heal a wounded people.

- ❏ Massage therapy can increase blood circulation, rejuvenate the body, manage pain, and stimulate the immune system by draining the lymphatic system.
- ❏ Deep cleansing facial treatments can help us stay youthful in appearance and alleviate stress and worry.
- ❏ Natural nail care can give us better self-esteem to feel better about ourselves.
- ❏ Self-care can evoke endorphins that make us feel and look good.

The beauty within can free our minds of low self-esteem and give us the respect and love for ourselves needed to free our minds and souls. So let us not give in to others' standards of beauty, but heal ourselves by accepting our own natural beauty that comes from an internal peace we are all seekers of.

Look into some indigenous traditions of makeup. Look for fashion and makeup magazines that cater to who you are in a natural way.

HOLISTIC SKIN CARE AT ITS FINEST

BY DR. KANIKA JAMILA

Cleanse

Cleansing Milk – This is a facial cleanser. Not always a foaming cleanser. Watch out for cleansers that foam a lot as they may contain detergents or surfactants that strip the moisture out of the skin and make your skin dry. Oilier skin types which have an oily T-zone, the area of the face that forms a t-shape, along the nose or middle of the face and forehead will tolerate a foaming facial cleanser. Combination skin types contain different levels of oil and hydration/water moisture in different areas of the face. One area may be dry while another area is oily. For example, an oily nose and dry cheeks.

Dry skin comes in two forms. There is water dry and oil dry. Most people have dehydrated skin due to environmental factors and because most of us just don't drink enough water. This can also be caused from using petroleum based products that rid the skin of moisture. Oil dryness usually occurs in dry winter months or in the aging process. The drier the skin the older its appearance is.

Exfoliate

A good exfoliator is essential to any skin care regimen. Depending on the type of exfoliator used, the frequency of exfoliation can be 2-3 days. Exfoliation is the shedding of the surface layer of the skin. We shed this skin naturally every day as our cells are constantly repairing and reproducing themselves.

There are exfoliates that are scrubs. They contain some type of gristle such as pumice, ground up nuts, or seeds to shed this layer of skin. There are also substances that breakdown the protein of the skin to shed the surface layer of skin such a s bromelain. This is an enzyme that is in papaya and pineapple. Enzyme peeling exfoliates can be used 2-3 times per week. A fine gristle scrub can be used daily on oilier skin types. These two types of exfoliates can also be used in combination.

Tone

After cleansing the skin, there is usually a tight feeling or a dry feel to the skin. This is because cleansers strip the skin's acid mantle which has a pH of about 4.5-6, normally. The alkaline nature of a cleanser will alter this state. The acid mantle is a protective barrier, therefore this pH must be restored to keep the skin in total health. The next step in your skin care regimen should consist of a toner or sometimes what we call a lotion. This product is water based. It combats dehydration of the skin and restores the skin's acid mantle.

The difference between a lotion and a toner is the alcohol. Alcohol is usually in toners. They may also contain an astringent such as witch hazel. Preferably an alcohol free lotion would be the best choice due to the drying effect of alcohol on the skin. Though alcohol has a cleansing effect the drying effect it has on the skin is not in the best interest of the skin. Essential oils of rose increase moisture in dry skin. Citrus extracts of grapefruit, orange, and lemon help combat oiliness. Problematic skin that is subject to breakout can use ingredients such as salicylic acid and glycolic to clear up blemishes.

Moisturize

Moisturizers are essential to skin care as well. They are water-based or oil-based. Oil-based moisturizers usually have a small water content providing more oil to dryer skin types. Hydration is needed in oilier skin types because there is no need for added oil. Facial creams for dry or sensitive skin also tend to be thicker than water-based moisturizers used on oily skin. Dry and sensitive skin moisturizers tend to be more creamy and white; while oily skin moisturizers have little to no oil with a more of a gel-like consistency. They are lighter in texture. It is very important that no products containing mineral oil or petroleum are used as moisturizers on our skin. It suffocates the skin depleting it of oxygen. It just sits in the pores thereby clogging them and making them larger and vulnerable to infection.

Shea butter based moisturizers are good for dry, sensitive. Oils rich in alpha lipoic acid such as olive oil and flax seed oil are good for stimulating the production of collagen in the skin which gives elasticity to the skin. Almond, evening primrose and jojoba oil are also natural oils that are food for the skin.

Add a cleanser, exfoliator, toner, and moisturizer to your daily or bi-daily routine. Seek to get all natural ones.

KILLIN' ME SOFTLY – TOXIC PERSONAL CARE
BY ANGET MARCUS PANAG

Beauty products ranging from makeup, lip balm, creams, deodorant, perfumes, toothpaste, hair products and others all contain tens if not hundreds of potentially harmful chemicals that we apply to ourselves almost daily. Matter fact…**The average American woman uses 12 personal care products daily that contain up to 175 unregulated chemicals and toxic materials!**

Back in 1938, the cosmetic industry decided that if less than 50 percent of laboratory animals die while testing a new ingredient, that ingredient is considered non-toxic. So basically, **if 49 percent of lab animals die from an ingredient, they label it nontoxic.** Most of the some 25,000 chemicals they use today ain't ever been tested for long-term effects. (Not that calling a product non-toxic means anything anyway.)

The average American is exposed to over 200 different chemicals every day, many of which are suspected of causing cancer or resulting in imbalanced hormones. Studies show that the stuff in personal care products and home care products are messing with hormones that control reproduction and development. In the same way nicotine patches (patch put on the skin to get nicotine for people trying to quit smoking), chemicals that come into contact with the skin are absorbed into our bloodstream and brought to our liver for detoxification. These chemicals can build up in the body and mess up your health.
Need more proof?

That don't mean there aren't alternative methods, you can follow the natural route. **For the ladies – most makeup got less than 10% actual pigment in it and the rest is all fillers, including harsh chemicals.** Mineral Makeup is the best alternative and can be bought almost anywhere that sell makeup, the zinc oxide in it is like a natural sunscreen. Drink that green tea if you dealing with wrinkles, just make sure to check the ingredients. Vitamin C can stimulate production of collagen, the connective tissue that keeps skin firm and taut.

Did You Know - More than 60% of what we put on our skin is absorbed into our bodies? Here's a partial list of things you should look out for:

Alcohol, Isopropyl (SD-40) or Rubbing Alcohol: Rubbing alcohol is in many products. Swallowing even a small amount can kill you. Exposure can result in severe headaches, dizziness, depression, nausea, vomiting, narcosis, and even death.

DEA, MEA, & TEA (Diethanolamine), MEA (Monoethanolamine) & TEA (Triethanolamine): These chemicals are banned in most European countries. But here they're used in shampoos, shaving creams, and bubble baths. Repeated application of these chemicals result in a major increase in the incidence of liver and kidney cancer. These chemicals are especially harmful for children.

Color Pigments: They are fake colors made from coal tar! They contain metal that deposit toxins in the skin causing skin sensitivity and irritation.

Fragrances (Perfume): Made up of mostly artificial ingredients, many are toxic if swallowed. A typical fragrance got more than FOUR THOUSAND separate ingredients! They can cause headaches, dizziness, allergic rashes, skin discoloration, violent coughing and vomiting. Studies show and prove that fragrances affect the central nervous system, causing depression, hyperactivity, irritability, inability to cope, and other behavioral changes.

Parabens: Many moisturizers and lipsticks got the chemical paraben, which is linked to breast and testicular cancer.

Mineral Oil: Made of petroleum products that cover the skin like a layer of plastic, clogging the pores. It interferes with the skin's ability to eliminate toxins, promoting acne and other disorders. Slows down skin function and cell development, making you look older then you are. Used in many products, Baby oil is 100% mineral oil.

You could run a Google search or go to www.cosmeticsdatabase.com and find a database of thousands of popular skin care products, the chemicals they got in em, and the health hazards of them chemicals.

Find healthy natural alternatives to toxic products you might be using. Ex. switch from perfumes to plant oils like peppermint.

DOES PROACTIV WORK?

It depends. If you're familiar with Proactiv, you know it's a serious daily routine involving multiple steps…and that's what makes it pretty expensive to keep up. But there's no magic ingredients in those little bottles, besides maybe benzoyl peroxide (and hydrogen peroxide works about the same, yet only costs a dollar). What makes Proativ so effective is the routine. According to Dr. Jeffrey Benabio:

The first step is to use a cleanser. The cleanser has tiny beads that help to physically exfoliate the dead skin cells, unblocking the pores. The cleanser also contains benzoyl peroxide. This is a powerful oxidizer that both exfoliates the skin as well as kills bacteria (similar to hydrogen peroxide).

The second step is to use a toner. The toner contains glycolic acid. This is a natural acid found in citrus fruits. It also works to exfoliate the skin and to unstick sticky-cells. It is a chemical exfoliator and compliments the physical exfoliator in the cleanser.

The third step is to use a repairing lotion. In actuality, it is another dose of benzoyl peroxide, now in lotion form. Again the benzoyl peroxide helps exfoliate the skin and kill the bacteria.

Although there are other anti-inflammatories, moisturizers, and botanicals in Proactiv, the main treatment is from the exfoliates and the benzoyl peroxide.

Proactiv is effective for many people with acne. The main reason why it works is because people actually use it. The system is designed to be used every day and over your entire face. The whole concept is for you to be "proactive" about treating your acne. It is also a good product because the benzoyl peroxide, which is one of the most effective treatments for acne, is a mild strength, only 2.5%. At this strength, the benzoyl peroxide is mild enough to not be too irritating, but strong enough to treat your acne, especially since it is used in two products and applied twice a day.

> Did You Know?
> Acne is not found among indigenous people who don't eat the crap we do. In fact, while acne afflicts 80-90% of all Americans and those eating a western diet, populations not eating processed foods have no acne. Medical researchers recently examined 1200 of the Black islanders of Papua New Guinea and found no acne at all. They concluded that acne rarely occurs in non-westernized societies and that they are looking for the reasons why this occurs. Dr. Joe Fuhrman has said that the reason why is because "the dismal American/Western diet-style that creates a cancer and heart disease epidemic...also sets us up for premature puberty, allergies and acne."

Ideas on How to Prevent or Treat Acne

In parts of Africa they use a facial mask of avocado, egg yolks, and honey for treating acne. Eggs are rich in retinol which helps heal the skin. Honey helps kill bacteria by hydrating them, and avocado moisturizes the skin. You can use yolks only if you have dry skin and whites only if you have oily skin. Mash and mix one avocado, eggs and a tablespoon of honey. Apply to the face and leave it on about 5 to 10 minutes. Rinse with water. Use this treatment about once a week.

"Vitality and beauty are gifts of Nature for those who live according to its laws." – Leonard Da Vinci

Here are some more approaches to getting the bumps off your face:

❒ Keep the skin clean by washing 3 to 5 times daily. But make sure it doesn't become too dry.

❑ To remove as much oil as possible, first wash the skin then apply a hot facecloth for 2 minutes (as Ghostface said). Afterward, splash with cold water and wipe gently with a cotton ball soaked in witch hazel, which is cheap as hell, and even available at the dollar store. Repeat as necessary. Always use a clean facecloth, towel and cotton ball to prevent the spread of infection.

❑ Drink plenty of pure water (not sodas, teas or juices). Water keeps things moving and helps flush out the organs so that there is less chance of toxins building up.

❑ Use gentle cleansers made from natural ingredients, rather than harsher chemical preparations. Wash the skin with natural soap such as African Black soap and/or clay soap. According to Tariq Sawandi and others, these are better choices for melanated skin.

❑ Women should avoid heavy or greasy make-up. Cosmetic products can also clog in the pores and trigger acne. If you do use makeup, remove it thoroughly every evening with a natural cleanser, and switch to natural cosmetics and skin-care products as soon as you can.

❑ Exercise. Sweating can clean the dirt that is clogged in the pores and trigger acne. Just make sure you clean that sweat afterwards.

❑ A traditional "Hood Remedy" is to put toothpaste on your face at night and let it dry until morning. Toothpaste makes acne dry fast and absorbs oil. However, this method shouldn't be done if you have a sensitive skin, because it can cause irritation.

❑ Get the stress out of your life. The biggest acne trigger is hormonal. That's why acne kicks in during puberty, but also can return during women's menstrual periods.

> **Did You Know?**
> An oily substance called sebum, produced by the skin's sebaceous glands, acts as natural lubricant for the skin. When too much sebum is produced, the glands can become blocked and inflamed, causing blackheads and pimples. Sometimes the blocked glands become infected. When this occurs, pus and sebum build up under the skin, forming larger pimples or cysts which can leave scars and pitting. The fluctuating hormone levels of puberty are known to have an important role in the onset of acne. The problem usually clears up as the sufferer reaches their early twenties. If not, you've got other issues.

This is what I was talking about in *How to Hustle and Win, Part Two*, in the piece titled "Bumps on Your Face":

Normally, you get pimples and acne when you're finishing up puberty. But I've been seeing more and more people in their 20s and 30s with bumps on their faces like connect-the-dots. My brother Lord Diligent gave me a theory on why that is. He admitted that whenever he held things in, like frustration, pain, sadness, or worry, he would notice that he would start breaking out. Once he started finding ways to channel that energy and get it out of his system, he would clear right up. It made sense. When I meet people who are cool and stress-free, they have clean complexions. When I meet people with f*cked-up faces, they're usually pretty f*cked up in the head too. Sometimes, people are able to hide it so well that no one can tell how miserable they are. But your face tells it all. Your eyes give away the pain on your mind, and your skin gives away how long you've been holding it in. Learn how to channel that energy and watch how quickly your eyes get brighter, teeth get whiter, and your skin gets clearer. Oh, sorry, but your breath won't smell better until you start eating right.

More Ideas for Natural Skin Healing

☐ Cucumber juice on scars will tighten pores, improving skin tone and reducing marks.

☐ Apply lemon juice on scarred areas twice a day, by means of a cotton pad. Alternatively, you can cut a fresh lemon and rub this on your skin, twice a day.

☐ Cocoa butter and Shea butter are natural skin healers. Apply the butter on your scars twice a day and massage it into the skin, until the skin completely absorbs it.

☐ Honey is one of the oldest remedies to heal wounds and burns, due to its healing properties. It also has anti-bacterial properties, and can help you remove stubborn scars in a few months, if applied twice daily.

☐ Aloe Vera is one of the best remedies to get rid of scars naturally. Application of this, twice a day, will give you noticeable results within a few days.

☐ Make a paste of raw garlic and rub this into your skin. it's a healer and also a skin toner.

☐ Mash a ripe banana thoroughly and apply on your skin for ten minutes. Wash off with cold water, for getting well-toned skin.

☐ Grate a potato and wrap it in soft, thin linen. Wait for the juice of the grated potato to start coming through the linen. Rub this over the scarred skin, leave for ten minutes and then wash it off with warm water.

☐ Crushed mint leaves can be applied to scars, to help the skin heal faster.

☐ Fresh tomato juice is an excellent skin rejuvenating agent and can help the skin heal faster.

☐ Essential oils, like Tea Tree Oil, eliminate acne scars and acne on the face. Tea tree oil (when applied correctly) is also effective in preventing the occurrence of scars.

☐ Herbs that are helpful in clearing the skin are chickweed, dandelion, ginger, red clover, yellow dock root, sarsaparilla, burdock and sassafras.

Create a daily "Face Care" routine, using whole foods like honey, eggs, avocado, and cucumbers instead of synthetic chemicals.

HOW TO REDUCE CELLULITE

Exercise. Duh. Exercise can help you lose fat while tightening muscles, which makes skin more healthy and toned. (See, "RBG Fit Club.")

Drink plenty of water. "Every time the skin is well hydrated, the skin will look fresh and healthy," says Dr. Lona Sandon. At the end of the crease where the thigh and the appearance of cellulite there are many fat cells. To destroy it, the body requires intensive training and liquids. Sandon recommends drinking eight glasses of warm water every day. In addition, eat fruit that contains a lot of water, such as grapes, apples or watermelon.

Eat more fruits and colored vegetables. Colored fruits and vegetables, like carrots, spinach, oranges, grapes, or tomatoes contain lots of vitamin

C which is important to prevent damage to collagen. Studies have also shown that vitamin C can help you burn 30% more fat during workouts.

Eat less bread. Excessive consumption of complex carbohydrates such as white rice, pasta and white bread, will be converted into blood sugar (glucose). The body tends to store surplus glucose to be processed into glycogen for storage, rather than burn it. It creates new fat cells, so that the fat is pushing on the skin and connective tissue cause cellulite.

Get some exercise ideas from our fitness chapter and get to it! Volume 1 of this book gets heavy into nutrition, read it!

HEALTHY HAIR
BY YVETTE GZ

It's a known fact that we Black women spend billions of dollars on our hair yearly, mostly on weaves and harmful products that we believe make us more appealing. What we don't realize is that there's a huge difference between healthy hair, and good-looking hair. Unfortunately the majority of us choose the latter, when we should be going for both since healthy hair automatically gives us good-looking hair.

Here are a few examples of how good-looking hair is NOT healthy hair:

☐ When you get it flat-ironed/blow dried and it looks silky and shiny, but after the third day it's splitting and breaking off.

☐ When you sew in a weave, but the "crown" of your head is shorter than the rest of your hair due to brittleness.

☐ When you relax and style it, but whenever you wet it, it looks dull and lifeless.

In short, relaxed/permed hair is NEVER healthy, no matter how silky smooth it looks. Relaxers break hair down to its weakest form, leaving it more prone to breakage and dryness. However, **did you also know that all those chemicals don't only sit on the surface of our scalp but get absorbed into our skin, and possibly into our bloodstream and brain?** Look it up. Relaxers contain phosphoric acid and ammonium hydroxide, which are pretty much considered health hazards. That's why the instructions on a relaxer pack discourage pregnant women from using it and carefully tell us to apply the relaxer at least half an inch away from the scalp.

I want to focus more on how to get healthy hair and saving money. In my experience, going natural was the cheapest way of maintaining my hair. On most days, water is the only thing used to style it. To achieve a "healthy look" on relaxed hair, you end up spending more money repairing damage than actually styling it. It doesn't have to be that way; you can still straighten natural hair without the harm of chemicals, and if you do it correctly it actually looks better and shinier than when it's relaxed.

As a person of color with loose or tight curls, your hair is normally dry and needs a lot of moisture. Now do not confuse moisture with grease/oils. They do two separate things. Moisture (from water, leave-in conditioners, nourishing sprays, etc.) penetrates the hair cuticle and nurtures it and oil (hair oils/mayonnaise, grease etc...) protects the hair from getting dry. If you apply oil to dry and un-moisturized hair, you're basically putting a band-aid over a gun wound because you're not treating the root and inside of your hair, and if you moisturize your hair without applying some protection, it will dry up faster. Once you really understand this concept, you've done half the work.

Moisturizing Your Hair

Water, surprisingly enough, is the best moisturizer. A warm bath followed by a quick cold rinse always does the trick. Warm water softens the hair and allows it to absorb moisture, and cold water locks the moisture in, leaving the hair shiny and frizz-free.

When using a shampoo, don't lather, rinse and repeat as the instructions say. It will dry your hair even more by stripping down the natural oils. A small amount and one rinse should be enough. If you have really dry hair, replace your shampoo with a cheap conditioner, then use a good deep conditioner afterwards. Don't worry, it will clean your hair just as good as a shampoo will.

For post-shower care, you can make your homemade leave-in conditioner by mixing 3 parts of distilled water, 1 part of light conditioner (any brand that works on your hair) and half part of oil (olive or almond). Pour the mixture in an empty spray bottle that you've saved from previous hair sprays and shake well. Spray on damp hair.

> **Did You Know?**
> When you wash your hair with one of those name brand "nutrient-rich" shampoos, most of the nutrients and active ingredients don't actually end up in your hair – they wind up down the drain (along with all the money you spent on the shampoo) because the shampoo molecules they contain are too large to penetrate the cells of hair and, more importantly, the tiny hair follicles where our hair actually grows. They sit atop the follicle until we wash them away. As usual, simple and natural are better than expensive and "miraculous."

Protecting Your Hair

All hair types produce a natural oil/protection called sebum. It's the oily substance on your scalp that starts to build up after a few missed shampoos. Some hair types produce it more than others, so if you have that, you need little to no oil/lotion to protect it or give it shine. For drier hair types, use the following as substitutes.

Shea butter: Very cheap, can be bought by the pound. Melt it at very low temperature or heat it by rubbing your palms and apply a small amount to the tips. it's best when used after a rinse on dried hair.

Olive/Jojoba/Coconut/Almond/Avocado oil: Massage and leave in hair for 30 mins. then rinse out. Almond and Jojoba oil also work as leave-in conditioners and can be applied as regular lotion.

Hair serums/silicone: Possibly the most effective way to protect your hair. Also lasts longer because a drop goes a long way. Apply to towel-dried hair.

You don't want to use heavy grease or vegetable oils because they weigh the hair down, suffocate it, and make a mess. Light oils like the ones mentioned above may be a bit pricey, but nowhere near the amount of money would you spend on a kit of products, monthly salon visits, and hair weaves.

Another way to help your hair is through diet. Foods rich in zinc, vitamin A, C and E strengthen hair cells, reduce hair loss, and are good for the scalp. Add carrots, green leaves, nuts, and beans to your regular meals. It won't make fragile hair strong overnight, but it can improve the overall well-being of your hair.

Get some of the suggestions from the above article and come up with a "healthy hair" routine that fits your schedule and needs.

GROWING OUR NATURAL AFRIKAN HAIR
BY DR. KANIKA JAMILA

It is with great pride that I can say that Afrikan hair is becoming less and less taboo. It has become a movement for independence, entrepreneurship, and a true expression of culture. **Many women are beginning to follow in the footsteps of Madame CJ Walker and producing products that promote healthy hair growth for us. No longer do we have to purchase products manufactured by Caucasians and other nationalities to groom Afrikan hair.** Contrary to popular belief, Madame CJ Walker did not invent the straightening comb, but the actual inventor was one of her associates. However, Madame Walker was an entrepreneur and educator of promoting healthy Afrikan hair growth and made an arguable million dollars selling these products in the 1930's before she passed on. A million dollars was more like a billion in her day.

Our hair is definitely unique in that it comes in all textures, curl patterns and varies from straight, wavy, to just plain nappy. We have been brainwashed to think that our hair is hard to manage. It hurts our children to get their hair combed, so they submit to the idea of straight hair being the best and most beautiful hair to have. Young boys keep their hair cut to feel assimilated and accepted. Thus, the concept of "good hair" and the "creamy crack" is born. Young children ages 3 and 4 are getting their "Just For Me" perms and Mama is happy because she doesn't have to comb the hair out any more. Because we don't know how to deal with our hair properly, we are victims of "creamy crack" and any other product that claims to change the naps to straight flowing hair.

Moisture

The key to keeping our hair in a manageable state is moisture. I remember my Mother using a brush with water on it to style my hair when I was a girl. I don't remember my head hurting after she did my hair. On the other hand, when I was about ten years old, I started to get my hair pressed by my grandmother. I remember crying after she would "comb out" my hair. Literally, she combed out clumps of hair out when she was done. I would have a piercing headache and sore scalp for days after. The water gave my hair moisture which was a natural "detangler". Usually Afrikan hair will do what you want it to do when it's moisturized. The hair should not be "combed out"/detangled when it's dry. Apply a moisturizer before this process. No moisture contributes to hair breakage and overall damage. (See, "Healthy Hair.")

Kare for Roots and Ends

Take care of the roots and ends of the hair. We are trained to oil the scalp, but tend to forget about the ends. It is important for the ends to be treated with care due to split ends. Trimming the ends of the hair regularly also helps avoid split ends. Just as a gardener or farmer will prune and harvest regularly to replenish growth we should do the same for our hair. Hot oil treatments help to infuse the hair with vitamins and soften and condition the hair as well. Vitamin E is another good oil for the hair. The scalp treatments are also good in a similar a fashion as the roots of a tree. There is a saying "If you have no roots your tree will bear no fruit" The same goes for the hair.

Too Tight

Our little girls suffer from traction alopecia (See, "Damn You're Going Bald!") because their hair is being pulled too tightly. This causes fine bumps along the hair line and eventually there will be hair loss. We fight with the hair to make it look different than its natural state. Pulling it as flat to the scalp as possible makes it look straight, so we shellac it back and pull it back with little rubber bands so the naps won't show. When the hair is braided and corn rowed, it's usually done too tightly as well. Then, the braids and extensions are added too tightly leading to stress on the scalp and hindering hair growth.

The best styles to have for tightly curled hair are braids, twists, and coils are similar in aiding growth as it gives the hair a resting period without abuse. So let's moisturize, add sheen with natural oils, and stop struggling with our hair. Become comfortable with the notion that Afrikan hair is good hair and embrace natural beauty!

Look up healthy, natural hairstyles and try them!

DAMN, YOU'RE GOING BALD!
BY SUPREME UNDERSTANDING

Most people have no idea that Tupac suffered from premature baldness. That's why he shaved his head. If only Chris Kelly of Kris Kross would do the same thing. To understand my point, you just have to see the video on YouTube where he explains all the bald patches in his otherwise braided head, confirming he has a condition called alopecia. Unlike male pattern baldness, alopecia causes you to lose patches of hair all over the place.

What IS Baldness?

The most common form of baldness is a progressive hair-thinning condition called *androgenic alopecia* or "male pattern baldness" that occurs in adult males. That's what Tupac had, along with damn near every other celebrity who's shaved their head for "cosmetic reasons." There's also the less common *alopecia areata* (or "spot baldness"), which involves hair coming off your head in random, usually round patches. That's what Chris Kelly has. It's an auto-immune disorder that causes your body to attack its own hair follicles. There's also *traction alopecia*, which is most commonly found in people with ponytails or cornrows that pull on their hair with excessive force (See "That Damn Ponytail").

Male pattern baldness affects roughly 40 million men in the United States alone. **Approximately 25% of men begin balding by age 30, and most others start sometime later.** However, plenty of teenagers are developing baldness these days. Females can go bald as well. This can be caused by pregnancy, chronic illness, crash diets, stress, or genetics (in old age), and now it's also occurring in women as young as 15 or 16. Considering how toxic our environment has become, I'm not surprised.

And baldness IS inherited (and both parents' genes are involved). **Either way, there is a 4 in 7 chance of getting the baldness gene.** What causes it? The trigger DHT, a sex hormone that turns *ON* your body and facial hair growth, but also (for some reason) can also turn *OFF*.

What are the signs you're going bald?

It all begins with a receding hairline, which can start setting in as early as your teenage years. The hairline can then recede ALL the way back (Anterior Male Pattern Baldness), or another bald patch may develop on top (Vertex Male Pattern Baldness or as it's known in the hood, The Moon Roof).

Male pattern baldness is classified on the Hamilton-Norwood scale, which you'll find here.

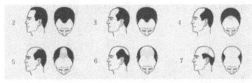

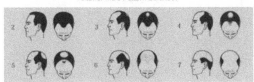

Anterior Male Pattern Baldness

Besides looking for yourself in the scale, there's another way (based on a recent study) to tell if you're losing hair (or even if you're at risk for it):

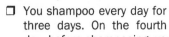

Vertex Male Pattern Baldness

❏ You shampoo every day for three days. On the fourth day, before shampooing, you comb your hair forward over a pillow case for 60 seconds. Then you count the hairs on your pillow case.

❏ Do it three days a month, and track it for six months. Make sure you use the same comb or brush each time, and make sure it's clean before you do it.

❏ The number of hairs on your pillow doesn't matter as much as whether that number remains almost the same each time you do it. Do it three days a month, and track it for six months.

❏ If the number of hairs on your pillow remains consistent each time, you're probably not over-shedding. But if there's an increase, you might be experiencing balding.

Below are a few natural remedies for baldness that are less expensive and, some say, more effective than prescription drugs like Rogaine or Propecia:

❏ Saw Palmetto - Blocks hormone DHT responsible for baldness.
❏ Ginkgo biloba - Improves circulation in scalp to regrow hair.
❏ Scalp massaging - Increases blood flow to the hair follicles to promote hair growth.
❏ Olive oil - Lifts dirt and trapped oil from follicles to promote hair growth.
❏ Vitamin B - Provides necessary nutrient for hair to grow.

Other natural approaches include honey, yarrow herb, green tea extracts, apple procyanidins (www.applepoly.com), and caffeine anhydrous powder, all of which you can find at a health food store and which can be applied to your scalp.[24] There are some people who will try to hide their receding hair using "spray-on hairlines" (sometimes known as "Beijing" in hood barber shops), but that will only work for so long. Pretty soon, you'll look ridiculous.

Instead, if all else fails (in terms of natural methods), just learn to love your baldness and buy a razor (get a thorough one like the *Mach 5*) and shave it all off. Rub in some tea tree oil (or aftershave) so your head doesn't bump up. Grow some manly facial hair and groom that instead.

---

[24] For more natural remedies, check out sites like www.natural-homeremedies.com or www.hairloss-reversible.com

HEALTHY NAILS
BY ROCHELLE KERR

Did you know our nails can tell a lot about us? From the kind of housework we do, if any, to most importantly the state of our health. Many of us do no not take time to study our nails, truly look after, love and protect them. Our nails could be so beautiful with the right amount of time care and attention. If we knew the signs to look for, we might not have to see a doctor as often because our nails health can give us an insight to the overall health of our body.

Our nails, which are made up of hard layers of protein known as keratin, were not by design for cosmetics reasons (at least not alone). They are primarily there to protect the sensitive nerves and tissues of our fingers. This is why it's imperative that we look after them the best we can.

The use of press on nail, gels, acrylics and even nail biting is a big no-no. They will eventually destroy our natural nails, break down the top layers and rob them of their natural oils, which can lead to nail fungus. Yes, fungus.

Nail fungus is caused by micro-organisms living, growing and feeding off of your nail. Signs of nail fungus are yellow or whitish spots building up under the tips of your nails. If left untreated, your nails can become brittle and can eventually die. Treatment for nail fungus includes apple cider, vinegar, laser treatment, anti-fungal medicine and tea tree oil. If all fails, the nail might possible have to be removed.

Nutrients for Healthy Nails.

Calcium (Almonds, oatmeal, rhubarb, spinach) Keep your nails from being dry, brittle and helps to strengthen them.

Amino Acids/Protein (Brewer's yeast, nuts and seeds) Supplies your body with sulphur, helps in building new substance for new nails to form, leaves your nails healthy and strong.

Folic Acid (Fortified cereal, oranges, bananas) Keeps nails healthy.

Hydrochloric Acid Natural salts (such as sea salt) are necessary in order to produce hydrochloric acid in your stomach. Other foods such as black olives, celery, ginger and lemon help to stimulate the production. A Lack of hydrochloric acid might cause your nails to split.

Iron (Avocado, beets, eggs, pumpkins and whole-grain breads) Lack of iron can cause you to be anemic, leaving you with pale nails, which can be easily cracked or broken.

Lactobacillus (The "Friendly Bacteria" found in cole slaw, cheese and yogurt) Lack of this can cause fungus to grow under and around your nails.

Linoleic Acid (Flax, mustard and hemp seeds, kale, collard greens and spinach) Lack of these might cause nails to be brittle, split and to flake.

Silicon (Asparagus, cabbage, cucumbers, parsnips and radishes, as well as whole grains) Promotes strong nails.

Other Nutrients Magnesium, Vitamin A, Vitamin C, and Vitamin D, are also fundamental for healthy and beautiful nails, skin, and hair.

Tips on Longer Lasting and Beautiful Nails

❑ Keep your hands moisturized. After a bath, washing the dishes or anything else that leaves your hands dry, dry your hands thoroughly and use a hand lotion.

❑ Your hand lotion should preferably be one that is rich in vitamin A, after which you can use some Vaseline to rub in to the cuticles and skin around the nails to keep them from getting hard and dry.

❑ It also good advice to wash your hands and moisturize them right before you go to bed.

❑ Wet nails tend to break easier, so definitely do not file your nails straight after a shower or bath.

❑ A good method of removing stains from nails is mixing one tablespoon of lemon juice with a cup of water, soak nails in the solution for a few minutes; remove, wash, dry thoroughly and moisturize.

❑ Give your nails a break in between polishing. Nail polish tends to leave a yellow stain on your nails, so a few days every now and then without will reduce the chance of this happening.

❑ When filing, do so in ONE direction, do not move the file back and forth, This will make your nails brittle.

❑ Buffing nails helps keep them strong and shiny. It also augments blood flow which in terms stimulates growth.

❑ Use essential oils. Tea tree, rosemary, Lavender and lemon on your hands, These will act as an anti-fungal, conditioning, strengthening and whitening treatment.

❑ Mix a few drops of each with a base such as sweet almond oil and massage them into your nails, between your fingers and hands. Keeping them nicely scented, soft and smooth

❑ If nails are too soft, soak them in olive oil for 20 minutes every other day to harden them

❑ If using nail polish remover, stick to those that uses acetate. Never acetone-based or formaldehyde-based removers. They can lead to splitting and breaking of nails and can be toxic to children.

Your Nails as Indicators of Possible Health Problems

Like other extremities (hair, feet, etc.), your nails can also be indicators of health problems. For more signs, see "What Your Body is Telling You."

❑ **Beau's line,** horizontal indentations that runs across the nails, can appear after the occurrence of a traumatic and severe illness, such as a heart attack or pneumonia.

- ❏ **Brittle** nails, soft nails, can just be down to ageing, but they may also indicate a thyroid, kidney or circulation condition.
- ❏ **Bumps** on nails is an indication of rheumatoid arthritis
- ❏ **Clubbed** nails or curled nails can indicate a problem with the heart, liver or lungs. 80% of people with clubbed nails have lung disease.
- ❏ **Dark spots** could be melanoma, a very dangerous type of skin cancer. If there is any bleeding of the spot into the cuticles or the nail folds, immediate medical attention is required
- ❏ **Deep blue** nail beds may be caused by asthma or emphysema.
- ❏ **Flat** nails can indicate Raynaud's disease.
- ❏ **Greenish** nails may be caused by a fungal infection and internal bacterial infection.
- ❏ **Half-white or Half-pink** can indicate possible kidney disease
- ❏ **Horizontal ridges** on nails is an indication of both psychological and physical stress. May also suggest that the person is susceptible to arthritis.
- ❏ **Nail shingling** is caused by exposure to harsh detergents and the frequent excessive use of nail polish remover.
- ❏ **Nail beading** may be a sign of rheumatoid arthritis.
- ❏ **Pale or bluish** nails: this may indicate anemia
- ❏ **Pink colour** when nail is squeezed indicates poor blood circulation
- ❏ **Pitted** nails are punched-out looking spots, which might indicate psoriasis.
- ❏ **Unusually wide, square** nails can be signs of hormone imbalance.
- ❏ **Raised** nails at the base with small white ends could be owing to a respiratory disorder such as emphysema or chronic bronchitis. This nail condition could also be hereditary.
- ❏ **Red skin** around the cuticles – indicates poor metabolism of essential fatty acids or Lupus
- ❏ **Spooning** are indentations that dips inwards, almost as if it's been scooped out and can hold a drop of liquid and be caused by low iron (anemia)
- ❏ **Thick** nail signs there could be problems with the heart, poor circulation and the weakening of the vascular system
- ❏ **Vertical ridges** indicate a kidney disorder, poor general health and nutrient absorption
- ❏ **White spots** can occur due to injury of the nail. It can also indicate cirrhosis of the liver, especially if you are a heavy alcohol drinker.
- ❏ **White lines** parallel to the lunula (not your cuticle) indicates there might be systematic problems with the whole body.
- ❏ **White lines** may be liver disease.
- ❏ **White** nails indicates possible liver, kidney disorders and/or anemia
- ❏ **White** nail with **pink** near the tips could be a sign of cirrhosis.
- ❏ **Yellow** nail might be the first sign of diseases such as the lymphatic system, respiratory disorders, diabetics, and liver disorders.
- ❏ **White moon area** of the nail is **red**, possible heart problems. If it turns slate **blue**, possible overexposures to metal or lung problems.

Add some "healthy nails" foods to your diet. Come up with a weekly or bi-weekly nail maintenance routine. And look for possible indications of "poor health" from your nails.

FIVE SIGNS THAT SPA OR SALON ISN'T SAFE

BY SUPREME UNDERSTANDING

In *What the Yuck: The Freaky and Fabulous Truth about your Body*, Dr. Roshini Raj lists the following signs to be wary about a spa or salon. These same rules can apply to barbershops as well:

No License. If a license isn't prominent displayed or if they aren't willing to produce one, you should go somewhere else. The "hood hookup" might hook you up with something you ain't pay for.

Iffy Foot Baths. Make sure the pedicure tubs are fully drained and scrubbed after every use. If you don't see someone scrubbing, bet on there being bacteria and fungus in that tub.

Scary Bathrooms. Restrooms are always a good indicator of the cleanliness of any business, whether it's a restaurant or a nail salon. If it's a mess, you can assume they're not too big on cleaning there.

Barely Sanitized Tools. If they aren't fully submerged in disinfecting liquid, they're still dirty. And if someone drops a tool and continues using it, you're in the wrong hands. Not only should the tools be sanitized, they should be well-maintained. That means scissors shouldn't be rusty, clippers shouldn't have teeth missing (you can feel the "scratching" from the missing metal teeth), and nothing should look "old."

> **Did You Know?**
> Not only do unsanitary nail salons (especially those in the hood) and fake nails put you at risk for bacterial infections, but the UV-light dryers used by many nail salons has now been linked to skin cancer on the fingers! Instead, choose the fan or air dry.

Strong or Funny Odors. If it smells like chemicals, even "good-smelling chemicals," the place isn't well-ventilated. This can cause YOU respiratory problems down the line, so think twice. Of course, it should be a dead giveaway that something is wrong when everyone there is wearing a face mask…except you.

Compare your salon, spa, or barbershop to these credentials. If they fail your inspection, find a new one in your community. You'll most likely get better service there as well.

AN INTRODUCTION TO MELANIN

BY ROBERT BAILEY

Melanin is a fascinating substance. Yet you're likely not taught much about it in school, except for it being a pigment that gives you your black appearance…oh, and that you've got it because it protects you from the sun, almost like a little accident. There's so much more to it. Our ancient ancestors knew much about this dark matter than we may know now. In fact, this organic Blackness was regarded as a divine attribute. Some Europeans eventually figured it out, but didn't announce it to the rest of us. Today, millions of dollars are spent annually on its study. This substance is now studied worldwide, largely by those with the least amount of it. This leads some of us to wonder about what we've been told so far, and how much we haven't been told. As Dr. Jewel Pookrum has noted:

> There is a club of scientists that do nothing but research on the melanin molecule. If you're not in that club and want access to that information they will send it to you for a cost. These 3 binders of books (the melanotropic peptides) cost $608. This is what I invested my money in. Because, see I understand that if I do not know who I am, then there are people that do know who I am, that can definitely alter my plans!

Scientific research on melanin (at least what has been published for the public) has gradually progressed over the past 100 years, although it was slowed in the past due to prejudices, false information, and the potentialities it unfolded for African peoples. At one point, it was even described as a waste product! Also, because of its extremely stable nature, it's hard to study. Melanin resists most experimental analyses designed by man. What we now know, however, is that melanin has fascinating potential, dozens of known uses, and tons still undiscovered.

What's in a Name?

Melano is Greek for black. The *"mel"* in *melanin* is derived from *melano*. *Anin* comes from amine, a hydrocarbon. So melanin is a black hydrocarbon amine. Carbon, a black element, is fundamental to all life, and your melanin.

Melanin is a complex, multifunctional biochemical found in the brain, the body, the environment, and throughout the blackness of space. There are several types of melanin. In our environment, it's found in the soil, plants, animals and in the waters of creeks, lakes, springs, seas and rivers. In plants and animals, melanin acts as a protective tool against invading organisms.

Functions and Characteristics

From the earliest stages of embryogenesis, melanin is present. In fact, the presence of melanin in sites of the neural tube where the brain and spinal cord are formed is integral for proper physiological functioning. The nerves for vision and hearing are both formed from the presence of melanin. Melanin in these parts of the body helps to provide extrasensory perceptive abilities. So if life is about enjoying what nature has to offer, experimental research on the biophysical properties of melanin suggests that this enjoyment can be enhanced by melanin. Consider these points: the absence of pigment in the inner ear would produce deafness, the absence of pigment in the retina would make us practically blind and without pigment in specific midbrain structures, our psychomotor abilities would be harshly damaged.

In the body, melanin's job is regulating all bodily functions and activities. It is located in important areas such as the central nervous system (which includes the brain and spinal cord), the autonomic nervous system (which regulates breathing, heart action and the movement of the intestines), the peripheral nervous system (which connects the central nervous system with the various tissues throughout the body), the diffuse neuroendocrine (glands) system (includes major glands responsible for manufacturing and secreting various chemicals into the blood stream, including the pineal gland, the pituitary gland, thymus gland, kidneys, thyroid gland, ceratoid gland, etc.), and the viscera's (major internal organs such as the heart, liver, arteries, eyes, ovaries, testes, nerves of the inner ear and more).

Melanin has both physical and chemical properties. Some of its physical properties include its color which ranges from golden brown to black, a pleasant odor which can be attributed to the highly fragrant amine and sulfur in its structure, its ability to resist x-ray diffraction and strong acids and alkaline agents. It has a tough but flexible arrangement. It can resemble a cloud, gas, wood, metal or liquid and take on many forms without losing its structure. A high thermal resistance enables it to maintain approximately 50% of its original properties when exposed to 1225° F.

As far as chemical properties, it can be transformed in the blood, concentrates nerve and brain information, and neutralizes free radicals. It responds to and absorbs light, sound (music) and electrical energy to fuel the body. It can convert light energy to sound energy, then back to light energy. It is centrally involved in controlling all mental and physical body activities. It is present at the site of tissue repair, regeneration and infectious diseases. It has shown semi-conductive properties outside the body, meaning it may conduct electricity.

This is evident in the appearance of melanin on sites where energy conversions occur. It may be a biological superconductor under certain conditions and behaves like an insulator in that it won't allow electrical current to pass through its structure. Melanin in the iris of the eye is directly related to an individual's reaction time/quickness of movement. It can bind and release most known elements. On a molecular level, by a process called resonance, melanin's molecular orbitals rearrange themselves to allow for new energy to come in, replacing sites of low energy.

When most individuals go out shopping for a new car, cell phone or other gadget, they look for the one with the most accessories. Chemicals molecules also have "accessories" which are called functional groups (FG). A chemical can do more work in the form of chemical reactivity as the number of these FGs increase. Melanin molecules contain many different FGs which undergo many chemical reactions at the same time. These chemical reactions show themselves in the highly expressive culture of Black people.

Black people have a highly energized sensory-motor network due to large concentrations of melanin. This expressiveness can be seen in rhythmically oriented activities such as dancing, rapping to a beat and any other task involving psychomotor skills.

Melanin in the Brain

Neuromelanin is an antioxidant that can prevent cellular damage; it can act as a semiconductor by increasing the speed of nerve impulses, and functions as an electrochemical transducer to transform physical stimuli into neural activity.

The impact of melanin in the brain or other internal organs (neuromelanin) isn't as well-known as surface/skin melanin. Although it's out of sight from the sun, the cortex is dark and rich in neuromelanin. T. Owens Moore states, "Melanin's capacity to interact with light and to transmute it to higher states of order and complexity, to transform it from one state to another, is seen as a crucial parallel to evolution itself." **The darker this neuromelanin has become through evolution, the more cognitively sophisticated our species has become.** Higher primates have more than lower primates, and man has most of all.

There is evidence that learning new skills increases neuromelanin concentration in certain parts of the brain. On the flip side, drugs, chemicals and the aging process can cause loss of neuromelanin containing brain cells. Although it's obvious that the amount of skin melanin varies between ethnic groups, it's more difficult to measure the different levels of neuromelanin. T. Owens Moore states:

> It is very significant to mention how ethnic differences are overlooked when evaluating the presence of neuromelanin. If the claim is made that brain melanin is programmed to function at different capacities depending upon a person's overall genetic capacity to produce melanin, then it is likely that brain melanin can vary between ethnic groups.

The amount of neuromelanin is determined by genetics. Melanin is produced by melanosomes located in cells called melanocytes. The amount of melanin produced, according to Carol Barnes, is controlled by catalyst concentration (the catalyst being tyrosinase, peroxidase and melanin-copper complex), catalyst chemical reactivity, electrical charge, melanin type and molecular weight. Neuromelanin and skin melanin DO NOT form in the same manner.

To biologically activate neuromelanin, it's important to eat the proper foods (natural, sun-rich foods). Research has proven the protective role of pigments in certain fruits that function as effective antioxidants. As a general rule of thumb, the darker the berry, the greater the antioxidant effect-think blueberries. Since neuromelanin functions as an antioxidant, its health is enhanced by that which has a similar role.

Neuromelanin is a double-edged sword. If you properly maintain the health of it, you can greatly enhance its effects in your life, if neglected; it can lead to neurodegenerative diseases such as Parkinson's.

Drugs and Melanin

One of the rules of chemistry is "like attracts like" and "like dissolves like." This means that if two chemicals have similar structures or FGs, they will bond, or chemically react with one another. After binding, the new mixture or chemical will show properties similar to both chemicals before the bond but properties different from any one of the two originals.

Drugs such as cocaine, LSD, marijuana and many others are very similar to melanin and the sub-units that make up melanin. These similarities cause the drugs to work at a faster pace, cause a user to experience higher "highs" and lower "lows" and to remain in the eumelanin (melanin-dominant) person's system for longer periods of time. Basically, **crack-cocaine, nicotine, and similar drugs "stick" to melanin, and this has been proven in studies.**

The new chemical formed from bonding drugs such as cocaine with melanin, cannot support life functions; however, the body will try and use cocaine to do the job of serotonin and dopamine because they are similar in makeup. **Cocaine use depletes melanin because melanin is essentially a storehouse of brain signals, which will get released into the body once other sources are gone.** Thus, when the body is used up by cocaine, it realizes the real chemicals in which it needs are gone, triggering the craving for cocaine because it thinks it's getting the chemicals (melanin, dopamine, serotonin, etc.) it has used up.

In addition, a chemical like cocaine has the potential to co-polymerize into the melanin structure. It can remain intact for a number of months until an event such as stress, poor diet, or some other significant event triggers the melanin structure to release the cocaine back into the body. When this happens, the amount of the drug released back into the body is not controlled by the individual and can cause an overdose, seizures or even sudden death.

More information on the harmful effects of drugs on melanin can be found in senior research chemist Carol Barnes first volume in his series, *Melanin: The Chemical Key to Black Greatness.*

The Pharaoh's Tomb

Dr. Richard King states in *Why Darkness Matters*:

> In the tomb of Pharaoh Tutankhamen, there are inscriptions that make reference to our pineal gland and its stimulation. First, in the 2nd shrine and

first group of divinities, there is a clear picture of star passing rays of light into the midforehead site of the pineal gland. The second group of divinities, fourth figure, named the neck of Horus, may define the location of the vocal cords. This is noteworthy because it is the site of production for the spoken word, which defined the ancient study of the role of music and harmonic resonance in elevating melanin systems. In the second group of divinities, fifth figure is a clear reference to the pineal gland. The second group of divinities, sixth figure, is "the doorway," as in "in the head, there is a doorway." Last, in the third group of divinities, the sixth figure, morning bark of Ra, may be a deeper aspect of the doorway, in that as the doorway ascends it becomes a vessel of vast travel, a literal star ship.

Suggested Reading

For more information, because this is not by any means a comprehensive look into this outstanding substance, check out *The Melanin Diet* by Deanne Meningall, *Melanin: the Chemical Key to Black Greatness* by Carol Barnes, and *Why Darkness Matters: The Power of Melanin in the Brain* by Edward Bruce Bynum PhD, Ann Brown PhD, Richard King MD and T. Owens Moore PhD. You'll want to read up on it as much as possible, as they've all had something more to add on to the subject and no two books were alike. Also, Dr. Jewel Pookrum is also releasing a revised edition of *Vitamin and Minerals from A to Z with Ethno-Consciousness*. It covers diet, food, vitamins and minerals specifically to suit melanin-dominant people.

Pick up one of the "suggested reading" books and keep your neuromelanin healthy by learning new skills, eating dark fruits and vegetables, getting good sleep, and healthy amounts of sun.

---

10. SURVIVAL TACTICS

While we'd love if everyone reading this book could embrace holistic health, a natural diet, and a lifestyle that doesn't resemble slow suicide...we know that most of us are still in basic survival mode. That is, most of are still scraping by from month-to-month, living check-to-check (include those of us in the so-called middle class), struggling to keep a roof over our heads and our children out of trouble...Trust me, we understand – survival is real. It's that lifestyle that forces us to make tough decisions between eating healthy or eating cheap and easy. Between exercising daily, or getting to it when we have time (never).

Between preventative medicine and over-the-counter medications. And it's a battle we've been losing. Though the hood has forced us to learn how to survive with little to nothing for resources, too many of us are still NOT surviving. And that's part of the plan. This system is designed for us to be destroyed, all while it appears that we destroyed ourselves. From the prison system to the economic system to the healthcare system, the odds are against us. It's not by accident, and – contrary to the "conservatives" among us – we didn't make it this way.

Free healthcare for all people would mean the game was changing, and it's not (why do you think poor white people get so angry about something that would actually help poor white people?). As author Amanda Marcotte noted:

> **I've long been a proponent of the idea that one reason that Americans don't have universal health care already – unlike every other industrialized Western nation – is that enough white people in power are so unwilling to share with non-white people that they'd rather go without than share.** History would certainly indicate this is the case. Ta-Neishi Coates pointed out that New Deal had to exclude black people to get passed, for instance.

As Dr. Vernellia Randall explains in her book *Dying While Black*, the health problems faced by Blacks in America are not simply disproportionate to whites (no matter what level of income, proving that it's about race more than about poverty), but in fact, this inequity can be traced back to slavery and has remained relatively consistent since then. So all these branches (inequities in incarceration, health, and economic) lead back to roots in conquest and exploitation (for all Original People, if you think about it). And it all adds up to being an issue of whether you are meant to survive or not. In short, you're not. At least, that's not how the system's set up. It's designed for you to fall victim…unless you start playing for the other side, of course.

So when we talk about "survival," we're talking about a lot of things. We're talking about healthcare, insurance, elder care, prison, and – here's the big one – what to do when it all hits the fan. We've got it bad enough as it is, but what the hell would we do if all hell broke loose today? We've already seen the worst-case scenarios in New Orleans and Haiti…so we don't have any reason to believe that the people of any hood, anywhere else, would do much better…which is why we've dedicated a good chunk of this chapter to THAT kind of survival.

Develop a list of life-saving techniques, methods, and principles from this chapter.

INSURANCE IN THE HOOD
BY SATORI ANANDA

Michael Moore went to great lengths to document how "sick" our healthcare industry is in the U.S., in his award-winning documentary *Sicko*. Now, you might have heard some great things about the recent healthcare bill, but American healthcare is still NOTHING like universal healthcare. Just check out this article from the June 14, 2010 edition of the *Huffington Post*:

> An unemployed Michigan woman who was unable to afford medical treatment for a searing pain in her shoulder took matters into her own hands last week, shooting herself in the shoulder in a last-ditch effort to get into the ER. Kathy Myers, 41, said she was pushed to the brink of desperation Thursday night because she was "crazy in pain," and the local hospital emergency room would give her no more than a handful of anti-inflammatory pills. "Pain will make you do silly, crazy things," the 41-year-old Niles, Mich., woman said in a YouTube.com interview with News 8 in Grand Rapids, Michigan. "I knew they wasn't going to do anything, again. They said if it wasn't life-threatening, no health insurance, you can't get any help." In the video, she reenacts how she covered her right shoulder and head with two pillows before pointing her .25-caliber handgun at her own body. "I took the gun and went 'Boom!'" she said. Myers was treated for the gunshot wound at Lakeland Community Hospital and released a few hours later, reports ABCNews.com. She said the self-inflicted wound did not help her achieve her goal. "It didn't take the pain away," she told News 8.

Uninsured in the Hood
You exercise regularly, eat a healthy diet, try to manage your stress levels and generally take care of your health as the best way of keeping yourself out of the doctor's office and hospital. But, accidents, unexpected illness, serious disease and injuries happen to even the most cautious of families and having access to the best care is critical.

Chances are like nearly 46 million other Americans, you have been without insurance, or maybe like 25 million of your neighbors if you do have insurance you are underinsured. **An estimated 1 in 4 (25%) Blacks are uninsured, compared to 10% of whites (But Latino Americans are the largest segment of the adult population most likely to be uninsured, at 41.5%).** The rates of employer-based health coverage are just over 50% for employed Blacks, compared to over 70% for employed whites. In 2007, 23.8% of Blacks relied on public health insurance, in comparison to only 9% of whites.

Studies have shown that being uninsured (or underinsured) leads to a 40% increased risk of death. That means no insurance can equal DEATH. People without health insurance or who are Medicaid recipients are generally younger, less likely to be white, more likely to have a lower income, and more likely to be admitted to the hospital through the emergency room. **If you are involved in an auto accident or victim of a gunshot wound and you don't have health insurance you are more likely to die of your injuries than if you have private insurance.** Additionally, if you compare people hurt in car accidents to gunshot patients, gunshot victims require more of everything: more surgery, more intensive care, more rehabilitation and more counseling. They have more complications that bring them back for care, sometimes for the rest of their lives. They also are less likely to have private insurance.

> Did You Know?
> According to a report published in the November 2009 *Archives of Surgery*, uninsured adults' higher risk of death results in approximately 18,000 more deaths per year. Uninsured patients have the highest rate of death following admission for any kind of traumatic injury. Uninsured patients may experience treatment delay and/or receive different care, including fewer diagnostic tests.

Under the healthcare reform act bills recently passed, insurance coverage will be made available to more American citizens. The new laws require U.S. citizens and legal residents to have qualifying health coverage. Those without coverage will pay a tax penalty. The new law will allow more people to be eligible for government and state medical coverage and help many families pay for insurance. The new laws don't go into effect until 2014 but some of the positive aspects of the new reform, like parents being able to keep their adult children on their insurance until age 26, has begun early on many plans.

Still, many of us don't currently have access to private insurance or can't afford it even if it's available through our employers. Listed below are websites that offer clinics based on sliding scares or free services depending on income. Also included are programs to help with the cost of medicine and long term prescriptions.

- ❏ www.wheretofindcare.com
- ❏ www.rxassist.org
- ❏ www.needymeds.org
- ❏ www.pparx.org

BLOOD AND GUTS

Natalie Cole – A Story of Hope

Natalie Cole, the daughter of legendary singer Nat King Cole, had been having kidney troubles since February of 2008, when she was diagnosed with hepatitis C. According to the singer, she contracted the illness from her long struggle with drugs such as cocaine and heroin. Today, she says she's sober after two stints in rehab.

Once diagnosed, Cole underwent chemotherapy to fight the virus. In March 2009, she appeared on CNN's Larry King Live, announcing that the disease has caused both of her kidneys to fail, and she was searching for a donor. "I couldn't breathe. I – I went into – literally, my kidneys stopped functioning. They stopped, you know, processing the fluid that was starting to build up in my body," Cole explained. Since her kidney failure, she was on dialysis three days a week. Without a transplant, she was likely to remain on dialysis for the rest of her life, which would most certainly be cut short. She explained to Larry King, "I'm on a very long [waiting] list, which is why we are looking to donors." During her appearance, dozens of emails flooded CNN's computers. They were from fans who were offering up their own kidneys to help save the 59-year-old singer.

According to CNN.com, King handed Cole a stack of paper. "These are all e-mails from dozens – dozens of people offering to be tested to see if they can match, who want to give you a kidney," King told her. Stunned, Cole responded, "There are some great human beings out there. That's all I can say." Today, she has a new kidney.

MC Breed – A Story of Tragedy

But all stories like this don't have happy endings. In September of 2008, Flint, Michigan-based rapper MC Breed was playing basketball in Atlanta when he collapsed and was rushed to a nearby hospital, where he was listed in critical condition. When Breed was admitted, his kidneys were only 30% functional. Breed needed a kidney transplant. A number of rappers were contacted about participating in a benefit concert to help Breed with his medical expenses. "We are hoping we can find Breed a kidney through this process, before it's too late," Breed's manager Darryl Morris told AllHipHop.com. Breed died November 22, 2008 of kidney failure, still waiting for a kidney transplant. He was 37.

What made the difference in who lived and died? Nothing, except who received and who didn't.

"Light bill, phone bill, plus my Granny's nerve pills/ Feel like I should be takin them, imagine how my nerves feel/ I want a new Bentley - my Auntie need a kidney/ And if I let her pass, her children never will forgive me"
– Young Jeezy, "Crazy World"

The typical waiting time for a white person in need of a kidney for transplant is 553 days. Meanwhile, the typical waiting time for a Black person is nearly double that, at 1,082 days! Why?

I was recently taking a test where – as a security measure – everyone had to put their driver's licenses out on the table in front of them. All the white people had "organ donor" stamped on theirs, but I didn't see *any* Black people with that mark. That made me think about facts like the numbers above. I thought about how Black people's bodies aren't compatible with everything in white people's bodies, so Black people usually need Black organs (and blood). I thought about all the Black people I know who need a kidney or a liver or a brain and can't get one. I thought about Alonzo Mourning *and* Walter Payton (ask somebody).

In 1982, Blacks were about 12% of the U.S. population, but only 3% of organ donors. A team at Howard University started a campaign to increase donor participation. Since then, the numbers have gone up, but not by much.

A study in Ohio of 1,283 subjects found that fewer Black people signed donor cards – 39% of Blacks, compared to 66% of whites. Other findings from the study revealed greater mistrust in medical system, with Blacks concerned that they wouldn't be revived if doctors realized they were signed up to be donors. While we know that Blacks get targeted by the medical industry for the worst of the worst (See "Are All Doctors Mad Scientists?"), the "worst" also includes needing a kidney and not getting one because a bunch of people were scared of being harvested for organs.

So here's my simple advice. When you get your state ID or driver's license, go ahead and check off the box for "organ donor." It's that simple. It don't cost you anything. All it means is that when you die, your organs can go to someone else who needs them. It's not like your dead ass is gonna need them for anything. Even if you believe in heaven, I'm sure you won't miss your kidney there. But that kidney from you could save another Black man's life.

Now that I think about it, what about blood? There's a lot of Black people who need Type O blood, but can't get it because Black people don't like giving blood. Matter fact, some cities don't have enough of ANY kind of blood. As *The Grio* reported in July of 2009:

In Chicago this weekend, a 12-year-old boy was critically wounded in a drive-by shooting, another victim in what has seemed like non-stop violence there lately. Things are so bad that one hospital emergency room has actually come close to running out of supplies of blood for incoming patients.

Over the Fourth of July weekend alone there were a reported 63 shootings and 11 murders. Staggering numbers push the trauma unit in public hospitals to the brink. With the number of homicides this year over 200, albeit a slight decrease over last year, for Mayor Richard Daley it is still a senseless loss. "That's a sad thing. Another funeral, another funeral. It's about time that people get outraged." **Chief trauma surgeon Andrew Dennis says his hospital recently came dangerously close to running out of blood for transfusions.** "This is the first time we've been critically short to the point where someone could perish because we didn't have the right product to give them."

Become a registered organ donor. Think about all the people you can potentially save. Also, get some friends and donate blood

---

PRISON IS BAD FOR YOUR HEALTH
BY SUPREME UNDERSTANDING
PUBLISHED IN LOCKED UP BUT NOT LOCKED DOWN BY
AHMARIAH JACKSON AND I ATOMIC ALLAH

Between 1987 and 2007, the U.S. prison population tripled. The majority of those inmates, as we all know, were Black and Latino men. Blacks are imprisoned at nearly seven times the rate of whites – mostly for drug-related, nonviolent offenses...despite the fact that whites typically use more drugs than Blacks. The only group going to prisons at a comparable rate is now Black women, following in the footsteps of their men.

And prison is bad for your health. Not just in the sense of the violence that goes on behind those walls, but in much deeper, long-term ways as well. Nearly all serious conditions and illnesses are in prison in greater proportion than on the outside. For example, **AIDS rates are five times higher and Hepatitis C rates are 10 times higher.** Additionally, overcrowding, unsanitary conditions, and improper ventilation can increase your risk of exposure to other infectious diseases. **In the largest outbreak of multi-drug-resistant tuberculosis in New York City in 1989, fully 80% of all index cases could be traced to jails and prisons.**

To make things worse, your conditions will probably get worse in prison. Jail and prison medical care is far below acceptable standards. **In most cases, the correctional system recognizes the high rates of disease among those incarcerated, but provides very little treatment, prevention, discharge planning or aftercare unless there is a legal threat or humanitarian influence.** That's why you hear about those legal cases where a prisoner is suffering "cruel and unusual punishment" because they are not receiving standard medical services for their preexisting conditions. In fact, some people say they deny healthcare to political prisoners on purpose.

Let's not forget the ridiculous number of mental health problems in most prisons. In fact, if those inmates weren't Black and Latino, many of them would be in mental health facilities and substance abuse programs instead of prisons. But not only are they all in there, they're not getting treated. Combine that neglect with the heightened stress of incarceration, and your end result is that these individuals come back to our communities even crazier than when they went in. And they continue to suffer…and our communities suffer with them.

As you can tell, the health consequences extend even beyond the time you're locked up. A 2009 study published in the *Archives of Internal Medicine* shows that young adults who previously served time in prison have a higher risk of developing high blood pressure and an enlarged heart than those who have never been incarcerated. The study found that ex-inmates are also less likely to have access to regular health care, including treatment for the health issues linked to their incarceration. In fact, you may not know exactly how hard it is to get health insurance or life insurance with a felony on your record. Just ask anyone who's tried.

You can get auto insurance, but forget about funding your future (or your children's future). In fact, once you get convicted, your insurance is probably going to get terminated. In addition to an increased risk for heart disease, a 2005 study found that imprisonment has a long-term negative influence on health that lasts until at least age 40 and is only slightly improved by marriage and employment. What's the solution? If you're in prison, demand adequate treatment. Take em to court if you have to. Demand treatment for your fellow prisoners as well. And if you're not in prison, don't go…because it's a sick, sick place.

If you're locked up with a medical condition, fight to get the medical attention you need.

TEN WAYS TO STAY HEALTHY IN PRISON
BY I ATOMIC ALLAH
TO BE PUBLISHED IN A FIRST TIMER'S GUIDE TO PRISON BY AHMARIAH JACKSON AND I ATOMIC ALLAH

When it comes to health in prison and even the "free world" for that matter, you must maintain it in three dimensions: mentally, physically, and emotionally. Personally, I stress mental health first however; for some it's going to take a gang of work in that department. So for them they may take to physical exercises quicker. It doesn't matter because eventually these three dimensions of health fuel each other. Physical health eventually fuels a desire for mental health (stability). That is; in most cases, there are still others who suffer a more severe degree of mental instability that is fueled by emotional turmoil. So when a man acts out fits of rage he does so because his emotions have taken over his rational thought patterns rendering him instinctual, thus other than self.

When I specify mental, I'm referring to logical (calculated) thought as opposed to emotional impulses (psychological suicide). Here are ten tips to help you establish and maintain a stable foundation for optimal mental health while locked up...and in the "free world."

Mental Health

Tips to maintain mental stability in the concrete and steel:

1. Awareness. First you must recognize that from day one you are in a mental war of sorts. The most important and lethal participant in this war is you. Either you can come out of this for the better or worse.

2. Mental Stimulation. Think of your mind as a muscle. Just like the rest of the muscles in your body, if you don't exercise it; it will start to deteriorate. Of course, the most proficient way to exercise the mind is by reading. More importantly though, is what you choose to read. Sometimes that can be more detrimental than not reading at all. I recommend *Knowledge of Self: A Collection of Wisdom on the Science of Everything in Life* as a first read. For a lot of cats locked down this is usually the time that they pick up their first book. *Knowledge of Self* is a must read. However, don't let this be the only book you read. Make it the first of many.

3. Critical Thinking. There are many activities that may seem like just games on the surface that serve as vital tools in the development of critical thinking skills while incarcerated. They are: chess, dominoes, scrabble, puzzles and things of that nature. The point is to not only occupy your mind but to strengthen it as well. Although these may seem like trivial pastimes, they're not! They also promote a more positive atmosphere for social interaction.

4. Fighting the Law. If you have been wrongly convicted, then most of your problems are going to surround the proof of your innocence. Most of your time should be spent in the law library. There's no high like finding precedents to support your case. This in and of itself puts you on a mental high. Knowing that you single-handedly are facing down the "most powerful judicial system on the planet" is somewhat liberating.

5. Find a Hobby. Lastly, I strongly advise that you find a creative outlet such as drawing, writing, rapping, singing, arts and crafts, tattooing, or something. This serves as a mechanism to vent frustrations, anger, and disappointments. In other words these activities will actually help you to harness irrational behavior into productive outlets and occupy a lot of time, something that you must occupy wisely!

Emotional Health

Since emotional health is so closely related to mental health, I only have a few tips dealing with emotional health. If you follow the advice of the tips I've already outlined for mental health, then you will be equipped with enough exercises to keep strokes of irrationality in check. However, like I mentioned earlier; there are still others who suffer a more severe degree of mental instability that is fueled by emotional turmoil (psychological suicide). If you fit into this category don't worry I got you covered.

6. Get Over It. You must get it into your head that you cannot stress the things you cannot change. So you just got divorce papers in the mail. You shanking somebody isn't going to stop your divorce. Get over it playboy. She's on to the next one. The best way to avoid situations like this and do your time with as little stress as possible is to totally sever all ties to the "free" world.

You're not going to be able to just sever all communications at first, but over a period of time you can stop calling as much, until you've completely stopped calling altogether. The same can be applied to mail. What this does is allow you to do your time, which is stressful enough and limits the incidents of impulsive rage.

7. Control Yourself. Now of course there are situations where tip #6 won't resolve. When it comes to the children of prisoners there's a delicate situation. What usually makes this situation so complex is the fact that more often than not, you have to deal with the emotions of the mother and the child (or children, for that matter). In this case, severing all ties won't be the smartest move. Situations like this take the highest degrees of self-control.

So anytime you anticipate interactions in this area you must prepare yourself to control the situation by controlling yourself! So approach these situations with measured steps. All it takes is for you to lose control and the next thing you know it's been two years since you last had a visit or mail from your child or children. Also keep in mind though, at some point you must accept what you cannot change due to your incarceration.

Physical Health

The final aspect for optimal health while in the belly of the beast is physical health. Now that you've been adequately equipped with the keys to mental and emotional stability, it's only right that I complete the cipher with tips for obtaining the best physical conditioning.

8. Diet. When people think of physical health they automatically think exercise and body building. Don't get me wrong, exercise is an extremely vital tool in achieving optimal physical conditioning. However, it's not the most important. The most important aspect of physical health is what you put into your body!! What you put in is what you get out. Ya dig?!? If you eat junk then you're going to feel like junk. Food is supposed to fuel the body. You're not supposed to want to lay down to rest after you eat. No!!! I strongly advise that you either become vegetarian or cut down your flesh intake as much as you can while incarcerated. In the free world too for that matter. My reason for saying this is actually two-fold.

First, the animals raised on these prison farms are never in the best of health. Most of them are suffering from debilitating ailments before they are slaughtered. So much so that the actual slaughter becomes something of a mercy killing. Now combine that with some of the savage acts the prisoners who "care" for these animals partake in with these animals and you shouldn't want to eat that sh*t anyway. Yes, I mean beastiality!!

Maintaining a vegetarian diet is not as hard as you would think it is in prison. The one thing you will learn very quickly while locked up, EVERYTHING has value to it in prison. I don't think that there is a bartering system in the world that is remotely comparable to the prisoners' barter system. So when meat items are served as the main course of your meal you can easily trade/sell it off for the vegetables on that menu. Or, you can sell it off for some item off the commissary (inmate store). Trust, there were many days that I ate very well trading meat for vegetables.

Now if you decide to go vegan which is no meat, meat byproducts, or dairy you may have a harder time. That's not to say that you can't maintain your diet. It's just that you're going to have to be extremely persistent in demanding the prison recognize your diet. In Georgia, there are three prisons that offer vegan menus. So if you're in prison in Georgia and you're vegan and the prison where you are being housed doesn't offer vegan alternatives, then you should request to see the prison chaplain and state your case. You shouldn't experience too much resistance in this area. There may be some laziness in the handling of it. However, if you're persistent you should be transferred within sixty to ninety days.

9. Physical Conditioning. Now we can go into physical conditioning. This is probably the most commonly associated aspect of prison life. Most cats start out doing pushups to either relieve stress, frustrations, or to kill some time. Whatever the case, these physical exercises serve more purpose than just cosmetic. They actually serve as another outlet to vent.

More than a few states have taken weights out of their prisons citing that the weights were a threat to the security of the prison. What that meant was that the prisoners were getting too big for security to handle them. Since weights were taken out, you're forced to find more creative ways to strength train. The most common is the water bag. It is just what it sounds like it is, a trash bag filled with water. The bigger the bag the more it's going to weigh. I have also worked out with two buffers tied together.

Whatever the case, pushups, sit ups, crunches, water bag, or buffers; I advise that you partake in some form of physical conditioning. It's far too easy to do your time just lying around deteriorating.

Even if you don't exercise using the methods I named, at least, when they call "yard call," go out and, if nothing else, walk the yard. You can even pick up a game of basketball. You must know, however, prison ball is a little more "intense" than street ball. If you're really feeling yourself, then run a few laps around the yard. This is such a therapeutic experience that once you try it a couple times, you may find yourself addicted.

10) Last but not least, masturbation. Hey, it is what it is. Masturbation is as much a part of prison life as concrete and steel. Sometimes you just have to get that off your chest. If you don't, you may find yourself exploding in fits of violence for no apparent reason. Now there is moderation to everything. Have enough respect for yourself and others to at least do this in the privacy of the shower. I'm just saying, not everybody has common sense. Whipping your sh*t out in the presence of others will get your head split the f*ck open.

Then again, you may not have to "jack." You may be able to let nature take its course and release that pressure via dream. This is the best. At least you get a good visual and the mind is so focused that it almost feels real. That is, until you open your eyes to the same cats you've been around for however many years, months, and days.

Be careful to not get caught up on feeling on yourself, though. There are cats that develop uncontrollable urges when it comes to "jacking." So much so that they become instinctual instead of intellectual. Meaning on any impulse they may act on the urge to "jack."

Develop mental and physical discipline and make the best of your time.

CARING FOR YOUR ELDERS
BY RODNEY JONES

The conversations we have with our elders help us see this world through a lens that is very different from what is often presented to us in the songs, television programming and movies of popular culture. The conversations we hold with our elders help us connect to who we were, are, and shall become as a people. This communication is necessary to our wellbeing, as well as the health of our elders. I remember a scene in the Tyler Perry movie *Madea's Family Reunion*, when the Great Grandmother rings the bell after watching the family fight, drink, gamble and de-class themselves. She then goes on to give them a little history lesson. Up until that point I don't think anybody even knew that she was there.

Health is one of the areas that becomes more and more important to deal with as our elders' age. Ensuring they have healthy lifestyles and diets becomes increasingly important as well. Unfortunately, the traditions of family meals and intergenerational communication in our communities are becoming frailer than osteoporosis stricken bones. During a recent conversation with a homeboy of mine, we discussed how when his grandmother became too ill to live alone, she began suffering from dementia and had to move in with his family. This elder in the family who would always have family gatherings in her home was soon forgotten by other family members. Once the immediate and obvious value of the family's interaction with her was removed so was the motivation to gather as extended family.

All too often, we basically forget about our elders and leave them to wither away and die in some f*cked up retirement home. According to some stats from the National Center of Health Statistics, Black people in America over the age of 70 report having trouble with everyday activities. Of all our elders, 11.5% report trouble with bathing or showering, 8.1% with dressing, 11.1% with getting out of bed, 25% with walking, 11.0% with getting around swiftly outside, and 3.0% with using the restroom.

This cycle is repeated again and again in the black and brown hoods across America. As we allow our cultures and customs to erode into a more European style we are losing the connections necessary to enjoy life as it was intended to be. This disassociation with our spirit and community is highlighted in old age. Too many of our elders are suffering in isolation in their last years with us. **The best way to care for our elders is to engage with them and their needs as elders. Other ways include:**

- ❐ Talk with their doctors and know what medications they are taking. Research these medications to know their side effects and look for healthier alternative treatments.
- ❐ Prepare meals with your elders. Siblings can take turns or the family can eat together. Nothing improves the health of our elders like involvement with family matters.
- ❐ Don't over work them. Too many of our elders, especially women are forced to raise grandchildren and great grandchildren. Interaction is one thing but raising children is the responsibility of parents.
- ❐ Take a class together. One great opportunity for people of color is the D'zert Club that teaches about Africa and the history of African people and culminates with a trip to Africa.
- ❐ Know the leading causes of death for elders in your community, the systems, and research methods of prevention and cure. Currently the leading causes of death among African Americans age 65 and over are: Heart Disease, Cancer, Stroke, Diabetes, and Pneumonia/Influenza

However, regardless of the initial thoughts invoked at the numbers and information above, there is TREMENDOUS hope among our community as far as caring for our elders are concerned.

In the Stanford University Ethno-geriatric study, Blacks were more likely to assist or take on the role of caregivers to their elderly friends. The study also mentioned that Blacks were more likely to have more contact with friends, family and neighbors; probably from living in areas that are more bunched and confined (turns out the "projects" served a positive purpose). Even with the use of informal caregiving (friends and family), there was shown to be no dropoff in formal caregiving (senior centers, rehabilitation centers).

In a study of African American caregiving for a relative with Alzheimer's disease, it was shown that caregiving, a traditionally female role, is not only a traditional family value, but an act of love, and that frequently, social supports served to lighten caregiver burden. Also, **Black caregivers report less depression than white caregivers and have greater self-efficiency in managing caregiving problems.**

When it comes to caring for our elders, we often can't afford to send them off to old folk's homes. So we do our best to handle what's needed, as far as diet, exercise, medicine dispensement and monitoring their health. However, not all of us are on our jobs like that.

"Be not slow to visit the sick." – Ecclesiastes

If you aren't, guess who is? THE CHURCH!!! In places that are more rural ("country" if you will), or with less community resources, the church plays a vital role providing a family-like feeling, ranging from bringing Sister Mabel a plate of black eyed peas, co'n bread and greens, to getting Brother Johnny Lee Jones out to the annual church picnic on Saturday, or just getting together for prayer meeting (and gossip) with Sister Jesse Mae.

Whatever the gathering be for that particular day, it provides the community-based infrastructure we often lack in the "secular" realms of our communities. The church members are often the go-to source for an elder who has no family in the area that they reside in. So for all you non-Christian folks trying to force Nana out the church, part of the reason why she ain't budging is because it's her support network. And if YOU ain't providing a better, more loving, more thorough support network, stop complaining and criticizing. ADD ON instead. You owe it to your elders to make sure their needs are met. So are you on your job?

There are many ways to bond with your elders, choose one. Just make sure they aren't neglected.

GET YOUR AFFAIRS IN ORDER!
BY SUPREME UNDERSTANDING

If we can learn anything from the tragic death of Hip Hop pioneer Guru, it should be that we MUST have our affairs in order before tragedy strikes. When Guru fell ill in February of 2010, we learned he'd been battling cancer for years. Some of his family members didn't know. That's not a good look. What's worse is that the person who assumed responsibility for his care was doing anything BUT taking care of him. Solar, Guru's business partner and producer had quickly assumed control of Guru's business affairs and even his damn MySpace page. While Solar was spinning Guru's illness in the media to his own benefit,  Guru laid in a hospital bed comatose, his face unshaved, his nails uncut. DJ Premier lashed out on Sirius radio after seeing his condition:

> If you love him, and you're taking care of him, why the f**k did his nails look longer than a f*cking ruler?! [And] a clump Afro?! I've taken care of people in the hospital [before]. You can wash their hair and clean their nails off. His feet were swollen and his toenails were really disgusting...I took the logo on my shirt and rubbed it against his whole body and told him a message from me about how much I loved him, and that we were for life and still were for life. Then I kissed him on his face and let him know that I was going to miss him because it seemed like he was already gone.

Goddamn, Solar, you could've taken a break from flirting with white girls on MySpace to at least cut the man's nails. Instead, Solar blocked Guru's own family members from seeing him. When Guru passed on April 20th, Solar released a "deathbed letter" supposedly written by Guru (while he was in a coma!). The letter placed all of Guru's business interests in Solar's hands and even gave a shout-out to a nonprofit that was supposedly Guru's...but which was really Solar's, and wasn't even an active nonprofit at that...just a way to collect donations from unknowing supporters.

In the letter, it also appeared that Guru was blocking DJ Premier, his former producer, from doing ANYthing in memory of his old friend and colleague. Primo wasn't buying it. Meanwhile, it appeared Guru was somehow buying and selling real estate! Records suggest that Keith Elam sold his home for $325,000 in March (while he was in a coma), and then bought another home. How? You figure it out. Thanks to the diligent investigative work of a number of Guru fans, one of whom hacked into all of Solar's online accounts, it soon became clear that the letter was a fake and Solar was a fraud.

But this kind of sh*t happens all the time, and you don't have to be famous for it to happen to you! Haven't you ever heard of someone "contesting the will"? I experienced it when my father passed away in 2009. All of a sudden, his ex-wife from 20 years ago wanted to pop up and claim that she was entitled to a piece of the pie. In fact, this wretched woman claimed she was entitled to EVERYTHING because of some crazy "irrevocable beneficiary" clause in their marriage contract. Fortunately, her argument didn't have a leg to stand on, so she didn't get a dime. But as I said, this kind of stuff happens quite often. When you fall ill, people will pop up in your life asking for money at the last minute (which they believe is your last minute), or trying to be extra nice to you (while you're conscious) so they can get in your Will. These same people will often neglect to take care of you while you're unconscious (in a coma or just too sick to speak up), or worse yet, they'll pull the plug on you like Gary Coleman's woman.

Can you imagine that? Somebody busting you over the head, claiming you fell, then pulling the plug on you and selling your photos for ten stacks?! But that's how dirty some people are! And unless you want to fall prey to those wolves, you'll get your affairs in order NOW. If not for your own sake, do it for your children and the loved ones you'll leave behind. Otherwise, they'll be fighting expensive legal battles instead of honoring you the way they want to. At a time of grief, they'll be stressed and stretched to limits they shouldn't have to be. Fortunately, my mother had me and a lawyer relative to help her. What about people who don't have those kinds of resources? So here are some ESSENTIAL things you need to start putting in place right NOW to avoid any future drama:

Get life insurance. At least $150K worth, especially if you'll be leaving behind young children who will need college money. Choose your beneficiaries wisely. If you don't feel safe telling your mate/spouse that they're gonna get paid if you die, why are you even with them?

Start a "Rainy Day" savings fund. While this can go towards a serious family crisis in an emergency, it can also be used to cover funeral costs (which can get quite expensive). It's always especially sad when a grieving family has to beg for money to cover someone's burial expenses. If you live a high-risk lifestyle, your rainy day fund better be BIG.

Don't leave behind a ton of debt. Speaking of money, you should know that your debt also transfers to your next of kin. So does the hospital bill and the nursing home bill and the funeral home bill. Either live healthy and die peacefully in your sleep (very few bills) or set aside a ton of money for when your lifestyle puts you in a condition that requires ongoing care (lots of bills).

Make your wishes known. When Tupac died, some people were concerned that he'd been cremated, which they claimed he didn't want. Don't leave those issues ambiguous. Let your loved ones know who is in charge if something happens to you, if you want to be cremated (much cheaper) or buried (much more expensive), as well as making sure you're leaving behind the money to cover whatever it is you want.

Prepare your Estate Plan. Whether married or single, rich or poor, young or old, you need an estate plan. Even if you don't have tons of property or businesses, you need to make it clear who will take care of your children or other dependents if something happens to you. Once it's done, you need to put a copy, along with all your important financial documents in a fire-proof safe or a safe-deposit box. The other copy goes to whoever you trust enough to have power of attorney and/or be the executor of your estate. Make sure those executing your estate plan know how to access those documents quickly.

Your Estate Plan

Here's a list of documents to consider when preparing your estate plan:

A Will: This handles all of your business when you go. You can keep it simple, and say that 100% of your estate goes to your next of kin (your spouse if living, and your children if not). Or you can get more specific, which can be necessary if your children aren't in your custody or have different parents. While it doesn't affect your life insurance or any financial accounts where you've already named beneficiaries, if you have business interests, accounts, or investments that most people don't know about, you should make sure you identify them here. Remember, you can't take it with you.

The Will also names your executor (the person who follows its instructions). If you die without a Will, the state of your last residence will distribute your assets as it sees fit. Really. A simple will for a single person generally costs between $400 and $600 ($600-$800 for married couples), but this is where getting a membership with Pre-Paid Legal (perhaps a "temporary" one) might make the most sense.

A Living Will: A Living Will covers all of your wishes in case you're unable to make decisions for yourself. It names who will be responsible, and under what conditions – if any – they can "pull the plug" on you. Make sure you get it legally notarized (if you can't afford to have a lawyer handle the whole thing) and that your loved ones know where it's kept. If you're having a lawyer prepare your Will, it can usually be added at very little extra cost.

A Trust: This is different from a Will in that it can pass down property and other assets to your beneficiaries in a more "protected" way. This is what rich folks use to avoid taxes, creditors, and other drama when they pass away.

Power of Attorney: This legal document empowers a spouse, relative, or trusted adult to conduct financial transactions for you, mainly if you become incapacitated. They can sign checks or make business decisions as if they were you. A durable power of attorney becomes effective immediately, while a medical power of attorney allows someone to make medical decisions if you become incapacitated.

You can check out the information at www.estateplanninglinks.com and www.nafep.com/estate_planning for more details and other resources.

Decide how you'd like you family to be helped after you're gone. Weigh the pros and cons, and determine what they'll need.

USING REPARATIONS TO REPAIR BLACK HEALTH
BY DR. VERNELLIA R. RANDALL
AUTHOR OF DYING WHILE BLACK

"Being Black in America is dangerous to our health!"

Historically, the enslavement of Africans was abnormally hazardous and there were health hazards and high death rates during every phase: during the interior trek, the middle passage, the breaking in period and the enslavement. The slave health deficit that was established during slavery was not relieved during the reconstruction period (1865-1870), Jim Crow Era (1870-1965), the Affirmative Action Era (1965-1980) or the Racial Entrenchment era (1980 to present). Thus, repairing the health of African Americans will require a multi-facet long term financial commitment and effort.

To many, both black, white and others, reparations is viewed as a paycheck, some undetermined amount of money for some long ago harm. In my view, that is an incomplete and destructive view of reparations. Rather, **reparations should be viewed as an obligation to make the repairs necessary to correct current harms done by past wrongs.** This is a much more expansive view than merely calculating the economic harm and writing a check. Under this view, reparations become a process that restores hope and dignity and rebuilds the community. The burden of a slave health deficit has been a continuous burden. That deficit will only be removed if the United States makes a significant and sustained commitment - undertaking whatever actions necessary. Specifically, to eliminate the slave health deficit, the government will need to:

❑ Eliminate the disparities in morbidity and mortality
❑ Assure access to health care
❑ Assure quality health care, and
❑ Eliminate racial discrimination in health care and health research.

Eliminate the disparities in morbidity and mortality. Eliminating the disparities in morbidity and mortality will require, among other things:

❑ A focus on education and prevention through targeted services;
❑ The provision of a live-able wage for all persons and families, and
❑ The elimination of environmental hazards in African American communities.

Targeted Services. The health disparities among African Americans have been well established and up until recently eliminating health disparities has not been a goal. For instance, the United States health population

---

goals in Healthy People 2000 focused on reducing the disparities and not eliminating it. It was not until Healthy People 2010 that eliminating health disparities became a goal and the same health goals for Whites were set for African Americans. **Targeting health care services to African-Americans would focus resources on the specific health problems confronting them.** States could take steps to target services toward African-Americans. In particular, a focused and sustained effort must be undertaken to eliminate health disparities in diabetes, cardiovascular disease, maternal and infant mortality, HIV/AIDS, cancer, oral health, mental health, drug, alcohol and tobacco addiction, asthma and violence (including domestic violence).

An essential public health approach will need to be taken which includes:

- ❏ Assurance of access to quality health care;
- ❏ Locating health facilities in the black community;
- ❏ Providing universal health care;
- ❏ Assurance of cultural competence of the health care workforce;
- ❏ Elimination of racial discrimination in health care and health research;
- ❏ Authorization/funding of the use of medical testers; and
- ❏ Requirement of data collection and reporting.

Eliminating the morbidity and mortality disparities will require access to quality care. Assuring access to quality care will require:

- ❏ Locating adequate health care facilities within the Black community,
- ❏ Assuring competent health care workforce in black communities,
- ❏ Assuring the cultural competence of the health care workforce, and
- ❏ Increasing the knowledge about health and health of black persons and translating it into effective clinical practice.

Historically, African-American communities attempted to address the problem by establishing African-American hospitals. At one point more than 200 hospitals were located in predominately black communities. African-Americans relied on these institutions to "heal and save their lives." Now, these institutions are almost non-existent. By the 1960s, only 90 African-American hospitals remained. Between 1961 and 1988, 57 African-American hospitals closed and 14 others either merged, converted or consolidated. By 1991, only 12 hospitals continued to "struggle daily just to keep their doors open". As a result of closures, relocations, and privatization, many African-Americans are left with limited, and difficult, access to hospitals.

Thus, reparations would provide for hospitals, clinics, alcohol and drug detox centers, dental health clinics and mental health clinics in the African American community.

Reparations could be used to increase the availability of providers in the community. This could be done by providing scholarships for blacks to enter health care professions, by providing grants to university and colleges to increase their graduation rate of persons who will work in urban area, by increasing the capacity of historically black colleges to train and graduate students, by increasing health care reimbursement for services provided to inner-city residents, and by providing economic incentives to doctors and other health care professionals to locate to African American communities.

One barrier to culturally competent care is the physicians' own negative perceptions about African Americans. Because they have differing needs and problems in accessing care, physicians may see African Americans as less compliant and more difficult to care for. The problem, however, is not African Americans, but the health care system's inability to provide effective care to diverse populations. If increased compliance and improved health status are the goals, then the health care system must be flexible enough to match a community's cultural, ethnic, lifestyle and socioeconomic needs. Through reparations culturally competent care can be assure by requiring:

- ☐ Health professional schools to train providers from a diverse background;
- ☐ All physicians to have a rotation during their internship and externship the focus on providing culturally competent care;
- ☐ Providers to take continuing educational units in cultural competency;
- ☐ Health care facilities and managed care organizations to complete and submit on regular basis a cultural competency assessment to a regulatory agency; and
- ☐ Health care be provided in accordance with realities of the needs of the various "classes" of the Black community.

Provide a Live-able Wage or Income. Poverty effects housing choice, job choice, food and education. Since African Americans are disproportionately poor, the elimination of poverty becomes essential to improving the health status of African Americans. Poverty is not the only problem, also a problem is the "working poor" also disproportionately African American. The working poor are people whose full-time, year-round earnings are so meager that despite their best efforts they can't afford decent housing, diets, health care or child care. Poverty and the problems of the working poor could be eliminated by assuring everyone in the United States a "live-able wage" and not merely a minimum wage. A "livable wage" provides enough income to pay for the basic necessities of daily living: shelter, food, clothing, health care, child care and transportation. Without a livable-wage income, people suffer not only a lack of dignity, but also a variety of social and health problems. **The San Francisco Department of Public Health reported livable wages diminish mortality rates, decrease unnecessary hospitalization of the poor, eliminate some costs associated with caring for the homeless, and saved lives.** Thus, livable wages become a cornerstone to eliminating the "slave health deficit and reparations could be in the form of assuring a livable wage.

Eliminate Environmental Hazards in African American Communities.
A critical component of health care is the location of environmental hazards and toxic dumps in Black communities, the workplace hazards and the hazards in the home. Studies have documented that hazardous waste landfills are disproportionately placed in African American communities while poor communities are not disparately burdened. (See, "Dying To Learn: Lead Poisoning And Environmental Racism.")

Reparations could be used to remove toxic dumps and landfills from African American communities or completely relocate the communities to safe environment; to make workplace safer and to eliminate lead paint from housing.

Conclusion

Reparations ultimately are about social justice since it's about undoing the harm that has been done to one group in society. Reparations is not a one way action, it requires the African American community to undertake action and to rebuild itself. Reparations will rebuild community and cleanse the soul of the nation. Most importantly, reparations could restore the health of people of African descent in America.

Know what to do with a large sum of cash. Know what it takes to build a hospital, run a university, open an urban gardening center or a free clinic, etc... Its way more exciting than opening a McDonalds.

EVERYTHING COSTS MONEY
BY TRUE ASIATIC ALLAH

Corporate Control (Neo-colonialism)

The New World Order is all about controlling Old World Resources. There truly is nothing new under the Sun.

There are many "old world" countries (Black, brown, and yellow nations) that are former colonies of European powers. Many gained their Independence through armed struggle, some were abandoned once the resources were depleted, and others were traded like cards between European neighbors (some more than 3 or 4 times). One thing remains constant, the resources that remain are controlled by corporate interests, who are typically still based in one of the former colonies, and hence they are still in control. Some of the biggest of these are as follows:

ADM (Archer Daniels Midland): ADM is a conglomerate based in Decatur, Illinois. ADM operates more than 270 plants worldwide, where cereal grains and oilseeds are processed into products used in food, beverage, nutraceutical, industrial and animal feed markets worldwide.

Monsanto: This U.S.-based multinational agricultural biotechnology corporation is the world's leading producer of the herbicide glyphosate,

---

marketed as "Roundup." Monsanto is also the leading producer of genetically engineered (GE) seed; it sells 90% of the US's GE seeds. It is headquartered in Creve Coeur, Missouri. Agracetus, owned by Monsanto, exclusively produces Roundup Ready soybean seed for the commercial market. In 2005, it finalized purchase of Seminis Inc, making it the world's largest conventional seed company.

Tate & Lyle: is a global provider of distinctive, high quality ingredients and solutions for the food, beverage and other industries. Though our large-scale, efficient manufacturing plants, we use innovative technology to turn raw materials into distinctive, high quality ingredients for our customers. These ingredients add taste, texture, nutrition and increased functionality to products that millions of people around the world use or consume every day

Cargill: Cargill is an international producer and marketer of food, agricultural, financial and industrial products and services. Founded in 1865, our privately held company employs 138,000 people in 67 countries.

Wal-Mart: Operates under its own name in the United States, including the 50 states and Puerto Rico. Wal-Mart operates in Mexico as Walmex, in the United Kingdom as Asda ("Asda Wal-Mart" in some branches), in Japan as Seiyu, and in India as Best Price. It has wholly-owned operations in Argentina, Brazil, and Canada. Wal-Mart's investments outside North America have had mixed results: its operations in the United Kingdom, South America and China are highly successful, while it was forced to pull out of Germany and South Korea when ventures there were unsuccessful.

Dupont: Pioneer Hi-Bred International, Inc., a DuPont business, is the world's leading developer and supplier of advanced plant genetics to farmers worldwide. We seek to increase customer productivity, profitability and develop sustainable agricultural systems for people everywhere. Innovative and customer-focused, Pioneer is a leader in the agriculture industry and upholds the highest standards. Headquartered in Johnston, Iowa, Pioneer provides services to customers in nearly 70 countries.

This is just a short list of who is really controlling the means of survival for you and your children. Understand that the less you know and do, the easier it is to lose consciousness and control concerning your food and other resources… and hence your ability to survive.

Solutions (Food for Thought)
☐ One of the best ways to prepare your family is to learn the science of agriculture: Urban gardens, rural farms, hydroponics, and rooftop planters.
☐ Wherever you are, learn what it will take to sustain yourself in any climate/season.
☐ Study the herbology and botany of your area, and find out what you can and cannot eat for sustainability.

- ❏ Teach the babies how to grow their own food as they love to see (and eat) the fruits of their labor. Educate them and expose them to farms (perhaps starting with pumpkin/hay rides in the fall season), especially ones where you can pick your own produce.
- ❏ Understand the water sources in your area. Even many urban areas have natural springs (many of which were sealed when they started bottling water).

Finally, learn about Solar and Wind Energy. For those (like myself) who have not (yet) gotten back to living strictly on the land, you should be heading toward "getting off the grid." **Monthly utilities are actually taking the bulk of many families' monthly income, some as much as 60-70% just for water, gas, and electricity.** It is no accident that to convert one's home to wind or solar runs in the 10's of thousands (out of range for most of us). This is because the utilities are a powerful global lobby that wants to keep sucking the blood out of us (I'm thinking "Matrix" again). **Keep in mind, if you can install Solar yourself you could save as much as 80% of the cost.** Solar produces more energy than wind (unless you are in an area with constant wind). I would suggest both, as some days of constant rain offer less sunlight, but more than likely offer strong winds instead.

> **Did You Know?**
> You cannot necessarily leave your children a job (at least not at someone else's company), but you can leave them land (and the skills to cultivate it) from which they can work and live off of. Dependence on corporate resources will make them a victim.

The Earth has all the necessary resources to manifest a holistic lifestyle for yourself and family. Become a cultivator, as the days of America being the "great producer" are over and done. We have moved from the Agricultural Age to the Industrial Age to the (so-called) Information Age, and now we're approaching the Service Age (which does not pay sustainable wages for the endangered so-called middle class), and all this has only been in the last 150 years. And it's all been a social experiment. The experiment is over, so let's get back to the land.

Write a list of things you don't want to rely on anybody for and do it yourself. It can be as small as growing your own basil and as ambitious as generating your own electricity.

FARMER'S MARKETS AND URBAN GARDENS
BY SUPREME UNDERSTANDING

There are about 4,800 farmer's markets in the country, the majority of which are seasonal markets. Many of those in urban areas are well-established and stable financially – staples of their communities. But in recent years, we've also seen the rise of smaller markets and stores, as well as people converting vacant land into urban farm sites and abandoned parking lots into open-air farmer's markets. Yet, according to food justice activist Ladonna Redmond, "We have yet to prove we can feed everybody...we need more vendors, more producers...communities of color still come up short."

While Black and brown farmers are quickly being wiped out of the actual farming population, they remain a significant presence at most farmer's markets. And Black people, especially people emerging from the Hip Hop generation are becoming more and more involved in proactive ways to bring fresh fruits and vegetables to the people who need it most. According to Redmond, "More people of color are getting involved. People who better understand the communities' needs." Even Michelle Obama recently broke ground on a sizable 1,100-foot garden plot on the White House lawn. Organic, of course.

Urban Farming is Local

Chances are good that you've got some urban farms and gardens springing up in your hood as well...many of them using hip hop to connect to the community.

In Detroit, "Peaches and Greens," uses ice cream trucks to push fresh produce in the hood. Volunteers grow the produce in nearby community gardens.

In St. Louis, "Hip Hop for Health" uses music to teach about healthy food choices, building school gardens, and the benefits of eating locally grown foods.

In Atlanta, HABESHA Gardens makes fresh food accessible to people in the hood of Mechanicsville. The director Cashawn Myers, told CNN:

> We invite people from the local community here, the immediate community but also from the greater Atlanta community...to come out, work in the garden; learn, reconnect with the Earth and also be able to take food home with them after the harvest...Not only are we teaching them about agriculture, [we're] teaching them about solar technology, rainwater catching...A majority of the food that was planted here was done by the youth in the after-school program. They helped to build the shed, they helped to build the greenhouse, they helped to build the shade nursery...They are very much a vital part of the process that goes on here...When you're poor, when you don't have access to resources, you have to create your own. So this is a way for people of African descent to use their creativity to grow their own food...[Starting] community gardens in local communities, specifically in urban areas, is important, so you create your own food security network...You're not relying on large grocery stores to provide food for everyone because if those grocery stores have problems, your access to food is done...We invite people from the local community here, the immediate community but also from the greater Atlanta community...to come out, work in the garden; learn, reconnect with the Earth and also be able to take food home with them after the harvest.

In Milwaukee, former pro basketball player Will Allen has turned urban farming into a million-dollar enterprise. He estimates that his

venture, Growing Power, Inc., is one of thousands of urban farms that have sprung up in recent years. "It's beyond a movement at this point. It's more like a revolution," Allen told CNN.

Even the CDC recently recommended making fresh produce more available and visible in poor communities as a means to combat obesity and disease. But most people in our communities have yet to understand the relationship between nutrition and illness. "We need to make the link between food access and health outcomes," says Redmond. And it's actually cheaper to eat this way. **Eating seasonally available local produce is 20-50% cheaper than eating fruits and vegetables trucked or flown in from many miles away.** But many local vendors tend to sell their produce in affluent (white) areas, where consumers don't mind paying more than they would in regular supermarkets. Meanwhile, people in the hood don't even have that many REGULAR supermarkets to go to. That's why the documentary "The High Cost of Being Poor" talked about how we have to resort to "corner stores" where we pay higher prices for lower-quality goods! As Will Allen said, "Minority people are affected by poor food, more than any other groups," and many inner cities lack access to quality fruits and vegetables. Our food system is broken."

All the more reason, Redmond claims, to use a hyper-local approach when creating urban markets and farm sites. It not only answers the food access question to "keep it in the hood," but also she says, "It creates jobs in the community and expands its economic capacity."

Urban Farming is Global

And it's not just happening here. It's happening in slums and ghettos throughout the world. In the crowded slums of Mumbai, India, Dr. R. T. Doshi's "city garden" methods have worked in the most cramped of spaces. Doshi's tools are mostly recycled garbage: sugarcane waste, polyethylene bags, tires, containers, cylinders, and soil. Dr. Doshi uses all of his household's organic waste and produces enough food on his roof to make his family self-sufficient in terms of food.

On the other hand, **a new program in Kenya may help people grow their own food and maintain the delicate ecosystem in which they live. The "Backpack Farm" provides everything a new farmer needs to start growing food, and it's all contained within a backpack. Each pack carries drought-resistant seeds, a collapsible drip irrigation kit, plant food, farm tools, training manuals, and a diary for keeping track of the farm's progress. The goal is to feed every hungry person and engender a sense of community while teaching self-reliance through farming.**

Personally, I hope this is the direction that Original people take throughout the world, because the secondary reason why the "Third World" is poor is because we've abandoned our traditional means for survival in pursuit of Western ideals, allowing European interests to come into our "backyards" to take advantage of all the natural resources and fertile land we lost sight of. It's time to take it back. Will we do the same in America? I can only hope (and educate) to see that happen…before it's too late. As Lupe Fiasco raps on "B.M.F. (Building Minds Faster):

> I got a fifth flow, call me brother man/ Africa's the set, yeah that's the motherland/ For that BP, I shed 50 tears/ In Nigeria that oil been spillin' for like 50 years!/ Fifty years?! Hell naww/ Hell yeahhh, tryina tell ya'll/ At this rate, niggas gon lose! Can't search for water, or grow your own food!/ Tell me what's gon' happen, when them stores close/ And ain't gon open up, no mo/ Yeah that's the realest sh*t/ You gon' feel dat, hunger's yo enemy/ But you can't kill dat!/ Survival of the fit, is what they aiming at/ And niggas ain't fit, fat as hell!/ Fat in mind, body fat as well

So what are YOU gonna do? You just gonna let Lupe clown you like that? Better question, you just gonna let Monsanto and all those other food corporations clown you when they decide what you can and can't eat? Or IF you can eat at all? Yeah, homey, this world is becoming a prison planet, and you're getting chumped off at chow.

But as this article (hopefully) shows you, it's not impossible to reverse these trends. Even though the government has tried cracking down on everything from backyard farming to rainwater collection, whenever the people are determined, we will find a way. My mother raised me in Jersey City, where we had NO backyard. We just had a little concrete lot behind our house. She filled that tiny space with over a dozen buckets, containers, and just about anything that would hold soil and plant life. She hung vines across clotheslines. And from that little urban garden, we ate organic tomatoes, cucumbers, eggplant, hot peppers, and even had mint leaves for our iced tea…yet I never appreciated or understood what she was doing, until now. When I was 20, I bought a house in Atlanta with over an acre of land behind it. Ten years passed and I never planted so much as a flower back there. That's gonna change. I've invited Cashawn Myers of HABESHA to help me put a full urban garden back there, complete with fruits, vegetables, herbs, rainwater collecting barrels, and even some fruit trees. You can check my progress at www.HoodHealthHandbook.com

But even if you don't have that much space, you've got all the resources you need. Look at what Dr. Doshi does in India. Or what my mother did in Jersey. It's called "container gardening." You can find tons of resources on how to make it happen (even in an apartment) at blogs like containergardening.wordpress.com and websites like insideurbangreen.org

---

Start an urban farming coalition in your hood, and get so gangsta about gardening that people will want to tattoo carrots on their face.

URBAN GARDENING IN YOUR OWN BACKYARD

BY SHA-KING CEHUM ALLAH

No matter where you live, having your own garden isn't impossible. In fact, it's fairly simple. Find a nice place that gets reasonable sunlight and start diggin'! If you live in an apartment or some congested community where there's no soil, you can put large containers to use as pots and plant beds. **It would be ideal to get the soil tested for mineral and chemical contents, this can be done via agri-agencies/businesses in the city. It only costs like $10!** I know this isn't practical for everyone, but it's a good idea because you could be tryin'a garden on some "worst part," mineral-deficient, contaminated soil. And while it may still produce crops, the crops will contain whatever is in the soil. If the soil is deficient or contaminated then you would have to take steps to revitalize it – via organic farming techniques like composting and planting certain plants that actually suck up the chemicals, like sponges.

If contamination isn't a problem, just start digging'. Choose which plants would grow best given the specific amount of sunlight you have access to. Some need direct sunlight, some don't. You can find out what will work best by asking the people who work wherever you're getting your seeds from.

You want to take off the top layer with the grass, which is easiest with a hoe. The tool, that is. This top layer contains weed and grass seeds. If tilled and turned over, it can result in more weeds/grass growing throughout the garden. So you have to take it off altogether. Once that is removed, use the hoe to break up the soil underneath, and start turning it over. This allows the moist soil underneath to be exposed and mixes up the soil.

At this point I recommend mixing in some fertilizer – compost or dog sh*t. My pops used to throw dog sh*t from our Chow Chow on our garden and the neighborhood used to be in awe at how "black" and fertile the soil was. Human feces could work but I wouldn't advise it, because our diets are usually more toxic than animals and there have been reports of people receiving heavy metal poisoning from using baby sh*t. My Taino Elder Ni Bon also advised me against it (and I trust him – he has a huge farm in Maryland – he's where I get my heirloom seeds from). And that's it! Plant! Plant your seeds ¼ to ½ inch below the surface.

Here are a few things that are easy to grow, along with some pointers on how to grow em:

❏ Peppers (from bell to cayenne and jalapeno), tomatoes, eggplants are easy. Plant about 6 -12 inches apart.

❏ Beans are pretty easy too, except that you need a stick or pole for them to climb up (they're like vines). Similarly, 6-12 inches apart.

❏ Strawberries and mint are easy, plus they grow back every year.

- ☐ Squash and melons are easy, but require significant ground space, as they spread out. They help suffocate "weeds to be" and keep them from coming up.
- ☐ Herbs like chamomile, cilantro, peppermint, lavender, aloe (just buy a plant and replant so it expands & grows), thyme, and sage – are all very easy and can even be grown on your windowsill.

Make gardening a weekly project. Get kids involved, have them help when they're already outside and dirty, so it won't feel like a chore.

IN THE LAND OF PLENTY...TOO MANY ARE HUNGRY
BY EBONI JOY ASIATIC

In America, the "land of plenty," you'd be surprised how many people go hungry every day. And it's more than the homeless. In fact, **14.6% of American households were "food insecure" at some point in the past year, including 5.7% (or 507,000 people) who suffered very low food security.** That means food sometimes ran out before they had money to buy more, they could not afford to eat nutritionally balanced meals, and/or adults in the family sometimes cut the size of their meals - or skipped them - because they lacked money for food.

People who are without an adequate supply of nutritious food are considered "food insecure" and those who have severe food shortages are considered hungry. Sound familiar now? That's not starvation or famine. But it's the American version of hunger, and it has no place in a country where investment bankers buy $80,000 mohair teddy bears...just because they can.

Almost 50 million people, including one in four children, struggle to get enough food to eat. 3.5 million children in America, ages 5 and under, are food insecure - meaning they lack enough food for a healthy, active life during the most critical stages of brain growth and development. Food insecurity is also more common – where else? – in large cities (aka the hood) and rural areas (aka the country), and its worst in the South, followed by the Midwest and West.

Also not surprising is that food shortages are even more common among single mothers – in 2008, more than one in three single mothers reported that they struggled to buy food for themselves and their children, and more than one in seven stated that at least one person in their household had gone hungry. Blacks and Latinos are even twice as likely as white people to report that food in their home was scarce.

So let's kill that stereotype myth of the "food stamp queen" who is just pigging out every day on "rack of lamb and gouda cheese." The reality is that people in poverty typically live in "food deserts" so it's more like "clearance rack Spam and cheese in a can."

And it's not getting better. **In 2008, nearly 17 million children (22.5%)**

lived in households in which food was scarce at times, an increase of 4 million from the year before. (Among Americans of all ages, more than 16% - 49 million people – went without nutritious food at some point in the year, compared with about 12% the year before.) The irony here is that more than half of the people surveyed who reported they had food shortages said that they had, in the previous month, participated in at least one of the government's largest anti-hunger and nutrition programs: The National School Lunch Program, Food Stamps Program (Supplemental Nutrition Assistance Program/SNAP), or the Special Supplemental Nutrition Program for Women, Infants, and Children (WIC).

So What Can Be Done?

Fortunately, there are programs out there to help people without adequate access to food.

Food Banks. In 2008, 4.8 million households got help from private food pantries, and about 625,000 households hit up local soup kitchens. (Only 7 people would later admit it, though.) Where do these places get their food? From food banks, which also supply childcare centers, homeless shelters, and senior citizen centers with food and goods critical to survival.

To find a food bank in your area – in order to seek help or donate goods and/or services go to www.feedamerica.org – they currently provide assistance to more than 37 million (1 in every 8) Americans receiving emergency food assistance through the more than 200 food banks that Feeding America assists.

If you need the help, don't be ashamed to go. And if you have the means, don't be too selfish to give. But keeping in mind the whole "critical to survival" part, they really don't need you to donate the crap you don't want (like that expired can of lentil soup), or the crap that nobody needs (like that half-opened pack of Starburst). The primary donations they need include:

❐ peanut butter (they really love that for some reason)	❐ 100% fruit juice
❐ canned tuna	❐ canned fruits and veggies
❐ canned beans	❐ macaroni and cheese dinners
❐ canned soups, stews and pastas	❐ whole grain/low sugar cereals

They also won't turn down personal hygiene products, diapers (not used), and other living essentials. Also, food banks, food pantries, soup kitchens, elderly centers and shelters are always looking for volunteers.

Food Drives. You can also help by donating to a food drive – or creating your own – and taking a hands-on approach to feeding the hungry. I work with a grassroots organization called the FTP Movement, which founded a national Feed the People Program in 2004, inspired by the Black

Panther Party's free breakfast program. Our volunteers come together to stuff brown lunch bags with sandwiches we've made, along with other donated goods like chips, fruit, pastries and bottles of water. We also put together hygiene kits of soap, toothpaste, toothbrushes, razors, sanitary napkins, baby wipes and diapers. And when we can, we distribute clothing, coats, blankets, socks, underwear, and even toys. If you've ever done something like this, then you know it can change your entire attitude about life. To get involved, join us at www.ftpmovement.ning.com or find our FTP Movement page on Facebook. To donate resources, you can contact us at defendingthepoor@yahoo.com

Know what free-food services you're city offers and where they're located. Knowing personally who runs these centers will put you in a better place to help people. Volunteering won't hurt!

URBAN SURVIVAL: PREPARING AN EMERGENCY PLAN
BY PATRA AFRIKA

With war preparations in "an advanced state of readiness", hi-tech weapons systems including nuclear warheads being fully deployed, the collapse of major banks, 14 million people unemployed, companies embarking on massive layoffs, people losing their homes, food prices soaring, inflation at an all-time high, and the US not giving up war to care for its people who have had enough…there's a lot for us to be concerned about. But there's no need to be scared if we're adequately prepared.

Another catastrophe like 9/11, Hurricane Katrina, a major power outage, or even a collapse in the economy could come any day. Whatever the circumstances, the solution is to have an emergency plan for what you're going to do in case of an emergency. So what will you do?

Awareness is a first step towards a solution – Educate yourself. If you are prepared, you will be less likely to panic. Even if you aren't, do not panic! If we succumb to fear, we will lose it all. Secure yourself, stay alert and remain vigilant.

Community Preparation
Once you know, it's your obligation to inform others. After establishing your emergency/evacuation routines with your family, make sure your friends have their own plans. Then you can reach out to the local community (churches, associations, etc.) to discuss the need for such plans.

What we need to consider in any emergency situation is that our neighborhood grocery stores and super markets can dry up in days, depending how frantic people are to get their supplies; you can expect there will be rioting, violence, confusion and pandemonium. If there is an economy crash, you will have problems finding food and gas and left at the mercy of the government if you don't start planning ahead. When folks are ready to rob or hurt you for food, you don't want to get caught out there alone. Also keep in mind, your emergency services will be overwhelmed and are not going to be there to handle what's coming at them. Neither will there be enough National Guards to police the whole nation (looking at Katrina when they had to bring in multiple states to handle their catastrophe).

Initially you and/or your family will want to **align with or start up a group to identify community target areas, e.g., neighborhood tenant and block association; community schools and houses of worship; neighborhood grassroots and street organizations and mainstream political groups.** Also special tactics and training such as street first aid and police/military occupation survival would be a plus.

Water

Water is going to be your most important commodity (Second will be food which we will get to in the end). When you don't have means to pump water from a source or a well, you're going to need some stored away. You'll need about a gallon per person, per day, for at least a two weeks supply. When you run out, you need to be prepared to treat whatever water you find so that it's safe for drinking. There's three main methods for this:

Boiling: Boiling is the safest method of treating water. Boiled water will taste better if you put oxygen back into it by pouring the water back and forth between two clean containers. This also will improve the taste of stored water. Let the water cool before drinking.

Chlorination: You can use household liquid bleach to kill microorganisms. Use only regular household liquid bleach that contains 5.25 to 6.0% sodium hypochlorite. Add 16 drops (1/8 teaspoon) of bleach per gallon of water, stir, and let stand for 30 minutes. The water should have a slight bleach odor. If it doesn't, then repeat the dosage and let stand another 15 minutes. If it still does not smell of chlorine, discard it and find another source of water.

Distillation: The most effective way to remove other contaminants like heavy metals, salts, and most other chemicals. Distillation involves boiling water and then collecting only the vapor that condenses. Tie a cup to the handle on the pot's lid so that the cup will hang right-side-up when the lid is upside-down (make sure the cup is not dangling into the water) and boil the water for 20 minutes. The water that drips from the lid into the cup is distilled.

Emergency Kits

The following is built around what you will need as a family when you are away from home. Either kit or backpack can be thrown in a vehicle without a problem. You, of course, can personalize your kit to make it better or to add other needs over time. It's always good to have extra items in your kit, just in case you come across someone else needing help.

Disaster Supply Kit: Keep at least one complete change of clothing and footwear per person in the disaster kit. If you live in a rainy or cold weather climate, also consider including an extra set of thermal underwear, hats and gloves, or rain gear. You'll also want to pack:

- ❑ a sleeping bag, blanket and extra clothing
- ❑ infant and small children's needs (if appropriate)
- ❑ first aid kit and manual
- ❑ personal hygiene supplies
- ❑ plastic garbage bags and twist ties (for personal sanitation uses)
- ❑ portable radio(preferably a hand cranked radio that doesn't use batteries)
- ❑ flashlights and extra batteries
- ❑ shovel and other useful tools
- ❑ money and waterproof matches in a waterproof container
- ❑ fire extinguisher

- ❑ compass and map of the area (for locating shelters)
- ❑ disinfectant/disinfecting wipes, hand sanitizer
- ❑ household chlorine bleach (really important for purifying water)
- ❑ non-electric can opener
- ❑ utility knife
- ❑ prescriptions (all to last two weeks)
- ❑ glasses/contact lenses
- ❑ copies of important documents (insurance policies, birth certificates, passports
- ❑ paper and pen
- ❑ whistle (in case you're trapped)

You'll also need one gallon of water per person, per day, to last at least two weeks, and food that isn't refrigerated: nutrition bars, breakfast bars, canned food, and dry goods. Check the contents of your kit every six months and replace these items (mentioned above) as needed: food, water, outgrown clothes, and weak batteries.

These items should be stored in a container that is easy to locate and carry. If the container is not waterproof, place individuals items in sealed plastic bags.[25] The kit should be stored in a safe, secure area that will still be easily accessible in the event of an emergency.

Food: Have a two-week supply of food on hand of nonperishable food in your disaster kit. Choose foods that are easy to carry, high in calories, nutritious and ready-to-eat. Individuals with special diets and allergies will need particular attention, as will babies, toddlers and the elderly, nursing mothers may need liquid formula, juices, and soups may be helpful for the ill or elderly. Include vitamin, mineral and protein supplements in your stockpile to assure adequate nutrition.

Backpack for Kids: When it comes down to it, even kids need to be in control and not to lose their head. Stay away from bright colors, bright

---

[25] You can make "Strike On Box" Matches waterproof yourself and spare the expense of purchasing them! There are several methods but nail polish works well with very little mess.

clothing and backpacks. Neutral colors will help you blend in with your surroundings better. Also, water restraint bags can be made easily with silicon spray. Your best bet: Glenwood Canyon Internal Frame Pack by Remington. For only $23, it has many of the same features found on packs that are at least twice the price. For what the kids will be lugging, this fits the bill perfectly!

Car Kit: There may come a time where you may have to leave without even being able to grab your bag. You never know what turn of events may take place causing you to evacuate! I hope you never have to use these, but it's better to have a "bare essentials" kit in your car just in case!

Firearms: The Second Amendment to the Constitution states: "A well-regulated Militia, being necessary to the security of a free State, the right of the people to keep and bear Arms, shall not be infringed." Persons who are not eligible to possess a firearm or ammunition are: fugitives from justice; illegal aliens; unlawful users of certain drugs; those committed to a mental institution; those convicted of crimes punishable by imprisonment for more than one year (which generally covers felonies); and those convicted of crimes of domestic violence. In most states, nearly everyone else over the 18 can own a rifle or a shotgun, and nearly everyone else over the age of 21 can own a handgun. However, it's not enough to have one. Without proper training, it's useless.

Last but not least, in addition to *The Hood Health Handbook*, you're going to need Supreme Design Publishing's urban survival manual, *When It Hits the Fan*, which will be released sometime in early 2011. Until then, you have this.

Do less consuming and store away. By doing so we've already taken major steps to being better prepared for an emergency.

SAVE THE WORLD...OR SAVE YOURSELF?
BY SUPREME UNDERSTANDING

I hope this book has inspired you to DO something...and to do it NOW. Wait too long and your inspiration will die. But what will you do? You gonna get healthy? Great. How healthy? Hopefully healthy enough to change the REST of the world, because we've got some serious problems out here, homey...and we need some soldiers on the frontlines who are physically fit and of sound mind. Of course, instead of taking the "new you" and working to create a "new us," you could always get so obsessed with becoming healthy that you basically go crazy. What I mean is that **it's crazy to preoccupy yourself with "perfecting" yourself to the point that you effectively DO NOTHING of consequence in this world.** Some of us are already there, and there's no saving them. So I'm talking to you. **I want YOU to change this world.** I want YOU to educate the hood. I want YOU to spread these ideas. I want you to NOT become obsessed with a journey that has no final destination. Because that's actually Unhealthy. As my elder brother and colleague Mwalimu Baruti has said, "Pretty soon, we'll have the healthiest generation of slaves ever." When I look around at some of these super-health-conscious folks, I totally understand. Some of these people are doing NOTHING to fix this world (even to help fix the hoods they live in), besides pushing the latest health fad on whoever will listen. That's NOT what we're about at Supreme Design Publishing, where our company motto is "Reinventing the World."

So do you want to save the world…or just save yourself while the world dies around you? Oh, you're on board? The motivational speech worked? Great! Now the question is…How? I suggest you TEACH the people. Sure, they're gonna be stubborn and defensive, but as long as YOU are shining as a living example, SOME will listen…and that SOME will grow too many. It worked for me. As long as you ain't got any personality disorder, it SHOULD work for you. Trust me, the ONLY way we'll save our world is by engaging, educating, and organizing the people living in it, from the lowest to the highest.

All them other approaches to "saving the planet" ain't gonna cut it, homey. Sure, you can try to "save" the animals by not eating them, but are you really saving animals that way? Of course not. **Your personal choice doesn't affect a global industry that kills animals to clear land, kills animals for lab research, kills animals for use in other industries, and kills animals just to feed other animals. Monsanto just killed 5,000 animals**[26] **while you read this sentence, and they don't care how many Boca burgers you eat!**

I'm vegetarian for my health's sake, not because I've deluded myself into thinking it's a political statement to "Go Veg." But I'm not saying you SHOULDN'T do such things. Just understand the bigger picture! Yes, go ahead and save water, but know that more than **90% of the world's water usage is in agriculture and industry, not people.** Go ahead and **recycle your garbage, but know that municipal waste accounts for only 3% of total waste production in the United States.**

It would be nice if you got a gas-friendly car and used those swirly light bulbs, but the vast majority of the world's energy consumption comes from the commercial, industrial, corporate, government, and military sectors. Less than 25% comes from our cars and homes. Are you still more concerned with your little carbon footprint than the massive crater

---

[26] Not as much of an exaggeration as you might think. Just ONE of their many subcontractors, Huntington Life Sciences, kills at least 500 animals a day just for routine testing.

being left by the giant corporations? **Even if all of us did everything the movie *An Inconvenient Truth* suggested (all "personal" solutions, and no challenges to the system), U.S. carbon emissions would fall by only 22%. Scientific consensus is that it's really got to drop by at least 75% worldwide to do us any good.** As Derrick Jensen writes in his article "Forget Shorter Showers: Why Personal Change Does Not Equal Social Change":

> Would any sane person think dumpster diving would have stopped Hitler, or that composting would have ended slavery or brought about the eight-hour workday, or that chopping wood and carrying water would have gotten people out of Tsarist prisons, or that dancing naked around a fire would have helped put in place the Voting Rights Act of 1957 or the Civil Rights Act of 1964? Then why now, with all the world at stake, do so many people retreat into these entirely personal "solutions"?...
>
> So how, then, and especially with all the world at stake, have we come to accept these utterly insufficient responses? I think part of it is that we're in a double bind. A double bind is where you're given multiple options, but no matter what option you choose, you lose, and withdrawal is not an option. At this point, it should be pretty easy to recognize that every action involving the industrial economy is destructive...
>
> So if we choose option one–if we avidly participate in the industrial economy–we may in the short term think we win because we may accumulate wealth, the marker of "success" in this culture. But we lose, because in doing so we give up our empathy, our animal humanity. And we really lose because industrial civilization is killing the planet, which means everyone loses. If we choose the "alternative" option of living more simply, thus causing less harm, but still not stopping the industrial economy from killing the planet, we may in the short term think we win because we get to feel pure, and we didn't even have to give up all of our empathy (just enough to justify not stopping the horrors), but once again we really lose because industrial civilization is still killing the planet, which means everyone still loses. The third option, acting decisively to stop the industrial economy, is very scary for a number of reasons, including but not restricted to the fact that we'd lose some of the luxuries (like electricity) to which we've grown accustomed, and the fact that those in power might try to kill us if we seriously impede their ability to exploit the world–none of which alters the fact that it's a better option than a dead planet. Any option is a better option than a dead planet.

So what are you REALLY gonna do with all this information? When?

It's not about being a busy activist, it's about being effective. Look deeper into the issues and fix the root cause of all these problems.

THE WORLD'S HEALTHIEST SLAVES

BY MWALIMU BARUTI, AUTHOR OF MENTACIDE

Perspective is important. Balance equally so. To know where we should be going as a people (and doing more to facilitate this process) is something to which every warrior of worth must give serious thought. **If we recognize that liberation, empowerment and sovereignty are**

critical to our sanity, and that we are one (meaning what impacts one of us impacts all of us, meaning that the group's power is the individual's, and not the other way around), **then we cannot expend energy selfishly, unless the work is designed to promote and secure the good of us all.**

This means that we individually cannot become so focused on self (or "individualism") that we become blinded to our obligations and duties in service to those who do not yet know and/or cannot do. We cannot place self in front of what we actually need to do to save Afrikan people from the terror of an ongoing physical, mental and spiritual genocide.

Mentacidal individualism has led more and more of us, who otherwise might be the strongest and most decisive of our warriors, to become unduly diverted from our missions by distractive appetites which cause us to focus more and more on "self" (and only self) for escape from the reality of responsibility. If we are not working to remove our enemies, we are working to sustain their control over us. There is no other reality in war.

A submission to fear and despair, or defeatism and lack of vision, at the most personal, subconscious level, has led many men and women of potentially enormous power to become slaves, frantically caught up in their individual survival. The singular focus on diet (like an overly excessive, all-consuming concern with one's spiritual elevation, intellectual capital, and/or physical well-being) is a perfect example of this debilitating flight from reality, into a denial of one's personal responsibility to save a people, especially our children, through selflessly building and defending what the community needs.

Of course, there is nothing wrong with having a good diet. Certainly, as Imhotep instructed us, those aspiring to good health should understand food as medicine and vice versa. Our temples must be in the best shape so that we can do the best work possible for our people. But, we must not, in a rationalizing compromise of our whole potential as warriors, mislead ourselves into believing that the temple, itself, is the work. The temple is a tool through which the work, in the physical reality, is done.

They say that a slave's fear drives him or her to have little to no concern for anything other than their own personal survival. If that be true, and it is, then, sadly, we are witnessing the willful production of the world's healthiest slaves. And, obviously, any halfway intelligent master would only object in pretense. For common sense would tell us that the healthier the slave, the greater and lengthier the service they provide their owners.

For every good piece of information, habit, and resource YOU acquire make the effort to share it with your people.

---

11. First Aid

First aid is an important aspect of health that many overlook and don't know too much about. First aid not only assists us with our outward injuries including burns, cuts, and sprains, but it can also assist those who have faced life threatening injuries internally including heart attack, seizure, and internal bleeding. It is important to know how to react in a situation with calm and clarity.

In this section you will learn more about first aid techniques that can help you or others when in a potentially dangerous situation. It will give you steps to follow so you do not find yourself in a panic or worst; in danger. Even knowledge of the most basic first aid can be an asset to your toolbox of health as an emergency can occur anywhere and at any time.

It's important to revisit and study this section often (and in some cases more often) than others as it will allow for you to be savvy and clear-headed enough to implement aid to those in need, including yourself. This chapter is truly one that should not be skipped and left for another day as it will become important to you when you least expect it.

Primary Assessment
BY PHYLIS IQBAL

Protecting Yourself
Never place yourself in a situation which might put you in danger. Remember, you cannot help a victim if you become a victim yourself. As you approach a scene, you need to be aware of the dangers which might be posed to you as a first aider, or to the victim. These can include obviously dangerous factors such as traffic, gas or chemical leaks, live electrical items, buildings on fire or falling objects.

Once you have assessed the scene for danger, you should continue to be aware of changes to the situation or environment that could present danger to you or your victim until you have left the scene. If there are dangers out of your control then STAY CLEAR and call the emergency services.

What has Happened?
Assess the Scene – Where are you? What stores, clubs, public buildings, etc. are nearby? Has anything here caused the injury? Does this area have motor vehicle traffic? What time of day is it? What are the weather conditions?

Look for Clues – Things that could help you determine the reason for the patient's illness or injury may be obvious or subtle (i.e. food poisoning or choking).

Get some History – If there are witnesses, ask them what's happened, gain information such as how long ago it happened, but be sure to start your assessment and treatment of the victim simultaneous with your history taking.

Be Sure to Listen – While working on a victim you may overhear information from witnesses in the crowd, but you may not see the person saying this. Everything should be taken into account should no witnesses want to become involved or you cannot ask questions. Note what is said and continue treatment.

Responsiveness

Once you are confident that there is minimal danger to yourself in the situation, the next step is to assess how well (if at all) your victim responds to you. This can be started with an initial responsiveness check as you approach the victim. The best result would be the victim looking at you and replying. This means that the victim is alert at this time.

The AVPU Scale

A – Alert: If the victim looks at you spontaneously, can communicate (even if it doesn't make sense) and seems to have control of their body

V – Verbal (Voice): If the victim is not alert, but you can get them to open their eyes, or obey a command by talking to them

P – Pain: Anything physical you do to elicit a response from your victim. The first and most gentle stimulus to use is a tap/shake of the shoulder. Three most commonly used:
- Sternal rub
- Nail bed squeeze
- Ear lobe squeeze

U – Unresponsive: A victim who is unresponsive will often require special attention, both due to the injury or illness causing their unconsciousness, and the fact that they are unable to provide any reason for them being sick or injured. If the victim is unconscious, the first aider should immediately call an ambulance. If there is more than one person injured, the rescuer must determine the order in which victims need care. In general, rescuers should focus on the victim with the most serious injury.

Develop a good sense of Situational Awareness. Knowing what's going on around you and someone you're helping is important.

CHECKING A VICTIM'S VITALS
BY PHYLIS IQBAL

As part of your ongoing assessment of the victim, and in preparation for the arrival of any assistance you have called, it's important to keep a check on a victim's vital signs. If possible, these recordings should be written down so that you can keep a record of any changes, and hand this over to the ambulance crew who take the victim from you.

It starts with the ABC's of **A**irway, **B**reathing, and **C**irculation, and continues with look of the skin, level of consciousness and pupil reaction.

Airway

Checking the victim's airway depends on whether the victim is conscious or unconscious. If a victim is conscious, ask him or her to speak. The ability to speak directly relates to the airway. If a person's airway is blocked, he or she can't speak.

Unconscious victims, on the other hand, require a closer inspection. Put your ear close to the victim's mouth and listen for breathing. Feel for air on your cheek and look at the chest to see if it or the abdomen is rising with each breath. At a basic level, opening of the airway can be achieved through manual movement of the head using the "head tilt – chin lift" technique.

Breathing

If you do not see, hear or feel normal breathing: start CPR immediately! If the victim is breathing normally, place him or her in the recovery position (See "Recovery Position").

Once you have ensured an open airway, and that the victim is breathing, count the rate of breathing. The easiest way to do this is to count the number of breaths taken in a given time period (15 or 30 seconds are common time frames), and then multiply to equal however many breaths that would be in a minute. The longer the time period, the more accurate it is.

In addition to rate, you should note if the breathing is heavy or shallow, and importantly if it's irregular. If it's irregular, see if there is a pattern to it (such as breathing slowly, getting faster, then suddenly slower again) and note whether breathing is noisy. These are serious concerns.

Circulation

It is important in monitoring the breathing victim to check their circulation. There are two methods for this:

Capillary Refill: The capillaries are the smallest type of blood vessel, and are responsible for getting blood into all the body tissues. If the blood pressure is not high enough, then not enough blood will be getting to the capillaries. It is especially important to check capillary refill if the victim has suffered an injury to one of their limbs. You check capillary refill by taking the victim's hand, lifting it above the level of the heart, and squeezing reasonably hard for about a second on the nail bed. This should move the blood out, and the nail bed will appear white. If the pink color returns quickly (and in a healthy victim, it may return before you even move your fingers away to look!), then this is normal.

Victims who have poor peripheral circulation, especially the elderly and hypothermia victims, may not demonstrate adequate capillary refill due to general lack of blood flow, making this test less valuable on these patients. A normal time for the pink color to return is less than two seconds. If it takes longer than two seconds for color to return, then this could indicate a problem and you should seek medical advice.

Pulse Check: As a first aider, you can also check a victim's heart rate by feeling for their pulse. There are three main places you might wish to check for a pulse:

❏ **Radial pulse:** This is the best pulse to look for. On a conscious victim, as it's non-invasive and relatively easy to find. It is located on the wrist (over the radial bone). To find it, place the victim's hand palm up and take the first two fingers of your hand (NEVER use your thumb, as it contains a pulse of its own) and on the thumb side of the victim's wrist you will feel a rounded piece of bone, move in from here 1-2cm in to a shallow dip at the side of the bone, and press your fingers in (gently), where you should be able to feel a pulse.

❏ **Carotid Pulse:** This is in the main artery which supplies the head and brain, and is located in the neck. This is best used on unconscious victims or those victims where you are unable to find a radial pulse. To locate it, place your two fingers in to the indentation to the side of the windpipe, in line with the Adam's Apple (on men), or approximately the location an Adam's Apple would be on a women.

❏ **Pedal Pulse:** The pedal pulse can be found in several locations on the foot, and this is used when you suspect a broken leg, in order to ascertain if there is blood flowing to the foot. When measuring a pulse you should measure the pulse rate. This is best achieved by counting the number of beats in 15 seconds, and then multiplying the result by four. You should also check if the pulse is regular or irregular.

Skin Color: The color of the skin is also related to circulation. Changes in circulation will cause the skin to be different colors, and you should note if the victim is flushed, pale, ashen, or blue tinged. It should also be noted if the victim's skin is clammy, sweaty or very dry, and this information should be passed on to the ambulance crew.

Level of Consciousness: You can continue to use the acronym AVPU to assess if the victim's level of consciousness changes while you are with them. To recap, the levels are:

❏ A - Alert
❏ V - Voice induces response

- ❏ P – Pain induces response
- ❏ U – Unresponsive to stimuli

Pupils: Valuable information can be gained from looking at a victim's pupils. For this purpose, first aid kits should have a penlight or small torch in them.

Ideally, the pupils of the eye should be equal and reactive to light, usually written down as PEARL: (P)upils (E)qual (A)nd (R)eactive to (L)ight

To check this, ask the victim to look straight at you with both eyes. Look to see if both pupils are the same size and shape (be sensitive to those who may be blind in one eye, or may even have a glass eye, although they will usually tell you).

To check if they are reactive, take the penlight, and ask the victim to look at your nose. Briefly (5 seconds or so) shield their eye with your hand from the light source where they are (sunlight, room lighting etc.), and then turn on the penlight, positioning it off to the side of their head. Move the penlight in over their eye quickly, and watch to see the size change. A normal reaction would be the pupil getting smaller quickly as the light is shined into it. Repeat on the other eye. If both pupils are the same, and both react, note this as PEARL, or else note what you did, or did not see.

Imagine how scary it is seeing a loved one unconscious on the floor. If you live with someone with health complications, prepare yourself.

SHOCK
BY PHYLIS IQBAL

Shock can refer to a range of related medical conditions in which the victim's heart, lungs and blood cannot deliver oxygen to the body properly. Shock is not a diagnosis or condition, it's always a symptom of a larger problem, and is a medical emergency that requires immediate attention.

- ❏ **Hypovolaemic shock:** Caused by the rapid loss of blood from the blood vessels, either inside or outside the body.
- ❏ **Cardiogenic shock:** Caused by failure of the heart to move blood adequately. This is typically caused by damaged heart muscle due to a heart attack.
- ❏ **Anaphylactic shock:** Caused by an allergic reaction which forces fluid out of the blood vessels.
- ❏ **Septic Shock:** Caused by a severe infection this poisons the blood vessels, causing them to enlarge.
- ❏ **Neurogenic Shock:** Caused by a spinal cord injury, preventing the brain from communicating with blood vessels.

Regardless of the type, the goals of the layperson rescuer are the same:

prevent blood loss and preserve body temperature.

Common Signs of Shock

- ❐ **Early Phase:** A fast pulse; pale, cool, clammy skin; sweating; flushed face; anxiety or agitation
- ❐ **Developing Phase:** Ashen or blue skin on lips and nail beds, cold, damp skin, weakness and dizziness, nausea and possibly vomiting, thirst, rapid, shallow breathing, weak, very rapid "thready" pulse, confusion, disorientation
- ❐ **Advanced Phase:** Lack of pulse in wrists or feet, restlessness and aggressiveness, yawning and gasping for air, unconsciousness
- ❐ **Final phase:** Multiple organ failure and cardiac arrest

Treatment

The most important treatment for shock of any type is to try and **maintain the blood flow to the body's vital organs (brain, heart, and lungs).** To do this, lay the patient flat on the floor and raise their legs about 6-12 inches off the ground. Do not incline the victim's head, chest, or pelvis.

Other important factors in the treatment of shock can be remembered by the simple mnemonic WART:

- ❐ W - Warmth
- ❐ A - ABCs (Airway, Breathing, Circulation.)
- ❐ R - Rest & Reassurance
- ❐ T - Treatment of underlying cause

Unconscious patients: Should a patient become unconscious, confirm that an ambulance has been called, and assess ABCs. Should any change occur, compensate with required treatment. For example, if patient goes into cardiac arrest, begin CPR (See "Basic CPR").

Get help when possible. If you must leave the victim, make sure blood flow is circulating to their upper body.

SEIZURES

BY PHYLIS IQBAL

A seizure occurs when the electrical activity of the brain becomes irregular. A seizure is a medical emergency. Seizures may be caused by either an acute or chronic condition such as epilepsy.

Risk Factors for Seizures

Head trauma, infections, malignant (or benign) tumors of the brain or spinal cord, epilepsy, stroke, drug use or withdrawal, hypoglycemia (Low Blood Sugar), heat stroke, and even some allergies.

Lack of sleep, excessive stress, fever, severe infection, hypoglycemia or dehydration (lack of sufficient nutrition), and exposure to bright light can all trigger seizures in those who have epilepsy or are otherwise predisposed to them.

Often before a seizure occurs, the victim may feel an aura, which is an unusual sensation that typically precedes seizures. Auras may come in many forms, such as a strange taste in the mouth, tingling in the limbs, or the visual disturbance of "flashing lights"; often if the person is epileptic, they may be aware that a seizure is imminent and may tell others or sit or lie down to prevent injury.

Typically seizures usually last no more than three minutes. Some common occurrences during a seizure include stopped or irregular breathing, body rigidness or convulsing, defecation, urination, and drooling. Some forms of seizure, such as Status Epilepticus or a "Status seizure" do not cease without medical intervention.

Never try to restrain the seizure. Never put anything in the mouth.

In the event of a Status seizure being noticed, as described above, it's important to get emergency help as quickly as possible – you should explain to any call handler or dispatcher that the patient is having a continuous seizure. These types of seizures can only be terminated by a trained EMS professional or doctor.

Care for Seizures

Call EMS or have someone call for you. Move anything the victim can injure themselves with away from the victim such as chairs or other objects. Gently support the victim's head to prevent it from hitting the ground. Request that all bystanders move away (persons having a seizure are often embarrassed after their seizure).

After the seizure has ended, roll the victim into the recovery position but only if you do not suspect a spinal injury. After the seizure, the victim will slowly "awaken." Ensure that bystanders are away and offer reassurance for the victim. Victims who have a seizure in public are often self-conscious about their condition. The victim will be very tired after his seizure. Continue to reassure the victim until he or she is fully aware of the surroundings or until EMS arrives.

Don't leave someone having a seizure unattended.

THREE DEGREES OF BURNS
BY PHYLIS IQBAL

- ❏ **First-degree (Superficial Burn):** Dry, red, may swell, may be painful, likened to sunburn.

- ❏ **Second-degree (Partial Thickness):** Red, may swell, very painful, blisters that may open and release a clear fluid which will make the skin appear wet.

- ❏ **Third-degree (Full Thickness):** May destroy underlying tissue including fat, bones, nerves, and muscle. Skin may be brown or black and will look charred. Tissue underneath may appear white. Either very painful or painless due to nerve endings being destroyed.

Types of Burns and How to Treat Them

❏ **Thermal (heat) burns:** Cool the burn with copious amounts of clean water until the pain is relieved. After the person feels better, cover the burn loosely with a sterile, dry (non-adhesive) dressing. Do not use butter, oils, creams, etc.; that traps heat and increases risk of infection. Do not use antiseptics that may aggravate sensitive skin. Ensure the victim isn't over-heated or chilled. Use Aloe vera extract, silverdene (Silver Sulfazdiazine), topical analgaesics, and NSAIDs (such as ibuprofen or aspirin) under the care of a doctor.

❏ **Chemical (wet or dry) burns:** If there is a dry chemical, brush it off the skin using paper, cloth, or with a gloved hand; not getting any on yourself or more on the patient. Once the bulk of the dry chemical is gone, flush with running water as above. Call EMS immediately. If the burn is caused by a wet chemical, flush with plenty of water for 15 minutes and while flushing, call EMS immediately.

❏ **Electrical burns:** Electrical burns look like third-degree burns. They always come in pairs: a smaller entry and a larger exit wound. Call EMS (Emergency Medical Services) immediately. Be prepared to give CPR or defibrillation. Care is the same for thermal burns.

❏ **Radiation burns:** Typically caused from a nuclear source, can include sunburn which should be treated as a thermal burn. For all nuclear radiation burns, call your local emergency number immediately. Radiation burns also come in the form of snow blindness (or other intense light burns to the retina). Cover the eyes with sterile gauze, and contact EMS immediately.

Always do whatever you can to keep the victim comfortable and calm.

HEAT-RELATED ILLNESSES

Condition	Symptoms	First Aid
Sunburn	Skin redness and pain, possible swelling, blisters, fever, headaches	Take a shower using soap to remove oils that may block pores, preventing the body from cooling naturally. Apply dry, sterile dressings to any blisters, and get medical attention.
Heat Cramps	Painful spasms, usually in leg and abdominal muscles; heavy sweating	Get the victim to a cool location. Lightly stretch and gently massage affected muscles to relieve spasms. Give sips of up to a half glass of cool water every 15 minutes. (Do not give liquids with caffeine or alcohol.) Discontinue liquids, if victim is nauseated.

Heat Exhaustion	Heavy sweating but skin may be cool, pale, or flushed. Weak pulse. Normal body temperature is possible, but temperature will likely rise. Fainting or dizziness, nausea, vomiting, exhaustion, and headaches are possible.	Get victim to lie down in a cool place. Loosen or remove clothing. Apply cool, wet clothes. Fan or move victim to air-conditioned place. Give sips of water if victim is conscious. Be sure water is consumed slowly. Give half glass of cool water every 15 minutes. Stop water if victim is nauseated. Seek immediate medical attention if vomiting occurs.
Heat Stroke (a severe medical emergency)	High body temperature (105+); hot, red, dry skin; rapid, weak pulse; and rapid hallow breathing. Victim will probably not sweat unless victim was sweating from recent strenuous activity. Possible unconsciousness.	Call 9-1-1 or EMS, or get the victim to a hospital immediately. Delay can be fatal. Move victim to a cooler environment. Removing clothing. Try a cool bath, sponging, or wet sheet to reduce body temperature. Watch for breathing problems. Use extreme caution. Use fans and air conditioners.

SPRAIN OR FRACTURE
BY PHYLIS IQBAL

Sprains, strains, dislocations, and fractures can all present with the same symptoms. If the patient has any of the following symptoms, you should treat for a possible muscle or skeletal injury:

❑ Deformity at the injury site

❑ A grinding or cracking sound when the affected area is moved, reported by the patient.

❑ Bruising and swelling

❑ No pulse below injury site

❑ Inability to use the affected body part normally

If the injury appears to be severe, EMS should be contacted as soon as possible. The treatment for any muscle, bone or joint injury follows the simple acronym "RICE": (R)est, (I)mmobilize, (C)old, (E)levation.

❑ **Rest:** Rest is very important for soft tissue injuries, both in the short term and for longer term care.

❑ **Immobilize:** Sprains, strains and dislocations can be slinged; fractures should be splinted and slinged.

❑ **Cold:** Ice should be applied periodically, for around 10-20 minutes at a time. You should then take the ice off for around the same time it was on for. In order to avoid problems, always place some fabric between the ice and skin.

❑ **Elevation:** Where appropriate, the injury should be elevated, as this may help reduce the localized swelling which occurs. Do not elevate if this causes more pain to the victim.

Once something has been injured don't put any more weight or pressure on it. Working through the pain can make things worse.

NATURAL REMEDIES FOR SMALL SCRAPES AND WOUNDS

BY QUEEN RIGHTEOUSLY REFINED

Unless you have been living in a glass bubble your entire life I am sure that you have experienced a scrape, scratch or cut or two. And although I am sure you may have outgrown some of the clumsiness we may experience growing up there are still occasions where we may get hurt or have children that may get hurt from time to time. If you are like me there is no way I will run to the emergency room for every razor nick or knife cut that I get. It could get quite expensive. If you're a man, it's just not a good look, anyway. So I'm going to give you a few ways to treat these superficial wounds that are inexpensive, natural, and yet quite effective.

The first solution I would suggest would be sweet honey. **The sugar content in honey kills off bacteria and provides a moist environment that helps wounds heal.** Using granulated sugar in a wound will do the same trick in terms of making the scar less ugly. **When choosing honey make sure that it's pasteurized. If it isn't, it may have germs in it that will cause more infection and disease.** Cover the area with a bandage, gauze or, if you have cornstarch, you can dust a little on to keep it from sticking to everything.

Another method is a sure fire way to stop bleeding in seconds. And when I say fire, I mean it. Try sprinkling some cayenne pepper on it. I know you are thinking ouch, right? Well it works wonders because **cayenne pepper is very high in capsaicin, which is essential for blood clotting. So if you put some on a minor cut or scrape, the bleeding will stop dang near instantly.** Of course, if you stab yourself and it goes pretty deep, don't pour hot pepper into the gaping hole. I assume that goes without saying, but you never know.

Now, on to Aloe vera. This remedy happens to be my personal favorite. No matter what type of minor injury it is, you can most likely use aloe on it. It can be a cut, burn, scratch or scrape. Aloe contains a colorless slimy gel like liquid. Take a bit of it and apply a generous amount to the area. Make sure you repeat about three to four times a day to speed the healing process. This remedy is natural, seals off the injury, relieves pain and is a fast healing agent.

Now please remember, while these are some great inexpensive yet effective ways to treat minor scrapes, cuts and scratches, please see a doctor if you notice any of the following:

☐ The cut is filthy and you have no way of getting it clean.

☐ Blood is spurting out of the wound like crazy, you may have a cut artery.

☐ The cut is large, deep and gaping open, and may need stitches.

☐ The wound develops red streaks or a red area that extends more than a fingers width beyond the edge of the cut

BLEEDING AND TYPES OF WOUNDS
BY PHYLIS IQBAL

Types of Wounds
☐ **Abrasion:** A graze that doesn't go below the skin

☐ **Laceration:** Irregular wound caused by blunt impact to soft tissue overlying hard tissue

☐ **Incision:** A clean surgical wound

☐ **Puncture Wound:** Caused by an object, such as a nail, needle or knife penetrating the skin and underlying layers

☐ **Contusion:** Also known as a bruise, this is a blunt trauma damaging tissue under the surface of the skin

Treating a Bleeding Wound
Recognizing external bleeding is usually easy, it should be remembered that blood may be underneath or behind a victim. If there is more than 5 cups worth of blood, then the situation is life-threatening.

As with all first aid situations, the priority is to protect yourself so put on protective gloves before approaching the victim and any blood or body fluids.

All external bleeding is treated using three key techniques, which allow the body's natural repair process to start. These can be remembered using the acronym mnemonic 'RED':

☐ **Rest:** In all cases, the less movement the wound undergoes, the easier the healing process will be, so rest is advised.

☐ **Elevation:** Direct pressure is usually enough to stop most minor bleeds, but for larger bleeds, it may be necessary to elevate the wound above the level of the heart (while maintaining direct pressure the whole time). Elevation only works on the peripheries of the body (limbs and head) and is not appropriate for body wounds. You should ask the victim to hold their wound as high as possible. You should assist them to do this if necessary, and use furniture or surrounding items to help support them in this position. If it's the legs affected, you should lay them on their back, and raise their legs.

☐ **Direct Pressure:** The most important of these three is direct pressure. This is simply placing pressure on the wound in order to stem the flow of blood. This is best done using a dressing, such as a sterile gauze pad (although in an emergency, any material is suitable). If the blood starts to come through the dressing you are using, add additional dressings to the top, to a maximum of three. If you reach three dressings, you should remove all but the one in contact with the wound itself (as this may cause it to reopen) and continue to add pads on top. Repeat this again when you reach three dressings. The reason for not simply adding more dressings is that it becomes harder to apply the direct pressure which is clearly needed if this much blood is produced.

Dressing: To dress a wound, use a sterile low-adherent pad, which will not stick to the wound, but will absorb the blood coming from it. Once this is in place, wrap a conforming bandage around firmly. It should be tight enough to apply some direct pressure, but should not be so tight as to cut blood flow off below the bandage. If blood starts to come through the dressing you've applied, add another on top, to a maximum of three. If these are all saturated, remove the top two, leaving the closest dressing to the wound in place.

Embedded Objects: If there is something embedded in the wound, do not remove it. Instead, apply pressure around the object using sterile gauze as described above. Rolled bandages are perfect for this. Be careful not to disturb the object, as moving it may exacerbate the bleeding. This doesn't apply to superficial splinters and such.

Amputations: If a body part has been amputated, immediately summon ambulance assistance, and treat the bleeding as above. Cover the amputated part with a moist dressing and get it into a clean plastic bag, and place this bag into a bag of ice and water, sending it with the victim to the hospital. (label date & time, what body part it is) You should avoid putting the part in direct contact with ice, as this can cause irreparable damage, meaning that surgeons are unable to reattach it. If the body part is partially amputated, do not detach.[27]

Wear gloves when dealing with someone else's blood. Remember to always disinfect the wound and your hands (before and after).

YOUR FIRST AID KIT
DO YOU EVEN HAVE ONE?
BY SUPREME UNDERSTANDING

What would you do you accidentally slit your wrist right now? Probably scream and cry and die. Well, not really, because cuts to the wrists aren't as deadly as they seem on TV. But my point is that you should be prepared for an injury, so everyone should have a well-stocked first aid kit. If not for yourself, at least for your children's sake. Matter fact, you should have one in your house, one in your car (nice cars like mine already come with one), and you should know where the kit is at your job (or better yet, bring your own).

First aid kits need to be kept well-stocked because supplies can expire and need to be replaced periodically. Consider creating a schedule for checking that the kit is stocked, and replacing any expired items as required. Put that little schedule on the outside of the kit, kind of like the little chart that shows when they last cleaned the Burger King bathroom. If possible, use a bright-colored, watertight plastic container. Tool boxes

---

[27] You can also find an excellent and easy-to-follow (and free) guide to emergency first aid at www.resus.org.uk/pages/bls.pdf

work as well (even the cheap plastic kind from the dollar store). You can also buy some good premade kits in many stores (or online), but definitely don't buy THAT at the dollar store.

First Aid Kit Essentials
A good first aid kit (for home and vehicle) should include:

- ❒ Antiseptic
- ❒ Assorted sizes of safety pins
- ❒ Cleansing agent/soap
- ❒ Hypoallergenic adhesive tape
- ❒ Latex gloves (2 pair)
- ❒ Moistened towelettes
- ❒ Needle
- ❒ Penlight/Small flashlight
- ❒ Phone Numbers
- ❒ Scissors
- ❒ Sterile adhesive bandages in assorted sizes

- ❒ Sterile gauze pads, various sizes (4-6 each)
- ❒ Sterile roller bandages, various sizes (3 rolls each)
- ❒ Sunscreen
- ❒ Swiss Army Knife/Penknife
- ❒ Thermometer
- ❒ Tongue blades (2)
- ❒ Triangular bandages (3)
- ❒ Tube of petroleum jelly or other lubricant
- ❒ Tweezers

Non-Prescription Drugs
- ❒ Activated charcoal (use if advised by the Poison Control Center)
- ❒ Antacid (for stomach upset)
- ❒ Anti-diarrhea medication

- ❒ Aspirin or nonaspirin pain reliever
- ❒ Laxative
- ❒ Syrup of Ipecac (use if advised by the Poison Control Center)

Note: The phone numbers should be on a durable card in legible writing or type. You should include EMS numbers as well as poison control, non-emergency ambulance, a cab company, and any emergency contacts (for home kits).

Make sure your family has a first aid kit, know how to use it, and a PLAN on what to do in the case of an emergency.

RECOVERY POSITION
BY SUPREME UNDERSTANDING

This position helps a semiconscious or unconscious person breathe and permits fluids to drain from the nose and throat so they are not inhaled. After performing the ABC's, move the person into the recovery position while waiting for help to arrive.

Note: Do not use the recovery position if the person has a major injury, such as a back or neck injury. If the victim has to be kept in the recovery position for more than 30 min, turn him to the opposite side to relieve the pressure on the lower arm.

1. Kneel next to the person. Remove the victim's glasses if they are wearing any. Place the arm closest to you straight out from the body. Position the far arm with the back of the hand against the near cheek.

2. Grab and bend the person's far knee.

3. Protecting the head with one hand, gently roll the person toward you by pulling the far knee over and to the ground.

4. Tilt the head back slightly so that the airway is open. Make sure that the hand is under the cheek. Place a blanket or coat over the person (unless he or she has a heat illness or fever) and stay close until help arrives. Check breathing regularly.

If you can learn the steps to a dance, you can learn these steps. And just like dancing, it's best to practice with a partner!

BASIC FIRST AID FOR GUNSHOT WOUNDS

BY DAN TRES OMI

If someone suffers from a gunshot wound, they are more likely to die of shock more than anything else. If someone could stop the excessive bleeding, one's chances of survival increase dramatically. When I learned those tidbits of information, my heart sank thinking of all the lives I could have saved if I knew these two things.

We all know what happens when you call 911 when it comes to living in economically deprived areas. The first few minutes after someone is severely wounded can be the determining factor of whether the victim lives or not. It is during the moments immediately after a traumatic injury where the injured can go into shock. Shock can be caused by reduced blood volume and low blood pressure.

The first order of business would be to find the wound. This will mean that you will have to remove and rip through clothing. **When rubber gloves aren't available, you may have to be resourceful and cover your hands with plastic bags** (like the kind provided by most grocery stores). And in these days and times, it would probably be best to "double-bag." This is the same with a stab, slash, or puncture wound.

Very simple articles of clothing can be used, such as a bandanna or a t-shirt. Roll the clothing into a ball and hold it down onto the wound. You might have to wipe away the blood to find the wound (this is even more common for a razor slash, where there is a tremendous loss of blood for a small wound). A t-shirt can be used like a towel to absorb the blood so that you can find the wound.

Once the wound is found, the next step is to stop the bleeding. There are pressure points on the body that you can hold with three fingers to slow down the flow of blood. Arteries spread through the armpits, between the forearm and triceps, jugular vein, and behind the knee. **Tying a flag behind the knees can stop the flow to the lower legs and tying around the elbows stops blood flow to the lower arms and hands.** You can make a tourniquet using a bandanna or strips of a t-shirt. In most cases, applying pressure will suffice to staunch the bleeding. But if a major artery is punctured, this may be the only way to stop the flow of blood. **An extremity where there is a bullet wound might have to be tied off with a tourniquet to keep the blood from flowing out.** The only drawback to a tourniquet is that the limb which is tied off might have to be amputated.

Once the bleeding is stopped, the next thing you must do is to keep the victim warm. We often hear the victim of a gunshot wound joke that he or she is feeling cold. This is actually true. **The body temperature, due to loss of blood, drops to dangerous levels.** This can lead to the shutdown of major organs and eventually death. **Wrapping the victim in a blanket or in some cases, extra clothing can keep him or her warm.**

Finally, you should try to maintain the blood flow to the upper body. **Raising the victim's legs about a foot off the ground will help keep the blood circulating through the major organs and help to maintain body temperature.** All of these steps can help the victim survive until a fully trained paramedic arrives on the scene.

It is advisable that you learn basic first aid and even take classes in CPR. Usually basic first aid classes can be found free of charge at a local community center or church. CPR classes are given at low rates at the

American Red Cross or the YMCA/YWCA. These classes are highly recommended.

Know how to SAFELY hold/use a gun. Create a set of steps to treat a gun wound and have a friend, pretending he's hurt, test you.

BASIC CPR

BY DAN TRES OMI

Cardiopulmonary Resuscitation, CPR, is an emergency procedure conducted on victims of respiratory or cardiac arrest. It is a very dangerous procedure that should only be performed by qualified personnel. However, living in economically deprived areas many of us don't have the quick access to medical emergency personnel.

It is also important to remember that once CPR begins, one must continue until qualified emergency response arrives to relieve the person performing CPR. Living in the areas we reside in, this can be an indefinite amount of time. It takes much energy to perform CPR even on a dummy during a CPR qualification course.

The first thing one should do is to lay the victim on his or her back. Tilt the head back to open up the air passageway. Check for breathing by listening or watching the victim's chest. If no air is coming up or the chest is not moving, check to see if the throat is clogged. Do a finger sweep to remove any food, debris, or blood. Also, check the victims pulse by placing two fingers on the jugular vein. Go ahead and give two breaths while pinching the victim's nose. Check to see if there is any air or if there is any pulse. If there isn't, position your hands on the center of the victim's chest and push down two inches 15 times.

You will hear cartilage breaking. The sounds you make while pushing down will be scary. Unfortunately, this will tell you that you are doing it right. It may sound crazy, but it's true. Again, check to see if there is a pulse or if the victim is breathing. If not, continue to perform the above steps until help arrives or the victim is breathing and has a pulse. It must be noted that, at this point, you are actually breathing for the victim and this is the reason why you must remain performing this procedure until help arrives or someone else is qualified to take over. **If there is more than one person present who is willing to help, another should take over CPR about every 2 min to prevent fatigue. But make sure you minimize any delay during the changeover of rescuers.**

Many worksites, gyms, schools, and other facilities have CPR kits available. Usually these kits are located in the main office or in the lobby. These kits come equipped with manual air pumps to be placed over the victim's mouth to simulate breathing while someone pumps the victim's chest. This is helpful since it alleviates having to breathe for the victim. And even without a kit, if you are trying to avoid mouth-to-mouth contact (for whatever reason), studies have shown that Hands-Only CPR (pushing hard and fast in the center of the chest, continuously a rate of 100 a minute.), can be as effective as conventional CPR. So you don't HAVE to put your mouth on a stranger to help them when no one else can. But FYI, there have been NO cases of HIV transmitted via CPR, and other forms of infection (SARS or TB) have been extremely rare.

Again, it's advisable that you seek CPR classes. Normally, there is a onetime fee for these classes and the qualification has to be renewed after 5 years. Some employments offer free classes or provide vouchers to take these classes

Get a CPR certification. It's always better when you sign up friends or family. Create a list of life saving skills and add this to the list

THE HEIMLICH MANEUVER
BY DAN TRES OMI

The Heimlich Maneuver, usually referred to as the Heimlich, was co-created by Dr. Henry Heimlich and Dr. Edward Patrick. It is used when someone is choking due to a clogged windpipe. It can also be used to purge water from a drowning victim. People also refer to it as abdominal thrusts. It's very easy to realize when someone needs the Heimlich Maneuver performed. Usually, they are signing in the universal symbol: clutching their neck with both hands as they turn colors.

The first thing you should do is ask the question folks always ask in a movie after someone is hurt: Are you okay? It sounds stupid, but you want to determine if that person can speak. If they can speak, breathe, or cough, then the Heimlich Maneuver should not be performed. **When a person is really choking, he can't cough strongly, speak, or breathe, and his face may turn red or blue.**

If they cannot speak, breathe, or cough, proceed to assist the choking victim. The next thing you should do is to perform a mouth sweep. You might not have safety gloves handy, so you **might have to stick your fingers in the victim's mouth and sweep around to see if you can dislodge the item that way. If you don't succeed, then stand behind the victim.** Place your arms around the victim's midsection and clasp one fist into the other palm. Make sure the thumb of the clenched fist is facing the victim. Place that clenched fist slightly above the sternum and below the rib cage and then thrust towards you. It might take a few thrusts to dislodge the item.

You can also conduct these abdominal thrusts to yourself if you find yourself choking. Stand behind a chair and bend over, placing your abdomen on the back of the chair. Then push into the chair using your abdomen. It will have the same effect as the Heimlich Maneuver. If you need more information, you can check online or even take a first aid class. Most community centers and schools offer basic first aid classes for free. Look up videos online to see it done then send links to your closest friends. When they can save your life, and vice versa, you're family.

EMERGENCY QUICK REFERENCE PAGE

	Blow to the Head	Poisoning	Sprain	Object in Eye	Bloody Nose
Situation	The skull is very protective, so hitting it rarely injures the skull itself. But great force can injure the neck, back, and/or the soft tissues inside the head.	Potential household hazards include cleaning supplies, carbon monoxide, and pesticides. Bites and stings can also be poisonous to some people.	Sprains occur when the ligaments surrounding a joint are pulled beyond their normal range. Often accompanied by bruising and swelling.	Anything that gets in your eye, whether it's a speck of sand or a chemical, can cause pain and could damage the cornea.	A nosebleed occurs when blood vessels inside the nose break. Because they're delicate, this can happen easily.
What to do immediately	If the person is unconscious, call 911. If the struck area is bleeding, treat it as you would any other cut, but follow up with your doctor, as there may be internal injuries. Icing a small bump can help reduce the swelling.	If a person is unconscious or having trouble breathing, call 911. In other cases, call the Poison Control Centers' national hotline (800-222-1222). Be prepared to tell what substance was involved, how much was taken and when, and the age and the weight of the victim.	Alternately apply and remove ice every 20 minutes for the first day. Wrap the joint with an elastic compression bandage. Elevating the limb may also help. Stay off the injury for at least 24 hours. After that, apply heat to promote blood flow to the area.	Try to dislodge a small particle by blinking several times. If it's not budging, rinse the eye by holding the lid open under a running tap (if possible, remove contact lenses first).	Lean slightly forward and pinch your nose just below the bridge, where the cartilage and the bone come together. Maintain the pressure for 5 to 15 minutes. Pressing an ice pack against the bridge can also help.
What not to do	Don't leave the victim alone, especially when he's sleeping. Wake him up every three to four hours and have him answer simple questions to make sure there's no brain injury, such as a concussion.	Don't give Ipecac or try to induce vomiting. The poison could cause additional damage when it comes back up. The victim shouldn't eat or drink anything, unless the hotline operator tells you otherwise.	Don't try to work through the pain. You risk doing more serious damage, like tearing the ligament.	Never rub your eyes. Even a tiny piece of dirt can scratch the cornea and cause an infection. Never try to remove an object that's embedded—leave that to the professionals.	Don't tilt your head back, or you may swallow blood, and potentially some could go in your lungs.
When to seek medical attention	Call 911 if the victim exhibits seizures, dizziness, vomiting, nausea, or obvious changes in behavior.	Don't wait until symptoms appear to call for help. If you have reason to think someone has been poisoned, immediately seek medical attention.	If the injury doesn't improve in a few days, you may have a fracture or a muscle or ligament tear; call a doctor.	If you have splashed a chemical (such as bleach) in your eye or have an object embedded in it, call 911. For minor irritants, call your doctor if your eye is still stinging or swelling after rinsing or if you have vision problems.	Call your doctor if you can't stop the bleeding after 20 minutes; if the nosebleed happened spontaneously; or if it accompanies a headache, dizziness, ringing in the ears, or vision problems.

You can save a drowning or choking victim by learning these basic techniques. Experts stress that people should take a class in CPR. For classes and lessons, contact your local American Red Cross or American Heart Association.

Basic CPR technique

The American Heart Association and the American Red Cross recommend the use of rescue breathing if a victim is not breathing and CPR if there is no pulse.

For adults

Call 911

Tilt head, lift chin, check breathing

Pinch nose shut and give two breaths

Check pulse

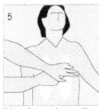

If there is no pulse, position hands in the center of chest

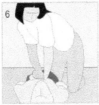

Place one hand over other and push down two inches on the chest 15 times

7 If there is no pulse, continue with two breaths and 15 pumps for one minute and recheck pulse – if no pulse – continue until help arrives.

The Heimlich maneuver

Do not perform the Heimlich maneuver if the victim is coughing, speaking or breathing. If the person cannot cough, speak or breathe, proceed as follows:

Choking

1. Stand behind the victim, wrap your arms around his or her waist.

2. Clasp your hands together in a double fist and place the fist thumb side in just below the victim's rib cage and above the navel*.

3. Press into the victim's abdomen (not the rib cage) with a quick, upward thrust.

4. Repeat thrusts until object is dislodged.

Alone
If you are alone and choking you can give yourself abdominal thrusts. Press your abdomen onto a firm object, such as the back of a chair.

Drowning
Dr. Henry Heimlich recommends the Heimlich maneuver to purge water from the lungs of a drowning victim.

Lying down
Place victim on his or her back. Turn face to one side, allowing water to drain from mouth.

Place hands together with the heel of the bottom hand on the abdomen*. Press with quick upward thrusts.

In deep water
Perform maneuver in deep water by wedging a flotation device between the rescuer's stomach and the victim's back. The rescuer bear-hugs the victim and performs maneuver.

NOTE: The American Red Cross and the American Heart Association do not recommend the Heimlich maneuver as the first or only step to save a near-drowning victim.

* Use the index and middle fingers of both hands to perform the thrust on infants or toddlers – do not use your fist or entire heel of hand.

CPR for infants and children

Brain damage can occur within minutes of a breathing emergency. It is essential that oxygen to the brain is restored quickly. Have someone call 911; if you are alone, use rescue breathing for one minute before calling 911. If there is a pulse, but the infant/child is not breathing, give 1 breath every 3 seconds. If the infant/child is not breathing and has no pulse, give cycles of 5 compressions and 1 breath. Infants from birth to 1 year of age receive slightly different care from that of children ages 1 to 8.

Puffs
If infant/child is not breathing. Tilt head back. Cover infant's nose and mouth, (child – pinch nose) give 1 slow breath until chest gently rises.

Check pulse
Check infant pulse on the inside of the upper arm. Maintain head tilt with other hand. On older children, take pulse on neck.

Chest compression
If there is no pulse, place two fingers below an imaginary line between nipples, not below sternum. Press gently 5 times.

Child 1 to 8 years of age
If there is no pulse, place heel of one hand about center of the breast bone and press 5 times.

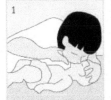

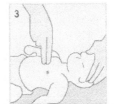

Continue with sets of 1 breath and 5 compressions – recheck pulse and breathing – if no pulse, continue CPR until help arrives.

APPENDIX

In the following pages, you'll find tons of resources to help you along your journey, including a list of free documentaries you can find online; a list of recommended websites to check out, and dozens of other things you'll want to use, possibly just to show off how smart you are. Whatever works for you.

RECOMMENDED VIEWING

FOOD AND HEALTH DOCUMENTARIES
BY JUSTICE RAJEE

The following is a list of exceptional films and documentaries related to the various topics in this book. You can find them at many places that sell or rent DVDs, or you can find out how to see them for FREE online at www.HoodHealthHandbook.com.

Addicted to Plastic – All about the growing role (and risks) of plastic in our daily lives.

Aerosol Crimes (aka Chemtrails) – Investigates chemical trails in our skies and the dangers they pose to our health.

Affluenza – Examines the high cost of achieving the most extravagant lifestyle the world has ever seen.

AIDS Inc. – An intriguing study of the economy surrounding HIV/AIDS treatment and diagnosis.

Architects of Control – Investigates the attempt to control the masses by economic elites.

The Beyond Within – A study of LSD.

Big Bucks, Big Pharma – Study of the influence of the pharmaceuticals industry.

Big Sugar – Explores the power and reach of the sweetener industry.

Bigger Stronger Faster – Intimate first person study of performance-enhancing drugs.

Blue Gold: World Water Wars – Looks into the future of water and its potential to be the center of conflict.

Busting Out – explores the history and politics of breast obsession in America.

Chernobyl Heart – Detailed investigation of the health aftermath of the Chernobyl nuclear radiation leak.

The City Addicted to Crystal Meth – Sobering study of the effects of meth addiction.

Consuming Kids – Kids and advertising.

The Corporation – Corporations and their new-found control of the people.

A Cow At My Table – Explores Western attitudes towards farm animals and meat, and the intense battle between animal advocates and the meat industry to influence the consumer's mind.

Deconstructing Myth of AIDS – Challenges accepted views on AIDS.

Dirt: The Movie – All about soil and its connection to our food and health.

The Disappearing Male – About one of the most important, and least publicized, issues facing the human species: the toxic threat to the male reproductive system.

Doctor, the Depleted Uranium, and the Dying Children, The – The film exposes the use and impact of radioactive weapons during the current war against Iraq.

Don't Swallow Your Toothpaste – Investigates fluoride and its negative effects.

The Drug Trial That Went Wrong – Study of a drug trail the resulted in multiple deaths.

The Drugging of Our Children – Investigation of ADHD, ADD, and the drugs prescribed to treat these conditions.

Dust to Dust: The Health Effects of 9/11 – This disturbing documentary asks whether the EPA's pronouncement of safety was based on science or politics.

Earthlings – Uses hidden cameras and never before seen footage to chronicle the day-to-day practices of some of the largest industries in the world, all of which rely entirely on animals for profit.

Exploring Life Extension – Investigation into methods to extend life.

Flotsam Found – Intriguing look at where our waste goes once it hits the ocean.

Flow – For Love of Water.

The Fluoride Deception – Short interview with author of the book of the same name.

Food, Inc. – A thorough study of our food system and the problems in it.

Food Matters – Food Matters sets about uncovering the trillion dollar worldwide 'sickness industry' and gives people some scientifically verifiable solutions for overcoming illness naturally.

Frontline: Poisoned Water – Short case study of our water systems and its threats.

Frontline: Sick Around America – Detailed investigation into the American Health System.

Frontline: Sick Around the World – Comparative investigation into healthcare around the world.

The Future of Food – There is a revolution happening in the farm fields and on the dinner tables of America, a revolution that is transforming the very nature of the food we eat.

The Garden – Story of one community farm and the fight to save it.

The Genetic Conspiracy: Following the Trail – GMOs and safety.

Genetically Modified Food: Panacea or Poison? – Study on the safety of GMOs.

The Ghost In Your Genes – Biology stands on the brink of a shift in the understanding of inheritance. The discovery of epigenetics – hidden influences upon the genes – could affect every aspect of our lives.

Gulf War Syndrome: Killing Our Own – Intriguing look at possible causes of an illness that affects many Gulf War Veterans

The History of Asbestos – Study of the industrial life of Asbestos.

HIV = AIDS, Fact or Fraud? – This documentary challenges the conventional thinking on HIV and AIDS.

Hofmann's Potion – A study of LSD and its creator Dr. Albert Hoffman.

Holes In Heaven? – Investigates HAARP.

How The Kids Took Over – A study of how direct marketing to children has affected families in our society.

Hoxsey: How Healing Becomes a Crime – Details the fortunes of Harry M. Hoxsey and his herbal treatment for cancer.

I Am A Man: Black Masculinity in America – A study of the challenges to Black male masculinity.

I, Psychopath – In this intriguing documentary, Sam Vaknin, a self-proclaimed psychopath, goes in search of a diagnosis.

In Lies We Trust – Proposes a connection between the CIA, Hollywood and mass media to influence fear in the public.

In Pot We Trust – The medical use of marijuana is examined from every side of a very complex issue.

Is Alcohol Worse Than Ecstasy? – How bad is alcohol really? This documentary tries to find out.

Jungle Trip – Investigates several powerful plants found in the Amazon.

Killer At Large: Why Obesity – Study of obesity and our future.

Killing Us Softly 3: Advertising's Image of Women – Groundbreaking analysis of advertising's depiction of women.

Life Running Out Of Control – A study of GMOs and the long-term dangers they present.

Making A Killing – Psychotropic drugs. It's the story of big money-drugs that fuel a $330 billion psychiatric industry, without a single cure.

Mind Control: America's Secret War – Looks at the use of messaging to engineer social outcomes

Modern Meat – FRONTLINE goes inside the world of the modern American meat industry and shows that this once simple product, the hamburger, is no longer so simple.

Money Talks: Profits Before Patient Safety – Where your health is traded to maintain profits.

Multiple Personalities – Deep investigation of a challenge mental health disorder

My Big Breasts and Me – In this documentary, meet three women who feel defined by their naturally big breasts, and find out what it's really like to have a cup size at the far end of the alphabet.

My Penis and Everyone Else's – Challenges society's stereotypes of masculinity as well as getting to the heart of why men are so fixated with their members.

Natural Mystery – A look into several naturally occurring phenomena.

Patent For A Pig – Monsanto's continued quest to patent life itself.

Philosophy – A Guide to Happiness – Multipart study of human emotion.

Poison In The Mouth – Startling documentary shows evidence of brain damage from Mercury in silver amalgam fillings.

Poison on the Platter – Looks at the threat to our health posed by GMO foods

Pandemic – Pandemic puts faces and personalities to the extraordinary profitable business of pornography today.

Prescription For Disaster – is an in-depth investigation into the symbiotic relationships between the pharmaceutical industry, the FDA, lobbyists, lawmakers, medical schools, and researchers, and the impact this has on consumers and their health care.

Psychopath – Equinox reports on techniques developed by psychologists to work out whether a person is psychopathic and shows how brain scientists are coming close to mapping the malfunctions in the brain that cause a person to be a psychopath.

Quiet Rage: The Stanford Prison Experiment – A study of how role and position changes behavior.

Run From The Cure – Covers the trial of Rick Simpson for offering hemp oil to treat many illnesses.

Sexy Inc.: Our Children Under Influence – A look into how adulthood is being pushed on our children primarily around sexuality.

Sicko – Comparative study of healthcare in the US vs. the rest of the world.

Simply Raw: Reversing Diabetes in 30 Days – its right in the name.

The Slow Poisoning of India – A short powerful look into the dangers of agricultural pollution.

Stephen Fry: The Secret Life of the Manic Depressive – Comedian, actor, author and film-maker Stephen Fry meets celebrities and members of the public who talk frankly about the impact the condition has on their lives.

The Story of Stuff – A very informative presentation of unsustainable consumption and what we can do about it.

Street Medicine – An informative look at health professionals taking healthcare to the streets of America.

Super Size Me – One man's quest to prove the ill effects of fast food.

Supermarket Secrets – In a two-part program, journalist Jane Moore investigates how supermarkets have affected the food on our plates and reveals the tell-tale signs that the food we buy may not have been grown in the way we think.

The Supermarket That's Eating Britain - Investigates the effects of Britain's largest Supermarket chain on public health and wellbeing.

Sweet Misery: A Poisoned World – Excellent documentary showing how dangerous artificial sweetener Aspartame is.

Sweet Remedy – A great study on how the PR industry convinces us that everything is okay.

The Beautiful Truth – Investigates how our bodies heal.

The Gerson Miracle – Study of a small clinic's cancer treatment method.

The Science of Healing – Structured investigation into how we heal.

Thin – This HBO documentary takes us inside the walls of Renfrew Center, a residential facility for the treatment of women with eating disorders.

Tough Guise – In this innovative and wide-ranging analysis, Jackson Katz argues that widespread violence in American society, including the tragic school shootings in Littleton, Colorado, Jonesboro, Arkansas, and elsewhere, needs to be understood as part of an ongoing crisis in masculinity.

The Truth About Vitamins – A great look into the vitamin industry.

The Union: The Business Behind Getting High – The title says it all.

Unnatural Causes – Detailed series showing the connection between poverty and ill health.

Vaccination: The Hidden Truth – Investigates vaccines and their possible negative effects.

Vaccine-Nation – Investigates vaccines and their possible negative effects.

Waiting To Inhale – Examines the heated debate over marijuana and its use as medicine in the United States.

We Become Silent – A look at the conspiracy to access to alternative treatments away from the people.

We Feed The World – In WE FEED THE WORLD, Austrian filmmaker Erwin Wagenhofer traces the origins of the food we eat.

Wegman's Cruelty – A short film about the inside of a Wegman's egg farm.

The World According to Monsanto – A strong look at Monsanto, GMOs and farming in the USA.

A World Without Water – Investigates the privatizing of water around the world

Liquid Measure Conversion				
				½ fl
			1/8 cup	1 fl c
			¼ cup	2 fl c
			½ cup	4 fl c
	¼ qtr.	½ pt.	1 cup	8 fl c
	½ qtr.	1 pt.	2 cups	16 fl
¼ gal	1 qtr.	2 pt.	4 cups	32 fl
½ gal	2 qtr.	4 pt.	8 cups	64 fl
1 gal	4 qtr.	8 pt.	16 cups	128

RECOMMENDED WEBSITES

www.HoodHealthHandbook.com
www.BlackHealthcare.com
www.All-Natural.com
www.WebMD.com
www.WrongDiagnosis.com
www.Mercola.com
www.PCRM.org
www.iHealthTube.com
www.MetropolitanWellness.com
www.HealthBookSummaries.com
www.HolisticMed.com
www.BlackHerbals.com
www.NaturalNews.com

www.HealthyTalkRadio.com
www.SoulVegFolk.com
www.Shirleys-Wellness-Cafe.com
www.NutritionData.com
www.EveryNutrient.com
www.WHFoods.com
www.DrFuhrman.com
www.DrWeil.com
www.DoctorOz.com
www.NaturalHealthMag.com
www.HolisticHealthTools.com
www.NaturalHealthWeb.com
the50besthealthblogs.blogspot.com

www.Fooducate.com
www.YumKid.com
www.GrowYouthful.com
www.Naturalpedia.com
www.NaturalNews.tv
www.CounterThink.com
www.ConsumerWellness.org
www.FoodInvestigations.com
www.HonestFoodGuide.org

www.HealingFoodReference.com
www.NaturalHealthLibrary.com
www.HerbReference.com
www.NutrientReference.com
www.GaryNull.com
www.DrLeonardColdwell.com
www.HealthFinder.gov
www.MentalHelp.net
www.HoodHealthHandbook.com

HOW TO CALCULATE YOUR BODY FAT

The following formulas will allow you to do everything from calculating your body fat to determining how many calories you need to eat daily in order to lose weight.

Body Fat Formula for Women		
Factor 1	(Total body weight x 0.732) + 8.987	
Factor 2	Wrist measurement (at fullest point)/ 3.140	
Factor 3	Waist measurement (at navel) x 0.157	
Factor 4	Hip measurement (at fullest point) x 0.249	
Factor 5	Forearm measurement (at fullest point) x 0.434	
Lean Body Mass	Factor 1 + Factor 2 – Factor 3 – Factor 4 + Factor 5	
Body Fat Weight	Total bodyweight – Lean Body Mass	
Body Fat Percentage	(Body Fat Weight x 100)/ total bodyweight	
Body Fat Formula for Men		
Factor 1	(Total body weight x 1.082) + 94.42	
Factor 2	Waist measurement x 4.15	
Lean Body Mass	Factor 1 – Factor 2	
Body Fat Weight	Total bodyweight – Lean Body Mass	
Body Fat Percentage	(Body Fat Weight x 100)/ total bodyweight	

NOTE: Doing stuff like this on paper develops your brain and sharpens your math skills, so stop Googling for "online body fat calculator" and do something to keep your brain alive.

HOW TO CALCULATE YOUR DAILY CALORIE NEEDS

Basic Metabolic Rate (How Your Body Burns Calories)

This is how you calculate your Basic Metabolic Rate (BMR). Your body burns calories even when it isn't doing anything. Your BMR is the number of calories your body burns at a state of rest. Your BMR decreases as you age. As a survival response, it also drops when you're depriving yourself of food, which makes it harder to lose weight if you're simply limiting your food intake. On the other hand, a regular routine of cardiovascular exercise can increase your BMR, improving your health and fitness while helping your burn off any unwanted calories.

BMR Formula	Subtotal		Subtotal
Women		Men	
(4.35 x weight in pounds)		(6.23 x weight in pounds)	
+ (4.7 x height in inches)		+ (12.7 x height in inches)	
– (4.7 x age in years)		– (6.8 x age in years)	
+655		+66	
TOTAL BMR		TOTAL BMR	

The Harris Benedict Equation is a formula that uses your BMR and then applies an activity factor to determine your total daily energy expenditure (calories). The only factor omitted by the Harris Benedict Equation is lean body mass. Remember, leaner bodies need more calories than less lean ones. Therefore, this equation will be very accurate in all but the very muscular (will under-estimate calorie needs) and the very fat (will over-estimate calorie needs).

Harris Benedict Formula for Daily Calorie Needs

To determine your total daily calorie needs, multiply your BMR by the appropriate activity factor, as follows:

Activity Factor	Calorie-Calculation
Sedentary (little or no exercise)	BMR x 1.2
Lightly active (light exercise/sports 1-3 days/week)	BMR x 1.375
Moderately active (moderate exercise/sports 3-5 days/week)	BMR x 1.55
Very active (hard exercise/sports 6-7 days a week)	BMR x 1.725
Extra active (very hard exercise/sports and physical job or 2x training)	BMR x 1.9

For example, if you are sedentary, multiply you're BMR (1745) by 1.2 = 2094. This is the total number of calories you need in order to maintain your current weight. Once you know the number of calories needed to maintain your weight, you can easily calculate the number of calories you need to eat in order to gain or lose weight:

❏ **Calorie Needs to Gain Weight:** Once you know the number of calories you need to maintain your weight (using the BMR Formula in conjunction with the Harris Benedict Equation), you can easily calculate the number of calories you need in order to gain weight. If you want to gain body weight, you need to consume more calories than you burn. One pound of body weight is roughly equivalent to 3500 calories, so eating an extra 500 calories per day will cause you to gain one pound a week. For optimum health, if you increase your calories to gain weight then (health permitting) gradually increase your level of physical exercise in order to maintain or increase your lean body mass. The benefits of exercise on physical and mental health are well documented and shouldn't be ignored.

- ☐ **Calorie Needs to Lose Weight:** There are approximately 3500 calories in a pound of stored body fat. So, if you create a 3500-calorie deficit through diet, exercise or a combination of both, you will lose one pound of body weight. (On average 75% of this is fat, 25% lean tissue) If you create a 7000 calorie deficit you will lose two pounds and so on. The calorie deficit can be achieved either by calorie-restriction alone, or by a combination of fewer calories in (diet) and more calories out (exercise). This combination of diet and exercise is best for lasting weight loss. Indeed, sustained weight loss is difficult or impossible without increased regular exercise.

If you want to lose fat, a useful guideline for lowering your calorie intake is to reduce your calories by at least 500, but not more than 1000 below your maintenance level. For people with only a small amount of weight to lose, 1000 calories will be too much of a deficit. As a guide to minimum calorie intake, the American College of Sports Medicine (ACSM) recommends that calorie levels never drop below 1200 calories per day for women or 1800 calories per day for men. Even these calorie levels are quite low.

An alternative way of calculating a safe minimum calorie-intake level is by reference to your body weight or current body weight. Reducing calories by 15-20% below your daily calorie maintenance needs is a useful start. You may increase this depending on your weight loss goals.

GLOSSARY

Abnormal: Unusual or unexpected, especially in a way that causes alarm or anxiety.

Adenosine Triphosphate (ATP): ATP is a molecule that serves as the universal energy source for all plants and animals. ATP is continuously being recycled by your body.

Amino Acids: See Protein.

Analgesic: Reduces pain (without inducing unconsciousness).

Anthocyanidins: See Flavonoids.

Anthocyanin's: Plant pigments that help protect you from heart disease.

Antibiotic: Any substance that can destroy or inhibit the growth of bacteria and similar microorganisms.

Anti-inflammatory: An agent that prevents or counteracts inflammation.

Anti-microbial: An agent that destroys microbes, inhibits their growth, or prevents or counteracts their pathogenic action

Antioxidant: A substance that prevents harmful molecules called free radicals from damaging DNA.

Antiviral: An agent that inhibits the growth and reproduction of a virus.

Aneurism: A fluid-filled sac in the wall of an artery that can burst.

Ascorbic Acid: See Vitamin C.

Astringent: A substance which draws tissue together, restricting the flow of blood.

Beta-sitosterol: See Sterol.

Bioflavonoids: See Flavonoids.

Body Mass Index (BMI): Body Mass Index is a standardized ratio of weight to height, and is often used as a general indicator of health or risk.

Calcium: The most abundant essential mineral in the human body, primarily related to bone development.

Calorie: A unit of measurement for energy found in food.

Campesterol: See Sterol.

Carcinogen: A substance or agent that can cause cancer.

Carbohydrate: A sugar, starch, or cellulose that is a food source of energy for an animal or plant.

Carnivore: Any animal that eats primarily meat.

Carotenoids: Antioxidant plant pigments that are converted to Vitamin A by the body.

Casein: A milk protein sometimes used in otherwise non-dairy products like soymilk, soy cheese and non-dairy creamer

Cholecalciferol: See Vitamin D.

Cholesterol: Cholesterol is a soft, waxy substance present in all parts of the body including the nervous system, skin, muscles, liver, intestines, and heart. It is both made by the body and obtained from animal products in the diet. It is transported in the blood to be used by all parts of the body.

Cobalamine: See Vitamin B12.

Copper: Copper is a trace element that is essential for most animals, including humans. It is needed to absorb and utilize iron.

Curative: Able to restore health

Daily Values (DV): Daily Values are the dietary reference values that are used on all current U.S. Nutrition Facts labels. These values were determined by the FDA to best represent the minimum needs of the general population.

Deprived: Kept from having something

Dietary Fiber: Indigestible fiber taken in through food or drink that usually comes from the thick cell walls of plants.

Dietary Reference Intakes (IDV): See Daily Values.

Diuretic: Something that causes an increase in urination.

Doula: A traditional midwife.

Ellagic acid: A chemical that controls bleeding.

Enzyme: A natural chemical produced by animal and plant cells that helps reactions and other processes to start.

Essential Amino Acids: Amino acid that the body cannot make and that must be obtained from food to maintain growth. Histidine, Isoleucine, Leucine, Lysine, Methionine, Phenylalanine, Theronine, Tryptophan, and Valine

Fatty Acids: An acid found in fats and oils in animals and plants.

Flavonoids (bioflavonoids): Flavonoids are a class of water-soluble pigments that are found in many plants. Many of these compounds serve as antioxidants and deter cancer in various ways.

Folate: See Folic Acid.

Folic acid: A B vitamin found in green vegetables and liver that helps prevent birth defects and lower levels of homocysteine, an amino acid linked to heart disease.

Free Radicals: a molecule that has an extra electron and can react very easily with other molecules linked to cancer and heart disease in the human body.

Fruitarian: One who only eats fruit.

Genetics: The study of heredity

Glycemic Index (GI): The Glycemic Index is a dietary index that's used to rank carbohydrate-based foods and predicts the rate at which the ingested food will increase blood sugar levels.

Glycemic Load (GL): Glycemic Load is equal to the Glycemic Index of a food times the number of grams of carbohydrates in the serving.

HDL: High Density Lipoprotein

Histidine: One of 9 Essential Amino Acids.

Hormone: A chemical substance produced in animals and plants that controls things such as growth and sexual development

Individualized Daily Values (IDV): See Daily Values.

Indoles: A crystalline compound found in plants and animals that help fight cancer.

Insoluble Fiber: A fiber incapable of being dissolved in a liquid.

Insulin: Insulin is a hormone that's secreted by your pancreas to help regulate blood-sugar level and promotes glycogen storage.

International Unit (IU): A measurement unit primarily used on nutrition labeling for vitamin A.

Iron: Iron is one of the human body's essential minerals. It forms part of hemoglobin, the component of the blood that carries oxygen throughout the body. Iron is also part of myoglobin, which helps muscles store oxygen.

Isoflavones: Organic Compounds found in legumes, especially soy beans, that act as weak estrogens (phytoestrogens), and may have positive effects against cancer and heart disease

Isoleucine: One of 9 Essential Amino Acids.

Isomer: An isomer is one of two or more compounds that have the same chemical formula, but have the atoms in their molecules arranged in a different way and have different properties from each other.

Isothiocyanates: Compounds, including sulphoraphane, that protect against cancer.

Kilo joule: 1000 units of work/energy

LDL: Low-density (LDL) lipoproteins. LDLs are considered the "bad cholesterol," since they can stick together to form plaque deposits on the walls of your blood vessels, leading to atherosclerosis.

Legumes: The vegetable family that includes beans, lentils, peas and peanuts, all of which are excellent sources of vegetable protein

Leucine: One of 9 Essential Amino Acids.

Lignans: Organic compounds found in legumes, especially soy bean that may have positive effects against cancer and heart disease

Lipid: A general classification to denote water-insoluble compounds, such as fatty acids and sterols.

Lysine: One of 9 Essential Amino Acids.

Macronutrient: those nutrients that form the major portion of your consumption and contribute energy to your diet that includes carbohydrates, fats, protein, and alcohol. Sometimes water is also considered to be a macronutrient.

Magnesium: An essential mineral for the human body. It is needed for protein, bone, and fatty acid formation, making new cells, activating B vitamins, relaxing muscles, blood clotting, and forming adenosine triphosphate (ATP).

Maltitol: See Sugar Alcohol.

Manganese: An essential trace mineral that is required in small amounts to manufacture enzymes necessary for the metabolism of proteins and fat. It also supports the immune system and blood-sugar balance and is involved in the production of cellular energy, reproduction, and bone growth.

Mannitol: See Sugar Alcohol.

Medical institutions: a place where people who are, e.g. mentally or physically challenged are cared for

Menadione: Vitamin K supplement in medicines and animal feedstuffs used as a fungicide.

Methionine: One of 9 Essential Amino Acids.

Microgram (mcg): A microgram is a unit of measure equal to one one-millionth of a gram (g).

Micronutrient: Any nutrient that is smaller than a macronutrient.

Milligram (mg): A milligram is a unit of measure equal to one one-thousandth of a gram (g).

Mineral: An inorganic substance that must be ingested by animals or plants in order to remain healthy.

Misdiagnosis: A wrong diagnosis

Moderate: Not large, great, or severe

Monosaccharide: A carbohydrates that consist of a single sugar molecule. Examples include glucose, fructose, and galactose.

Monounsaturated Fat: Fats and oils are made mainly from vegetable oils. They are considered to be healthier than those made from saturated fats.

Mutations: The actions or processes of something being changed

Niacin: A B complex vitamin found in meat and dairy products. Deficiency of niacin causes pellagra. See Vitamin B3

NLEA Serving: A standardized serving size that arose from the U.S. government's Nutrition Labeling and Education Act to restrict the typical serving size that can be claimed on a U.S. Nutrition Facts label

Nutrient Density: Nutrient density is the measurement of the amount of a nutrient per fixed portion of food. Nutrition Data calculates nutrient densities based on a 200-Calorie serving size.

Nutrient: A substance that provides nourishment (e.g. the minerals that a plant takes from the soil or the constituents in food that keep a human body healthy and help it grow)

Nutritional Yeast: A health supplement grown on molasses, sugar beets or wood pulp. A rich source of vitamin B12 and protein

Omega-3 fatty acids: A type of fat that reduces the risk factors for heart disease.

Omnivore: An animal that eats both plants and meat.

Organosulfides: Substances that help lower cholesterol.

Pancreas: a large elongated glandular organ lying near the stomach.

Pantothenic Acid: A B complex vitamin that is present in many foods and is essential for growth. See Vitamin B5.

Pescetarian: Someone that eats no meat except for fish.

Phenylalanine: One of 9 Essential Amino Acids.

Phosphate: Phosphorus combined with oxygen.

Phosphorus: Phosphorus is an essential mineral that is usually found in the human body in bone.

Phylloquinone: See Vitamin K.

Phytoestrogen: Plant-based compound similar to human estrogen It helps protect against certain cancers, while providing many of the same heart-and-bone-protective effects as human estrogen.

Phytonadione: See Vitamin K.

Phytosterol: Phytosterol is any plant-derived sterol. (See Sterol)

Polysaccharides: Polysaccharides are complex carbohydrates, made up of multiple sugar molecules. Examples of polysaccharides include cellulose, starch, and dextrin.

Polyunsaturated Fat: A class of fats, especially plant oils that are less likely to be converted into cholesterol in the body. See Unsaturated Fat.

Potassium: An essential mineral that helps regulate heart function, blood pressure, and nerve and muscle activity.

Premature: Before due time.

Probiotic: A substance containing live microorganisms that claims to be beneficial to humans and animals, e.g. by restoring the balance of micro flora in the digestive tract.

Protein Quality: The general standard or grade of protein.

Protein: One of the basic components of food and makes all life possible. They provide for the transport of nutrients, oxygen, and waste throughout the body. They provide the structure and contracting capability of muscles. They also provide collagen to connective tissues of the body and to the tissues of the skin, hair, and nails.

Pseudoscience: A theory or method doubtfully or mistakenly held to be scientific.

Quackery: Bad medical treatment from doctors who are not very good at their job, or from people who cheat other people by pretending to be doctors

Recommended Dietary Allowances (RDA): See Daily Values.

Reference Daily Intakes (RDI): See Daily Values.

Rennet: An enzyme from the stomach of slaughtered calves, used to coagulate cheese. Found in many, but not all dairy cheeses.

Retinol Activity Equivalent (RAE): A unit for expressing vitamin A activity.

Retinol: See Vitamin A.

Riboflavin: See Vitamin B2.

Ruptured: A break in something.

Saccharide: A sweet-tasting, water-soluble carbohydrate

SAMe (S-adenosyl-L-methionine): A natural metabolite of the amino acid methionine, which plays a key role in dozens of chemical reactions in the body.

Satiety: Satiety refers to the feeling of satisfaction or "fullness" produced by the consumption of food.

Saturated Fat: A saturated fat is a fat or fatty acid in which there are no double bonds between the carbon atoms of the fatty acid chain. Common saturated fats include butter, lard, palm oil, coconut oil, cottonseed oil, and palm kernel oil.

Seitan (wheat gluten): A vegetarian replacement for meat, made of protein (gluten) extracted from flour.

Selenium: An essential trace mineral that may help protect the body from cancer.

Sodium: Sodium is a mineral, an essential nutrient. It helps to maintain blood volume, regulate the balance of water in the cells, and keep nerves functioning.

Soluble Fiber: Dietary fiber that is dissolvable in liquid.

Sorbitol: See Sugar Alcohol.

Soy cheese: A cheese-like product made from soybeans. However, some soy cheeses are not vegan as they contain the animal protein casein.

Soybean: A legume, which is an excellent, inexpensive vegan source of protein and iron. Soybeans are used to make a number of vegetarian and vegan substitutions for meat, dairy and eggs.

Soymilk: A milk-like product made from soybeans, with the same amount of protein and less fat than cow's milk. However, some soymilks are not vegan as they contain the animal protein casein.

Starch: A flavorless white substance found in rice, potatoes, and other vegetables. It is a type of carbohydrate that gives you energy.

Sterol: A sterol is any of a class of solid cyclic alcohols, found in both plants (e.g., campesterol, stigmasterol, betasitosterol) and animals (e.g., cholesterol).

Stigmasterol: A sterol found in plants. Used in the manufacturing of progesterone.

Sugar Alcohol: Carbohydrates that are more slowly or incompletely absorbed by the human digestive system than sugars. Common sugar alcohols include sorbitol, mannitol, maltitol, and xylitol.

Supplements: Additions to something to increase its size or make up for a deficiency.

Symptoms: Indications of a disease or other disorder, especially one experienced by the patient, e.g. pain, dizziness, or itching, as opposed to one observed by the doctor. A sign

Synonymous: If one person, thing, or idea is synonymous with another, there is an extremely close connection between them, so that you cannot think of one without also thinking of the other

Tempeh: A replacement for meat, made from fermented soybeans.

Textured Vegetable Protein (TVP): Made from soy flour, TVP is commonly used in vegetarian restaurants as a substitute for ground beef.

Theobromine: An alkaloid compound with a molecular structure similar to. Theobromine has a mild stimulating effect on humans, and is found in certain foods, such as cocoa and chocolate.

Theronine: One of 9 Essential Amino Acids.

Thiamin: A natural chemical in many types of food that your body uses to make your nerves work correctly. It belongs to the B vitamins.

Tocopherol: One of a group of fat-soluble compounds that make up vitamin E, present in vegetable oils and leafy greens.

Tofu: A replacement for meat, eggs and cheese, made from curdled soymilk and pressed into blocks. Tofu can be eaten fresh or cooked in many different ways and is an excellent source of protein.

Tryptophan: One of 9 Essential Amino Acids.

Unsaturated Fat: An unsaturated fat is a fat or fatty acid in which there are one or more double bonds between carbon atoms of the fatty acid chain.

Valine: One of 9 Essential Amino Acids.

Vegan: Someone who chooses not to eat anything derived (made) from animals or fish, including eggs, milk, and cheese.

Vegetarian: Someone who chooses not to eat meat or fish.

Vitamin A (Retinol): A fat-soluble vitamin with multiple functions in the body. It helps cells differentiate, an essential part of cell reproduction.

Vitamin B1 (Thiamin): A water-soluble vitamin that the body requires to break down carbohydrates, fat, and protein. Vitamin B1 is also essential for the proper functioning of nerve cells.

Vitamin B12 (Cobalamine): A water-soluble vitamin needed for normal nerve cell activity, DNA replication, and production of the mood-affecting substance SAMe (S-adenosyl-L-methionine).

Vitamin B2 (Riboflavin): A water-soluble vitamin that helps the body process amino acids and fats, activate vitamin B6 and folic acid, and convert carbohydrates to adenosine triphosphate (ATP). Vitamin B2 can sometimes act as an antioxidant.

Vitamin B3 (Niacin): Vitamin B3 is required for cell respiration and helps release the energy in carbohydrates, fats, and proteins. It supports proper circulation and healthy skin, functioning of the nervous system, and normal secretion of bile and stomach fluids. It is used in the synthesis of sex hormones, treating schizophrenia and other mental illnesses, and as a memory-enhancer.

Vitamin B5 (Pantothenic Acid): Vitamin B5 is a water-soluble vitamin involved in the Kreb's energy production cycle.

Vitamin B6: Vitamin B6 is a water-soluble vitamin that plays a role in the synthesis of antibodies by the immune system and it helps maintain normal nerve function and also acts in the formation of red blood cells. Deficiency of this vitamin can cause mouth and tongue sores, irritability, confusion, and depression.

Vitamin B9 (Folate): Vitamin B9, also known as folic acid, is a B vitamin necessary for cell replication and growth. Folic acid is most important, then, for rapidly growing tissues, such as those of a fetus, and rapidly regenerating cells, like red blood cells and immune cells.

Vitamin C (Ascorbic Acid): Vitamin C is an essential water-soluble vitamin that has a wide range of functions in the human body. One of vitamin C's important functions is acting as an antioxidant.

Vitamin D (Cholecalciferol): Vitamin D is a fat-soluble vitamin that helps maintain blood levels of calcium, by increasing absorption from food and reducing urinary calcium loss.

Vitamin E (Tocopherol): Vitamin E is an antioxidant that protects cell membranes and other fat-soluble parts of the body. Vitamin E has been shown to directly affect inflammation, blood cell regulation, connective tissue growth, and genetic control of cell division.

Vitamin K (Phylloquinone): Vitamin K is necessary for proper bone growth and blood coagulation. It helps the body transport calcium.

Vitamin: Natural substances found in food that are necessary to keep your body healthy.

Xylitol: See Sugar Alcohol.

Zinc: Zinc is an essential mineral, needed to repair wounds, maintain fertility in adults and growth in children, synthesize protein, help cells reproduce, preserve vision, boost immunity, and protect against free radicals, among other functions.

AUTHOR BIOGRAPHIES

BRANDI L. DAWSON aka "BranDIVA" is the owner of Liberation Coaching & Consulting. She is a sought-after business/personal success coach, empowerment speaker, and proud special needs parent. To bring Coach Brandi to your company or organization, contact her at 706-225-9217 (Monday-Friday 10AM-5PM). For additional information, contact details, or empowerment resources, go to www.liberationcoaching.com

BRYAN OGILVIE is a writer, public speaker, and webmaster of DoTheKnowledge.com, which hosts his daily blog, "Today's Transcendence." On the blog, Bryan helps you improve your productivity, strengthen your confidence, attain greater self-discipline, enhance your ability to focus and concentrate, master your subconscious mind and much, much more...check him out at www.dotheknowledge.com/transcend

DAN TRES OMI is a freelance writer and lecturer. Currently, he tutors children of all ages and teaches capoeira in Dayton, Ohio. He is a long-standing member of the Universal Zulu Nation and the Imani Foundation.

DR. KANIKA JAMILA WARD, ND is a holistic day spa owner, skin care specialist, naturopath, professional beauty educator, cosmetics manufacturer and author is a true expression of being young, black, female and beautiful. Her commitment to enhancing the natural beauty from within has been the driving force behind her businesses Khemistry Kosmetiks, Kosmik Publishing, and Kosmik Kare Day Spa, 633 W Capitol Drive, Milwaukee, WI 53212, (414) 264-3401, www.kosmik-kare.com

DR. SUPREME UNDERSTANDING is an author, activist, educator, and student. After acquiring Knowledge of Self at 15, he began a long journey toward healthful living that continues today. He is a vegetarian working towards quitting processed foods, a drinker working on quitting cheap beer, a relatively healthy person working on quitting Western medicine, a husband working on quitting being a jerk, and an Original man in America working on quitting the psychological instability that comes with being an Original man in America. Somewhere along that journey, he earned a doctorate in education, focusing on alternative methods for reaching at-risk learners. This work led to the development of Supreme Design Publishing, which provides affordable, accessible non-fiction titles tackling real-world problems, including *How to Hustle and Win, Real Life is No Fairy Tale, Knowledge of Self, Black Rebellion,* and *From Poverty to Power.*

DR. VERNELLIA RANDALL is one of our nation's most distinguished legal scholars and analysts on issues involving race and healthcare. A tenured professor of law at the University of Dayton, she has published numerous scholarly articles on race, healthcare and legal education. She also spent 13 years in nursing, including serving as the Maternal-Child Health Nurse Coordinator for the State of Alaska. She has received numerous awards, honors and citations including being selected for Marquis Who's Who in the

World, the Chairman's Award from the Ohio Commission on Minority Health, Who's Who in American Nursing, and a Commendation from the Ohio House of Representatives. Her book *Dying While Black* provides understanding and insight into the bias of healthcare service based on race in the United States.

IATOMIC ALLAH is a tattoo and piercing profession with years of experience in the industry. He is also coauthor, with Ahmariah Jackson, of the book *Locked Up but Not Locked Down: A Guide to Surviving the American Prison System.* (www.guidetoprison.com) He can be reached at studio7ink@gmail.com

JAMIL SULEMAN is a soul in the cipher appreciating the present moment...and dreaming his next creation. His vision is to see a world of abundance and free expression. His mission is to share his talents in assisting humanity's transition from the mind to the heart. growitheflow@gmail.com

JUSTICE RAJEE is a writer, advocate, educator and father. He works with youth and their families connecting them to resources to help them reach healthy outcomes and pull the best out of themselves.

LANDRIA CARR is an 18-year-old student at Florida Atlantic University majoring in Biomedical Sciences. She is pursuing studies leading to a medical degree, specializing in Pediatrics or Gynecology, with a minor in journalism.

MECCA WISE has been studying holistic health for the past eight years, focusing on natural remedies and affordable cures for common problems. Before taking the helm of Sales and Fulfillment at Supreme Design Publishing, she worked for a national research organization conducting clinical trials in breast and colorectal cancer. She is currently working on a book on relationships with Stic.man and Afya Ibomu, detailing her experiences living with the disorder known as Supreme Understanding.

NASIM ALLAH is a writer, photographer, activist, member of the Nation of Gods and Earths, and personal trainer. NasimAllah@gmail.com, facebook.com/Nasim.Allah, or @DigitalTysonMedia.

PATRA AFRIKA is the founder of NIA (Neighborhoods In Action) Collective. In 2008, she joined ranks with People Survival Program (PSP) in Harlem, aimed at promoting Food Drives, expanding Food & Farmers Cooperatives, Community Gardens & Nutrition Programs and Emergency Preparedness Training. She can be reached at nia.collective@gmail.com

PHYLIS J. IQBAL has been a writer since she was twelve years old. She combines this love with her desire for justice, health and wellness. She's been a vegetarian for several years and has just begun to practice yoga. You can find her on Facebook, SoulVeg, Twitter, and Yelp. You can read her blog at cametowrite.blogspot.com.

QUEEN EARTHIASIA is a mother of two whose journey of motherhood has shown her the necessity of developing holistic health practices. The longest journey always begins with one step, and that is how she acquired her knowledge of how to prepare foods medicinally and flavorfully – one step at a time. Health and wellness will always be our greatest asset.

ROBERT BAILEY is a writer, Kung Fu San Soo practitioner, aspiring actor, and overall growth-oriented individual. Wondering why our people have the health complications that we do, he made a proactive decision to become more informed regarding his health and well-being and became a vegetarian in the summer of 2009. He is striving gradually towards raw foodism. He can be reached at greatone9101987@yahoo.com

ROBERT L. WILLIAMS, CPS was diagnosed and treated for Schizophrenia at the age of 15 and re-diagnosed with Bi-Polar at age 23. Since then he has overcome the symptoms associated with either diagnosis and hasn't had the need for psychiatric medication for several years. He has proven to himself that such diagnosis can be reversed by Holistic Healing methods and he is available to share his story and methods. He was once a consumer for mental health care and he is now an administrator of mental health care. He is certified by the Georgia Mental Health Consumer Network as a Certified Peer Specialist, assisting people with Mental Health diagnoses to become educated about their symptoms and to learn that they can recover and live the lives of their choosing. He also specializes in Sober Living Support from drug and alcohol addiction. tawabliss@gmail.com or 404-914-6429

ROCHELLE KERR has been studying holistic living (including using natural substitutes for everyday products and making soap) in London for the past 5 years. She exercises regularly by walking skipping and practicing yoga and Pilates. She runs a local business RebelJewel (www.rebeljewel.com) where she demonstrates her natural jewelry-making skills with original designs.

SATORI ANANDA works with the community through The People's Lunch Counter in Dallas, as an advocate for food justice and sustainability. The PLC provides a holistic approach to ending food insecurity and focus on a healthy body and mind through education, gardening and environmental awareness. They can be reached at plcdallas@gmail.com or facebook.com/plc Satori can be followed at twitter.com/satori06

SHERIESE NICOLE TANAHESI is a community activist and holistic counselor working with children and families for 12 years. She specializes in holistic child development, family creative arts programming, and holistic lifestyle transitions. To get more information on current health, wellness, and youth arts events/programs, visit www.ItiopiOnline.com

STIC.MAN is one-half of the revolutionary rap duo Dead Prez. Stic.man does it all: rapping, producing, writing and publishing books, and training in the martial arts. Besides the critically heralded albums he's recorded as a member of Dead Prez, the Florida native published The Art of Emcee-ing and Balogun O. Abeegunde's Afrikan Martial Arts: Discovering the Warrior Within. Stic.man is also the founder of .Ammo Magazine, Boss Up Inc. (www.BossUpBU.com), and the RBG Fit Club (www.RBGFitClub.com). In 2010, Dead Prez teamed up with DJ Drama to release the mixtape, *Revolutionary But Gangsta Grillz*, available free at www.DeadPrez.com.

TAMIKA HOGAN is a single mother of three, living in New York City. She is a Community Liaison responsible for educating the community on the issues of domestic violence and teen violence. She also provides individual and group counseling for victims of domestic violence, victims of other crimes as well as to at-risk teens. Ms. Hogan holds a BS in legal studies, a MS in Psychology and is active in youth-oriented and other community organizations with an emphasis on females, who suffer from and display deficiencies with self-esteem, low awareness on health issues and issues relating to relationships, education and/or the lack thereof.

TESNIM HASSAN is a Registered Respiratory Therapist, currently living and working in Omaha, Nebraska. She is a native of Los Angeles, CA and came into Knowledge of Self during her studies at the Museum In Black under the mentorship of the Warrior Teacher, Brian Breye. Tesnim is a proud wife and mother to seven children. She has a firm understanding that life's successes are rooted firmly in mental and physical health.

TRUE ASIATIC ALLAH is presently living in Puerto Rico with his Queen Skai and their seeds. He is a co-founder of Paradise Wellness Center, a volunteer for the Luquillo Surf and Rescue, and teaches History on the secondary level at The Fajardo Academy. He is currently working on "getting off the grid." He can be contacted at trueasiatic@gmail.com

WISE INTELLIGENT of the legendary rap trio Poor Righteous Teachers, hails from Donnelly Page Homes, a low income housing community in Trenton, New Jersey. Wise Intelligent is an activist, author, MC, entrepreneur, and a firm believer in African American solidarity and self-sufficiency. Through his Intelligentseedz youth media organization, Wise Intelligent works closely with urban youth and like-minded community organizations. While commandeering Intelligent Media Group, LLC – a media company that includes a record company, film production, an online magazine and not-for-profit division – forever loyal to his Hip Hop constituents and roots, Wise Intelligent continues to release some of the most relevant studio albums of the times.

YVETTE GZ is a full-time civil engineering student, writer, and third world affairs connoisseur. She has lived in Ivory Coast, Liberia, Palestine/Israel and Austin, TX and visited many other countries, all the while going through five African and Middle Eastern wars. Her experience in those regions brought her much knowledge on politics, social issues and, of course, diets, health, and lifestyle choices. Yvette now resides in Brooklyn, NY.

If you have Volume Two, MAKE SURE you get Volume One!

DIET & NUTRITION • SICKNESS & DISEASE • HEALING & PREVENTION • HYGIENE

THE HOOD HEALTH HANDBOOK

A PRACTICAL GUIDE TO HEALTH AND WELLNESS IN THE URBAN COMMUNITY

VOLUME ONE

EDITED BY
C'BS ALIFE ALLAH and SUPREME UNDERSTANDING

Volume One focuses on the status of health in the urban community, the "wrong foods" that make us unhealthy, the history of diet and healthcare among Black and brown people (focusing on how things changed for the worst), the diseases and illnesses that plague our communities, and holistic (natural) methods to heal and treat ourselves into wellness.

What should you do now that you're done reading?
Here are some suggestions:

☐ Complete any activities mentioned in this book, especially the discussions. See any of the films mentioned, but with others.

☐ Tell somebody about this book and what you've learned. Invite them to come read it. Don't let them steal the book.

☐ As another option, let them steal the book. It might help them.

☐ Mentor some young people or teach a class using this book as a handbook or reference.

☐ Talk about this book online, but don't stay on the Net forever.

☐ Join an organization or group that discusses concepts like the ones in this book and get into those discussions.

☐ Leave this book away somewhere it will be picked up and read.

☐ Identify the people in your community who could use a copy of this book. If they're people would want to buy a book like this, let em read a few pages and see if they can afford to buy a copy.

☐ If they're people who don't normally buy books – but you know that givin em a copy could change their life – give em a copy and tell em to come see you when they're ready for another one. This is why you can order copies at wholesale rates at our site.

We hope this helps you keep the knowledge contagious.

ALSO FROM OUR COMPANY

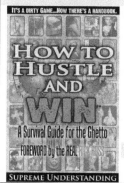
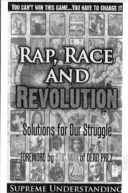

The Hood Health Handbook, Volume One (Physical Health)

Edited by Supreme Understanding and C'BS Alife Allah, Foreword by Dick Gregory

Want to know why Black and brown people are so sick? This book covers the many "unnatural causes" behind our poor health, and offers hundreds of affordable and easy-to-implement solutions.

CLASS	PAGES	RETAIL	RELEASE
PH-1	480	$19.95	Nov. 2010

ISBN: 978-1-935721-32-1

The Hood Health Handbook, Volume Two (Mental Health)

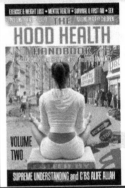

Edited by Supreme Understanding and C'BS Alife Allah

This volume covers mental health, how to keep a healthy home, raising healthy children, environmental issues, and dozens of other issues, all from the same down-to-earth perspective as Volume One.

CLASS	PAGES	RETAIL	RELEASE
MH-1	480_	$19.95	Nov. 2010

ISBN: 978-1-935721-33-8

A Taste of Life: 1,000 Vegetarian Recipes from Around the World

Edited by Supreme Understanding and Patra Afrika

This cookbook makes it easy to become vegetarian. In addition to over 1,000 recipes from everywhere you can think of, plus over 100 drink and smoothie recipes, this book also teaches how to transition your diet, what to shop for, how to cook, as well as a guide to nutrients and vitamins.

CLASS	PAGES	RETAIL	RELEASE
W-1	400	$19.95	Jun. 2011

ISBN: 978-1-935721-10-9

La Brega: Como Sobrevivir En El Barrio

ISBN: 978-0981617-08-4

By Supreme Understanding

Thanks to strong demand coming from Spanish-speaking countries, we translated our groundbreaking How to Hustle and Win into Spanish, and added new content specific to Latin America. Because this book's language is easy to follow, it can also be used to brush up on your Spanish.

CLASS	PAGES	RETAIL	RELEASE
0-1	336	$14.95	Jul. 2009

Locked Up but Not Locked Down: A Guide to Surviving the American Prison System

ISBN: 978-1935721-00-0

By Ahmariah Jackson and IAtomic Allah
Foreword by Mumia Abu Jamal

This book covers what it's like on the inside, how to make the most of your time, what to do once you're out, and how to stay out. Features contributions from over 50 insiders, covering city jails, state and federal prisons, women's prisons, juvenile detention, and international prisons.

CLASS	PAGES	RETAIL	RELEASE
J-1	288	$14.95	Jul. 2012

The Science of Self: Man, God, and the Mathematical Language of Nature

ISBN: 978-1935721-67-3

By Supreme Understanding and C'BS Alife Allah

How did the universe begin? Is there a pattern to everything that happens? What's the meaning of life? What does science tell us about the depths of our SELF? Who and what is God? This may be one of the deepest books you can read.

CLASS	PAGES	RETAIL	RELEASE
I-4	360	$19.95	Jun. 2012

The Science of Self: Man, God, and the Mathematical Language of Nature (Hardcover Edition)

By Supreme Understanding

A beautiful hardcover edition of the bestselling work, *The Science of Self.* Under the full-color dust jacket is an embossed clothbound hard cover. Autographed and numbered as part of a special limited edition series, this book also includes the 16 full-color inserts found in the paperback edition.

CLASS	PAGES	RETAIL	RELEASE
I-4	360	$34.95	Jun. 2012

Only available direct from publisher.

365 Days of Real Black History Calendar (2012 Edition)

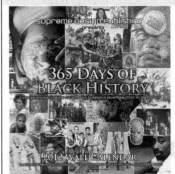

By Supreme Understanding and Robert Bailey

A calendar that'll never be out-dated! Over 365 important facts and quotes covering little-known, but important, moments in Black history. Written in brief chunks and easy language for all audiences.

CLASS	PGS	PRICE	RELEASE
I-2	26	$2.95	2011

Only available direct from publisher.

365 Days of Real Black History Calendar (2013 Edition)

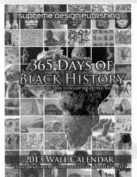

By Supreme Understanding

Our 2013 calendar and planner was also designed to be timeless, as it's a beautifully-designed companion to *When the World was Black*. You'll find dozens of striking full-color images that help tell the stories of global Black history.

CLASS	PAGES	PRICE	RELEASE
I-2	26	$4.95	2012

Only available direct from publisher.

When the World was Black, Part One: Prehistoric Cultures

By Supreme Understanding
Foreword by Runoko Rashid

When does Black history begin? Certainly not with slavery. In two volumes, historian Supreme Understanding explores over 200,000 years of Black history from every corner of the globe. Part One covers the first Black communities to settle the world, establishing its first cultures and traditions. Their stories are remarkable.

CLASS	PAGES	RETAIL	RELEASE
I-3	400	$19.95	Feb. 2013

ISBN: 978-1-935721-04-8

When the World Was Black, Part Two: Ancient Civilizations

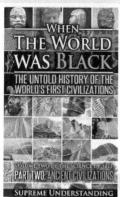

By Supreme Understanding

Part Two covers the ancient Black civilizations that gave birth to the modern world. Black people built the first urban civilizations in Africa, Asia, Europe, and the Americas. And every claim in these books is thoroughly documented with reputable sources. Do you want to know the story of your ancestors? You should. We study the past to see what the future will bring.

CLASS	PAGES	RETAIL	RELEASE
I-3	400	$19.95	Feb. 2013

ISBN: 978-1-935721-05-5

When the World was Black, Parts One and Two (Hardcover)

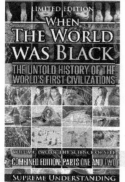

By Supreme Understanding

An incredible limited edition that combines Part One and Part Two into a single book, cased in an embossed clothbound hardcover and dust jacket. Autographed and numbered, this collector's item also includes both sets of full-color inserts.

CLASS	PAGES	RETAIL	RELEASE
I-3	800	$19.95	Dec. 2013

Only available direct from publisher.

Black Rebellion: Eyewitness Accounts of Major Slave Revolts

Edited by Dr. Sujan Dass

Who will tell the stories of those who refused to be slaves? What about those who fought so effectively that they forced their slavers to give up? Black Rebellion is a collection of historical "eyewitness" accounts of dozens of major revolts and uprisings, from the U.S. to the Caribbean, as well as a history of slavery and revolt.

CLASS	PAGES	RETAIL	RELEASE
P-3	272	$14.95	May 2010

ISBN: 978-0-981617-04-6

The Heroic Slave

By Frederick Douglass

Most people don't know that Douglass wrote a novel...or that, in this short novel, he promoted the idea of violent revolt. By this time in his life, the renowned abolitionist was seeing things differently. This important piece of history comes with *David Walker's Appeal*, all in one book.

CLASS	PAGES	RETAIL	RELEASE
P-3	160	$14.95	Apr. 2011

ISBN: 978-1-935721-27-7

David Walker's Appeal

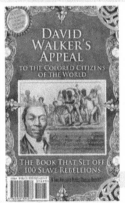

By David Walker

This is one of the most important, and radical, works ever published against slavery. Rather than call for an end by peaceful means, Walker called for outright revolution. His calls may have led to over 100 revolts, including those described in *Black Rebellion*. This important piece of history comes with Douglass' *The Heroic Slave*, which it may have helped inspire.

CLASS	PAGES	RETAIL	RELEASE
P-3	160	$14.95	Apr. 2011

ISBN: 978-1-935721-27-7

Darkwater: Voices from Within the Veil, Annotated Edition

By W.E.B. Du Bois

This book makes Du Bois' previous work, like *Souls of Black Folk*, seem tame by comparison. *Darkwater* is revolutionary, uncompromising, and unconventional in both its content and style, addressing the plight of Black women, the rise of a Black Messiah, a critical analysis of white folks, and the need for outright revolution.

CLASS	PAGES	RETAIL	RELEASE
I-4	240	$14.95	Jun. 2011

ISBN: 978-0-981617-07-7

The African Abroad: The Black Man's Evolution in Western Civilization, Volume One

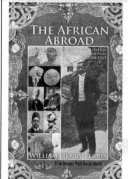

By William Henry Ferris

Who would think a book written in 1911 could cover so much? Ferris, chairman of the UNIA, speaks up for the Black man's role in Western civilization. He discusses a wealth of history, as well as some revolutionary Black theology, exploring the idea of man as God and God as man.

CLASS	PAGES	RETAIL	RELEASE
I-5	570	$29.95	Oct. 2012

ISBN: 978-1935721-66-6

The African Abroad: Volume Two

By William Henry Ferris

The second volume of Ferris' epic covers important Black biographies of great leaders, ancient and modern. He tells the stories of forty "Black Immortals." He also identifies the African origins of many of the world's civilizations, including ancient Egypt, Akkad, Sumer, India, and Europe.

CLASS	PAGES	RETAIL	RELEASE
I-5	330	$19.95	Oct. 2012

ISBN: 978-1-935721-69-7

From Poverty to Power: The Realization of Prosperity and Peace

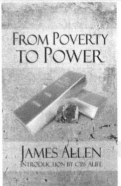

By James Allen

Want to transform your life? James Allen, the author of the classic *As a Man Thinketh,* explores how we can turn struggle and adversity into power and prosperity. This inspirational text teaches readers about their innate strength and the immense power of the conscious mind.

CLASS	PAGES	RETAIL	RELEASE
I-3	144	$14.95	May 2010

ISBN: 978-0-981617-05-3

Daily Meditations: A Year of Guidance on the Meaning of Life

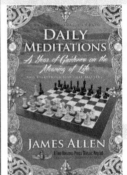

By James Allen

Need a guidebook to a productive and healthy year? This is it. James Allen delivers another great work in this book, this time offering 365 days of inspiration and guidance on life's greatest challenges. This book includes sections for daily notes.

CLASS	PAGES	RETAIL	RELEASE
C-3	208	$14.95	Apr. 2013

ISBN: 978-1-935721-08-6

The Kybalion: The Seven Ancient Egyptian Laws _

By the Three Initiates

Thousands of years ago, the ancients figured out a set of principles that govern the universe. In *The Kybalion*, these laws are explored and explained. This edition includes research into the authorship of the book, and where the laws came from.

CLASS	PAGES	RETAIL	RELEASE
C-4	130	$14.95	Oct. 2012

ISBN: 978-1-935721-25-3

Real Life is No Fairy Tale (w/ Companion CD)

By Sujan Dass and Lord Williams

Looking for a children's book that teaches about struggle? Written for school age children, this full-color hardcover book is composed entirely in rhyme, and the images are as real as they get. Includes a CD with an audio book, animated video, review questions, and printable worksheets and activities.

CLASS	PGS	RETAIL	RELEASE
CD-4	36+	$16.95	Jun. 2010

ISBN: 978-0-9816170-2-2

Aesop's Fables: 101 Classic Tales and Timeless Lessons

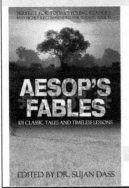

Edited by Dr. Sujan Dass

What's better to teach our children than life lessons? This easy-to-read collection of classic tales told by an African storyteller uses animals to teach valuable moral lessons. This edition includes dozens of black-and-white images to accompany the timeless fables. Color them in!

CLASS	PAGES	RETAIL	RELEASE
CD-3	112	$14.95	Feb. 2013

ISBN: 978-1-935721-07-9

Heritage Playing Cards (w/ Companion Booklet)

Designed by Sujan Dass

No more European royalty! This beautiful deck of playing cards features 54 full-color characters from around the world and a 16-page educational booklet on international card games and the ethnic backgrounds of the people on the cards.

CLASS	PGS	RETAIL	RELEASE
CD-2	16+	$6.95	May 2010

UPC: 05105-38587

Black God: An Introduction to the World's Religions and their Black Gods

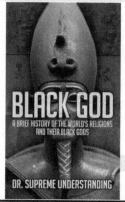

By Supreme Understanding

Have you ever heard that Christ was Black? What about the Buddha? They weren't alone. This book explores the many Black gods of the ancient world, from Africa to Europe, Asia, and Australia, all the way to the Americas. Who were they? Why were they worshipped? And what does this mean for us today?

CLASS	PAGES	RETAIL	RELEASE
C-3	200	$19.95	Jan. 2014

ISBN: 978-1-935721-12-3

Black People Invented Everything

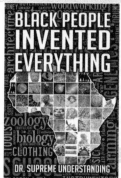

By Supreme Understanding

In *The Science of Self* we began exploring the origins of everything that modern civilization depends on today. In this book, we get into specifics, showing how Black people invented everything from agriculture to zoology, with dozens of pictures and references to prove it!

CLASS	PAGES	RETAIL	RELEASE
I-3	180	$14.95	Feb. 2014

NOT YET PUBLISHED

The Yogi Science of Breath: A Complete Manual of the Ancient Philosophy of the East

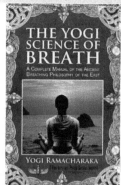

By Yogi Ramacharaka

A classic text on the science of breathing, one of the most ignored, yet important, aspects of our physical and emotional health. This book has been used by both martial arts experts and legendary jazz musicians. This edition explores the "secret science" of breath, and where its mysterious author learned such teachings.

CLASS	PAGES	RETAIL	RELEASE
PH-4	112	$14.95	Apr. 2012

ISBN: 978-1-935721-34-5

How to Get Our Books

To better serve our readers, we've streamlined the way we handle book orders. Here are some of the ways you can find our books.

In Stores

You can find our books in just about any Black bookstore or independent bookseller. If you don't find our titles on the shelves, just request them by name and publisher. Most bookstores can order our titles directly from us (via our site) or from the distributors listed below. We also provide a listing of retailers who carry our books at www.bestblackbooks.com

Online (Wholesale)

Now, you can visit our sites (like www.supremeunderstanding.com or www.bestblackbooks.com) to order wholesale quantities direct from us, the publisher. From our site, we ship heavily discounted case quantities to distributors, wholesalers, retailers, and local independent resellers (like yourself – just try it!). The discounts are so deep, you can afford to GIVE books away if you're not into making money.

Online (Retail)

If you're interested in single "retail" copies, you can now find them online at Amazon.com, or you can order them via mail order by contacting one of the mail order distributors listed below. You can also find many of our titles as eBooks in the Amazon Kindle, Nook, or Apple iBooks systems. You may also find full-length videobook or audiobook files available, but nothing beats the pass-around potential of a real book!

By Mail Order

Please contact any of the following Black-owned distributors to order our books! For others, visit our site.

Afrikan World Books
2217 Pennsylvania Ave.
Baltimore, MD 21217
(410) 383-2006

Lushena Books
607 Country Club Dr
Bensenville, IL 60106
(800) 785-1545

Special Needs X-Press
3128 Villa Ave
Bronx, NY 10468
(718) 220-3786